Charles McMoran Wilson was created 1st Baron Moran of Manton in 1943. During the 1914–18 war he was awarded the MC during the Battle of the Somme and the Italian Silver Medal for Military Valour for a raid. He was for twenty-four years Dean of St Mary's Hospital Medical School. In 1945 he published his observations of men under the stress of war in *The Anatomy of Courage*. He became Winston Churchill's doctor in 1940, as the curtain was rising on one of the greatest dramas in our history, and from 1941 to 1950 he was also President of the Royal College of Physicians. *Winston Churchill: the Struggle for Survival* was first published in 1966, a year after Churchill's death. In his war memoirs, Winston Churchill called Lord Moran 'a dev⸺ personal friend' to whose 'unfailing care I probably owe

Praise for the first edi⸺

'A Churchill treasury . . . a personal memoir, recollections from ⸺ vation, brilliantly written and deeply felt.'   *Publishers Weekly*

'Of overwhelming interest to the general reader . . . Lord Moran's devotion to Sir Winston shines through everything he writes.'
Cyril Connolly, *Sunday Times*

'Clear-eyed, revealing, intensely human memoir . . . In all of the books written about Churchill so far, I have read nothing which tells me so much about the man as this informal, candid, astonishingly insightful portrait . . . What [Lord Moran] saw and heard he recorded as it happened, and when it happened, neither enhancing the achievements nor glossing over the failings . . . Immensely absorbing. If you read no other book about him, make sure you read this one.'   John Barkham, *Saturday Review Syndicate*

'This is Churchill in his slippers, off guard. But how little history would tell us if its great figures were shown only in their public attitudes!'
George Malcolm Thomson, *Daily Express*

'The world should be grateful . . . that the full story of Churchill as a human being with frailties at times in proportions to his strengths, should be brought out by so sensitive and knowledgeable a companion.'
Herbert Black, *Boston Globe*

'The most magnificent portrait of Winston, his strength and his weakness, yet drawn.'
Edward Weeks, *Atlantic*

'Will prove to be a valuable contribution to the history of our times.'
British Medical Journal

'It is a book of high quality and unflagging interest, a priceless witness to the history of our time.'
Daily Express

'Lord Moran's eloquent and amazingly forth-right chapters will undoubtedly change many a reader's opinions of some wartime leaders, but they can only add to Winston Churchill's stature . . . He emerges from this book clothed in greatness of spirit . . .'
Henry C. Wolfe, *Chicago Tribune*

'Delightful literary style . . . the precious intimate record, by the perfect chronicler.'
Katherine Gauss Jackson, *Harper's*

'As a contribution to history it is of the first importance . . . it adds very greatly to our knowledge of one of the foremost figures of modern times.'
Sir Charles Petrie, *Illustrated London News*

'Humour, urbanity, penetrating analysing of the motives which moved men on important occasions . . . love and sympathy for the man who was his patient – all these are present in this book.'
Barrie Pitt, *Book Society*

'We have nothing comparable to this about either of the Pitts, Fox, Burke or Walpole.'
Terence de Vere White, *Irish Times*

'Lord Moran has a respect for history and his record of the years through war and peace with the Prime Minister make a contribution to the history of that time . . .'
Library Journal

'An amazingly intimate portrait . . . a story from the wings of history's stage.'
Miles A. Smith, *Associated Press*

CHURCHILL

THE STRUGGLE FOR SURVIVAL 1945–60

LORD MORAN

ROBINSON
London

Constable & Robinson Ltd
3 The Lanchesters
162 Fulham Palace Road
London W6 9ER
www.constablerobinson.com

First published in the UK as
Churchill: The Struggle for Survival 1940–65
by Constable and Company, 1966

This abridged and revised edition published by Robinson, an imprint of
Constable and Robinson Ltd, 2006

A copy of the British Library Cataloguing in
Publication Data is available from the British Library.

ISBN 1-84529-297-9

Printed and bound in the EU

1 3 5 7 9 10 8 6 4 2

To *DOROTHY*
who has been given back to me
and to *JOHN & GEOFFREY*
who in their different ways
are not unlike her

Contents

Acknowledgements

I have to thank Her Majesty the Queen for permission to print her letter to Mr Churchill. I am grateful to General Eisenhower and to Mr Max Aitken for permission to use letters.

I wish to express my thanks to Mr Richard Church for his help in keeping this book within manageable proportions. I am grateful to Professor Terence Spencer of Birmingham University for his valuable advice while I was writing this book. I have been able to turn to him whenever a doubtful point arose.

Mr Henry Laughlin of Houghton, Mifflin Co., of Boston, USA, has followed my story as it unfolded, and I have found his sustained interest heartening. Mr Craig Wylie has read the text and has given me the benefit of his careful judgement. I have, too, been fortunate in my London publisher, Mr Ben Glazebrook of Constable and Co. He has met me at every point and has made things easy for me. And here may I pay tribute to Mr Denis Hamilton's warm encouragement.

I have to thank the late Professor Una Ellis-Fermor and Professor Muriel Bradbrook for criticism and counsel. I have come to rely on the frank criticism of my son, John Wilson: at every stage he has helped me to settle points of difficulty.

I would like to thank my wife and Miss Marian Dean for the time and care they have given to correcting the proofs.

When I put down my pen, I wish to be sure that I have reported faithfully those who have talked to me about him. I trust that in checking those conversations I have forgotten no one.

Made by Lord Moran in the original edition

Introduction

Published in 1966 over a year after Churchill's death, but in preparation for some years, *Winston Churchill: The Struggle for Survival, 1940–65*, was a detailed portrait of the 'greatest living Englishman', very much warts and all. The quickest of looks through even a handful of the many books written about Churchill demonstrates the importance of *The Struggle for Survival*. In the post-war volume of Martin Gilbert's official biography, Moran fills up virtually a column of the index alone.[1] Roy Jenkins, in many ways critical of Moran, uses his account to understand Churchill's declining years.[2] Two recent books studying the Churchill legend by John Ramsden and David Reynolds have also examined Moran's work in depth.[3] The importance of Moran is clear: whereas the story of Churchill the statesman has been told and retold, not least by the man himself, the story of Churchill the man has always been more elusive. Moran was the first to show the human Churchill, singing his praises and noting his shortcomings, and it remains the best intimate account.

---

[1] Martin S. Gilbert, *Winston S. Churchill, 1945–65: 'Never Despair'*, (London: Minvera, 1990).

[2] Roy Jenkins, *Churchill*, (London: Pan Books, 2002), pp. 862–912.

[3] John Ramsden, *The Man of the Century: Winston Churchill and His Legend Since 1945*, (London: HarperCollins, 2002); David Reynolds, *In Command of History: Churchill Fighting and Writing the Second World War*, (London: Penguin, 2005).

It is certainly richer in human detail than the rather dry volumes of the official biography. Moreover, many of the aspects of Churchill's working practices that have become almost legendary – his sleeping patterns, his use of amphetamines – are known to us through Moran.

Born Charles McMoran Wilson in November 1882, Moran was ennobled in 1943, serving as President of the Royal College of Physicians from 1941 to 1950. One of Britain's most eminent doctors, Moran became Churchill's doctor in 1940, remaining close to him until the end, and seeing him through a series of medical crises: from pneumonia and a heart attack in the war years, to a series of debilitating strokes from 1949. The wartime section of Moran's work was republished by Constable & Robinson as *Churchill at War, 1940–45* in 2002. I was commissioned in the summer of 2005 to help prepare an edition of the post-war section of the original book, using previously unpublished material from the Moran archive relating to people still alive when the original book was published. Much more than the wartime volume, it shows Churchill as an ailing figure. It documents his literal struggle for survival. Also, it contains more of the material deemed objectionable by Moran's attackers in the very public controversy caused by the book's publication: Churchill's bouts of depression, his ill-heath, and the laziness which characterized his second premiership between 1951–54. Moran's account provoked a group of other Churchill insiders to write a panegyric on Churchill at work. *Action This Day* was edited by the historian John Wheeler-Bennett, and included contributions by men who appear here, such as Churchill's Private Secretary, Jock Colville, and the Cabinet Secretary, Sir Norman Brook. The result was relatively anodyne, largely forgotten by the general public. It is the work of Moran which has dramatically shaped the historical memory of Churchill, and it has been used by historians as a key source for his life ever since.

The book, however, was immensely controversial when it was published, and continues to be almost equally so among historians. In 1966, Moran's apparent flouting of the Hippocratic Oath caused an outcry that split the medical world, with the *Lancet* attacking, and the *British Medical Journal* defending Moran's reputation. The British Medical Association censured the then very elderly Moran but refused, despite pressure, to expel him. Moran's son, the present Lord Moran, explained in his lucid and intelligent account of the controversy, that Moran's 'defence was that it was permissible to write about the great historical figure after his death, and that he had told Churchill what he proposed to do'.[1] Attacks on the book were spearheaded by the Churchill family, who objected to the intimate portrayal of Churchill. But, in a *Sunday Times* review eventually used on the back of Sphere Books' paperback edition (1968), Cyril Connolly noted that 'Lord Moran's devotion to Sir Winston shines through everything he writes'.

It will be obvious to all readers that Moran idolized Churchill. Sphere Books actually seized on the ethical controversy as a marketing tool. Along with Connolly, space was given to extracts from a Randolph Churchill letter to *The Times* and the Hippocratic Oath. This treatment of the book, as well as the pre-publication serialization of the most controversial passages in the *Sunday Times* heightened the impression that Moran's book was throughout a kind of exposé of the Churchillian way of life, instead of what it was: a detailed, compelling and humane account of his last years. How this ethical controversy is linked to the historical one can be graphically illustrated by the words which appeared on the cover of the paperback edition just underneath the title: 'The diary of Churchill's personal doctor is a masterpiece – which many have condemned as the gross betrayal of a patient's trust'. The 'gross betrayal' description sold books, as did the 'diary' status of the book. As an insider's account, a diary (as opposed to a retrospective memoir) conveys the impression of intimacy, honesty and poignancy.

The problem for historians has been that the 'diary' nature of the book was a result of a complex process of composition, a

[1] Lord Moran, 'Introduction', in Lord Moran, *Churchill at War 1940–45*, (London: Robinson, 2002), pp. xxi–xxii.

process first explained by Moran's biographer, Richard Lovell.[1]
From an examination of the Moran papers held at the Wellcome
Library in London, one can see that Moran often jotted down
thoughts and consultations with Churchill in notebooks. Some of
these were dated but not all. Also in these notebooks, there would
be more reflective sections, containing observations of Churchill
evidently written some months after the event, but containing
detailed observations. Finally, there were sections which amounted
to essays on various aspects of the Churchill persona. All these
three strands – the absolutely contemporary, the near-contempo-
rary and the essay material – were mingled in the same notebooks.
Often the same material would be reused in each strand. In addition, Moran often wrote his thoughts on loose pieces of paper or
the backs of envelopes. In all, the manuscripts amount not to a
'diary' in the truest sense of the word but rather the notes for the
book on Churchill Moran always intended to write, in a near-con-
stant state of flux and revision. These notes were typed up in diary
form, and this first draft contains some identifiable, dated, notebook entries mixed with other material. But this early typed version
was revised heavily and often, for a number of reasons. One was
the realization that not everything contained in them could be published. The second was stylistic: entries were rewritten to improve
the overall quality, and some entries were removed, cannibalized,
and redistributed, with parts of some entries being added on to
others. Most commonly, a single entry which contained Moran's
account of two different days with Churchill would be split into
two, one with a new date, giving the misleading impression Moran
wrote the entry that night. But aside from some dates going awry,
there seems to be no evidence that falsehoods have found their way
into Moran's work.

   This had been established as Moran's mode of working when he
was working on his first book *The Anatomy of Courage*, a brilliant book

[1] Richard Lovell, *Churchill's Doctor: A Biography of Lord Moran*, (London: Royal
Society of Medicine Services, 1992)

about his experiences as a Regimental Medical Officer in the First World War (he won the MC at the Somme), examining the limits of human endurance in the face of all the horrors of modern warfare. That too had a 'dual nature' of diaries and essays (although it is fair to say that the division is much more clearly marked). One of the results of the constant revisions of *The Struggle for Survival* was the dispersal of some of the essay material into the 'diary' entries, again helping to create a misleading impression about the nature of the book.

But the content of the book is more interesting than discussions of its composition. This volume, though containing entries from 1945 to 1960, concentrates on the period of Churchill's second government of 1951–55. This period has been neglected historically. As Peter Hennessy has noted, Churchill's peacetime administration has the feel of the conscious recreation of the wartime years. Old allies were summoned to new or old posts: Jock Colville, Lord Cherwell, 'Pug' Ismay, and Field Marshal Lord Alexander all returned to the colours, although Lord Portal resisted the call.[1] This has led to it being called the 'recidivist', or 'Indian summer' premiership.[2] The inclination of Churchill scholars to neglect 1951–55 is strengthened by the picture Roy Jenkins paints of Churchill being 'gloriously unfit for office',[3] an impression largely gained from *The Struggle for Survival.* Moran shows an apparently dying Churchill holding desperately on to office. Obviously, Moran mostly spent time with Churchill when he was ill, or thought he was, as John Ramsden notes.[4] But, as Peter Hennessy argues, 'one has to be careful not to overdo the depiction of the old warrior in his final premiership as a kind of walking off-licence-cum-pharmacy'.[5] Churchill here is often

[1] Peter Hennessy, *The Prime Minister: The Office and Its Holders since 1945,* (London: Penguin, 2001), pp. 181–2.
[2] The phrases were coined, respectively, by Roy Jenkins and Anthony Seldon. See Hennessy, *The Prime Minister,* p. 179.
[3] Jenkins, *Churchill,* p. 845.
[4] Ramsden, *Man of the Century,* p. 534.
[5] Hennessy, *The Prime Minister,* p. 181.

shown on top form, with sparkling conversation, cutting comments and pithy phrases to the fore, whether discussing the contemporary political situation, current colleagues or adversaries, his reading habits, or recollecting episodes from the war. Classic Churchillian vignettes pepper this volume.

In his summary of the second Churchill Government, Jenkins argued that 'with the exception of one issue which increasingly dominated his mind, the saving [of] the world from destruction in a reciprocal holocaust of H-Bombs, his struggle to prolong his life in office became more important than any policy issue'.[1] In fact, the main reason Churchill gave for holding on to office was his determination to end the Cold War. These twin concerns: the Cold War, and the desire to stay in office, are, along with the accounts of his illness, the main themes of Moran's book, which is the only firsthand account to weave these strands together adequately.

On the first of these themes, one quickly realizes whilst reading the book that Churchill's 1951–55 government was dominated by the Cold War. Much of Moran's time with Churchill was spent on trips to America, and his attempt to organize summit meetings with Eisenhower and the post-Stalin Soviet leadership looms large in Churchill's conversation. This pursuit of personal diplomacy came to a head in July 1954, when, onboard the *Queen Elizabeth*, Churchill sent a telegram to Molotov (see the entry for 2 July 1954). Sent over the heads of his Cabinet, it caused a political row on his return home. Churchill's mammoth push to end the Cold War may appear to some to sit at odds with his reputation for anti-Communism earned from the 1920s and enhanced at Fulton in 1946, but it was inspired by a genuine abhorrence of the destructive power of nuclear weapons. And it was the realization of the enormity of the hydrogen bomb in 1954 which inspired that year's desire to meet with both the Americans and Russians (for example, from 8 April 1954: 'they will say, of course, that I may get a snub. I don't care. What does a snub matter if you save the world'). Yet it was the

[1] Jenkins, *Churchill*, p.846.

hydrogen bomb which led to one of Churchill's major personal reverses of the post-1945 years, and introduces the second theme: his ill-health.

A key moment in Churchill's premiership came during the House of Commons debate on the hydrogen bomb on 5 April 1954. Attlee, still Labour leader, gave what Churchill himself called a 'thoughtful and inspiring speech', and although Churchill began by carrying on, in Moran's words 'the high argument', he then, 'when the whole house was still silent, seemingly numbed by the tragic issue confronting the world . . . shocked Tory and Socialist alike by making it a party matter, to be won on points'. Briefly, he attacked the previous Labour Government for giving up the British veto on the American use of nuclear weapons he had secretly secured at the 1943 Quebec conference. But rather than the substance of the attack (which Churchill had in fact badly mishandled), it was the partisan tone, so at odds with the occasion, which caused the outcry. As the House bayed at him to 'withdraw' or 'resign', Moran, watching from the gallery, was worried:

> I viewed the turn of events with growing concern. I marvelled that this man, in his eightieth year, and only half recovered from a stroke, could stand at the box for a full hour in all that uproar and tumult, in the face of such bitter hostility, and yet remain apparently unmoved. He had bungled the business. All the same, it made me very miserable to sit there watching him without being able to help. I wondered how it might affect him in the Party. Would he have another stroke? . . . When they allowed him to finish his speech in silence, in some strange way it seemed to increase my fears. All expression had gone from his voice, which quavered into the high-pitched speech of a very old man; he had somehow to get through a set piece before he sat down, and he gabbled through it as if his only purpose was now to get to the end.

At the time, and since, Churchill's poor performance in this debate stood as an eloquent example of his declining powers – the point when many openly questioned his ability to carry on. Macmillan noted in his diary that 'Churchill's failure was due to two things.

First, the contrast between the general "non-partisan" character of the debate and the damaging revelation was too horribly made and was inartistically led up to. Second, his power of recovery has gone . . . He was "knocked off his perch" '.[1] *The Times* leader ('insufferably pontifical', Macmillan called it)[2] argued that 'the Prime Minister's sense of occasion is one of his greatest strengths in the House of Commons. It deserted him sadly yesterday'.[3]

Yet, as Moran's entry tells us, this was a speech made by a man recovering from a serious stroke: and it is the story of that illness, his recovery, and Moran's hand in it, which forms what is essentially the central episode of this book. Churchill suffered a stroke on 24 June 1954 (he had also suffered one in Monte Carlo in 1949), affecting his speech, movement and ability to concentrate. From then on, it was clear that unless the Prime Minister could deliver his annual conference speech that year in Margate on 10 October, he would be finished. Churchill's determination to fight on, and Moran's fears for his life over those four months, are almost painfully poignant. The book also details the operation undertaken to keep Churchill's condition secret, something Moran participated in wholeheartedly. His abhorrence for the idea of Churchill's stroke becoming public is explained in the entry for 11 July 1953:

> Suppose he is obstinate and appears in public now, everyone will know he has had a stroke. He thinks that does not matter. I believe it matters a great deal. When people hear someone has had a stroke they feel that something has happened [to them] . . . which leads to paralysis and some deterioration of the mind. The man may perhaps go on living for a while, but for serious things he is finished.

It was this impression Moran was attempting to guard against, and it was remarkably successful. One reason for this was the 'gamble'

---

[1] Peter Catterall (ed.), *The Macmillan Diaries: The Cabinet Years 1950–57* (London: Macmillan, 2003), pp. 304–5, entry for 6.4.1954.
[2] Ibid.
[3] 'The Gulf', *The Times*, 6.4.1954.

over the medical bulletin issued over Churchill's health. Detailed in
the entry for 26 June, the original bulletin by Moran and Sir Russell
Brain was doctored by Lord Salisbury and R.A. Butler to avoid all
talk of 'a disturbance of the cerebral circulation' and instead used
tiredness as an excuse. This bulletin put off rumours of a stroke, but
would have proved very controversial if he had died in the summer
of 1953.

Although Churchill's conference speech in October 1953
allowed him to carry on until April 1955, and despite his failure
in the Commons in April 1954, it is important not to see the June
1953 stroke as an absolute division between a 'healthy' and an
'unhealthy' Churchill. Private doubts had been raised about
Churchill's ability to do the job before 1953 and after this second
stroke, there were days where his powers seemed almost fully
restored (see the entry for 25 August 1953). But there can be no
doubt that Churchill was generally less able and less willing to do
the arduous work of prime minister from 1953 onwards. For
example, after his first stroke in Monte Carlo in August 1949,
Moran wrote, in an entry not fully published until now, that the
1945 election, on top of the strain of the war years, had done him
no good:

> Something of the old vitality had oozed out of his wounds, the old confi-
> dence in himself had gone. However as the months passed I think my fears
> were half forgotten; he seemed to get back his interest in life, vigour
> returned and he appeared to put the past behind him. And then it began
> to dawn on me that he was descending into old age. The unmistakeable
> signs of his years were now present. All the same his stroke took me com-
> pletely by surprise (25 August 1949).

Another striking example of the concern over his health was the
attempt by Moran and senior members of the Conservative Cabinet
to persuade Churchill to lighten his load in February 1952 after a
mild cerebral disturbance. The day after it occurred, Moran decided
(entry for 22 February 1952):

If the P.M. comes safely through the next few days I've got to square up to him after the Budget and persuade him to be sensible. He won't listen to anybody, and I don't overrate my chances, but it is my job as his doctor. I think I know the turn of his mind as no one else does. I shall hate doing it, but it's the only thing I can do for him.

On the same day, Moran had an extraordinary meeting with Jock Colville and Lord Salisbury to talk about reducing his load, in which Colville said: 'I hate to be disloyal, but the P.M. is not doing his work. A document of five sheets has to be submitted to him as one paragraph, so that many of the points of the arguments are lost'. The solution was to be radical: sending Churchill to the House of Lords as Prime Minister. Salisbury 'felt sure he could go to the Lords and remain Prime Minister'. Moran doubted that it would work, and, sure enough, it came to nothing. Yet, this episode makes it clear that even when Churchill had been Prime Minister again for less than four months, senior colleagues and officials believed he was not fully up to the task of being Prime Minister. Reading this volume and understanding the array of sleeping pills, amphetamines and sheer will power it took for Churchill to even deliver a speech, it is hard not to conclude that Churchill should never have become Prime Minister for a second time. Moran himself, however, had no doubt that he was useful to the country, believing that 'unpopular decisions have to be made . . . he will make them'. Moreover, Moran was clearly concerned for his patient if he was forced to retire, often mentioning his belief that Churchill would not last long beyond his retirement date.

This secret meeting with Colville and Salisbury was the first of many which would take place with the object of persuading Churchill to slow down, or later, to resign. This is the third great theme of the book. Throughout the second half of 1953, all of 1954 and the early part of 1955, until Churchill finally resigned in April, the prospect of his going dominated the political discussion in internal Conservative Party circles. The views of many Churchill insiders are given here. One illustrative example (all the more impressive because it emanated from the personally disinterested and highly respected Cabinet Secretary) is Sir Norman Brook's comment to Moran on 1 April 1954, just before the débâcle of the hydrogen bomb debate, that he believed there would be a Party 'row' if Churchill did not resign in July of that year: 'They are thinking of a General Election in the autumn of 1955. If the P.M. pulled out in July that would give Anthony nearly a year and a half before the election . . . They want younger men, full of energy and drive.'

Another previously unpublished entry shows Christopher Soames, Churchill's ultra-loyal son-in-law expressing his concerns (on 8 April 1954, after the hydrogen bomb debate): 'Christopher was certain that he had seen a steady deterioration in Winston during the past two months: "He knows he is not up to it. He must pull out". Christopher thought Whitsuntide was the time for him to go. "You know Charles, you are the only person who can persuade him he ought to go"'. But despite the alleged tantrums of Eden, Churchill clung on, partly because of his increasing uneasiness about Eden's ability to do the job. Some of the newly published material shows members of Churchill's inner circle disparaging Eden. For example, Anthony Montague Browne, a private secretary of Churchill's, told Moran that 'if Eden does become Prime Minister I am afraid the people he will get round him will just echo his opinions. He's like that' (6 August 1954). He also told Moran (5 October 1954), that 'when you work here at No.10 it is for a great historical personage', but with Eden, 'you are working for a great hysterical figure'. Moran's own opinion was that 'Anthony is either very sweet or very angry, he can't be quiet and firm' (30 July 1954).

Other material new to this edition was removed from the original because its subject was still alive, such as his remarks on 'Pug' Ismay. In the 30 December 1951 entry, he noted that 'when the P.M. happens to look in his way his face slips as quickly into creases and folds, like a pug dog – whence Lord Ismay's nickname. But if you look more closely there is no mirth in the eyes which are cool and watchful'. In the 2 December 1953 entry, detailing the journey to the

Bermuda Conference, a new section praised Eden: 'his judgement of men was discerning'.

> Anthony isn't like Winston, he looks behind the façade. He isn't taken in by Pug's little ways as most people seem to be. Pug went about saying that he must retire from N.A.T.O. but, said Anthony smiling, "he's there for life. Nothing will get him out. He put it about that he couldn't get away to Bermuda and then he moved heaven and earth to get an invitation. But it doesn't alter my affection for Pug".

Another new story is Moran's account of Harold Macmillan's attempt to persuade Churchill to resign (9 January 1955). A heavily revised version of it exists in the original book. Moran lunched with Macmillan, who had come around to the view that Churchill should go: 'You know Moran, Winston ought to go . . . he can no longer handle these complicated matters properly. He can't do his job as Prime Minister as it ought to be done'. Moran was shocked, and the final paragraph of the edited entry runs:

> All this is not what I had expected. I have looked on Harold lately as an ally of the old man. Tory Prime Ministers have been overthrown by palace revolutions before, and the P.M., since he became aware that something of the kind was brewing, has taken counsel with his supporters – with Harold Macmillan more than anyone else. Now, though Harold is devoted to the old man, he feels that he is no longer up to the job.

This gives one the impression of Macmillan's principled belief that, though 'devoted to the old man', Churchill should go. But in the original manuscript, and in this edition, the final line was missing. Moreover, the entry carried on with the following paragraphs:

> Perhaps Jane Portal was right; Macmillan, she thinks, likes to be on the winning side; he must see that Anthony's time is coming, and that it can only be a matter of months before Winston goes. She doesn't like Harold, doesn't trust him, and thinks him disloyal to the P.M. Anyway he is very

indiscreet and talks too much. In politics at the top there is no quarter. All the same I do not bother my head about Macmillan's fidelity. Indeed I sometimes think that Winston's ignorance of what other people are thinking is a source of strength.

It transpired that when Harold Macmillan failed to get anything out of me he had gone to Clemmie. He said to her that Winston ought to resign, that he was no longer up to his job. Clemmie, according to Brendan Bracken, listened to what Macmillan had to say and then coldly retorted that he ought to say this to the Prime Minister and not to her. When Harold had gone Clemmie told Winston what had happened. The P.M. sent for Macmillan and told him shortly: "if in the future you have anything to say that you deem of importance, pray say it to me", and then dismissed the embarrassed minister. These clever people are always getting themselves into a mess.

This paints a different picture of Macmillan's actions: gone is the reference to his 'devotion' to Churchill, instead we have Macmillan the backhanded fixer, betraying Churchill's confidence and seeking his removal for his own personal gain. Clearly, when revising the manuscript, Moran attempted to smooth over many of these controversial accounts of living, though retired politicians. (It is interesting to note that in Macmillan's account of the same meeting he referred to Moran as 'a man of great shrewdness and wit').[1] It also clarifies a part of the next entry (20 January 1955): 'Harold's intervention has left a bruise. The P.M. had come to depend on him and counted on his support if it came to a row. After all, it was Harold who encouraged him to hang on . . . And now he had gone over to the other camp'. The title of the chapter this episode appears in explains Moran's feelings: 'Et tu, Brute'.

It is also now clear that Moran used his position as Churchill's doctor in an attempt to influence Churchill's choice of Minister of Health. In the original edition of the book, Moran bemoans how doctors in September 1951 (before the election which looked like

---

[1] Catterall (ed.), *The Macmillan Diaries*, p.380, entry for 6.4.1954

returning, as of course it did, the Conservatives to power) believed he could influence Churchill:

> Everything the doctors dislike in the Health Service they put down to me. They have heard that a certain politician, who is in their bad books, may be given office if the Conservatives win the election, and it is even going round that he will be the new Minister of Health. They come to me as if I could help. "Why don't you tackle Mr Churchill? He won't listen to the likes of us". They only smile in a knowing way when I protest that Winston will not ask my advice before he appoints a new Minister of Health.

Then, 'uncorked and bubbling over', Moran says: 'If you appoint this man as Minister of Health you will affront the doctors. I do think it would be a mistake'. But in the original draft, and in the present edition, the scene begins:

> It is said that Winston will not let a man do his job, but what the best elements in the party fear most is that if the Conservatives win the election he will gather round him the old gang.

And when Moran is 'bubbling over', he says: 'If you appoint Walter Elliot as Minister of Health you will have to get another doctor'. This is breathtaking, as Moran himself knew. The manuscript entry ends with 'I wanted to end the conversation. I had said more already than a doctor should, since his business is to build up and not to sap his patient's reserves'. And of course, the scene was heavily censored by a man who knew he was on shaky ground. Therefore, Moran expressing the concerns of 'the best elements in the Party' becomes 'the doctors', something he obviously felt more qualified to do. Walter Elliot's name is not mentioned, and Moran's extraordinary step of threatening to resign his position is quietly dropped. Also dropped was Moran's hope, expressed in his notebook for 21 February 1952, that 'just for a second it crossed my mind that he might after all ask me to take on the Ministry [of Health]'. This hope was never expressed in the original book, but was used maliciously against Moran in the controversy over its publication. But we have to remember that the idea of Moran as Minister of Health was by no means ridiculous. He had, after all, been President of the Royal College of Physicians for nine years, and he was no less qualified for the post than Lord Alexander had been when he became Minister of Defence only nine days later.[1]

In summarizing the picture of Churchill's later years in *The Struggle for Survival*, John Ramsden writes that

> Churchill appears as a pill-popping hypochondriac, petty and jealous with colleagues, maudlin about his own decaying powers, and quite outrageously lazy when in office as Prime Minister after 1951. But it also presents a warm and plausible human being, full of life and vitality (if decreasingly so as he moved through his eighties – but that likewise was all too plausible).[2]

Much the same could be said for the impression of Moran – this revised edition restores some of Moran's faults. It shows us his hopes and fears, but it also shows Moran as a rounded, humane, intelligent doctor, keenly aware of his obligations not only to Churchill the man, but also Churchill the politician. Mostly, of course, we now see Moran as a supreme political observer. It places Moran at the centre of Churchill's entourage and sheds immeasurable light on the working life of Churchill. *Churchill: The Struggle for Survival 1945–60*, therefore, is both a controversial and an essential book for anyone interested in Churchill the man and the statesman. But it is also an invaluable source for anyone interested in understanding the doctor, as well as his patient.

Matthew Grant, Queen Mary, University of London

[1] Ramsden, *Man of the Century*, p. 534.
[2] Ibid.
Acknowledgements: I would like to thank Tracey Loughran for lending a friendly ear and a critical eye throughout the writing of this introduction; the staff at the library of the Wellcome Institute, Lord Moran, and Becky Hardie at Constable & Robinson Ltd.

Preface

It happened that in both the German Wars I was plucked out of a busy life and left with time on my hands. In the First War I found myself in the trenches in France, where for nearly three years, apart from a battle or two, it was my task to help the men of my battalion to see the business through, although they were better fitted for war than I was. To fill the day and to save myself from the awful sameness of those years of trench warfare I began to keep a diary.

It was not a diary in the ordinary sense of the word. My job was to keep men in the line. What was happening in men's minds? How were they wearing? Those were the only questions that seemed to matter during my years with the battalion in France, and in my diary I set out to find the answers. Entry after entry was taken up with reflections on morale, which after a lapse of thirty years found their way into print in *The Anatomy of Courage*.

In the Second War, in May 1940, a few days after Mr Churchill became Prime Minister, he accepted me, though without enthusiasm, as his doctor. When I began to travel with him my practice vanished; it did not return, and I was able to give all my time to my unusual task. In a sense it was not unlike my job in the First War, only I was concerned now with the effects of stress and strain on a single individual, Winston Churchill.

He came to me more than once in the last years of the war

complaining of exhaustion, and it was plain that he was nearly burnt
out. But it was after the war, when he was fighting inch by inch to
keep his place in political life in the face of a series of strokes, that
he was really in need of help. 'It is the state of my mind that troubles me,' he complained. 'You have studied these things. Surely you
ought to be able to do something for it.'

Winston knew that if he was to help me he must not keep anything back, and it became my custom as I drove away from No. 10
or Chequers or Chartwell to note, sometimes on the back of an
envelope, anything that he said which might help me to get to the
bottom of his troubles. From these notes I wrote out the conversations with Winston the same night [. . .] had at that time no thought
of writing for publication.

A long time later, I attended a dinner at Caius College,
Cambridge, to celebrate its foundation six centuries earlier. I sat
next to Dr G. M. Trevelyan. I did not know him, and neither of us,
I suppose, is at our ease with strangers. For a long time we sat in
silence. Then, perhaps, it occurred to him that I was a guest from
London. At any rate, he fired a question at me about Churchill as if
he were not interested in my answer. When I replied he turned his
chair towards me, and for half an hour directed at me a stream of
questions. I dealt with them as best I might. 'This is history,' he said.
'You ought to get it on paper.' I tried to tell him that the trouble was
that I was Winston's doctor. He interrupted me, and, taking me, as
it were, by the scruff of the neck, proceeded to tell me that I knew
some facts about Winston which were not known to others, and that
it was my duty to make them available to posterity. 'It is inevitable
that everything about this man will be known in time. Let us have
the truth.' . . .

It was not until some years later that I came to see that it is not
possible to follow the last twenty-five years of Winston's life without
a knowledge of his medical background. It was exhaustion of mind
and body that accounts for much that is otherwise inexplicable
in the last year of the war – for instance, the deterioration in his
relations with Roosevelt. Masefield ascribed the diffuseness of

Winston's *The Second World War* to the same reason. It is certain that the onset of old age and the succession of strokes explain in part why he was not more effective as Leader of the Opposition, and later as First Minister of the Crown. While Winston counted politically these details are part of history and ought not to be left out of his story. It is as plain that only a doctor can give the facts accurately.

After his retirement in April, 1955, Winston made little effort to hide his distaste for what was left to him of life, and the historian might conclude that this reveals a certain weakness in moral fibre. Such strictures will, however, carry little weight unless due allowance is made for the way in which his will was sapped by old age and disease. It is therefore proper, and only fair to him, that the reader should be given the details of his mounting decrepitude.

When, however, Winston ceased to count in politics, when in a sense he could no longer be said to be responsible, I began to question whether there was any purpose in preserving a chronicle of his failing powers. During the last five years of his life I continued from habit to make notes in my case-book, but apart from the two alarming accidents when he broke his spine and fractured his femur, the short entries in my diary add little to the record. I have thought it proper to omit the painful details of the state of apathy and indifference into which he sank after his resignation, because they are no longer of historical significance, and so I bring my story to an end five years before his death.

Winston, as I shall tell, once asked me whether he ought to have retired earlier. I did not answer, but in turn myself asked a question: 'What will be said in fifty years' time of the part I have played?' I was, I think, alone in urging him to hang on, though I knew that he was hardly up to his job for at least a year before he resigned office. His family and his friends pressed him to retire; they feared that he might do something which would injure his reputation. I held that this was none of my business. I knew that he would feel that life was over when he resigned, and that he would be unhappy when there was no purpose in his existence. It was my job as his doctor to postpone that day as long as I could.

It was said of Chatham that his countrymen were so conscious of what they owed to him that they did not want to hear about his faults. That may be true of Winston Churchill. And yet he is already a part of history. A biographer, it is said, is on his oath, and once I decided to write this book its nature could not be in doubt; I cannot tamper with the facts any more than I could fake an experiment in the laboratory. In extreme old age a man is still sensitive to praise or blame, but he has come to see that if he can get at the truth much will be forgiven him.

'However, all things of this nature must be submitted, as this is, with great deference to the judgement of the equal reader.'[1]

Taken from Lord Moran's Preface in the original edition

---

[1] Clarendon, *History of the Rebellion*, preface to 1st edition.

PART ONE

Fall from Power

CHAPTER ONE

The Big Blow

London, July 26, 1945

Today as I walked along Pall Mall to the College of Physicians, where I was lunching, I met Jock Colville. He said there had been a landslide 'like 1906'. Brendan, Harold Macmillan and other Ministers were out.

After the Comitia, when Fellows were having tea in the hall of the College, Dorothy brought me the three-o'clock results given on the wireless, which I read to them. They were so taken aback they stood there in complete silence. One Fellow so far forgot where he was as to emit a low whistle. A little later the four-o'clock results confirmed the rout.

I walked down to the Annexe. The P.M. was with Alan Lascelles; I wrote him a note. He sent out a message that he would like to see me. He was sitting in the small room next to the secretaries', where I had never seen him before, doing nothing. He was lost in a brown study. He looked up. 'Well, you know what has happened?' I spoke of the ingratitude of the people. 'Oh, no,' he answered at once, 'I wouldn't call it that. They have had a very hard time.'

I expressed my fears that it might end in Stalin's being given too much of his own way. But the P.M. replied that Attlee and Bevin would stand up to Stalin: 'I do not feel down at all. I'm not certain the Conservative Party could have dealt with the labour troubles that are coming. It will be said Max brought me down,' he mused, 'but I shall never say that. He is far harder hit by this result than any of us.'

I said what I could to comfort him: that there was great unrest in the country; that demobilization, housing and unemployment would add to it; and that it was inevitable that the Government in power would get the blame. I said that I had dreaded the next two years for him. I think this brought him a little comfort, but he said nothing. At last he spoke. 'The public will be staggered when they hear tonight at nine o'clock that I've resigned. Labour will be in for four years at least. They may make it difficult for the Conservatives to come in again. But I think the financial consequences of their policy will be their undoing. This is not necessarily the end.'

I said that if he went abroad for health or other purpose I would like to go with him as I had done during the war, and that I should be hurt if he did not make use of me. He rose and thanked me for what I had done for him. 'If it hadn't been for you I might not be here now,' he said with tears in his eyes.

He blamed no one. He was very sad as he talked quietly about what had happened. I left him, for I did not want to add to his distress by showing my own feelings. For some time I have had a growing disquiet that he has lost touch with the way people are thinking; but I was not prepared for this debacle. I was so sure that we should return to Berlin that I left my luggage there. Now I must arrange for its recovery.

July 27, 1945

This morning, calling at the Annexe at 9.45, I found everything strangely quiet. The place seemed deserted. Sawyers told me before I went to his bedroom that Winston had been giddy before retiring. But when I went in he said at once: 'I'm very well.' He spoke very quietly; he was sad but quite composed. He had been 'stunned by the result'. He felt there was 'some disgrace in the size of the majority'. If it had been thirty or forty it would have been different. The soldiers had been noticeably cool when he opened the 'Winston Club' in Berlin. They had been told to cheer, but it was obvious that they had voted against him. The Army, he went on, had had a big say in these events. At his age there could be no question of a comeback. I asked him if he was going to take a holiday.

'There is no difficulty about holidays now,' he said with a wistful smile. 'The rest of my life will be holidays. It will be worse in three days, like a wound; I shall then realize what it means. What I shall miss is this' – pointing to the red box full of papers. 'It is a strange feeling, all power gone,' he mused. 'I had made all my plans; I feel I could have dealt with things better than anyone else. This is Labour's opportunity to bring in socialism, and they will take it. They will go very far.'

August 8, 1945

It is a fortnight tomorrow since we heard. Winston has been very brave and gentle under the blow. Before it fell he did not see that the nation was no longer in the mood to accept everything he told them. The result of the General Election gave him back his sight. Once in the First War I stayed in a ruined farm with a wounded officer until he died. His life had not been careful, and his face had become fleshy. As the days followed one another and nothing but water passed his lips, his face became thinner and thinner, until at the end the features had regained the chiselled refinement of his youth. Since the election it has seemed to me that Winston has been purged of the frailties which have prevented so many of his immediate colleagues from fully accepting his greatness – and when you get beneath the self-indulgence which he has allowed himself throughout his life, there is a fine character, staunch and truthful, loyal and affectionate.

Now he has the more difficult task of swallowing the bitterness of second thoughts. When I called on him at Duncan Sandys's flat in Westminster Gardens I found him sitting in his silk vest on the edge of the bed, looking at the floor. I asked him how he was sleeping. He said he kept waking about four o'clock in the morning and had to take a 'red' to get to sleep, or 'futile speculations' filled his mind.

'It's no use, Charles, pretending I'm not hard hit. I can't school myself to do nothing for the rest of my life. It would have been better to have been killed in an aeroplane, or to have died like Roosevelt. After I left Potsdam, Joe did what he liked. The Russians' western frontier was allowed to advance, displacing another eight million poor devils. I'd not have agreed and the Americans would have backed me. I get fits of depression. You know how my days were filled; now it has all gone. I go to bed about twelve o'clock. There is nothing to sit up for. What is that knocking? Will it go on all day? I can no longer stop it at will.'

He hates whistling, or the sound of knocking, and someone used to rush off to silence the blasphemous sounds. I asked him once more about his plans. He wanted to get back to Chartwell. He had got his paints out. He thought he might go to the south of France about the first week in September; it was all under Eisenhower's command. Ike [Dwight D. Eisenhower] would be glad to let him stay there indefinitely. Perhaps he wouldn't come home until the autumn session. He'd leave that to Eden. 'If I'm ill you could fly out.' With a wry smile, 'I think the Government would arrange that for me.' Sawyers came into the room; Winston waited until he went out.

'They want me to go to Australia and New Zealand, but I haven't the heart or strength or life for it. They keep offering me the freedom of places, but I won't bother.' Under his breath he muttered something about ingratitude. 'If Eisenhower will have me, I think I'll go to the Riviera. I don't mind if I never see England again. Ah, Charles, blessings become curses. You kept me alive and now – '

He turned his back, and when he looked at me his eyes were full of tears.

August 23, 1945

Called on Winston at Westminster Gardens. He was in quite good form. Mrs Hill tells me he is much rested. But he said: 'It has been a horrible experience. When I left St Paul's on Sunday there was a lot of cheering. No Minister got any. But what's the good of it all? I don't know where I stand with the public. I have not even ceased to reproach myself for wasting time whenever I play a game of cards. I find I do not want to sleep in the afternoon now. You ought to put your mind to that and what it means. I needed the afternoon sleep then; I don't seem to now. I am very happy at Chartwell. I can paint for three or four hours without getting tired. I'm just touching up old pictures, a new sky perhaps. Yes, I was standing all the time. I think I must get some sort of high stool so that I can paint sitting. I am going to Italy – to Alex – on the first of September.'

August 26, 1945
I read today a letter of Chekhov: 'There is a sort of stagnation in my soul. I explain it by the stagnation of my own personal life. I am not disappointed. I am not tired. I am not depressed, but simply everything has become less interesting.' I feel like that.

CHAPTER TWO

The Beginning of Convalescence

September 1, 1945

Winant telephoned to me in his pleasant, diffident way: 'Would you like to help me?'

It was not Winant but Sarah Churchill who needed help. She may have some difficulty, it is thought, in getting leave from the Air Force to go with her father to Italy. Winston would be away a month, and it would help if I said that she ought to go to look after him. I was not sure whether Winston would like his health used as a pretext, and, as Sarah shared my doubts, Winant in the end agreed that it would be better to apply for leave on other grounds. Winston has never had any compunction about taking Mary or Sarah away from their units to accompany him on his travels – nor did he ever hesitate to ask the captain of a battleship, or an Army chieftain, to put them up. His word was law then, none dared to dispute it. But now that he has come down in the world they have to ask for leave like any other member of the Forces. There is hurt enough in his change of fortune without this. I telephoned to Clemmie and asked her if Winston was quite happy going off to Italy without me. She said at once she was sure he was, that he was very well and I need not worry. But after I had gone to bed I was awakened by the telephone bell. It was Clemmie; she had told Winston what I had said, and he had rather jumped at the idea that I should go with him; it would, she said, be a great comfort to her too.

September 2, 1945

We left Northolt this morning in Alex's Dakota and arrived at Milan after a flight of five and a half hours. All the time Winston remained buried in a printed copy of the minutes which for five years he had sent out month by month to the Chiefs of Staff and the Cabinet. Even during luncheon he went on reading, only taking his eyes from the script to light a cigar. I drove with him to the house on Lake Como that had been prepared for him.

'People say my speeches after Dunkirk were the thing. That was only a part, not the chief part,' he complained. 'They forget I made all the main military decisions. You'd like to read my minutes, Charles.'

I asked him had they worn well. He smiled comfortably.

'They are mine. I can publish them.'

He was still going over the minutes in his head.

'Brookie was covering the retreat to Dunkirk with three divisions; Bulgey Thorne, commanding one of them, suddenly found himself faced with a large number of tanks, and thought to himself: this isn't too good, it may go hard with our fellows. Then the tanks had suddenly disappeared; they had gone to finish off Calais. I had given orders to the Calais garrison to fight to the last man, to give time for the troops to embark at Dunkirk. This saved the situation. Calais made the evacuation at Dunkirk possible.'

Winston's face became set and resolute as he followed the drama.

'If Calais had surrendered, those tanks and the troops around Calais would have turned on our men retreating to Dunkirk, and they would probably never have got away. It was my decision. When I made it I had a feeling I was going to be sick.'

He stopped and turned to me.

'Tell me, Charles, how does emotion stop the stomach digesting?' Winston continued:

'At one time I thought we should be lucky if forty thousand men got away. Next morning my price went up. The small boats taking away our army; it is an epic tale.'

Winston lisped as he followed the men down the beaches into the water until, breast-high, they stretched out to sea, like a black pier under the gathering night.

Major Ogier, the officer from the 4th Hussars, sent to meet us at the airfield, had been at Dunkirk, and during dinner Winston questioned him closely. He wanted detail, facts.

'What took you off the beach?'

'A destroyer, sir.'

'How long were you on the beaches?' Winston persisted.

After two days a destroyer had sent boats to take them off and finally landed them at Ramsgate. Next morning they found themselves at Bristol with a great crowd of other units, but every single man had eggs and bacon for breakfast. As Ogier talked, Winston nodded vigorously and began to speak of 'the magic carpet' by which this great host was collected from Dunkirk and distributed, overnight as it were, all over the country.

I made him tell again how he called his Ministers to his room at the House of Commons and told them how the fate of the Army in France was in the balance. 'But even if things come out against us, if not a man returns, we shall fight on. At that at least half of them jumped up from the table and came running to my chair and patted my back.' It was like that in 1940.

When he talks of the deliverance of Dunkirk, Winston has the invasion at the back of his mind. 'It was my job,' he said, 'to keep the Germans out.' He had, in fact, good reason to be exhilarated and uplifted by the Army's escape.

'Dunkirk was a turning-point. In a month after their return to England these men became a formidable army. It was one thing to plan an invasion of England before Dunkirk, with a hundred thousand men; quite another when perhaps half a million would be needed to break down the defences of this army.'

We were sitting on the balcony after dinner looking across the lake at the lights twinkling out of the darkness. It brought back to me the Embassy lawn at Cairo and the talks with Smuts. I said so. There was no response. Then after a long pause Winston murmured:

'Smuts sent me two heartfelt telegrams after the election, but I haven't answered them.' A pause. 'I was offended by the telegram he sent Attlee about his "brilliant victory". Brilliant indeed.' His voice rose. 'If he had just congratulated him on his victory it would have been different. Why brilliant?' The word stuck in his gorge. 'It wasn't brilliant at all.'

He looked across the lake for a long time in silence.

To turn his thoughts I asked him about Portal's future.

'If I'd gone on I'd have made him a Governor-General. He has everything which is needed. But what is the use of all these ifs?' he said impatiently.

The conversation lapsed again. His cigar smoke went straight up. I watched it vanish.

'I have a very difficult time ahead,' he said half to himself.

I said I hoped he'd write and give politics a rest. He replied that he wasn't in the mood for writing. 'Besides,' with a smile, 'I shan't write while the Government take all you earn. Dr Johnson said that only a fool wrote when he wasn't paid for writing.'

He reverted to the election. He had hesitated for a long time whether to wait until the autumn, as the Labour Party had suggested. It was discussed by the Cabinet, but most of them felt it would be difficult to go on with the Labour Ministers undermining everything that was done.

'But,' Winston added, 'Hudson[1] didn't agree. I remember he interjected from the far end of the table that he didn't think the Prime Minister ought to be pressed when he was so reluctant. I believe, too, he was thinking of the harvest. Of course, the autumn would have paid us, as things turned out. The Jap war would have been over and I should have had another six months. I enjoyed it so much,' he added half to himself; but he went on: 'We have had some luck too.'

I tried again to turn the conversation. 'Will Russia be a nuisance in the future?' I asked him.

[1] R. S. Hudson, Minister of Agriculture and Fisheries.

He answered: 'Russia has altered her tune since the atomic bomb. She sees she can't just do what she likes with the world.'[1]

He got up and went in. In the first room he entered there was a great glass bowl which became a fountain when it was inverted. He sat down and watched it. In his soft black hat, dark overcoat, white duck trousers and bedroom slippers, he made a strange picture as he gazed at the bowl.

'Marvellous,' he muttered. 'Turn it on again. I really call it remarkable.'

At last he went to bed.

September 3, 1945

We had planned to set out about ten o'clock to reconnoitre the surrounding country for a scene which Winston could paint; however, it was noon before we set off. As we drove by the lake, he kept his eyes open for running water, or a building with shadows playing on it, but we stopped for a picnic lunch before he had found what he wanted. The 'picnic' arrived in a covered shooting brake with his chair and a small table. A score of Italian peasants gathered in a circle and watched us eat. He was in high spirits.

'The greatest change in my condition that I notice is that I need do nothing I don't want to. I need not get up if I don't want to, and yet the days seem to pass speedily by.'

He went on with a whimsical look,

> *The world is so full of a number of things*
> *I'm sure we should all be as happy as kings.*

When he was satisfied that he had found something he could put on canvas, he sat solidly for five hours, brush in hand, only pausing

---

[1] Two atomic bombs were dropped on Japan, the first on Hiroshima on August 6, 1945, and the second on Nagasaki, three days later. The Japanese offered to surrender on August 10, thus preventing the need for an Allied invasion and the presence of Russian troops. Russia did not declare war on Japan until a few days before the capitulation.

from time to time to lift his sombrero and mop his brow. When he had done, I could only hope that he would come to no harm as he drove in an open car through the chilly night air, while he nursed his hat.

After dinner Winston was ready to talk of anything; he only mentioned the election once. Duff Cooper, he said, had a devil of a temper. When he got into gear his veins stood out, he looked as though he was about to have a seizure. Once someone told Duff that he was the worst Secretary for War in living memory. 'How dare you say that?' Duff had hissed. 'How dare you say that,' he had repeated with intense passion, 'in the presence of Jack Seely?'[1] Winston made guttural sounds as he savoured the full humour of Duff's remark. He did not want anyone to miss the point, 'You see,' he added, 'Seely was there.' At that he gave a great yawn; when we thought he was about to go to bed he broke into a hymn and sang three verses of 'Art thou weary'.

September 4, 1945

All morning Winston has been immersed in his minutes. He has not looked at them for a long time; now he wants to know how he comes out of it all. When you go into his bedroom he looks up, but he does not put down his bound copy. It is as if he was saying: 'Yes, yes, but I'm very interested. Could you return?' He is finding his role of prophet, as painted in these telegrams and minutes, very reassuring and gratifying.

September 5, 1945

In a sense Winston is tough, yet he is hardly ever out of my hands. His eyes, his ears, his throat, his heart and lungs, his digestion and his diverticulitis have given him trouble at different times. Some little thing goes wrong and apprehension and impatience do the rest. And if his doctor cannot bring relief, well, he ought to. This morning he sent for me. He had discovered a swelling in his groin. He was keyed

[1] Secretary of State for War, 1912–14.

up and waited anxiously while I made my examination. When I told him he was ruptured he seemed relieved it wasn't anything worse, but he immediately fired at me a stream of questions. Was an operation necessary? Would it become strangulated? Would it get worse? How long would it be before he got used to a truss? Why should he get a rupture at his age, when he hardly took any exercise? Brigadier Edwards, the consulting surgeon for the Army in Italy, said he would get him a truss in Milan, and now all is set fair again. Besides, Winston has been painting well today, so tonight he is all smiles.

September 6, 1945
We have been six days without a single letter, telegram or newspaper; they seem to get held up at Naples. If this had happened in the old days, what a terrific uproar Winston would have made! Telegrams would have been sent off, peremptory orders flashed back, abashed officials would have read, 'I will not be treated like this.' Now he hardly seems to have noticed the absence of news for, as he confessed tonight, he had found the solution of his troubles in his paint-box, just as he had thirty years ago when he was thrown out over the Dardanelles.[1]

In adversity Winston becomes gentle, patient and brave; always magnanimous to his enemies, he is content if he is justified by the event. But when the sun shines his arrogance, intolerance and cocksureness assume alarming proportions. At Hendaye, before the blow had fallen, hardly a day passed without some rather childish outburst of petulance, whereas nothing of the kind has marred the even serenity of these autumnal days. However, his sanguine spirit will not let him accept defeat for long, and it is plain from his conversation that he has made up his mind to cut his losses. He will not spend the rest of his days brooding on the past. Whatever happens,

---

[1] The failure of the Dardanelles campaign in 1915 had serious political repercussions. Before the evacuation had been decided, Asquith's Liberal administration was superseded by his coalition government. Churchill, the chief architect of the venture, resigned from the cabinet and went to France to command an infantry battalion.

nothing can hold up for long the stream of ideas that rush bubbling through his head. And if his thoughts keep turning to the past, it is not to the election, which he scarcely mentions, but to the war and the tremendous events of those 'wonderful years'. All his life, he has come to believe, was but a preparation for that epic struggle – the grand climacteric of his career – and naturally the chief actors in that drama are much in his mind.

Particularly Stalin; for in Winston's imagination he is already one of the great figures of history. On the other hand, apart from some passing tribute to Roosevelt, he seldom seems to allude to him in his conversation. In Washington, perhaps for a week or more, Winston would immure himself in the White House, where he would talk to the President for hours at a time, but he never tells us of Roosevelt's views, nor are we regaled by what he said, or by stories about him. The cast of Roosevelt's mind – I am thinking of his preoccupation with social problems and the rights of the common man – struck no sparks in Winston's mind. The war was all they had in common. Whereas Stalin was a type Winston had not met before; he interested him, notwithstanding his deliberate rudeness and his rough speech. 'In spite of everything I'd like that man to like me.' They are Winston's own words, addressed to us in August, 1942, and they explain much that is otherwise obscure. Stalin's stories, his ways, his habits, kept leaking out in Winston's talk; the man had caught his imagination, so that the P.M. had looked forward to the meetings in the Kremlin. Tonight he told us of a conversation with Stalin that I had not heard before. It was late at night, after Winston had dined in the Marshal's private apartments. Stalin asked: 'Why are you afraid of us Russians? You need not be. We have no intention of conquering the world – though we could if we wished,' he added. Uncle Joe had never been so frank before.

'You see,' Winston said, 'we'd both had a good deal to drink. I wanted to say to Stalin, "Don't you be too sure. Ribbentrop said something of the sort to me before the war. But England is a curious country. We have a way of finding the world on our side, and the world is a big place." But everything had to be translated, and before

I could say what I wanted to say, Stalin had gone on to speak of something else. Stalin had never been so candid before. The American armies were vanishing, ours were dwindling, there seemed nothing to stop the Russian armies marching where they pleased. And then the atomic bomb altered all that.'

September 8, 1945
Golfed in the morning and got back a little late for luncheon, but in time to hear Winston on the Boer War. Alex asked him about Buller. Was he a good General? Winston hedged. But he went on to tell how they had secured an important height and Buller was urged to pursue the beaten foe. 'Pursuit be damned,' Buller said with emphasis: 'Why, we wanted this place badly, and if we pursue they may return.' Somebody asked him if a few squadrons of cavalry might follow, and Buller grudgingly agreed; Winston went with them, to meet the starving defenders of Ladysmith. We heard once more how Lord Granard had made Buller promise that if he ever went on a campaign he would take him with him. Granard had great wealth. He picked some of his very best champagne, and to ensure that it was not stolen, labelled each of the six cases 'castor oil'. When it did not arrive, Granard grew anxious and telephoned to the base. Enquiries were made and the answer came back: 'Cases cannot be traced. Probably used in hospitals, but am sending six similar cases.'

After luncheon Alex departed. As he drove away, Winston stood on the doorstep, waving after the retreating car and shouting: 'Remember Friday. Don't forget. Do try and come.' A smiling Alex waved back, gracious but noncommittal. So tonight we are a family party, Winston, Sarah and I, with Ogier and the officer in charge of the Guard. In the old days I should have been fearful lest he should be bored, but everything is different now. As he says, he has not been so happy for a long time. Of course there had been high moments of glorious exultation after some victory, but they did not last.

This quiet, serene content is something new. That it is more than a passing phase of his convalescence I can hardly credit, for Winston is not built on these lines. Nevertheless, Winston told me today:

'With my painting I have recovered my balance. I'm damned glad now to be out of it.'

He looked for a long time across the lake, and then he added:

'I shall paint for the rest of my days. I've never painted so well before. The papers seem to bore me; I just glance at them.'

The pictures were placed where he could gaze at them as he dined. I told him a story – always a foolhardy thing to do. He listened, but his eyes were on the pictures.

'That new colour they found in Milan is wonderful. I've got it in the roofs of the houses.'

After dinner he asked for gramophone records. Ogier, who is musical, put on Edward German's *Merrie England*, but he would have none of it.

'Dreadful,' he exclaimed. 'Give me something with a tune in it.'

Then he began to waltz with Sarah. He went round for quite a long time, with a mischievous twinkle and half-suppressed smile.

'You boys, do you dance?'

Tim, who is in charge of the Guard, had gone straight from school into the Army. He didn't dance.

'When I was young,' Winston continued, 'I didn't either. It was a great mistake.'

He began to recite from *Childe Harold*. He spoke about Byron's life, but his mind is not really analytical. He never says anything about people which throws new light on them; he only tells me what they did on such and such an occasion. He spoke of Macaulay's orations as having been the greatest inspiration of his life and quoted a few tags.

And then he gave us a tremendous chunk of Pope, to whom he generally turns when I begin to quote the things I love and best remember. His face was pink, his eyes twinkled, he was a child again, radiantly happy. It was nearly two o'clock before he went to bed.

September 9, 1945
A wet day, and Winston has had to fall back once more on touching up his canvases in his bathroom, which is also his studio. When

I went to his room in the late afternoon I found him in a sombre mood.

'I am very depressed,' he said; 'The papers' – pointing to a lot of newspapers littering his bed.

At that moment Sawyers came into the room and he said no more. Sarah told me later the Press had got into the house he has bought in Hyde Park Gate,[1] and, finding it was being redecorated in a manner denied to lesser folk, had made a song about it. All his good spirits seemed to have evaporated. He sighed heavily, sitting on the edge of the bed as if he was too exhausted to rise and dress. But during dinner he began to recover his morale. The flies were troublesome. He rose from the table with a mischievous glint in his eyes; then, biting his lip as if he was about to spring on some animal, he raised his napkin and for a moment stood poised, ready to strike, before with a smack he destroyed a fly on the wall. Soon, armed with our napkins, we joined in the assault. Every time a fly fell dead its corpse was placed on the table, until there were thirty dead flies laid out in a line.

The records were brought out; the 'Blue Danube' reappeared. Winston led Sarah on to a space which Ogier had cleared, and they gravely waltzed round the small area.

Then Winston had an idea. On the wall there was a picture representing a lake and its wooded shore. There was no light in the picture. Winston would repair its artistic shortcomings. But the picture had been let into the wall. At Winston's suggestion, Ogier got up on a chair and finally, as the plaster fell on the floor, the picture in its frame was wrenched from its socket in the wall. Then Ogier prised open the glass which covered the painting, and Winston, seizing the panel, bore it in triumph to his bathroom. Sarah had doubts about this assault on the property of the absent steel magnate; it was just doing damage for the fun of the thing, the kind of thing the Russians and Germans do. With a little encouragement from me, she hurried after her father to lodge her protest.

[1] 28 Hyde Park Gate, Churchill's London house.

It was waved aside. Winston was already busy with his brushes. It was after midnight; there was no more to be done, so I went to bed.

In the morning Sarah told me how the picture had been transformed; a sunset had been introduced, while the water gave him a chance to use the new paint which lit up whatever it touched. It was great fun, she said, forgetting her first reaction. But second thoughts often come to Winston's rescue. He isn't one of those people who instinctively do the right thing. On the contrary, he often does something foolish, but long experience has taught him a little caution. It occurred to him now that if people heard of this exploit it might be used against him even more effectively than the decorating of his new house. With turpentine he proceeded to remove every trace of the painting which he had superimposed on the dull, lifeless composition; the picture was secured again in its socket in the wall, and, except for a few small white holes on the light-green wall, where plaster had fallen, no one will suspect the assault.

September 13, 1945

A slight relapse in morale this morning. The election is again in his thoughts. Perhaps it is the weather; anyway, Winston has kept to his room all day, painting in the bathroom. The arrival of Montag, who represents Switzerland in Paris as Fine Arts Commissioner, helped to dispel the gloom. Winston has asked him to stay for a few days, and hopes that Montag will give him a few tips about painting. Montag, if he did not arrive laden with spices, came with a lot of beautiful brushes and twenty small boxes, each containing four or five tubes of paint. Winston said it must have cost his visitor sixty or seventy pounds. He was like a child, squeezing out a little paint from each tube, one after the other, on to his finger-tip, to savour the colour. After dinner Montag talked a great deal: his theme was that the decadence and fall of a nation can be predicted by the state of its art. Winston has seen too much of the world to take such a thesis very seriously.

Before he went to bed there was a message from Alex that his days are so full that he is sorry he cannot pay us a second visit.

CHAPTER THREE

A Year of Recovery

London, January 4, 1946

When a man is in the seventies, he throws off the effects of a surgical operation very slowly, very imperfectly. He appears to recover, but things are not the same as they were, and in the end his life may be shortened. The result of the General Election last summer left a mark on Winston which I can only liken to the scar of a major operation. It is true that he came safely out of hospital and went abroad for a period of convalescence, and that now he has come back ready for work. But it is a different Winston. The supreme self-confidence of the war years has been undermined, something of the old *élan* has evaporated. The wound appears to have healed, but there is left an ugly scar.

Winston – incredible as it may seem – is out of a job, looking for something to do, anything to keep his mind away from the past. He asked me this morning if I would be prepared to issue something to the Press which could be used both in America and in England.

'There are lots of flies buzzing round this old decaying carcass. I want something to keep them away. I want sun, solitude, serenity and something to eat' – a pause and then a grin – 'and perhaps something to drink.'

But what he really wants is something quite different. Looking up at me, he said:

'I think I can be of some use over there; they will take things from me. It may be that Congress will ask me to address them. I'd like that. Our Parliament can't. I'm a controversial figure, but they might. It's a funny position. I feel I could do things and there's nothing to be done. I'll go to Florida, avoiding New York; it's too cold there at present to go through the streets with one's hat off.'

And on top of this gnawing sense of frustration the humiliations of old age vex him. Not that the old man is impatient or unreasonable; he is in fact much more gentle these days.

He murmured something about his gratitude for all the trouble that had been taken, and then, just as I was leaving, he asked me about his eyes. When they began to bother him he had been told that ingrowing eyelashes were acting as a mechanical irritant and were the cause of his conjunctivitis. At first he found satisfaction in this diagnosis, and relief when they were removed. But at Yalta he had burst out:

'My eyes are no better, there must be something else causing the trouble. Surely it should not be beyond the resources of medicine to get to the bottom of this conjunctivitis.'

So, on our return, Whiting[1] was called in consultation. He came armed with a kind of telescope which threw a powerful light on the P.M.'s eyes, making the smaller lashes more visible. But the bright light hurt his sore eyes and presently, rising from the chair, he stalked over to the fire, with his face full of displeasure and the hurt, sulky look of a child. Whiting thought the inflammation was due to a microbe and that the lashes only contributed to the trouble. He said so without any finesse. Whereupon the P.M. exclaimed:

'Do you mean to say I've had a bug all this time that hasn't been found?'

Whiting proved right. In the tears microbes were found, which rapidly vanished with a penicillin ointment. And now, after some months of peace, his eyes have begun to trouble him again, and this

[1] Ophthalmic Surgeon to the Middlesex Hospital.

time the microbes have been found to be insensitive to penicillin. The new situation defeats even Winston:

'I have brought all my wits to bear upon this problem. It's like this: these bugs are the sons and grandsons of the sensitive ones; do sensitive bugs breed insensitive sons? And how long do they remain insensitive? We must ask Fleming.'

His instinct is to think everything out, and then he is quite sure that he knows all about it – far more than any doctor or soldier or sailor can tell him.

June 27, 1946
It is nearly a year since the election. Winston told me today he could do a good deal without getting tired.

'Yesterday I dined out and sat talking till two o'clock, and on my way home I saw a light in the Commons and found them sitting. I listened for half an hour, and then I made a very vigorous speech. I don't see why the Government shouldn't be beaten up. They've made an awful mess of this bread business. By August or September there may be no bread in the shops. They are very worried about it. Why, if we'd failed to bring in the wheat we should have been for it.'

For the first time, perhaps, the thought of a come-back flashed through his mind. He poked his nose in my face as he stopped pacing the room:

'A short time ago I was ready to retire and die gracefully. Now I'm going to stay and have them out.' With great vehemence: 'I'll tear their bleeding entrails out of them. I'm in pretty good fettle,' he went on in a more subdued tone. 'The Jerome blood.'[1]

'You would,' I mocked, 'ascribe to natural causes what is due to my art.'

'Ah, no, Charles,' he said warmly. 'I saw Alexander Fleming about my eyes. He wasn't interested in me as a patient, but in a very unusual bug in my nose, a staphylococcus, which was very resistant

[1] Leonard Jerome, Churchill's American maternal grandfather; died 1891.

to penicillin.' With a grin, 'The bug seems to have caught my truculence. This is its finest hour.' His face clouded. 'I asked the
Government for a plane to go to Metz – the French want me to take
part in a function there – and the Government said yes, if I was prepared to pay £200. Rather shabby, wasn't it? Of course it couldn't
be called a public duty, though the Foreign Office said it would do
good and are in favour of it.'

July 6, 1946
When I called on Winston today he seemed in poor heart – one of
his black moods.

'I'm fed-up,' he said. 'Victory has turned to sackcloth and ashes.'

August 8, 1946
Winston is happy at Chartwell, as happy as he can be when the
world has gone all wrong. I found him in the studio, the walls of
which are covered with his canvases. When he had greeted me he
climbed on to a big chair on a kind of platform, and surveyed the
canvas he was painting, which was at the other end of the square
room.

'My desert is too hot,' he said descending from his throne and
applying a white paint with a few bold strokes of a fat brush.

I said he had been busy.

'Yes, it gives me something to do – an occupation.' He paused to
take in his handiwork. 'And I must have an occupation. Elliott
Roosevelt has been writing a foolish book; he attacks me.'[1]

He advanced to the easel and made two or three quick strokes
with his brush.

'I don't care what he says,' he added almost absent-mindedly and
with his eyes glued to his picture. 'He's not much of a fellow. Elliott
says I delayed the cross-Channel invasion of Europe for two years.'
He turned to me. 'A short time ago I asked Monty whether we could

[1] Elliott Roosevelt, *As He Saw It* (Duell, Sloan & Pearce, New York, 1946),
p. 253.

have invaded France before we did. Monty answered: "It would have been madness. We could not have done it without the landing craft." '

Winston seemed to be thinking more of the picture than of Elliott Roosevelt. This was the real Winston, magnanimous, refusing to be ruffled by the small change of politics. The telephone rang. It was Clemmie summoning us to lunch. He put on a waterproof over his boiler suit, and walked very slowly up the slope to the house. I admired the fine setting.

'Ah, you should see it when the sun is on the Weald.'

He stood still to get his breath. I asked him how he had been.

'Two nights ago I was arguing with Randolph at two o'clock. We got heated. I bellowed and he counter-bellowed, and I felt things weren't right here.'

He pointed to his heart. I asked him if it was pain. He hesitated.

'No, but I was conscious of my heart; it was like the ghost of what happened at Washington when I tried to open the window. But I'm very well if I keep within my limits. I think I can make plans for some years yet. I feel much better than when I was Prime Minister.'

Winston did not seem to expect me to intervene. When he came to the house he pulled himself wearily, step by step, up to his work-room, where he picked up a little book and asked me if I would like it. I looked over his shoulder at the title: *Secret Session Speeches by Winston Churchill.*

'It has just come from America. I'm very pleased with it.'

The secretary spoke to him of 'Baby Winston'.[1]

'Why do you call him "Baby"? He is six years old.'

'Master Winston,' she corrected herself in a subdued voice.

They came to tell us that lunch was ready. There were just the three of us. Winston spoke gloomily of the future.

'You think there will be another war?'

'Yes.'

[1] Son of Randolph Churchill; born 1940.

'You mean in ten years' time?'

'Sooner. Seven or eight years. I shan't be there.'

I asked him if it would be between Russia and her satellite countries and the Anglo-Saxon countries.

'Yes, with France and Scandinavia and Belgium and Holland on our side.'

I wondered how England could take part in an atomic war when she was so small. He said:

'We ought not to wait until Russia is ready. I believe it will be eight years before she has these bombs.' His face brightened. 'America knows that fifty-two per cent of Russia's motor industry is in Moscow and could be wiped out by a single bomb. It might mean wiping out three million people, but they would think nothing of that.' He smiled. 'They think more of erasing an historical building like the Kremlin.'

His cigar had gone out; he fumbled in his pockets for a match.

'The Russian Government is like the Roman Church: their people do not question authority.'

I made some passing reference to Potsdam. 'Ah,' he said sadly, 'that was when the blow fell.'

He said nothing for a little, and then observed, half to himself:

'It was a blow.'

At length he rose from the table.

'Let's see if there's any news,' he said as he strode into the secretaries' room.

October 24, 1946

Called at Hyde Park Gate. Winston is full of his speech in the Commons on the danger of the Russian Army, which has not been demobilized.

Winston: 'The situation is grave.'

Moran: 'You mean there might be war in two or three years' time?'

Winston: 'Perhaps sooner than that, perhaps this winter. They have two and a half million men in the occupied countries, and we have about twelve divisions. They could march to the Atlantic in a few weeks, practically unopposed. They've got forward dumps of arms everywhere. The Swiss are most perturbed. Only the atomic bomb keeps the Russians back. They're making rockets to fire on us when they get to the coast.'

Moran: 'I doubt whether there will be war.'

Winston: 'I don't think there will be.'

Moran: 'At any rate conscription isn't an answer to this threat; if we are to be formidable it must be by mobilizing our scientists.'

Winston: 'We must have men.'

I was about to tell him of the dearth of recruits taking up science during the war, but I saw that he had lost interest in the subject. He wants people to listen to him, not to argue with him; he has learnt nothing from the election. I found Clemmie in her room. She told me that Camrose was pressing Winston to get on with his memoirs. They ought to be ready by Christmas 1947; after that they would not be worth so much. Several Oxford dons, she said, had agreed to devil for Winston. She thought the book would be a good thing; at any rate it would prevent him wandering over the Continent collecting honorary degrees.

November 30, 1946

Fifteen sat down to Winston's birthday party. We were summoned for eight-fifteen, but in the manner of the house it must have been nearly nine before dinner was announced. Brendan proposed Winston's health. He spoke in hyperbole and went on saying the same thing for quite a long time. Winston was much moved when he got up to reply; a big tear gathered beneath his left eye. His emotions are always near the surface, but they are never manufactured. He said very simply that it was a comfort to him at the end of the journey to have around him those for whom he cared. Then he exclaimed:

'But we are the past, and that is done with. Mary is the future.'

He went on to speak, very shortly, of her coming marriage, and sat down; the old man at his affectionate best. Mary said she hoped, with Christopher,[1] to found another English home, and went on to speak of what she owed to her own home, which would always be the greatest influence in her life. When the ladies had retired, Brendan belittled Smuts. Winston retorted:

'My faith in Smuts is unbreakable. He is a great man.'

Later someone referred to Winston's book, when he said:

'I should like to put down, without malice and without vanity, what happened.'

The butler came in and asked Winston if he could get the table ready for Harry Green, an actor, whose thought-transference stuff had gripped Winston. I retired with Green to a room, where he gave me a pencil and paper, and asked me to put down some serious thought. He then left the room. I wrote, 'Shall I write another book?' and folded the paper up several times. When he came back he took it from me, but without undoing it, held it against my forehead and repeated what I had written. Winston also retired and wrote: 'Shall I go to Chicago in the spring?' He was astounded when Green repeated this. Leslie Rowan then went out and asked: 'Shall we be at war with Russia within ten years?' Green not only got the words right, but went on to say, 'No.' Whereupon Winston pointed out that he was much impressed by the fact that he had got Leslie's words right, but he was not at all impressed by his views as to whether there would be a war with Russia or not. Winston found it easier to swallow magic than the conjurer's claim to views, as if ordinary folk ought not to have views at all.

In the past twelve months his spirits have risen and his vigour has come back. He has put vain regrets away; once more there is a purpose in life. He is very happy at Chartwell, farming and painting and dictating his book. In short, it has been a year of recovery.

---

[1] Christopher Soames was at this time Assistant Military Attaché, British Embassy, Paris.

CHAPTER FOUR

A Preview of Old Age

February 22, 1947

Winston telephoned to say that he was 'wheezy'. I said I would call on him, but he answered: 'No, I'll call on you.' His brother, Jack,[1] was in a poor way, and when he and Clemmie visited him they would be next door to me.

Winston was sad about Jack. He has a tender heart.

'He may not get through this turn. As you get older these things seem less tragic. In any case, there is not much time left.'

But it would be 'like the lash of a whip across my bare and quivering heart'. For a time he was silent, and then he said: 'Jack may go out with the tide.' Jack's malady had eaten into the wall of the main artery of his body, causing an aneurism, or bulging, which throbbed under his breastbone like a great engine. He knew that at any moment it might burst and kill him. But he went his way as if he had no care in the world. Every night during the war he dined in the Annexe in a mess set up for Tommy and the secretaries, and was the life of the party.

Winston sat gazing into the fire. 'You know, I'm six years older than Jack.'

He got up abruptly.

---

[1] Jack Churchill, younger brother of Winston Churchill.

'I cannot help being interested in politics; the Government is doing so much harm. Of course, it's all anticlimax.'

He cannot shake off the world of affairs.

February 23, 1947
Winston has just telephoned. 'Jack is dead. I was with him a quarter of an hour before. Yes, he meant a lot to me. I thought you would not mind my telephoning you. Good night, my dear Charles.'

June, 1947
It is nearly two years since Winston sent for me one morning because he had discovered a swelling in his groin. After examining him, I said that he had ruptured himself. Next day we began to search for a truss; the search has gone on ever since, with small success. Lately the hernia has got much larger, it is increasingly difficult to control with the truss, and is hardly ever out of his mind. He seems to look on it as a particularly humiliating hint – anyway to those who can read – of the impermanence of things. The very integument which confines his vital organs has, he protests, given way; it can, of course, be patched, stitched and strengthened to hold for a little longer, but only for a time.

Dunhill[1] rather funks an operation on a man of his age and eminence. He is a simple soul, though a fine craftsman, and regards Winston with awe and reverence as the man who saved this country from defeat. He won't hear of any question of payment whenever I have called him in to see Winston; he sees him at any time of day which suits the patient, scratching all his other appointments without a word, and he cut his summer visit to Norway by nearly a fortnight to fit in with Winston's arrangements. It is an attractive side to his character, but I am not sure it is a sound attitude for a doctor towards a patient. The only safe rule is to treat Winston exactly like any other patient. I had at last to put a blunt question to Dunhill: was there any real chance that he would be able to live the

[1] Sir Thomas Dunhill, Sergeant Surgeon to Her Majesty Queen Elizabeth II.

rest of his life without an operation? Dunhill thought it most improbable, and I decided forthwith to push Winston to a decision, so that the operation might be done while the going was good. If he must have it done, now is the time. So, after months of indecision, a date has been fixed.

Even now Winston havers; he would make a last determined effort to get used to the truss and put up with the skin irritation. When I thought I had persuaded him that he would get a good dividend for the small risk he was taking, a new trouble arose. With his liability to contract pneumonia, the surgeons are apprehensive of complications after the anaesthetic; they are jibbing at his cigars. At last they screwed up their courage to tell him that in men over seventy statistics proved that pulmonary complications after an anaesthetic were seven times more common in smokers than in non-smokers. Winston declared positively he could give up smoking whenever he liked; he would certainly not smoke for a fortnight before the operation if that was what the doctors wanted. It is true that he did make a feeble and abortive attempt to keep his word; then he decided to cut down the number of cigars to half; finally, he contrived to see Dunhill alone, and soon persuaded him to say that if Winston didn't mind the extra risk he, Dunhill, didn't.

I marvel how he dominates men. Like a ventriloquist, he puts words into the mouths of his dolls, the doctors. Then we had a skirmish over the place where the operation was to be performed; Winston made a strong plea for his own house, but this time the surgeons stood their ground. So it is all fixed for Wednesday, June 11. I went down to Chartwell on Sunday to see if anything was wanted, and had to submit to a close cross-examination. What anaesthetic would be given? Would it be injected into his veins? How long would it be before he went off? I said, before he could count fifteen. Whereupon he at once asked: how did the anaesthetic cause unconsciousness? Would he be very uncomfortable afterwards, and if so for how long? Would he have much pain?

He arrived at the nursing home with two big volumes of Macaulay's essays as a solace. I found him immersed in them on the morning of the operation. They soothed him, he said. He asked me to pass him the other volume, when he began to read from Macaulay's review of Ranke's *History of the Papacy*:

> There is not, and there never was on this earth, a work of human policy so well deserving of examination as the Roman Catholic Church. The history of that Church joins together the two great ages of human civilization. No other institution is left standing which carries the mind back to the times when the smoke of sacrifice rose from the Pantheon, and when cameleopards and tigers bounded in the Flavian amphitheatre.

He went on reading, savouring the opulence of the language, so much of it pure Winston, while Thomas Dunhill leant over the end of the bed to catch the words, his lips parted with pleasure, not so much in Macaulay's measurement of the achievement of the Catholic Church, as in pure joy at his fortune in hearing a great historic figure talk and pay tribute to another master of words. 'A fine piece of English writing,' Winston concluded, as he closed the volume. 'A fine bit of word painting.'

An operation for hernia can be, and usually is, a simple affair, but a surgeon never can tell what difficulties may confront him when he opens a belly. Winston was on the table for more than two hours. Adhesions, the legacy of the operation for appendicitis years ago, made technical difficulties. I could see that Dunhill, his assistant and the anaesthetist were engrossed in their job; but I was only an idle spectator, and as time passed and the twenty minutes the operation was to take became an hour, and then two hours, I kept glancing at the anaesthetist; and when from time to time he put his hand under the white sheet to feel the pulse I wondered if everything was all right.

Winston, however, experienced little discomfort after the operation, though he did say on the third day that it seemed 'a frightfully long time since the operation, almost before the last war'. He confessed now that he had not liked the idea of surgery, though he had said nothing. One thing interested him: he found the day before the operation that he had discarded thoughts of any kind, his mind was just vacant, 'as I imagine it is before you die'.

When Winston is well he does not think about his health, but when he is ill, particularly when he is in pain or has a temperature, he becomes impatient, and frets if his doctor seems content to be only a spectator of the course of his illness. He welcomes any active treatment, he likes to feel something is being done, and he is puzzled by my scepticism about drugs. Once, apropos of nothing, he suddenly said, with a mischievous smirk:

'Charles does not believe in any medicines, but he thinks it's only decent to put a label on before the end.'

He is always poking fun at my preoccupation with exact diagnosis. 'You are so desperately negative, Charles,' he complained. Every time he gets a cold in the head and finds his temperature is up he becomes apprehensive; those three attacks of pneumonia are always at the back of his mind.

December 7, 1947

It has been plain for some time that Winston is becoming restive. He cannot persuade himself that he is serving a useful purpose in opposition, nor for that matter does it add to the attractions of the Front Opposition Bench that most of his colleagues are so anxious to push him off it. If he were in office it would be another matter. Then he could put away his books and, with half a dozen clever young men to do the donkey work, feel that he was doing something really worth while. Of course he is right. For, like his father before him, he is at once more sober and altogether more responsible as a Minister with Civil Servants around to steady him and keep him on the rails. I was therefore not at all taken aback when Winston announced that he was stale and had decided to go to Marrakesh.

'I don't need rest. I like my mind to be active. But psychologically one needs change from time to time – different lights, different scenes, and especially different colours. Colour plays a great part in life.'

He mused for a little.

'Look at the greys and browns of a miner's life.'

When he spoke of miners it seemed to put the next General Election into his head. He thought if there was an election now it would come out fifty–fifty, and that would mean a coalition. But he did not think there would be an election yet; perhaps it would not come for two years. He would not be too old then, he thought. Meanwhile he must get on with his book. But how could he do this while he was leading his present life? It was then that he realized he was stale. Soon he had persuaded himself that he must be free for a time from the distraction of the House of Commons – that is, if his book was to have a chance.

Clemmie had been doubtful about Marrakesh. It was so remote if he were taken ill. However, Winston, brushing aside her doubts, went off in high spirits. He liked change, and at first, Sarah wrote, the holiday was a great success. Each morning he had dictated in his bedroom, so that in the afternoon he could go off to the mountains with his paint-box and a clear conscience. But when luncheon was at an end he would loiter for a long time in the garden of the hotel, dozing in the sun, and when at last he arrived at the appointed place in the foothills there was not time to finish his picture before the sun went down and a chill night air crept up out of the valley.

When the inevitable cold in the head came in retribution it hung around and would not go; and worse still, a low, smouldering fever persisted; and his doctor seemed so vague about everything. Winston began to say: 'I wonder, if Charles were here, whether he would find a patch on my lungs.' He was not happy in his mind, and one day he telephoned to me in London. The line was bad and he is a little hard of hearing; presently he rang off impatiently, but our Embassy in Paris had talked to him. They left me in no doubt that he wanted me to go. That was how one morning Clemmie, Dorothy and I set off for Marrakesh in a 'Dove' which Brendan had procured.

Winston greeted my arrival by holding out both his hands in an affectionate gesture. I had come a long way to help him, and he was all agog to hear my verdict. There was not much amiss, and when I had satisfied him that he had not got pneumonia he seemed to forget all about his illness. He began to come down to the restaurant for luncheon and dinner, and in a day or two had taken up his life just as it had been before he took to his bed a fortnight ago.

At night he would read aloud to us a chapter of his book, and when pressed he would read another. Winston is too self-conscious to read well, but that did not seem to matter. What would he pick out of this first volume, which he would have liked to call *The Downward Path*? What did he think was most vivid and arresting? He began with the fighting in Norway. The indecision and pusillanimous nature of these events would not in any case have commended them to Winston, but his distaste for the whole episode had been sharpened by the feeling that if he had been Prime Minister it would have happened differently. Roger Keyes had come down to the House in full Admiral's uniform, with all his medals, and had denounced the Government for their cowardice. He asked only to be allowed to attack, to force a landing. But Dudley Pound hated him, and Winston said that if as First Lord he had given Keyes the command there might have been resignations; the price was too high for this particular risk.

This will be stuff for the serious student of war. Winston's next chapter, however, will grip the most casual reader. It tells how Chamberlain resigned and Churchill was invited to form a Government. Winston called his account a proem. He did not want to alter it. He could add a lot more detail, but it was better as it stood. Winston went on:

'I was summoned to No. 10. Halifax was there already. I could see from what the Prime Minister said that he wanted Halifax to succeed him. He looked across the table at me, but I said nothing, and there was a very long pause. Then Halifax said that it would be difficult if the Prime Minister was a peer. I could tell that he had thrown in his hand.'

Brendan Bracken had described the scene to me and explained why Winston said nothing. Early in the evening of May 9, 1940, word reached Brendan that Winston had come to an agreement with Lord Halifax that he would act as his second in command if Halifax became Prime Minister. Brendan thought this would be disastrous, that if it were carried out we should lose the war. He went about London searching for Winston. At one o'clock in the morning he found him. 'You cannot agree to this,' Brendan spluttered, but Winston was obdurate; he said that he could not go back on his word. 'Well,' Brendan persisted, 'at least you must promise you will not speak first when you get to No. 10. Promise?' At last Winston said he would promise. Brendan went to his bed mollified. He knew that Winston would keep his word, and he knew that when Halifax spoke first he would have to suggest Winston as Prime Minister.

I was thinking of Brendan's story when Winston broke in:

'Halifax's virtues have done more harm in the world than the vices of hundreds of other people.'

Chamberlain had at least believed in Munich. Halifax did not, for the Foreign Office had drilled the facts into him. But he weakly agreed.

'And yet when I meet him, I can't help having friendly talk,' he added reflectively.

'When I was appointed Prime Minister,' he went on, 'it was an immense relief; I could discipline the bloody business at last. I had no feeling of personal inadequacy, or anything of that sort. I went to bed at three o'clock, and in the morning I said to Clemmie, "There is only one man can turn me out and that is Hitler."'

When the chapter was at an end, Clemmie looked serene; we were all silent while, for a time, he turned the pages of the American edition. Presently he looked up brightly.

'June the 6th, 1940, was one of the most fertile days of my life. I put down on paper everything that we should need for a successful invasion of France. I did this two days after Dunkirk. Dr Johnson said: "When a man is going to be hanged it concentrates his mind wonderfully."'

He looked up at me to see if the point had gone home.

'It was a pretty grim moment, but it's all down here – the tank landing craft and the Mulberry Harbours.'[1]

It took his mind back to the drama of those days.

'They were very wonderful,' said Winston half to himself.

Dorothy asked: 'Which year of all your life, if you could relive one twelvemonth, would you choose?' Winston: 'Nineteen-forty every time, every time.'

He seemed miles away, and then he said:

'I wish certain people could have been alive to see the events of the last years of the war; not many: my father and mother, and F.E., and Arthur Balfour, and Sunny. Sunny and I were like brothers. I have stayed for months with him at Blenheim.'

Winston had given chapters of his book to a dozen different people to read: to the Prof. and to Henry Luce, the head of *Time* and *Life*; to Lord Camrose and to Walter Graebner, and to Sarah. And here was Clemmie, pencil in hand, giving her views. She thought he had used initials too much. They would convey nothing to the average reader. Winston ought to replace these initials by the full name of the organization in question. He looked up impatiently with a pained expression. He doesn't really want criticism; he wants reassurance.

But he had asked for help, and I lay awake for a long time turning over possible pitfalls in my mind. His books before the war were immensely readable, but there was now a danger that he might be too anxious to convince posterity that he was right in everything, and that, in consequence, some of his text might be indigestible.

---

[1] Churchill was entitled to a measure of complacency. He actually described these landing craft and the Mulberry Harbours in a paper to Lloyd George bearing the date July 7, 1917, nearly thirty years before the Normandy landings. The tanks were to be transported in special ships and landed in flat-bottomed boats, the bow of which was designed as a drawbridge so that the tanks could crawl ashore on the beaches. They were to be used in a scheme Winston had prepared for the capture of the Friesian Islands of Borkom and Sit. This is the work of a creative mind.

PART TWO

The Prime Minister Falters

CHAPTER FIVE

The First Stroke

I left Winston at Marrakesh in December, 1947, living in the past and impatient of change. I could see then that he was sliding, almost imperceptibly, into old age. There is an undated entry in my medical notes that must have been written early in the New Year:

> When I examined Winston's retinal arteries with my ophthalmoscope, I found definite hardening of the vessels, but not more than one would expect after the stress of the war years. There is plenty of evidence that his circulation is sluggish.

It did not affect his tenacity of purpose. He kept his nose in his book, *The Second World War*, though a certain diffuseness in the second volume could be ascribed to his years. After Marrakesh there is a gap in my diary for eighteen months.

August 24, 1949
Dr Gibson telephoned from Monte Carlo this morning:

'I think Mr Churchill has had a stroke. I would like you to see him as soon as you can.'

When I arrived at the airfield at Nice, Max told me what had happened:

'He was playing cards at two o'clock this morning when he got up and, steadying himself with his hands on the table, bent his right leg several times as if it had gone to sleep. "I've got cramp in my arm and leg," was all he said. He kept closing and opening his right fist. Then he went on playing, but when he woke this morning – it would be about seven o'clock – the cramp was still present. A little later he found he could not write as well as usual. Dr Gibson was called, and he got on to you. It's a true bill, I am afraid,' Max added after a pause. 'But let's go and see him.'

With that he took me to his bedroom. When Max left us Winston said: 'I am glad you've come; I'm worried.' I could find no loss of power when I examined him; his grip was strong. Later, when he squeezed paints out of their tubes, he could not do it as well as usual. Max had told me that he was not sure whether his speech was affected. Winston was certain that it was not, and there was nothing I could detect. I asked him about his writing. Reaching for his pen, and steadying a bit of paper against a book, he wrote very slowly and carefully:

'I am trying to do my best to make it legible. It is better than it was this morning. W. Churchill.'

He handed me the paper, which shivered as he held it out – I felt he was watching my face as I read it.

'What has gone wrong, Charles? Have I had a stroke?'

'Most people,' I explained, 'when they speak of a stroke mean that an artery has burst and there has been a haemorrhage into the brain. You've not had that. A very small clot has blocked a very small artery.'

'Will I have another?' he demanded at once. 'There may be an election soon. An election in November is now more a probability than a possibility. I might have to take over again.' He grinned. 'It feels like being balanced between the Treasury Bench and death. But I don't worry. Fate must take its course.'

His memory did not seem to be impaired. He was quite calm, though perhaps a little fearful.

Moran: 'Do you notice anything different?'

Winston: 'Yes, there seems to be a veil between me and things. And there's a sensation in my arm that was not there before.'

Moran: 'What kind of sensation?'

Winston: 'Oh, it's like a tight feeling across my shoulder-blade.'

I told him he had done enough talking and that I would come back later. When Max heard the verdict he at once said:

'Oh, he must go on with things; he wouldn't agree to rust out.'

It hardly seemed the time to make decisions of that kind. The Press, Max said, were waiting at the gate.

'You must say something to them. It is no use,' he insisted, 'trying to fool them. You were seen at the aerodrome. They are all agog.'

He handed me a message which he had concocted. It was ingenious, but I was sure it would only excite their suspicions.

'Why say anything at all? Tell them that I am your guest for a few days, that I've brought my golf clubs. We'll produce him in a day or two, and that will convince them there is nothing wrong.'

Max wasn't persuaded, but when he saw my mind was made up he said no more.

August 25, 1949

Winston is never content with a diagnosis, he demands an explanation of the pathology of every malady; it must all be reasoned out. This morning I had to expound how the tracts, as they pass down from the surface, or cortex of the brain, to the spinal cord, come together at one point at the base of the brain, so that a small haemorrhage there can result in an extensive paralysis. At that point the tracts, or nerve paths, passing to the muscles are situated in front of the nerves carrying only sensation. He had had the great good fortune that the small vessel blocked had not touched the motor area, so that there was no paralysis; it had only cut off the nutrition of certain central cells concerned with sensation, and that was why he had a sense of tightness over his shoulders.

'Sensation doesn't matter,' I said.

He interrupted: 'Life is sensation; sensation is life.'

*

But he soon came to think he had had a lucky escape, and that what had happened belonged to the past. And when some days later he lunched at the Hôtel de Paris, and everyone rose to their feet as he entered and no one noticed anything, he gained confidence. He was, to be sure, irritable at times. Next day, when we dined at another restaurant where the service was slow, he said in tones which carried that he had never been in a worse restaurant. And when an American lady at another table came across and asked him to sign her menu he exploded. Could he not have even his dinner in peace? He wanted to get home, but he had misgivings that when he got out of the aeroplane in England the Press would notice that he did not walk straight. He devised a plan – I suspect with Max's assistance – by which the Press would be sent to Northolt while he arrived at Biggin Hill. It seemed a mad thing to do, and would have given rise to all kinds of stories. Eventually I managed to scotch this plan. When, however, we arrived at Biggin Hill and he saw all the photographers with their cameras, he was certain they would notice that something was wrong with his gait, and he waved them away with an angry gesture. A little later at Chartwell he said to me:

'I'm not the man I was before this happened. I had to see Cripps at No. 11 about devaluation.[1] It was an act of courtesy on his part. He was cool and debonair, but I was in a twitter. I shall never be able to believe a word Cripps says in future. Why, only in July he said he would sooner die than do this; now he says it will be an advantage.' And then his face brightened: 'When I arrived at Downing Street there were five people; when I left there were five hundred.'

Winston was in his seventy-fifth year. The shock of the election, coming right on the top of the strain of the war years, had done him no good. Something of the old vitality had oozed out of his wounds, the old confidence in himself had gone. However, as the months passed I think my fears were half forgotten; he seemed to get back his interest in life, vigour returned, and he appeared to put the past behind him. And then it began to dawn on me that he was descending into old age. The unmistakable signs of his years were at last apparent. All the same his stroke took me completely by surprise.

---

[1] September, 1949. The pound was devalued by the Labour Government from 4.03 to 2.80 dollars.

This is the beginning of trouble. He will not give in without a great struggle, but there can be only one end to it. How long it will last is only guesswork; he might hang on for some years yet, but this is certain: my task is just beginning.

January 24, 1950
Five months have gone by and nothing has happened. Winston has been so buried in the third volume of *The Second World War* that my fears had been set at rest until this morning when he sent for me. I went at once. He told me:

'About an hour ago everything went misty. There was no warning. I could just read, with difficulty. What does it mean, Charles? Am I going to have another stroke?'

I reassured him:

'You seem to get arterial spasms when you are very tired.'

He looked up sharply.

'You mustn't frighten me.'

In fact, I am more frightened than Winston. This is a grim start to the racket of a General Election.[1]

February 5, 1950
An election like this might well flatten a younger man, and I keep wondering how Winston is wearing under the strain. It was very late last night when he got back from Leeds, but when I called at Hyde Park Gate early this morning I found him reading the *Manchester Guardian*.

'Did Leeds tire you?'

'Oh, no, Charles. Speaking to five thousand people through a microphone is no more tiring than talking to a hundred. It doesn't bother me. I'm not overawed by them. I've got used to it. But I do worry over what I say and what I don't say. I felt invigorated by the

---

[1] The Labour Government decided to dissolve Parliament on February 3 before the Budget. The General Election was held on February 23, 1950, and resulted in the Labour Government majority being cut to 6.

meeting, brutalized as I am by fifty years of it. Of course, when it was all over I was tired.'

He appeared absorbed in his own thoughts. Then he muttered:

'I'm glad I've not to live my life over again. There is a dreadful degradation of standards.'

February 6, 1950

I went to Winston because Miss Sturdee[1] told me that he was taking on more speeches. After Manchester he is going to speak for Randolph at Plymouth and at Oldham. I wanted to persuade him that it was not necessary to stump the country making speeches. I tried to say that broadcasting had made other forms of appeal to the electorate of secondary importance, that argument had been replaced by little word pictures which humble folk would remember. Morrison had said that if food subsidies were taken away it would mean to a woman with two children that she would have to pay fourteen shillings more a week for her food. That went home to people. It must be met by similar methods. I saw he was hardly listening. He isn't going to learn any new techniques; he isn't interested in them.

'We, too, have our broadcasters,' was all he said.

I begin to see that we must let things take their course. I must be sensible. After all, if anything does happen he would prefer to go out fighting a General Election, with plenty of cheering and booing and heckling.

May 25, 1950

Winston is quite sure that the tightness over his shoulders has increased. He can't get the stroke out of his mind. To reassure him I called in Russell Brain.[2]

'The cells in your brain,' he explained, 'which receive sensory messages from your shoulder are dead. That's all. It's a bit of luck that sensation only is affected.'

[1] Secretary to Churchill.
[2] Sir Russell Brain, later Lord Brain, President of the Royal College of Physicians.

He seemed relieved by Brain's air of finality, and began talking about his dyspepsia. For ten years he had been 'tortured' by it; then he heard of Courtlandt MacMahon's name.

'He cured me by his breathing exercises. Why, after his third visit there was an enormous difference in the whole structure of the body.'

June 21, 1950

Took Winston to Negus[1] for increasing deafness. He found that the higher notes were lost.

Negus: 'You won't be able to hear the twittering of birds and children's piping voices.'

Winston: 'Are you going to hurt me?' He was watching Negus as he fiddled with his tuning forks. 'You must tell me if you are.'

Negus: 'Can you hear a clock ticking in your room?'

Winston: 'I won't have a ticking clock in my room.'

---

[1] Sir Victor Negus, consulting surgeon to Ear, Nose and Throat Department, King's College Hospital.

CHAPTER SIX

The King's Illness

I am unhappy about things. When the struggle for power is at an end and his political life is over, Winston will feel that there is no purpose in his existence. I dread what may happen then, and it is my task as his doctor to put off that day as long as I can. On the other hand, if he wins this election[1] and goes back to No. 10, I doubt whether he is up to the job. In the fourteen months since my last entry he has lost ground and has no longer the same grip on things and events. Moreover, his cares multiply.

September 18, 1951
When I saw Winston a fortnight ago he told me he had been shocked by the King's appearance. He questioned me closely about him. I explained that I could judge only by the bulletins, but they were rather disturbing – there was a possibility of cancer of the lung. Winston listened with a grave and anxious face. Tonight at eight o'clock he telephoned me saying a bulletin would be read in the nine o'clock news, intimating that 'investigations showed structural changes had developed in the King's lung.' What did it mean? I asked him who had signed the bulletin; I wanted to know if a chest surgeon was included.

'I can't remember. It will be in the nine o'clock news,' he said.

---

[1] Another General Election was to be held in October, 1951.

'Would you give me a ring when you have heard it? Don't mention the King. Just refer to your friend.'

He repeated this twice before he rang off. When I heard the news, I knew before I telephoned that he would expect me at Chartwell.

'How long will you take?' he asked.

'Forty minutes, about,' I answered.

'Do come.'

I found him playing cards with Randolph. The room was half in darkness; the light of a solitary lamp near the small card-table fell on the green baize. He put his hand down at once.

'Ah, Charles, come and sit here. What do you make of it?' he asked anxiously.

'I don't like it at all,' I said. 'The doctors would not have used the bronchoscope if they had not been worried about a possible cancer. But much more disturbing is their failure to say a single word of reassurance after the bronchoscopy. And why do they go into details in their brief bulletin? Why tell us that the Queen is returning to London, that Queen Mary has called at the Palace and stayed an hour and a half, and that the Prime Minister has seen the King? Surely this is to prepare the public. Why nine doctors?'

He picked up a bit of paper and handed it to me. Price Thomas[1] had obviously carried out the bronchoscopic examination. I said that my fears had been strengthened by an article in the *Sunday Express* on the King's health. Plainly someone had given Max information; the article talked of an operation and hinted that it was cancer.

Winston, almost absent-mindedly: 'Max said he knew someone behind the scenes.'

Randolph interrupted several times, eagerly asking questions, until Winston said:

'Oh, do let Charles finish his argument.'

---

[1] Sir Clement Price Thomas, chest surgeon to Westminster and Brompton Hospitals.

He was very grave, and said: 'If it's cancer, can he recover? How long can it go on?'

I told him what I could, and he turned it over in his mind slowly and painfully.

'Poor fellow. I'll pray for him tonight,' he said.

September 20, 1951

Winston telephoned after breakfast that he had had a very important letter. Where was I? At Marshalls?[1]

'Then could you run over? I'd like that.'

Winston had a letter in his hand from Lascelles, the King's secretary. He put it down and was silent for a time.

'He says that the King has a growth in his lung. It means an operation – on Monday. The King did not know that Lascelles was writing to me. Poor fellow, he does not know what it means.'

Winston questioned me about the implications of the letter. He seemed distracted, and told me that he was 'all of a twitter'. He 'got like that sometimes'. This was an older Winston. It was not his habit to get in a twitter during the war. He said that he had a lot on his mind.

He meant the election. I said to him that if things went well, he would have to think out how he was going to get through his work. He retorted:

'Oh, well, we're not there yet. Besides, I like most of the day in bed; dictating directives would be just like writing the book.'

I asked him, with misgiving, about the part he intended to play in the election campaign. He would have to write the Conservative manifesto, he said, and make a couple of broadcasts and perhaps five speeches up and down the country.

'I shan't overdo things, Charles.'

He said Labour had made such a mess of things in the hospitals that they were employing far more laymen – more secretaries, more typists – than in the old days. I told him that I had brought him a

[1] Marshalls Manor, Maresfield, Lord Moran's home in Sussex after the war.

few notes on the Health Service. He put them in his pocket without reading them.

'We don't want detail,' he protested impatiently. 'We propose to give the people a lighthouse, not a shop window.'

He was very restless and did not seem able to settle to anything; he kept walking up and down the passage at Chartwell. 'Have the photographers gone?' he demanded – he didn't want them to see me. He came back into the studio.

'I shan't be able to finish them,' he said, with a glum look at three canvases.

'It's a big job to take on at my age,' he continued, 'but there's no alternative. It's my duty.'

He strode to the secretaries' room.

'Has anything come in?' he asked.

We were back in the war years again. And when I came out of the house there was the old feeling of activity, the Press cars, the sense of things afoot. But we were ten years older.

CHAPTER SEVEN

Back to No. 10

September 29, 1951

Winston: 'The reports are good, we ought to win. Max is talking about a majority of a hundred and fifty, or at any rate a hundred.'

Moran: 'You surely don't take Max seriously as a prophet? He has no judgement in these things.'

Winston (*scowling*): 'The circulation of his papers runs into millions; he must know what people are thinking.'

Moran: 'Anyway, he has been completely off the map in the last two elections.'

Why do I argue with him? Shall I never learn that Winston likes to have around him sanguine, hopeful people? If they are of good heart, and make the best of things, he will not count it against them if their calculations prove to be ill-founded.

Max may be right, but the Tories are full of doubts. On all sides they are saying that Winston is too old and will never take advice – and surely he needs good counsel, for men who measure their words speak gravely of the economic position of the country. Last night J. J. Astor[1] said to me:

'We've had a mouthful of green sea-water; we've got to keep afloat.'

---

[1] John J. Astor, chief proprietor of *The Times*.

It is said that Winston will not trust a man to do his job, but what the best elements in the party fear most is that if the Conservatives win the election he will gather round him the old gang. One particular bad hat, they have heard, is certain to be given office, and it is going round that he will be the new Minister of Health. People come to me as if I could help. 'Why don't you tackle him, he won't listen to us,' and they only smile in a knowing way when I protest that Winston will not ask my advice before he appoints a new Minister. That, I suppose, explains how I came to blurt out to Winston what was in my mind. I had not got far when a secretary brought in the early editions of the evening papers. He picked up the *Star* and handed me the *Standard.*

'Let's see the news,' he said.

'That's the trouble. You will never listen to anybody.'

'I've done a lot of listening in my time,' he mused.

I was uncorked and bubbling over.

'If you appoint Walter Elliot Minister of Health you will have to get another doctor.'

It seemed to come out involuntarily. I was shocked by my own violence and want of reason. Winston looked up quickly:

'I've no intention of giving him any appointment at the Ministry of Health. We mustn't count our chickens before they are hatched.' He added in a kindly way: 'I've never seen you upset before, Charles. You mustn't let anything I say upset you.'

'I only want to help,' I said. 'There's a good deal of talk in the party which doesn't reach you.'

'What kind of talk?' he asked sharply.

'Oh, critical stuff.'

'But what kind of criticism?' he persisted.

'They say you will never listen to them, that you are very opinionated.'

A whimsical look crossed his face.

'Oh yes, I'm opinionated. You won't offend me. Tell me what they are saying,' he reiterated.

'Oh, it would take a long time and you are busy.'

'Now, Charles, you cannot say there's a lot of talk, and leave it like that. You must make out your case.'

I told him what McGowan[1] had said; that he could talk to Attlee about industry, but that Winston would not listen to him; that Winston tried to go on running everything himself as he did in the war; that he ought to retire.

'Who said that?' he demanded.

'A friend of yours,' I answered.

No one in their senses would fire stories at Winston, but I saw that for once his curiosity was aroused.

'He wasn't speaking for anybody,' Winston grunted.

'I'm not so sure about that; a good many want you to retire. But there! You know political life better than I do. Everything is in a mess, and you'll need a Cabinet of all the talents to carry people with you.'

He lit a match and held it under the end of his cigar.

'We're not going to have just the old gang as you call them. But the time hasn't come yet to parcel out the posts.'

I wanted to end the conversation.

I had said more already than a doctor should, since his business is to build up and not to sap the patient's reserves.

October 11, 1951

Winston will argue of course, but he is aware that there is something in what people are saying. Behind his bluff he is eaten up with misgivings. This morning when I arrived at Hyde Park Gate they told me: 'He was all in last night when he got back from Liverpool,' where he had gone to make an election speech. And when I went to his room, before I could say anything he admitted:

'I had a considerable reaction yesterday. I was glad I had nothing to do today.'

---

[1] Lord McGowan, Chairman, Imperial Chemical Industries.

He had been impressed by the X-rays; it was a 'wonderful machine'. Turning to MacKenna,[1] he said:

'Immediately I had it I felt the benefit; I believe they will cure the bloody itching over my shoulders. I would like another dose today.

'*The Times* is very favourable to me, more so than it has been for a long time.'

He told me how Liverpool had cheered him, and as he spoke of the 'love and affection of the people' his eyes filled with tears. 'There was rapture in their eyes. They brought their children. I'm not conceited,' he said, 'but they wanted to touch me.' He spoke humbly, as if he was just an instrument of the Almighty.

When MacKenna rose to take his leave, Winston asked me to stay. As the door shut he said that he had a 'muzzy feeling' in his head:

'Oh, it's nothing to do with alcohol; it comes on generally before luncheon. Aspirin helps it. If it's due to the circulation in my head, can't you think out something, Charles, that would be more effective than aspirin?'

He sat huddled in his chair, gazing gloomily at the carpet.

'I am not so sure as I was that I shall be able to see things through.'

I was disturbed that he said as much; it was not like him. He knew that the incident at Monte Carlo, when his arm suddenly became 'funny', was a notice to quit the world. In a few days he would be seventy-seven.

'I'm not afraid to die,' he said after a time, 'but I want to do this job properly.'

I told him I knew of no nostrum that would rejuvenate the circulation in his head. If he wanted to stay the course he must cut out things; he could not do everyone's job as he had done in the war; nobody wanted it. He interrupted:

'If I win the election I shall take on the Ministry of Defence.'

I retorted that he ought to get that idea out of his head. He had

[1] Mr R. M. B. MacKenna, dermatologist, St Bartholomew's Hospital.

never felt any desire to share with anyone the burden that he carried in the war. But now things were changed; he was an old man. I tried to argue with him. He answered that he had asked Portal to do it, but Portal had replied that he would do almost anything for Mr Churchill except to get involved in political life. He would have liked Alex to take it on, but he was not free.[1]

I wondered what was passing through his mind. He has always coveted office, probably he always will, but why does he want to be Prime Minister when, as he knows, he is not the man he was?

'You look tired and sad, Charles,' he said, interrupting my thoughts.

October 15, 1951
Today at twenty minutes to one o'clock Winston telephoned to say that he had a temperature.

'What is it?' I asked.

'Oh, ninety-nine degrees,' he answered, 'but it may go up tonight.' He was leaving Euston at one o'clock.

'Could you come and see me at the station?'

Ninety-nine degrees was nothing, but there was the question of morale, for he is always impressed by a temperature. I asked him if he would like me to come with him to Huddersfield.

'I would like that very much, Charles.'

I found him apprehensive, but when the train had started and I took his temperature it was normal. He was rather disconcerted. Was the thermometer wrong? Was it all a false alarm? Would my plans be badly upset?

Winston asked me in the train to vet his speech, but I knew that my function was to comfort and reassure; it was too late to reconstruct.

We drove to the meeting from the train. There were seventeen hundred people in the hall; a thousand of them Conservatives and seven hundred Liberals. Some, when they could not get admission,

---

[1] Field-Marshal Alexander was Governor-General of Canada, 1946–52.

had said, 'No seat, no vote.' The P.M.'s speech was in no way exceptional. When he stuck to his text his voice was strong and he spoke
with vigour and conviction. But he kept introducing asides, and this
he did in a very uncertain and hesitant manner which was anything
but impressive. Winston, of course, is a born writer, but in speaking
it is only by blood and sweat that he has become as effective as he
is. Lady Violet Bonham Carter,[1] on the other hand, has the address
of a natural orator. When he had done and she began to speak he
sat apart on the platform as if he were by himself; his head had sunk
into his shoulders, and in the hard light of the hall his face and scalp
appeared devoid of hair; the monolithic lines of the great skull and
jowl were somehow familiar; yes, he was like Mussolini. His eyes
gazed vacantly into the distance out of the expressionless mask of a
deaf man. There was a political meeting going on, but he was not
part of it; only when the laughter in the hall caught his ear would
he turn for enlightenment to his neighbour, and twice he took out
his watch and looked at it in a puzzled way, as if these speeches were
going on for a long time.

When it was all over we returned to the train, where we sat
down to a late supper – Winston cheerful and talkative, as is his
way after a speech. The deaf old man, who only an hour ago sat
by himself on the platform, huddled up and forlorn, was gone,
and in his place we saw a rejuvenated Winston, with his pink face
and his boyish spirits. His political agents and advisers had vanished, his worries had resolved, and in the little family party of
Lady Violet and Lord Layton,[2] he could relax and allow his
thoughts to go back to the past. Lord Layton spoke of his orderly
administration.

'You don't often get the credit for this, Winston,' he chuckled.

Winston smiled his gratitude. Layton felt things were going well;
he might even venture a little.

---

[1] Lady Violet Bonham Carter, daughter of Herbert Asquith, Liberal candidate for Huddersfield West, was supported by Churchill in the absence of a
Conservative candidate.

[2] Lord Layton, Deputy Leader of the Liberal Party.

'Tell us, Winston, what was your biggest mistake – what do you yourself consider now was your biggest mistake in the war?'

'I've no doubt at all,' Winston replied at once. 'Not going to meet Truman after Roosevelt's death. During the next three months tremendous decisions were made, and I had a feeling that they were being made by a man I did not know.'

There was a long pause, and then he added:

'It wasn't my fault. I wanted to cross the Atlantic. But Anthony put me off. He telegraphed from Washington that they did not want me.'

He could say what he liked now, he could throw caution to the winds, and to Lady Violet he freely admitted that for his part he wanted an independent Liberal Party. If the Tories and Liberals were united on a social policy, then he would have no fear of Socialists, but he did fear the vulnerability of the Tories if they were alone. The truth is that he is not happy with diehard Tories, any more than was his father before him. Lady Violet was bitter about the National Liberals.[1]

'Now, Violet,' Winston gently interposed, filling her glass with champagne with a whimsical pucker, 'you mustn't be too hard on them. I have only managed to live so long by carrying no hatreds.'

It is indeed true: he is completely without rancour. I asked what Max was up to.

'Oh, he flits about everywhere. He wants the jockey to win, but he hates his horse. The Tories,' Winston added sadly, 'hate him and he hates them. Max says we shall get a bigger majority than we deserve. If we are beaten,' mused Winston, 'I shall retire. There is a kind of argument going about that I am too old. I don't feel old, and I don't think I look old, though I'm on my way to eighty.'

---

[1] The Liberal Party joined Ramsay MacDonald's National Government in 1931, but was soon split over the Government's tariff reform proposals. The Free Trade Liberals left the Government in the following year, but Sir John Simon remained with the National Government along with his Protectionist followers. They became known as National Liberals, but soon became difficult to distinguish from Conservatives.

He had received assurances from several men prominent in trade-union circles that if the country gave a definite, unequivocal verdict they would respect the constitutional issue.

His mind wandered back to the war. He had 'had great influence over President Roosevelt until about three months before Yalta; then he ceased to answer my letters.' Winston defended the President; he was not to blame for Yalta. Stalin was the villain. He spoke of the tragedy of Potsdam, of giving Russia all that she demanded 'instead of having a show-down' as he wished, which would have prevented a third world war. He was bringing forward evidence in his book that he had taken steps to postpone the demobilization of certain units until we got a satisfactory solution. 'Of course,' he added, 'Russia might not have taken all this lying down.'

It was after midnight; everyone but Winston appeared a little jaded, but he was eager and gay, and talked all the time. Lady Violet said she must go to bed.

'Ah, no, Violet, not yet.'

She put her hand on his shoulder.

'I must, Winston, I'm so tired.'

He rose reluctantly and the party broke up. When we were alone he began telling me how some Catholic bishops had come to see him. The Labour Party had made them promises, and they came to him to see what the Conservatives would do. Winston had said to them: 'This is not a spiritual way of doing things.' They had a look, he said, of the other world.

'I belong to this world,' he paused, 'but . . .' I waited. He did not finish the sentence.

October 27, 1951

Winston has crawled back into Downing Street – his majority over all other parties is eighteen. After all the talk of a majority of a hundred and fifty it must be a great disappointment to him. But when I asked one of the secretaries whether he was upset by the figures, she replied: 'Oh, I don't think so; he's relieved he is in.'

November 8, 1951
Found Winston in poor spirits.

'I have had to fill seventy-five offices – it has worried me, particularly the junior appointments. If anyone is left out, it is probably the end of his political hopes. You know how unhappy it makes me to hurt others.' He sighed deeply. 'The last fortnight has been more tiring than anything in the war. There were great decisions then, of course, but I was swept along by events.'

CHAPTER EIGHT

An American Journey

The Queen Mary, *December 30, 1951*

The lady after whom this ship is named was talking to a friend who had forgotten something and was looking for her spectacles. They could not be found, and her old bones grumbled when she attempted to rise from her chair.

'The disabilities as one gets older, Ma'am, are horrible.'

'Damnable,' said the old Queen.

Ten years have gone by since we first travelled with Winston in the *Queen Mary*. Yet tonight we might be back again in the war; the P.M. is still talking and there, opposite to him, is Pug, still listening to him with his mouth open, as if he would not miss a syllable, uttering the same throaty, gurgling sounds of mirth. Pug anyway has not changed, and when the P.M. happens to look in his way his face slips as quickly into creases and folds, like a pug dog – whence Lord Ismay's nickname. But if you look more closely there is no mirth in the eyes, which are cool and watchful. Everything else seems different. The indomitable spirit of the P.M. of those years, battling against a deadly threat to the world's freedom, is now struggling only with the humiliations of old age and with economic problems that are quite beyond his ken.

Jock brought in a paper which he handed to the P.M.

P.M.: 'In all my life I have never seen so bewildering a situation.'

Eden: 'It is complicated.'

P.M.: 'Bewildering. And this war could easily have been stopped. At Locarno[1] it was nearly stopped. Russia would have fought at Munich.'

Moran: 'Isn't that true of both wars?'

P.M.: 'Oh, no, Charles. The first war was different, it would have been difficult to prevent it. The French were out for *revanche* and the Germans for glory, and England said, "We don't want to fight, but by Jingo if we do." There was a lot of glory about. Even I' – and there was a mischievous smirk – 'with my very different feelings, was thrilled. You know, Anthony, if a grandson of the Kaiser had been left on the throne after 1918 Hitler would never have seized power. But it's no use saying this to the Americans. The only King they think of is George III. Look at Austria. Why, all the countries which threw off her yoke, Czecho-Slovakia and the rest, have suffered endless, cruel tortures.'

The Prof. wondered whether in Washington he would get any information about the manufacture of atomic bombs.

P.M.: 'The Labour Government spent a hundred millions on atomic research without telling anyone, without any Parliamentary sanction whatever. Their Party knew nothing about it. I could not have done it. How was it done? Oh, they just divided the money between seven or eight departments. And they called me a warmonger!' he said angrily. 'Tell me, Anthony, about Roger Makins.[2] You like him? He is good?'

Eden: 'Yes, I think he is very able. But the Prof. here knows all about him.'

Prof.: 'He passed into the F.O. at the top of the list after a brilliant first at Oxford. He is a Fellow of All Souls.'

Eden (*smiling*): 'And he's sensible in spite of that.'

---

[1] Locarno Pact – a series of agreements in 1925 between Germany, Britain, France, Italy and Belgium to keep the peace in Western Europe. Germany renounced the use of force to effect frontier changes in the West and agreed to arbitration in her eastern border disputes.

[2] Sir Roger Makins, Deputy Under-Secretary of State, Foreign Office.

January 1, 1952

All the P.M.'s party – the three Cabinet Ministers, Norman his valet, his two detectives, the Prof.'s cook – were summoned last night to go to his sitting-room at ten minutes before midnight to toast the New Year. When the clock had struck twelve times the P.M., whose thoughts seemed a long way off, pulled himself out of his chair, put down his glass and, crossing his arms, began to shout Auld Lang Syne. When this had been sung he tried to give the note for 'God Save the King'. Then he resumed his seat as if his part in the proceedings had been safely accomplished. After a little the room began to thin – youth went off to dance – till none were left but the Prof., Pug, Slim[1] and Norman Brook. For some time the P.M. sat lost in his thoughts and no one spoke.

'I cannot tell you,' he said at last, 'how much happier I shall be when I have worked out the substance of what I shall say to Congress. The speech might not come off,' he mused, 'but I shall do my best whatever happens. I feel bewildered in my mind. The three thousand seven hundred millions of pounds which was to be spent on rearmament has gone up to five thousand two hundred millions. We have not stopped the rise in wages. Anyway, I'm not going to beg.'

He sat glowering at the carpet.

'We shall have to make great sacrifices,' the P.M. murmured without looking up. Then his face brightened. 'How much would it mean to the country,' he asked, 'if everyone gave up smoking? I would not hesitate to give up my cigars.'

He got up and I went with him to his room.

'I have done very little today,' he said as he kicked off his slippers so that they skidded along the floor. 'I am not so good mentally as I used to be. A speech has become a burden and an anxiety. Tell me, Charles, the truth. Am I going slowly to lose my faculties?'

He asked me to take his pulse; it was rapid and irregular.

[1] Field-Marshal Sir William Slim, Chief of the Imperial General Staff, 1948–52.

January 4, 1952

'It was late last night,' the P.M. admitted, 'when I settled in; I am glad I shall have a light day. Discussions don't tire me. I should look forward to every hour of this trip but for these two speeches. They hover over me like two vultures. What to say worries me. I dip into the well whenever anything is needed and generally find something there, but it does not come as freely as it did; it is harder work.'

'What is today?' he asked. 'The fourth? On the seventh the terrible announcement will be made.[1] People will be told that, if we go on spending as we are doing, by June there will be no money left. I'm glad I cannot be held responsible for it,' he said gravely. 'Never in my life have I faced an ordeal of this kind. It is worse than 1940. In Washington they will feel we are down and out. We have to tell them that if the rearmament is not spread out over a longer time the nations of Western Europe will be rushing to bankruptcy and starvation. When I have come to America before it has been as an equal. If, late in the war, they spoke of their sacrifices we could retort by saying that for a year and a half we fought alone; that we had suffered more losses.' He sighed deeply. 'They have become so great and we are now so small. Poor England! We threw away so much in 1945.'

I tried to argue that it was in the interests of America to meet us halfway. If the P.M. failed in his attempts to stabilize our finances, there would be a swing to the left in England and we should give up any attempt to rearm, so that Germany would be thrown into the arms of Russia. He did not agree. If England and Western Europe pulled out, America would rearm Germany. America alone could defeat Russia. I turned the conversation to his speech. He seemed a little happier about it; he was picking up points from the discussions.

January 5, 1952

A driving rain kept me below until the last minute, and when I came on deck I saw three tugs, the *Mary Moran, Gertrude Moran* and *Alice*

---

[1] The announcement of a large fall in our dollar reserves was made on January 7, and further import cuts, reductions in rations and other restrictions were imposed on January 29, when Parliament reassembled.

Moran, preparing to pilot the great monster to her berth. I wish I were as sure of my bearings as I try to guide my master on his journey. When we landed he was delivered up to the Press, who were tumbling over one another to get at him. After the P.M. left the shed I drove with Leslie Rowan to the aerodrome. Nobody, I suppose, saw more of the P.M. during the war than he did – he was his private secretary until the General Election of 1945, and his ability is such that everyone seems confident that he will one day be head of the Civil Service. I asked him whether he noticed many changes in Winston.

'Oh, yes,' he answered rather sadly, 'he has lost his tenacity; he no longer pushes a thing through. He has lost, too, his power of fitting in all the problems one to another. Of course in the war he would run a pet scheme, but it was always fitted into the whole plan. And he forgets figures. In the war he never did. Why, the other day I mentioned a figure he had used in the House of Commons. "Did I?" he asked, puzzled. Besides, the problems are different now. Questions of economics. He was not brought up on such things.'

I asked Leslie if he had noticed any physical changes. He seemed surprised that I should ask such a question.

'Yes, of course.'

'How?' I persisted.

'Oh, the way he walks – slowly, like an old man. Even his handling of the Press Conference today was different. It was good, of course, but not so good as it used to be in the war.' Leslie smiled. 'But he can still coin phrases. He referred yesterday to the Standing Group who deal with a future war as "Chiefs of Staff vitiated by the intrusion of the French".'

We drove between two lines of sandwich-men bearing boards: 'England bleeds Americans.' 'Money for Imperialists, but none for Veterans.' They were Irish, or perhaps Communists, picketing the Cunard Pier. At the airfield the P.M. climbed slowly into the aircraft 'Independence', lent by the President. During the short flight he appeared absorbed in the newspapers, but when we came down outside Washington he looked up and said:

'It is fifty years since I came here first. Mark Twain was my host.'

The world was full of his exploits then, like his escape from the Boers, and the Americans were eager to hear his story. They are still interested in him. He picked up his hat and gloves in one hand and his gold-headed cane in the other and stood at the head of the ramp, gazing down at President Truman and his Administration, who were waving to him from the tarmac. The feeling that things were about to happen came back; he pricked up his ears; he did not feel so old, after all.

It had been arranged that the visit to Washington should begin with a trip on the President's yacht on the Potomac River, but this afternoon a bitter wind caught the breath, and when the time came his little party gazed doubtfully at the grey, bleak prospect; rather anxiously they wondered how the Prime Minister's party manners would respond to such a searching test. However, we were quite wrong, and those of us who welcomed the returned reveller, when he appeared at the Embassy in the small hours, were startled to find something like the Winston we had half forgotten. He was full of the evening.

'Oh, I enjoyed it so much; we talked as equals.'

Franks:[1] 'It was a good beginning.'

Eden was more cautious. Truman, who had been very lively before dinner, had, it seemed, never opened his lips until the coffee appeared. They debated whether this had any significance. The P.M. brushed aside their doubts:

'There were twelve of us round a table, the guidance of the world was in our hands, not for domination but to work for the good of mankind.'

It was not, it seemed, that they had reached agreement on any specific issue, but rather there had been an atmosphere of friendliness which had given him pleasure.

'I do hope,' said the P.M., 'that Anthony will meet the Americans over China, which really does not matter to us. Then they in turn

---

[1] Sir Oliver Franks, British Ambassador in Washington, 1948–52.

might meet us about Egypt or Persia, which matter a lot. After all, what Conservative in England is in favour of Chinese Communists?'

But the Foreign Secretary held his peace, and a few minutes later he said firmly that it was time for bed. When we were alone in his room the P.M. talked with animation. Then his face fell. On January 7 the adverse trade balance would come out. 'It will do a lot of harm.'

January 7, 1952
At breakfast this morning there appeared to be some disquiet about the rigidity of the American attitude. The P.M., according to Norman Brook, is so glad to be in Washington that he'd be happy even if they threw bricks at him. He doesn't mind rough stuff in the course of discussion; in fact, he rather likes it. But Eden is more sensitive, he seems to take it more to heart.

January 8, 1952
I had gone to my room before luncheon, when the Ambassador put his head through the door. He began by saying he was afraid he had been a poor host, and then he came to the point. He does not want the P.M. to outstay his welcome in Washington; while he is here Truman and Dean Acheson[1] would have him on their minds. The Ambassador had seen signs that he might stop on. He ought to get away by the 19th. If he wants to stay longer it must be in New York – not Washington.

Franks is unlike anyone here. For one thing, he does not seem tired. The clarity of his pronouncements reminds one that he is a scholar, the product of a discipline to which no one here except the Prof. has been subject. He is, too, an exile, only waiting for his release to return to Oxford, so that no man is his master – and he thinks for himself. As the P.M.'s host, he is at once firm and polite. He thinks only Clemmie can persuade the P.M. to retire. He hopes she will not try. He was not a politician, he said, but he hoped this

---

[1] Secretary of State in President Truman's Administration.

government might stay in office for three years. I said the P.M. felt the inequality with the United States.

'Yes,' Franks interjected, 'the humiliation.'

I doubted whether it could be changed until we had put our house in order economically.

'Exactly,' he snapped.

No one else here would have used that word; everyone seems to dislike precision as they would a commitment. Franks agreed that if the P.M. had no knowledge of economics, at any rate he would have the guts to tell the people the truth when the solution of our financial problems had been given to him. Not that he thought poorly of Eden, who, he said, has good judgement in spite of appearing a little on edge – in fact, in spite of his façade.

'Yes, the Prime Minister is tough,' Franks rapped out; 'after a rough night he eats a breakfast like a boy – surely no one at seventy-seven can require so much. Come,' he said, 'it is time we went down.'

Franks is an individual; he says things which those of us who have worked in a team refrain from saying. He said to Eden before we sat down to luncheon:

'The Foreign Secretary this morning was not allowed to answer for foreign affairs. If I had been Foreign Secretary I should have been very angry.'

Eden: 'I was angry.'

The only guest at lunch was Senator McMahon, Chairman of the Senatorial Atomic Energy Committee. The P.M. sent for the original document which set forth the terms of agreement with President Roosevelt about the atomic bomb.[1] When it was brought to him, he handed it to McMahon. The Senator read it.

---

[1] Roosevelt and Churchill agreed at the Quebec Conference, 1943, that Britain and the United States should exchange their information on the technical developments of atomic weapons. In 1946, however, Senator McMahon, who was unaware of the agreement, sponsored a Bill in the American Congress which severely curtailed this mutual exchange. The Labour Government failed to press home British rights in this matter and the Bill became law.

P.M.: 'We have been grossly deceived. There has been a breach of faith.'

The Senator: 'If we had known this the Act would not have been passed. Attlee never said a word.'

P.M.: 'No. The Americans are not an unjust people. I've learnt a lot during the voyage. I had not read many of the papers since I came into office.'

It was now three o'clock, and Franks tried to persuade the P.M. to adjourn to the drawing-room to allow the servants to clear the table.

P.M.: 'Cannot we sit here a little longer? I regard this time after lunch as an island of peace in a stormy sea.'

Tonight he said he would not come down to dinner; he would rest in bed. He had slept for more than an hour and felt refreshed, but he said:

'I am still weary. Why, Charles, since I left London I have been kicked about; I hardly know night from day; it's all right for a younger man, but I am an immense age. It's not so much going to meetings, it's thinking out what you say.'

Down below, Eden, Franks and Roger Makins sat picking the communiqué to pieces.

'Every paragraph,' Eden complained, 'begins "The Prime Minister . . ." or "The Foreign Secretary was instructed . . .". No one instructs me. The Prime Minister and I are colleagues.'

Makins: 'It ought to be "we".'

So it was changed, but when the communiqué was taken to the P.M. he was scornful. They had 'clothed themselves in wool and fed on pap'.

'Take it away,' he said. 'I can make nothing of this.'

January 9, 1952

The P.M. has developed a habit – I cannot put a date to the tendency – of making a spot diagnosis of a man, a kind of surface impression, which is rather disconcerting; he will dismiss from his mind quite considerable folk if the first impact is unfavourable.

Roger Makins, Norman Brook and I lunched with him on the train
to New York, when he spoke scornfully of the First Sea Lord's inef-
fectiveness. He had no grasp of things. Before him he remembered
a long line of First Sea Lords; they had all been great sailors. The
P.M. falls for swashbuckling fellows – it is not necessary to ask
which he admired more, Beatty or Jellicoe. Vian had impressed him
at Bristol – 'at least he has fire in his belly; if he had been with us
when the Atlantic Command was discussed things would have
taken a different turn.' Norman Brook interjected that McGrigor
had a great reputation in the Navy, but the P.M. pursued his own
thoughts. If Vian was brought in as First Sea Lord perhaps
McGrigor could be given the Portsmouth Command. 'We must go
into this,' he said with an air of finality. He spoke about Troubridge
turning away from the *Goeben*, and then excusing himself by saying
he had not enough fuel. He was told to use up all he had and he
would be towed back. Jellicoe himself had a streak of this – three
times in the Battle of Jutland he turned away.

'When a man cannot distinguish a great from a small event he is
no use. Now Slim is quite different. I can work with him.'

When Slim says something which he thinks matters his jaws snap
together like a steel trap, while McGrigor is so diminutive, so hesitating in his address, that the romantic Winston Churchill, who
keeps a small bust of Nelson in his room at Chartwell, is quite put
out. He has never possessed any gift for the measurement of men.
Now he seems ready to scrap his First Sea Lord, whom he met for
the first time on this voyage, merely because he did not support him
on this issue, in which the P.M. is in a minority of one.

On the outskirts of New York the P.M.'s host, Bernie Baruch,[1]
boarded the train.

'Bernie!' Winston exclaimed as he hurried up the saloon to greet
him.

For the moment it appeared as if he was about to embrace him.
What manner of man is this, I wondered, who is acclaimed by other

---

[1] Bernard Baruch, American financier and adviser to successive Presidents.

men in the States as completely disinterested? He wants nothing for himself, so it is said, and all recent Presidents have been glad to turn to him for advice. At any rate, that was the position; I am not sure whether it still is. Bernie Baruch is a Jew, now in his eighty-first year, but neither his years nor his deafness appear to cut him off from his fellows: his intense interest in people is undiminished and his alert features keep relaxing into a friendly smile. It is as if he said: 'I don't know what you are saying, but I am sure you are having great fun and I want you to feel quite at home.'

Winston cannot be bothered as a rule to introduce his friends to his 'circus', but tonight during dinner he seemed to feel he would like others to know more about Bernie.

'Can I tell them about your early days?' he enquired.

Bernie smiled. Perhaps he heard the P.M.'s question.

'Bernie's fortune,' the P.M. said, 'began this way. One day, it was a Friday, the eve of the Jewish Sabbath, he saw the opportunity had come to make his fortune. He instructed his broker to buy heavily. But next day he was torn in his feelings; he always spent Saturday with his mother; he determined to keep to his custom and deliberately cut himself off from the market, declining all telephone calls. Then when the sun had gone down and the Sabbath was at an end, he found he had made seven hundred thousand dollars in a day.' The P.M. loved the story. 'If it had not been for the Jewish Sabbath,' he said, 'you would probably have cashed in and sold at, say, a hundred and fifty thousand dollars. You would not have hung on.'

Once only was the pleasing harmony between the two men in danger. Britain ought to be consulted, the P.M. contended vigorously, before an atomic bomb was sent off from airfields in East Anglia. Baruch at once broke in:

'But a considerable proportion of our bombing personnel are in Britain, and they would in that case be subject to your veto. If that is maintained it might be wise to withdraw them.'

The P.M. (*with some vehemence*): 'If the American Government take the line that they need not consult us, then they had better begin removing them now. Have you seen our agreement with Roosevelt?'

Baruch: 'No, I haven't.'

P.M.: 'It laid down that neither America nor Britain would release bombs without the consent of the other Government.'

Baruch: 'Cadogan made no objection.'

The P.M. thought the Russians were frightened of us and that there would be no war, but he spoke of October, 1952, as if it might be touch and go. Baruch agreed.

January 10, 1952

Today Bernie summoned three pundits of the Press to lunch with the P.M.; he wants him to get the feel of opinion before he addresses Congress. There were General Adler and Sulzberger of the *New York Times*, and Daniel Longwell, who holds *Life* together under Henry Luce. We had hardly taken our seats when the P.M. said without warning:

'What other nation in history, when it became supremely powerful, has had no thought of territorial aggrandizement, no ambition but to use its resources for the good of the world? I marvel at America's altruism, her sublime disinterestedness.'

All at once I realized Winston was in tears, his eyes were red, his voice faltered. He was deeply moved. Sulzberger broke the silence.

'I think, Prime Minister, it was hard-headedness on our part. I mean it was thought out, not emotional. Anyway, I hope it was, because emotion soon passes, whereas a thought-out plan might last. What view is taken in Britain about German unity?'

P.M.: 'I always felt in the war that we must strike down the tyrant, but be ready to help Germany up again as a friend. I have been doubtful about a European army only because I was concerned with its fighting power. It will not fight if you remove all traces of nationalism. I love France and Belgium, but we cannot be reduced to that level.'

And then the P.M. began to plead for a token American brigade, or even a battalion of Marines, to be sent to the Suez Canal.

P.M.: 'Now that we no longer hold India the Canal means very little to us. Australia? We could go round the Cape. We are holding the Canal not for ourselves but for civilization. I feel inclined to threaten the Americans that we will leave the Canal if they don't come in.'

General Adler: 'Could not America be invited to send this token force? If this is not done, I doubt if Congress will play.'

P.M.: 'I want it as a symbol that it is a United Nations project. Stalin was responsible for the United Nations and for the coming together of the two great English-speaking peoples; without him it might not have happened for generations. The architect of the Kremlin "builded better than he knew".

'Since Persia, the Egyptians have felt that America would not support Britain.[1] A token brigade would convince them they were wrong.'

Government House, Ottawa, January 11, 1952
The P.M. has been looking forward to his stay with Alex, who has a great hold over his affections, and his interest was quickened when General Templer arrived in order to be vetted for the command in Malaya.[2] After the business of the First Sea Lord, we are all a little apprehensive about Templer's fate. Alex was quite sure he was the man for this job of rooting out the Communist guerrillas from the jungle and Monty, too, had sent a letter, so we are hopeful that all will go well. Before I went to bed Templer told me he had talked with the P.M. for two hours.

'Winston began: "I am an old man. I shall probably not see you again. I may be sending you to your death." When he said this he almost broke down. And then he said to me: "Ask for power, go on

---

[1] When Persia nationalized her oil industry and with it the Anglo-Iranian Oil Company on May 2, 1951, the Americans failed to support the British Government's protest.

[2] At the end of the war well-armed Communist guerrillas, who had led the opposition to the Japanese, turned on the British in Malaya. A series of atrocities culminated in the assassination of Sir Henry Gurney, the High Commissioner of the Malayan Federation, on October 6, 1951. He was succeeded by Sir Gerald Templer.

asking for it, and then – never use it." At the end the P.M. smiled: "Here am I talking to you for all this time when I have two speeches on my hands." '

Templer turned to me:

'What is there about this man which no one else has?'

He did not seem to expect an answer, and I had none to give. He began to talk of his task in Malaya.

'The military problem is nothing. The police question can be set right; the civil service difficulty can be solved. What we have to do is to get the Malay and the Chinaman, with their different languages and religions, the followers of Confucius and of Islam, to say: "This is our country." '

Then Templer spoke of morale.

'There was something wrong with the British soldier in the last war; he would not have stood up to what happened in the First War. Are we going soft as a nation? But I feel it can be put right. The death penalty is necessary.'

He went on to recount a night operation:

'We were crossing a swollen river under heavy fire. I collected twenty men who would not face it. I told them that they would have to carry ammunition up a slope raked by fire. They wouldn't do it. I said I would return in an hour and then they would have to do it. In an hour they still refused. I had them court-martialled for mutiny. But at that moment I was whisked away to Anzio, and six weeks later, when I tackled Alex, he said: "They cannot be condemned to death now, the delay has been too long." So no example was made. Twenty-five divisions could have produced similar examples. You have studied these things. What is the explanation of this decay in morale?' he said, turning to me.

When I got a chance, I put Templer's question to Winston. He gave me a look as if I had accused him of spitting in church. He did not believe in all this stuff about nerves.

'But,' I persisted, 'surely courage has a social significance? A man who is ready to risk his skin is an unselfish man. Suppose, for the sake of argument, that the morale of the Army in this war was not as good as in the First War, then it means that men on the whole were not willing to behave as unselfishly.'

He gave a great snort.

'You've got some very queer views,' he said angrily and, taking up a book, he began to read.

I always give myself a black mark when I get drawn into an argument with Winston.

January 14, 1952

The P.M. said to Templer during luncheon:

'General, your doom will be announced tomorrow. It is a big job if you bring it off. Good luck to you.'

Whereupon he turned away to his left-hand neighbour and spoke no more to him. Alex rose. The General, he said, was an old friend, and in his judgement the Government could not have got a better man. He invited us to drink the General's health. Templer said to me under his breath:

'I need not say anything, need I?'

But I could see that the P.M. was looking at him and expected him to get up.

Templer said simply: 'I know nothing of this job. I will do my best because I recognize its importance.'

When he sat down the P.M. raised his glass to him, murmuring something about his 'dangerous mission'.

All day the P.M. has been working at his speech. He has a feeling that he can add something even now which might make all the difference. I think he must have infected me with his doubts and hesitations. Anyway, tonight when he rose to speak at the dinner given by the Prime Minister of Canada, I was so worked up I might myself have been making the speech. We had no need to be jittery. The fervour of his reception was a tribute, not to anything he had to say, but to his own corner in the hearts of the Canadian people. Afterwards he sat all crumpled up, but happy, receiving, like a Pope, the homage of the faithful. They were brought up to him one by one, and he gave them his hand, beaming upon them.

'Now,' he said to me, 'I'm not afraid of the Congress speech. When this speech is safely over it's more than half.' He turned to the Prof. 'Don't despise little things. I mean to appeal for a thousand young men to come over here to cut wood, so that we can build ten thousand houses above what Parliament has arranged. They'll have just enough wages to keep them going. And the same with steel. These are flash-lights in the sky.'

The representatives of the Press came up to him and said things which gave him pleasure. Later in his bedroom he said to me:

'They have never let me down. No friend has ever betrayed me.[1] I have come to believe in the brotherhood of man.' A whimsical smile flickered over his face. 'Now I'm making another speech.'

And with that he settled in his pillow.

January 16, 1952

Washington once more. This speech has become an obsession; it has hung over him, like a dark cloud, since the day we left England. At first he seemed to be on the verge of panic whenever it came into his mind. And then, as day after day he became familiar with the issues he must handle, as over and over and over again they were discussed by experts in committee after committee, he began to see what he ought to say. The experienced speaker knows when he has got what he wants, and so as time went by the P.M. became calmer, less irritable; the prospect of standing up before Congress no longer worried him. Once he went so far as to admit he thought it would be all right on the day. If the speech had been made a week ago he might have been jittery. Now there are moments when he even looks forward to it. I find that I am no longer jumpy, as I was in Ottawa. He will bring it off.

When the P.M. is not thinking of his speech to Congress he seems preoccupied with the security of his country.

'In 1940,' he said, 'three-quarters of a million Germans would have been needed to give invasion any chance of success; in 1941

---

[1] 'In all my life I found no friend but he was true to me' – *Julius Caesar*. One often catches Shakespearian echoes in his speech.

the number had risen to a million and a half. If Hitler had turned on all his factories to making landing craft . . . If . . .' He thought 1941 was the critical year for invasion. 'If,' he mused, 'the Almighty were to rebuild the world and he asked me for advice I would have English Channels round every country. And the atmosphere would be such that anything which attempted to fly would be set on fire.'

The P.M. went on to speak of war with Russia. Americans in Washington appeared anxious that Russia should know what the position was. There were detailed preparations for atomic bombing, the routes for aeroplanes. It was thought that in a month to six weeks three-quarters of Russia could be immobilized. He discussed the three American Chiefs of Staff with Roger Makins. Makins said it was a terrifying thought that three men could press a button to start another war. But the P.M. dwelt on the elemental forces in America: they were enormous; the preparations for war in the past eighteen months had been striking; in three years they would be irresistible.

If, however, the P.M. appeared for the moment to take the prospect of war with Russia rather lightly, he is obsessed with the precarious existence of Britain. There were, he said sadly, fifty million inhabitants, and we produced only enough food for thirty million; the remaining twenty millions must depend for food on our ingenuity in selling our exports. No great power had been so pre-cariously balanced, poised on the pinnacle of Victorian greatness. There would not be time for emigration to help. 'Poor England,' he said with a sigh. He keeps returning to this; it seems to haunt him.

Winston asked Franks about Cripps. Was it true that when he was staying at the Embassy three years ago, at the time of devaluation, Cripps rose at 5 a.m. and ran round the garden with nothing on?

'Nothing?' repeated Winston. 'Not even bathing drawers?'

The First Sea Lord, the P.M. said, had sent him a very fine paper on the Atlantic Command.

'I shall use it tomorrow when I go into action. I suppose,' he reflected, 'he wrote it himself.'

The First Sea Lord was recovering some of the ground lost at first contact.

January 17, 1952

Gladstone might have taken Congress off its feet with a vision of the better world for which the American people were striving, but Winston is not built that way; he must take the problems which interest Congress, and seek to persuade Members to see them through British spectacles. This he did as well as it could be done. He began by setting their suspicions at rest:

'I have not come here to ask you for money to make life more comfortable for the British people. Our standards of life are our own business, and we can only show our native and enduring strength, and keep our self-respect and independence by looking after them ourselves. I have come here to ask you not for gold but for steel; not for favours but for equipment.'

Britain could no longer bear the whole burden of the defence of the Suez Canal.

'We do not seek to be masters of Egypt. We are there only as the servants and guardians of the commerce of the world.'

He went on to speak of deterrents against a third world war. In solemn tones he admonished members of Congress:

'Be careful above all things not to let go the atomic weapon until you are sure and more than sure that other means of preserving peace are in your hands.'

Members had kept their heads – only now, when he spoke of the atomic bomb, was there any real warmth in the applause. But it is election year. Many members were conscious that the eyes of those in the galleries were on them, watching what points in the speech they applauded; they could not respond to his sentiments just as they felt; so they listened in silence while Winston went grimly on his way. (There would be no more elections for *him*. One thought alone gripped his mind: he was fighting for the survival of his country.) Winston has always had the feel of his audiences in America, even when he has lost touch with his own people, and now he ended as they would wish:

'Bismarck once said that the supreme fact of the nineteenth century was that Britain and the United States spoke the same language. Let us make sure that the supreme fact of the twentieth century is that they tread the same path.'

As he resumed his seat there was great applause, as there had been when he rose; whatever they might think of his views, they wanted him to know that he was a favourite son of America in his own right.

When it was done the P.M., flushed and happy, was like a man who has been granted a reprieve. He slumped back in the car, gazing vacantly out of the window; his cigar had gone out; he yawned contentedly. It had gone well, he thought; anyway, they had been very kind before he left the Senate. General Marshall, who had come by air from South Carolina specially to see him, awaited him at the Embassy. Winston was deeply touched; he admires Marshall as a great soldier. He hurried to take both his hands.

Marshall: 'It was a great success, Prime Minister.'

P.M.: 'I think they liked it. All the great speeches in history have had a simple theme; mine had not. I had to take a number of points. Lloyd George used to say that oratory is the art of successful dilution. I never hurry; it is a great mistake. Truman says a hundred and forty words in a minute. It's too fast. You must speak slowly, and you must not be afraid of repetition.'

Marshall, turning to us: 'The most wonderful speech I have heard the Prime Minister make was at Carthage; it was an inspired speech – and there is no record of it. The amphitheatre was full of troops, many in kilts, and then when he stopped the soldiers swept down upon him and he disappeared among them.'

General Marshall knew that every speaker, when he is back in his seat, has the same craving; he wants to know, in Mr Churchill's words, if he has hit the target. They could now talk of other things.

Marshall: 'What is said here in America is criticized by a million critics, but what is said in Russia has no critics. That is a terrible difference.

'Our basic training is sound, but you need some good professional soldiers to stiffen the "dull mass" of conscripts – your words, Prime Minister.'

P.M.: 'Glorious mass.'

Marshall, regarding Winston with a whimsical smile: 'That is politics.'

January 19, 1952

Today the P.M. is lying fallow. As the train bowled along towards New York he sat looking out of the window. I could not help noticing this, because usually he is impatient to do things, to read the papers, or play cards, or to dictate. Even when he is working on a speech or his book he cannot sit and think things out, he just says aloud what comes into his head, and then at the end he will take the typescript and correct and recorrect it many times. As his mind wandered lazily over the past, from time to time he dropped unconnected fragments. To piece these together appeared to be too much trouble; besides he was too tired to pursue any subject for long; he could not concentrate on anything.

'Baldwin was a remarkable man. I like to make people do what I wish. Baldwin liked to do what they wanted. But he was a great party organizer.

'I loved dining with Joe Chamberlain; he was a sparkling animal, attractive and fascinating, but he was a disrupter' – there was a pause to light his cigar – 'a bad element. The Conservative Party was mad to adopt the raw doctrine of Imperial Preference.[1]

'This visit to America has been a gamble. But it has come off, I think. It will do a lot of good. We have taken up old friendships and made new ones. I like Truman fearfully.'

I regretted that he had not persuaded Peter Portal to be Minister of Defence, and wondered if he still felt that Peter 'had everything', for often with the P.M. to be out of sight is to be out of mind. The P.M. assured me that nothing would induce Portal to leave life in the

[1] After the Imperial Conference of 1902 Joseph Chamberlain managed to persuade the Tory Cabinet that closer political union of the Empire would come only with tariff preferences, and more particularly the purchase of dearer grain from the Dominions. The prospect of an increase in the price of bread and other goods was a factor in the landslide Tory defeat in 1906.

country. This means that Portal has lost ground since he refused to be Minister of Defence.

There will be three hundred thousand houses next year. He would like each of them to have a little garden, because people at home love flowers. The Americans, he claimed, have no gardens to speak of; the climate is against them.

The Queen Elizabeth, *January 26, 1952*
It was eleven o'clock in the morning. The P.M. was asleep in his cabin, with his arm across his face, when he woke up with a start.

'I have been dreaming; it was extremely vivid,' he said.

'What did you dream?' I asked.

'Oh, I could not walk straight or see straight.'

He threw off the clothes and got out of bed, and very deliberately walked across the cabin to see if he could walk straight.

What have I learnt about the P.M. during this American visit that I did not know before? He is still better informed than any of his Ministers on any question affecting the armed forces of the Crown. It had taken a long time to settle the Atlantic Command, and his obstinate refusal to yield had provoked even members of his own little party. But in the end he salvaged more out of the dispute than anyone thought possible. British anti-submarine forces were, he argued, the key to action in the Atlantic, and he insisted that our naval staff should retain control of any action fought within the 'hundred-fathom line' – Shinwell, he said with contempt, had never heard of the line.

'Our writ will run in the western approaches; two hundred miles west from Plymouth and the St George's Channel; a hundred and fifty from Belfast and the Mull of Kintyre and more than a hundred miles from Scapa Flow.'

No other man could have achieved so much when the Americans were disposed to give so little.

CHAPTER NINE

In Which I Practise My Calling

February 7, 1952

King George VI is dead. Before the Prime Minister made his broadcast on the death of the King he sent for his ear man to syringe his throat. Often before, C. P. Wilson had been summoned for the same purpose, but this time it was different. This is what he said to me:

Wilson: 'Usually he has made some light remark, perhaps "Another brandy would do no harm," but now he asked abruptly: "What is the time?" "Twenty minutes to nine, sir," I replied. "No, it's seventeen to nine," he rapped out irritably. "We must hurry." I sprayed his throat with normal saline. When I had done he stalked out without a word. "He is terribly upset, sir," the valet said. "But nothing to lunch-time. Then when he was reading his speech he broke down." After the broadcast he came out of his study and without looking to the right or left made for the Cabinet Room, where he shut himself in.'

The P.M. had spent the whole day preparing his broadcast. He told me about it.

'It was short, but much was expected and much had been said. I wanted to make it a little different. It was only a week ago when I saw the King at the airfield when the Princess left. He was gay and even jaunty, and drank a glass of champagne. I think he knew he had not long to live.' Winston brooded for a time. 'It was a perfect ending. He had shot nine hares and a pigeon a hundred feet up, and then he dined with five friends and went out in the night. What more could any of us ask? I hope, Charles, you will arrange something like that for me.' He smiled. 'But don't do it till I tell you.'

He seemed to have done, and then he added:

'No institution pays such dividends as the Monarchy. Why, Canada is quite touchy about being called a Dominion, but look what happened when the Princess went there.'

February 12, 1952

Tonight at six-thirty the P.M. will have his first audience with the young Queen.

'Terrific things are happening,' Winston murmured. He spoke of his broadcast; there were letters from all kinds of people. They had liked 'walking with death'. There was nothing original in it, but it seemed 'to help people'. The troops at the funeral had had to wait fifty-five minutes, but no one had fainted or fallen out. He seemed to think this strange and unusual, and connected it vaguely with the occasion. A card, attached to the Government's wreath, bore the inscription: 'For Valour'.[1] Lord Athlone[2] told me that it was in Winston's handwriting; he said the Royal Family loved the words.

February 21, 1952

This evening, when I was about to go down to dinner, the telephone rang; it was Winston's voice. Usually the secretary calls me to the telephone before he comes.

'Where are you, Charles? I'd like to see you.'

I looked at my watch; it was seven-forty. I got into a taxi. 'Take me to 28 Hyde Park Gate.' Was the P.M. going to consult me about the new Minister of Health the papers were talking about? Would he bring up Walter Elliott's name again? It was not his custom to telephone like this just before dinner. Was anything wrong?

---

[1] 'For Valour' is the inscription on the Victoria Cross.
[2] Brother of Queen Mary and Governor-General of Canada, 1940–6.

The taxi pulled up at 28 Hyde Park Gate. A strange face opened the door.

'I want to see the Prime Minister.'

'This is the Cuban Embassy, sir. The Prime Minister left here some time ago. He is at 10 Downing Street.'

When I got to No. 10 I found him sitting on his bed in his boiler suit. He looked at me intently as if he were interested in me and wanted to know what I was thinking – so different from his usual detached and almost absent-minded greeting.

'I am glad you have come. I took up the telephone when I woke an hour ago, and I couldn't think of the words I wanted. Wrong words seemed to come into my head, but I was quite clear what was happening and did not say them. This went on for about three or four minutes. Then the operator asked, "Do you want the Private Office?" What does it mean, Charles? Am I going to have a stroke? If this happened again I'd have to pull out. It might come on in a speech. That would be the end. My pulse was all right,' he said, putting his finger on his radial artery. 'Take it now, Charles.'

I told him it was good and regular.

'Is the blood pressure up? Bring your instrument tomorrow and see if it's up. Can you do anything?'

I said I would get some trinitrin medicine.

'What will that do?' he enquired.

'It dilates the vessels and brings more blood to the spot.'

'Will it do me any harm?' he asked a little apprehensively. 'It won't burst an artery? Tell me, Charles, what happened? Why couldn't I find the words I wanted?'

I explained that some of the small vessels in his head had gone into a state of spasm, contracting so that the circulation to the speech centre was diminished.

'You'll have to pull out or arrange things so that the strain is less.'

He listened attentively and then said:

'I keep having to make important decisions, terrible decisions. It never stops. It is worse than the war.'

He rose.

'What shall I say if I run into Clemmie?' I asked.

'Oh, come, we'll go and tell her everything. She's in bed with a cold.'

He told her what had happened. She listened in silence; she was grave but quite composed. He offered to send me home in his car, but I thanked him and said I would walk some of the way. I wanted to do a little hard thinking. In the past I have taken great risks when I let him carry on at Washington after the heart attack, and again at Monte Carlo, two and a half years ago, when he had a stroke. But now something must be done.

This might, of course, be the first warning of a stroke; if it were I could not help, events would settle themselves. In a few days, however, we could put that behind us. Then if no clot formed and it was only spasm of the arteries, in a man whose cerebral circulation was no longer what it was, we should be faced with a difficult decision. Ought he to resign, or could we do anything to patch him up for a little? With a vote of censure hanging over him, and the prospect of a row in the House over the Budget, I knew he would hate pulling out at this moment. Aneurin Bevan and his gang would say that he had run away from trouble, for, as the P.M. put it, there was a lot of venom about. I knew, too, that he had set his heart on seeing the young Queen crowned before he gave up office. That it was a bad time for Anthony to take over was clear to him; he would be held responsible for the unpopular austerity measures. Was the P.M. more likely to get a stroke in the next six months if he carried on? No doctor could tell; it was mere guess-work. Even if I went to him and said, 'You must get away from this grind or you will have serious trouble,' it would get us nowhere. The P.M. is not easily frightened off his course. I was beginning to see that it was not the moment for him to go.

February 22, 1952
When I had slept on things there seemed only one course to take. If the P.M. comes safely through the next few days I've got to square up to him after the Budget and persuade him to be sensible. He

won't listen to anybody, and I don't overrate my chances, but it is my job as his doctor. I think I know the turn of his mind as no one else does. I shall hate doing it, but it's the only thing I can do for him.

It was in that frame of mind that I called at No. 10 this morning. He had had a good night and was in the mood to look upon the incident as closed. Perhaps it did not mean very much, after all. Anyway, I saw that he didn't want to talk about it and I got away in a few minutes. Downstairs I sought out Jock Colville. He has come back from the Foreign Office to share with Pitblado the duties of Principal Private Secretary to the Prime Minister; he is a friend of the family, knows Winston's ways, plays cards with him for hours at a time – and idolizes him. There is not much gratitude in the political world, and my first care must be not to put sharp weapons into the hands of anyone who might use them to hurt him. I wanted to hear from someone in the Cabinet whether the duties of Prime Minister could be cut, and I have no doubt that the man to make me wise is Lord Salisbury. His complete detachment and single-mindedness, with his lack of personal ambition, give me a comfortable sense of security. I told Jock what had happened, and asked him to arrange an appointment with Salisbury.

Two hours later I was shown, with Jock, into Lord Salisbury's room at Gwydyr House. I said my piece: I asked if the Prime Minister's work could be lightened.

'A Prime Minister cannot shed his responsibilities,' Salisbury replied.

Jock thought the Honours List and Ecclesiastical preferment might be done by Salisbury with Harry Crookshank. Perhaps even the Budget proposals could be simplified and summarized a little more before being shown to the P.M.

Salisbury: 'Of course, I don't know how far they are peptonized already.'

Jock: 'I hate to be disloyal, but the P.M. is not doing his work. A document of five sheets has to be submitted to him as one paragraph, so that many of the points of the argument are lost.'

I pointed out that this had happened in the last years of the war when Martin, Rowan and Bridges in turn had complained that he was not mastering his brief.

Salisbury: 'His work seems to vary enormously from day to day.'

Jock: 'Yes, that's true. Only yesterday I simplified something and he burst out, "Can't I read?" He was right on the spot.'

Salisbury: 'Another time in the Cabinet he will talk about something for two and a half hours without once coming to the point.'

Jock: 'Yes, Egypt, for example.'

The real difficulty, I said, was that he hated delegating anything.

Salisbury (*sympathetically*): 'We are all the same; the more tired we get, the more we seem to feel we must do the thing ourselves.'

As they talked I saw that even if Winston were willing to turn over a new leaf all this tinkering would come to nothing. Then Salisbury said suddenly:

'Of course he ought to go to the Lords – oh, yes, remaining Prime Minister.'

Jock: 'Eden would lead the House and would be virtually Prime Minister. In 1952 no one but Winston could be Prime Minister in the Lords. He would be the grand old man of politics, coming down from time to time and making a great speech to their Lordships.'

Salisbury felt sure he could go to the Lords and remain Prime Minister.

'We are beginning to see light,' he added cheerfully.

My heart leapt; this was a solution that had not occurred to me. But Jock's face had become serious.

'He won't do it,' he said gloomily. 'I did once suggest to him that he should go to the Lords, and thought at first he was taking it seriously, when he said: "I should have to be the Duke of Chartwell, and Randolph would be the Marquis of Toodledo." I saw that he was laughing at me.'

Salisbury, ruefully: 'No, I am afraid he regards us in the Lords as a rather disreputable collection of old gentlemen.'

Jock: 'Three years ago he would not have gone to the Lords because he would have thought it might ruin Randolph's political career. Now he has given up Randolph.'

They fell to discussing who could put it to him. No one has the least influence with him; he does not listen to any of the Cabinet. The Prof.?

'Oh,' said Jock, 'he'll listen to him on guided missiles, but not on politics. He does listen to Christopher Soames, he has a great affection for him; he seems to have taken Randolph's place as a son.'

I had not much faith in Christopher's discretion.

Winston is still remarkably quick at spotting a plot. A loose word, and he will tumble to everything. The conversation was ceasing to be helpful. I listened to them, but I knew in my heart that it would not work.

'There is only one person,' I said at last, 'who could get him to do this, and that is the Queen.'

They thought it a good idea.

Salisbury: 'Things are beginning to take shape.'

Jock: 'There is one person – and only one – I'd like to consult – Tommy Lascelles.'

Salisbury: 'Yes, he might help, and he's as close as the grave.'

When I saw Lascelles this afternoon at Buckingham Palace I began by admonishing him that if, when I had done, he felt that the P.M. ought to retire, he must forget what I had said; for if I could not help my patient I must see that nothing I said did him hurt. With that prelude I told my story.

Lascelles followed carefully what I said, without a word of comment. At the end he said:

'Well, listening to what you have told me, I would say at once the Prime Minister ought to resign and be content to be the elder states-man in the Commons or the Lords – better perhaps in the Lords. I have been expecting for some time to see you in this room. It is true that sometimes the Prime Minister is all on the spot, and then I say to myself: Why am I worrying? But at other times he doesn't seem able to see the point of a discussion.'

The conversation was not taking quite the line I had intended.

'Don't you think,' I said, 'he is still useful to the country? Unpopular decisions have to be made over finance; he will make them. I can't see most of the politicians I know risking the displeasure of the electorate. Besides, this is not the moment for Anthony to succeed. He would get all the blame for the Budget and it might even be felt that he had pushed Winston out.'

Lascelles seemed impressed by this line of thought. Then Jock intervened. The P.M., he said, had told him a few days ago that he would like to hang on until the Coronation in May of next year. After that he would resign. Lascelles appeared to agree that if we could bring him through this year it would be the best plan.

'Of course nobody,' he reflected, 'but Winston could go to the Lords and remain Prime Minister, but he could. He is a law to himself and is still a great figure in the country. He might of course, in that event, have to get rid of some of the Peers in the Cabinet, Leathers and perhaps the Prof. – that is a question of detail. But how are you going to get him to the Lords?' he enquired dubiously.

Jock: 'He once refused the Garter. Now he thinks he'd rather like it.'

Lascelles: 'He can have it tomorrow if it helps.'

Jock: 'It would fit in with the Lords.'

I interrupted at this point:

'Winston isn't worldly. If you want him to do this you must prove it is for the sake of Eden or the country or the Queen.'

Lascelles: 'Yes, that's true; he isn't worldly.'

Jock then brought up my idea about the Queen, but Lascelles said he did not think anything would come of that.

'If she said her part, he would say charmingly: "It's very good of you, Ma'am, to think of it –" and then he would very politely brush it aside. The Queen could not compete with him in dialectic. The King might have done it,' Lascelles added thoughtfully, 'but he is gone.'

Various names came into his head; he dismissed them one by one, though for a moment he hesitated when he said 'Pug.' It was at length agreed that nothing should be done till the Budget was over; we should only add to his worries if we brought this up now – we must gamble on nothing happening in the next few days. Then I am to deliver a medical ultimatum that he cannot go on at the present pace, that he must either throw in his hand or in some way cut down his work. Lascelles wanted me to go to him and say outright that he must go to the Lords, but I maintained that he would listen to me on the medical argument, but that when I began on politics he would switch off. Jock agreed. I said I would try and get him into a state of mind so that he saw something must be done – it is for others to suggest that something. Lascelles agreed reluctantly. Then he seemed to go back upon the plan; the P.M. ought to resign if he were not fit to carry on. I dealt with this.

'Very well,' he said. 'I shall hear from you in ten days' time and know what success you've had.'

February 23, 1952

This morning I called on the P.M. at Chartwell. I did my stuff and was out of his room in five minutes. I knew he did not want to talk about what had happened, but I knew, too, that it was there at the back of his mind; he had been warned – and Winston is still quick enough to take his leads. He was subdued. If he was left to himself there was still a chance that he would listen to reason. For my part I had no desire to talk; it might only do harm. Jock told me on the telephone that the P.M. had been discussing the Defence debate and that Jock thought it was a good opportunity to 'put in a word'. So he had suggested that the P.M. should leave the Defence speech to Anthony Head. [1] The P.M. turned on him like a flash:

'Have you been talking with Charles?'

Jock had brazened it out, but he was shaken.

[1] Secretary of State for War.

Chartwell, February 25, 1952

Found the P.M. chastened, but still uncommunicative. Another of his black swans had been killed in the night by a fox; he would have to make totally different arrangements. His speech was finished.

'I have to make my own speeches; what they give me is silly stuff. The country,' he mused, half to himself, 'is divided into two equal parts. If they worked together they might survive. But they won't; they are set on tearing the heart out of each other.

'I knew something had happened when I could not get my words on the telephone. I didn't like it. I was frightened. Oh, not frightened,' he corrected himself, 'I'm not frightened of anything. But I'm all right now. Why, you couldn't tell by examining me that anything had happened.'

He wanted me to tell him that he could put the incident at the telephone out of his thoughts.

'But the fact remains you've had notice to go slower.'

'I don't mind dying in harness,' he said rather defiantly.

'That won't help anyone,' I said. 'You've got a certain stock of energy, mental energy, and you can either spread it out over a period of time or just use it up recklessly – and in that case it won't last long.'

He didn't even frown at me, he seemed to feel that if he tried to argue the facts were against him. Anyway, I'd planted the seed, and to change the subject I pulled out my stethoscope and began to examine him. I have not given up hope yet.

February 26, 1952

When the P.M. had replied to Herbert Morrison's speech in moving a vote of censure he went to his room in the House, and I joined him.

'I was alarmed at lunch-time; I seemed to have no wits, and I was very tired and shaky before getting up to speak, but I felt stronger as I got under way. Now I feel quite all right. How did it go?' he asked eagerly. 'I feel it has gone well. Morrison was really very feeble. Where is Christopher? Send for him. He will know what the Lobby thinks.'

Christopher said the speech had been well received; the point that the Labour Government had spent more than a hundred million pounds on manufacturing an atomic bomb without disclosing it to the House, and then called the Conservatives warmongers, had gone particularly well. And the disclosure that Morrison was committed to reprisals if our aeroplanes in Korea were attacked by planes from central airfields in China was a most effective thrust. Christopher did not seem so certain what view members would take of the P.M. using a Cabinet document. Winston pooh-poohed this; he had been at the game for fifty years, and knew what could be done. I advised him to go home and have a bath and dine before returning to the House. But he said he would return to the House for a short time. He really wanted to know what people thought of his speech. He was excited. His pulse was 112. I have a feeling that the chance of translating him to the Lords has gone.

February 27, 1952

I called at No. 10 about half-past five, hoping to see the P.M. before he retired for his rest. But I learnt he had already gone to his room. I opened the door very gently, but the curtains had been drawn and the room was in darkness. I closed the door as quietly as I could, but Norman said he had only just settled, and went in and asked him if he would like to see me; he said yes. I found him animated, very different from the subdued Winston whose future has never been out of my mind since the difficulty with the telephone.

'You know, Charles, yesterday was a great success; the papers have been most kind. Attlee came up to me today after Questions and was positively gushing; he asked me about the Queen. He seems to have been pleased when he was found out manufacturing his atomic bomb like a good patriot. I think he's made up his mind to cut away from Bevan. But it doesn't seem to fit in with their vote of censure on me. Now there are new troubles – new decisions,' he corrected himself.

February 29, 1952

Visited the P.M. after breakfast. He said:

'Since the speech I have felt better and more cheerful about things. During luncheon that day I was stupid, dull and muzzy, and I wondered if I could make a speech at all. But we put them on their backs,' speaking with animation. 'Why, it was one of the meanest things in public life to withhold from their followers their commitment over Korea, and then bring in a vote of censure on me. I only quoted Cabinet directives, not Cabinet documents.'

I asked him if a long Cabinet tired him.

'Oh, no, I get excited; my appetite thrives on what it feeds on. I get muzzy in the head about lunch-time, and then I get better as the day goes on.'

He once more stressed the innumerable questions that came up for decision: the future of the B.B.C., for example. He had not been able to get off to sleep yesterday afternoon as he had always done. Could I not give him something to 'curl him up'? I saw again that the telephone incident had been relegated to the past. The success of his reply to Morrison and the way the vote of censure had fizzled out had given him a little breathing space; he has got back his nerve.

'Perhaps,' he said, 'I was hardly awake when I telephoned.' With a smile, 'You can't expect to live for ever.'

March 6, 1952

Called at No. 10 at nine this morning. The P.M. was full of the debate in the House.

Winston, reproachfully: 'You ought to read the papers. They are very interesting, if you like politics. The Bevan group sat all together in one part, and Attlee's supporters were gathered together in another group. There they were, glowering at each other. The split might deepen and lead to a coalition. I should not be against it. I would retire if necessary.'

I asked him if he had been less tired. He answered:

'If I don't get my sleep in the afternoon I cannot sit up late and work. I get muddled and tired.'

March 12, 1952

The game is up; nevertheless, I decided to warn the P.M. and put it on paper that he might absorb it.

My dear Prime Minister,

I have given careful thought to the significance of the little disturbance when you went to the telephone on February 21st. It was of the same nature as the sudden mistiness which you had within a fortnight of the Leeds speech in the 1950 election, namely due to spasm of the cerebral arteries. And these were first cousins of the blocking of a little artery at Monte Carlo in August, 1949. All three point to some instability in the cerebral circulation, which must be increased by excessive mental effort. On the other hand if it were possible to lighten the load without giving up being Prime Minister, which on medical grounds would not be wise at the moment, then you ought to be able to carry on more or less indefinitely. Of course if you would like confirmation of my interpretation of events, we could get Russell Brain at any time, but they are really capable of no other explanation.

If there is any point that I have not made clear, I will of course come at any time you want. I feel sure that you would like the medical facts put down for your consideration. When I saw Clemmie about your deafness I told her my view.

Charles

I explained to Clemmie what I had done.

My dear Clemmie,

There seem to me to be two dangers attendant upon this letter. Firstly, that he may resign, and it is our medical experience that to take a man out of a very active mental life into retirement is often – I might almost say always – accompanied by profound changes. And I would dread them here.

Secondly, that he may just take no notice. In this case we have to remember that it is not really putting the whole case when he talks about dying in harness. What one dreads much more is an attack which leaves him disabled.

I have not the slightest doubt that though there are risks in any course, to remain Prime Minister and to go to the Lords for a year or so is much the safest course medically.

I know it would be a sacrifice on his part, but I am sure it would be best for the Monarch, the country and his successor, and I think the country would look on it as a noble gesture, paving the way for the succession.

Charles

March 13, 1952

Clemmie telephoned: 'He was not angry when he got your letter; he just swept it aside. I mentioned the Lords, but he would not consider it. Charles, I'm glad you wrote. It may do good. Instead of going to the House this afternoon and listening to Mr Thorneycroft,[1] he has gone to bed.'

But I am under no illusions. We have failed.

March 23, 1952

A week ago the P.M. said to me:

'I got your letter. I don't want you to worry. You really needn't. One has got to die some time.'

At that moment MacKenna came into the room, and that was the end of my attempt to translate Mr Churchill into the House of Lords. I was sure I should hear no more of it; but today when I called at four o'clock he said he was just about to lie down and asked me if I would come to his room. As he undressed he said:

'I have noticed a decline in mental and physical vigour. I require more prodding to mental effort.' He smiled. 'I get a good deal of prodding. I forget names. I might even forget yours – people whose names I know as well as my own. I'm as quick at repartee in the House as ever I was. I enjoy Questions there. Do you think I ought to see Brain?'

---

[1] President of the Board of Trade.

I replied that it was no use seeing him unless he was ready to take his advice. The P.M. himself thought it would be a bad thing if he retired now. I said Brain would certainly advise cutting down what he had to do. He protested that he already devoluted a good deal of work. Rab[1] and Anthony, for example, did a lot – and they worked in a broad field. There were others, such as Lord Salisbury. He had worries, of course. He was worried over Egypt, and whether we were going to be blown up, and whether we should be able to solve our financial problems, and about houses and food.

'I'm halfway in my seventy-eighth year, and one can't expect to live for ever. I really don't think you need worry. I soon get tired physically; when I have fed the robin and the swans, and perhaps walked three-quarters of a mile, I have had enough. I dislike standing, except when making speeches.'

Then he began telling me about a poor woman whose husband had left her three lorries, and the local council, which was dominated by Labour, restricted the radius over which they could be used. He was very angry about it. It appeared that even Parliament could do nothing without legislation. He had just had a meeting with Leathers and others, lasting an hour and a half, and they were going to bring in a Bill. He took up the telephone.

'The Private Office. Pitblado? Will you get Christopher to come across, and tell him what has been done? Tell him in detail. He has been very fully into this.'

Twice I made a move. I told him he would not get to sleep if he roused himself. But each time he said:

'No, sit down. I want to talk.'

Now I rose and made for the door, and he settled in the pillow.

---

[1] R. A. Butler, Chancellor of the Exchequer.

CHAPTER TEN

Muddling Through

April 16, 1952

'This miserable cold has settled on my chest,' the P.M. telephoned this morning. 'Bring your stethoscope.' When I listened to his chest it was like a musical box.

'I have not much in reserve,' he said. 'How shall I know if it develops into anything?'

Winston seemed in poor spirits. He wanted to go to Newmarket, where two of his horses were running; as long as he has no temperature, he feels he can ignore anything that may be wrong with him. I told him there was a risk in going to Newmarket, though the risk was small. When I had said my say he picked up the house telephone and began talking to Clemmie, who was in her room.

'Charles is with me; he says there is not much wrong and sees no objection to my going, but I don't think I shall go. I've lost heart.'

It was not like him to admit defeat, and I was seeking an explanation when I met Miss Sturdee on the stairs. She told me Mrs Churchill had taken a strong line about Newmarket.

'He couldn't get any harm, Lord Moran, could he? He would meet all his buddies who have horses running, and get away from his worries.'

April 18, 1952

From Chartwell last night word came that he had made up his mind to take part in the debate in the House on railway fares; he was coughing, and they were not happy about him. I found him, however, in better spirits, he spoke indeed with animation. His pulse and temperature were normal – he had taken them himself. When I had listened to his chest he said: 'Well, is there anything there?'

I told him that he was better in himself, but that he was still full of bronchitis. He threw himself on his face.

'Listen again, my dear Charles,' he demanded. 'You may have examined me at a bad moment. I can't believe there's much wrong when I feel so much better in myself. Now, Charles, it's no use you telling me not to do things; you don't know what I must do. *The Times* has a stupid leader on the Government's action. You haven't seen it? Oh, well, don't bother to read it.'

I told him I wasn't interested in politics; my job was to tell him the medical position.

'Well, what is it?' he demanded.

'The trouble is in your tubes now – the larger tubes – if you take care of yourself it won't go lower down. If you don't it may spread to the smaller tubes.'

'Is that halfway to the old trouble?' he asked. Without waiting for an answer, he said cheerfully: 'Anyway, I shall be all right tomorrow. Come and sound me. Come to luncheon – and bring Dorothy.'

April 19, 1952

The P.M. sat in his place, glowering at his plate. This transport muddle has driven the threat of another attack of pneumonia out of his head. Leathers[1] was bright and apparently untroubled, but Maclay's[2] face was drawn, his cheeks sunken – he appeared to be a sick man. The P.M. said:

[1] Lord Leathers, Secretary of State for Co-ordination of Transport, Fuel and Power, 1951–3.
[2] J. S. Maclay, Minister of Transport and Civil Aviation, 1951–2.

'When I was told I had no power to alter these fares, fury arose in my breast. I was not responsible for this rise in fares, but I am getting all the blame. I feel I must protect the people from these nationalized industries.'

He turned to Maclay, who seemed too tired to listen:

'This is a great issue, more important even than steel. It's a great opportunity. We have a very strong case.'

Presently Lord Leathers, perhaps stimulated by my presence, or it may be to get away from the depressing transport talk, said across the table:

'When I was forty-six I began to get headaches which lasted sometimes as long as three weeks; they were so severe that I was left prostrate. I saw all kinds of specialists, but I got no better. Then in despair I was persuaded by a friend to see his osteopath. I went without faith. He said to me, "Get up here," indicating an elaborate surgical table. "Now put your head under my arm, like this" – he was a big fellow, perhaps six foot three. Then he began turning my head this way and that, with great rapidity. "I'm breaking down adhesions," he said. Finally, he gave a terrible wrench, there was a loud click – I thought he'd broken my neck. But I have never had a headache since.'

He looked at me in a challenging manner. The P.M. leant forward eagerly:

'Now, Charles, I call that a very remarkable story. You really ought to put aside your prejudices and go into it.' He turned to Leathers: 'A year and a half ago I went to an osteopath without telling Charles, and he knocked me about, but I was not a pin the better. I suppose it all depends on what is wrong with you.'

They were waiting for my answer. But I had no mind to be drawn into an argument with the P.M. and Leathers on faith healing. It seems strange that a man who is a director of 52 companies can be so credulous. At the first opportunity I took my leave.

The Government seemed to blunder out of one crisis into another, and the P.M. was plainly feeling the strain of it all. I debated what could be done to help him. No one envied him his task, but this weakness in administration had taken everybody by surprise. It was plain that if John Anderson, now Viscount Waverley, had been in charge of the home front, as he was in the war, none of this confusion would have arisen. He was the man they needed. I wondered if it was too late. But if I was going to butt into this business I must be sure of my ground, for the Prime Minister, when criticized, has a way of putting out his claws.

June 1, 1952

Lunched with Viscount Waverley at West Dean. While I was waiting for an opening he asked me:

'How long have you known Winston?' 'Oh,' he said, 'that's not a long time. I have known him since 1906, when he was Under-Secretary to the Minister for the Colonies, Lord Elgin.'

Winston, he said, had marked a document, 'I can take no responsibility for this measure.' Underneath, in a lady-like hand, Lord Elgin had written, 'I take responsibility.'

'Winston,' Waverley ruminated, 'was not autocratic, he was really quite humble; he would go over what had been done with an open mind.'

'He needs wise men round him,' I added.

Waverley interrupted: 'That's not enough; he must have congenial men about him, like Freddie Guest.'

I said I thought Winston was unhappy: the political ground on which just now he had to make runs wasn't his wicket. Waverley agreed.

'He was not happy in the old days when he was at the Treasury, and now, faced by economic questions, he is not at his ease. And his colleagues,' Waverley went on, 'are not happy either. Leathers has not learnt to handle an assembly like the Lords.'

I said: 'Winston will need all the help his friends can give if he is to come through with any credit. If you'd been a Minister,' I ventured to affirm, 'this transport muddle would never have occurred.'

Waverley looked down his nose and said nothing – he looked like a prim elder of the kirk.

'He needs you in the Cabinet,' I persisted.

Waverley said quietly that he could not afford to join the Cabinet.

June 2, 1952

Today at Chartwell I found the P.M. in an amiable mood and said to him:

'If I had had to make a Cabinet when you did I'd have begun, I think, with Waverley.'

'I asked John,' he retorted. 'I couldn't do more. He said he was over seventy, and that if he joined the Government he would not be able to get a job when he left office. He couldn't afford to give up his present posts, which brought him in a good income, and take office at £4,000 a year.'

June 20, 1952

The P.M. was dictating a memorandum when I called at No. 10. He sent out a message: would I make myself comfortable in the drawing-room for a few minutes? He would not be long. Then he forgot all about me. It might have been an hour later when a secretary discovered me. Winston seemed quite upset about it. He had never done this before. He said his memory was 'awful'.

I asked him how he had been. He looked up wearily:

'As well as I can be. I'm not what I was – not mentally overflowing. I don't want to dictate a memorandum,' he smiled. 'Of course I have written some quite serious papers.'

I asked him if he had any plans for a holiday.

'What can I do?' he answered a little impatiently. 'I cannot go abroad as the guest of *Life* while I am Prime Minister. I must find some interest.'

'Do you mean your book?'

'Oh, no; I must superintend things at Chartwell. I don't mean I am going to cut down trees – I promise you I won't do anything foolish – but I can direct others cutting them down. I don't know why, but I love Chartwell; somehow it's home to me.'

The P.M. gloomily contemplated the papers on his bed-rest.

'It is a most perplexing time, much worse than the war. All talk and no co-operation. Attlee and his people are behaving badly – currying popularity by attacking America. It's easy to pick out things there to attack in an election year.'

All this, of course, does not mean that Winston is thinking of retiring. It is his way of seeing if, as his doctor, I can help. He can't talk about his disabilities to anyone else. It seems, too, to relieve his feelings to go over the difficulties he has to overcome with someone not in the political world, though my part is only to listen; he does not want my views. But there is no weakening of purpose.

'I told the 1922 Committee,'[1] Winston continued, 'that they must trust the Government and that they must trust me too. I said they could be assured that I would not stay if I found I was failing physically or mentally. They took it all right. There is no movement to get me out. Anthony is absorbed in his work at the Foreign Office. It would be madness to move him.'

The P.M. thought his health was better than it has been for some time. He was not so stupid in the head in the middle of the day as he had been five months ago.

'Now, Charles, it is nearly three years since the trouble at Monte Carlo. Did you think then that I should be here now?'

He put his hand on my arm.

'You found the pulse good? I can still hold my own in the House. I can put anyone on his back if it is necessary.'

It is no more than the truth. His answers at Question Time in the House of Commons, particularly to Supplementaries, have the old merit of unexpectedness.

He seemed to want to talk, and rambled on in a way that was not at all like him in the early morning. It became obvious that he wanted to persuade himself that he was fit to carry on.

---

[1] A committee set up in 1922, comprising all back-bench Conservative Members of Parliament.

'I drink a great deal,' he said, 'it keeps me going. Oh, not too much, Charles.'

Last night, he returned from the 'Other Club'[1] hilarious (Camrose took him home), and at Chartwell on Sunday Jock said the P.M. spoke of his pranks at Sandhurst; Jock had not laughed so much for a long time.

July 30, 1952

When I entered his bedroom this morning the P.M. threw the morning papers on the floor in great disgust. I knew from the set of his jaw that he was looking for trouble. I asked him, was he rested?

'Yes,' he answered grimly. 'I'll knock hell out of anyone. You would think, from the way Attlee's supporters carry on, that they weren't responsible for the awful mess we found. There will have to be more cuts to keep the country from bankruptcy.'

In the afternoon I went to the House of Commons to hear him speak on rearmament. He had a very noisy passage, but what could he expect when he deliberately trailed his coat to Shinwell? I left the Chamber with Alex, who is now Minister of Defence. He said he would be glad to be done with it all.

'I would never have taken this job on if I had known what the House of Commons was like. They shout at each other. I think, Charles, it is lamentable. Do you consider that the English people have deteriorated? I don't believe the House was like that before the war.'

During tea Trenchard supported Alex; he thought it wrong that the Commons should treat Winston like that, he had done so much for the country. At that point the waitress gave me a bit of paper. It was a message from Jock. He was rather worried about the Prime Minister. He had been very shaky after his speech. He looked grey.

---

[1] F. E. Smith and Winston Churchill founded the 'Other Club' in 1911 in a fit of impatience with 'The Club'. The Other Club had a strong hold on Churchill's affections, and on more than one occasion when he was abroad and Lord Moran had to persuade him that he was not fit to travel to attend a dinner there was a stormy scene.

'Could you pop over – but you must not say I sent for you – he's in his room in the House of Commons.'

I found him slumped in his chair with a whisky and soda.

'I didn't tell them anything,' he said, smiling.

'Are you tired?'

'Oh, no, I feel quite well.'

This racket in the House, day after day, is doing him no good, but he can no longer do without it. He will go on squandering what is left of his capital until he goes bankrupt.

September 30, 1952

The P.M. was back from his holiday at Monte Carlo and says he feels better for it; he has more vigour. 'I had no money to gamble at the tables, but I did three pictures while I was away, and worked five hours every day at my book.'

In France he got a second wind. He said to me today:

'The Government position is stronger than it was a year ago. I have not yet decided when to resign. It might do me no good when the curtain is down.'

Then, as if the subject were closed, he added:

'I am going to Balmoral tomorrow. I felt I ought to see the Queen. I have not seen her for two months.'

November 13, 1952

I asked the P.M. how he had slept. 'I dream a lot. Why do I do that? The dreams are always pleasant, so that I am sorry when I wake. I want them to go on. They are extremely complicated. I dreamt last night about ten cigars. They were of enormous size, and each had attached to it a piece of paper with the history of that particular cigar.'

The unmistakable signs of old age are at last apparent; they seem to bother him, and yet he has no intention of giving up. This is an unequal contest, and I shall hear more of it.

He pushed away his plate and rang a bell, when Walter came in with a particularly big pear and a glass of orange juice.

'You know Fred Woolton?[1] I want to talk to you about him. You know he has been ill?'

The P.M. had forgotten that when he heard Lord Woolton was seriously ill he had been much concerned and had sent for me. He was, he said, very fond of Fred, and had been very much upset when told how gravely ill he was. But the political mind is essentially practical. The work of the Lord President of the Council would be greatly increased by the Coronation, and the Prime Minister had a growing feeling that Woolton would not be up to it.

P.M.: 'I don't believe he can be fit in four months' time, but I don't want to discourage the poor man, and put him back perhaps, by writing and asking him to put his office in my hands. I know he wants to do the Coronation. He likes pomp and ceremony. Of course he will have to give up being Chairman of the Party, but that was going to happen in any case before his illness. But I would give him a step in the Peerage. He wants that. Can you help me about him, Charles?'

---

[1] Lord Woolton, Lord President of the Council.

PART THREE

Never Give In

CHAPTER ELEVEN

A New Lease of Life

February 18, 1953

P.M.: 'Yesterday I was worried about my chest when I asked you to call, but I think my cold is subsiding. The poor Cabinet has been afflicted. Lord Salisbury has gone away for a month. He is one of those in my orchestra whose note I value.'

Moran: 'He is, of course, full of sense, but he has got a bee in his bonnet about the reform of the House of Lords.'

P.M.: 'We may revoke the Parliament Act,[1] if they are not too timid. Everyone is timid nowadays. It is all appeasement. I don't like it.'

His mind went back to the old conflict of 1911 with the House of Lords. He spoke with great severity of their conduct at that time.

P.M.: 'In a few minutes they had undone all we did in a session.'

Moran: 'Attlee, it seems, wanted to hold a conference on the reform of the House of Lords; at any rate he did not wish to return a direct refusal, but after Jennie Lee[2] had spoken the meeting turned it down.'

P.M.: 'We may do better on our own. At any rate we should restore the two years.'

---

[1] The Liberal Government's measure in 1911 to reduce the power of the House of Lords after the latter's persistent baulking of the administration's bills.

[2] Jennie Lee, M.P., wife of Aneurin Bevan.

Moran: 'It's too late. All this will lead to the abolition of the House.'

P.M.: 'I doubt that. The public are, I think, more friendly to your House than you imagine.'

The House of Lords means nothing to him. The history of England, its romance and changing fortunes, is for Winston embodied in the Royal House. He looked at a new photograph of the Queen. She was in white, with long white gloves, smiling and radiant.

'Lovely,' he murmured, 'she's a pet. I fear they may ask her to do too much. She's doing so well.

'I feel,' he said, 'that if I retired now it might do me a lot of harm. I could, of course, write another book. I might divide what I have between those near to me, and go abroad for five months in the year – Jamaica perhaps. But I might dislike what the Government did when I had left it, and I might say so, and there might be the hell of a row.

'I must not trouble you, Charles, to come with me to America. But I am very grateful for your generous offer. I think I'll take a chance this time. I suppose something will happen to me some day. It's bound to. But I'm not in bad condition. I haven't seen you since I replied to the vote of censure. I was glad to leave things in the House like that, because it showed them I was as good as any of them. Our people were cheering all the time, while most of the Opposition sat silent. I told them just what I thought of their charge of war-mongering.

'I hate this foggy stuff,' he grumbled, 'I never go out. I stay most of the time working in bed. They are saying, Charles, that I am going to get something out of Ike.[1] Well, we mustn't pitch our hopes too high. But I might. And if I did it would be good for this country and for America too.'

February 19, 1953

Found the P.M. absorbed in George Orwell's book, *1984*.

'Have you read it, Charles? Oh, you must. I'm reading it for a second time. It is a very remarkable book. But you came to tell me

---

[1] General Eisenhower was elected President of the United States on November 4, 1952.

about poor Smith. You know, Charles, I don't like psychiatrists. One of them said that insulin produces a state of coma, and when I asked if there was any danger in the treatment, he talked of "irreversible coma"'. (With great contempt:) 'Irreversible coma, indeed, when he means death.'

Moran: 'I saw Woolton in the Lords today.'

P.M.: 'He looks a wreck. Fred himself told me the doctors gave him up. He was not fit, they argued, for a general anaesthetic. So they could not explore his chest for an abscess. And then a young surgeon came along. He used a local anaesthetic and plunged his knife into Fred's side so that matter gushed out. Fred said to him: "You are the most brutal surgeon I've met," but from that moment he began to get well. Do you know, Charles, about the Duke of Newcastle and the Glove?'

Moran: 'No.'

P.M.: 'Well, as Lord of the Manor of Worksop he had the privilege of giving the Queen a glove when she is crowned. But as the Manor has been made a company, the Committee of Privileges has decided that it reverts to the Crown. I asked them to give it to Woolton. It is a dignified little ceremony. He will like it.'

Lord Woolton had passed from his mind, when there came to him, as an afterthought, the kindly idea of a consolation prize – of the Glove. Perhaps it may comfort Woolton when he thinks of the fat part in the ceremony he had to relinquish through illness.

The P.M. asked me today if he could see another eye specialist.

'I have stuck to Juler for so long,' he told me, 'because he did discover the ingrowing eyelashes when no one else did. At that time my eyes were so bad I could not read, even official documents. But he is stumped now, and we must change the bowling.'

February 24, 1953
Yesterday the P.M. spat up a little blood, so this morning I packed him off, vigorously protesting, to be X-rayed. I am sure nothing will be found, for he is just now in terrific form.

P.M.: 'What is this they are saying about smoking and cancer of the lungs?'

Moran: 'It is not proven.'

P.M.: 'You always give me a careful answer.'

Moran: 'You have smoked all your life, and I have never tried to make you give it up.'

A smile lit up his features.

'When I think of all the great causes you have championed, I think you were wise not to add that to your labours.'

For some time he has been hanging on to power while his strength was failing. And now, without any apparent reason, he seems to have taken a new lease of life.

'I'm much better than I was a year ago,' he said gaily. 'I can bite now, really hard.' And he snapped his jaws together. 'After our trip to America I was in poor form. Gladstone[1] lived to be eighty-eight; I might go on another eight years. If I do it will be very tiresome for those who manage my finances. Things are already getting very complicated. You see, Charles, during the war I retired from business, but by the end of the war I had become notorious; and all sorts of things, such as film rights and the copyright of my books, gave me quite a bit of capital. For the first time in my life I was quite a rich man. But the income-tax people take it all. I let Hyde Park Gate for £2,000 a year – 2,000 sixpences.'

I have said there was no reason for this renaissance, but it can be traced back, I think, to the day when Eden went sick and the P.M. took over the Foreign Office. Since he became Prime Minister he has been submerged by one economic problem after another, to which he could see no obvious solution; in this field he was ill at ease, and his discomfort became plain to his colleagues and to the House. And then suddenly he found himself at the F.O. dealing with questions which were familiar to him, engaged in work which he could do as well as anyone. He was more sure of himself; he had

---

[1] William Ewart Gladstone (1809–98), retired from office as Prime Minister on March 3, 1894, and died four years later from cancer after a painful illness.

long ago learnt how to handle the House; now he was also master of his theme.

P.M. 'Anthony has aged a lot. When Rab goes to America I shall be Chancellor of the Exchequer – not that I shall do much – and also Foreign Secretary.'

Moran: 'Good Lord.'

P.M.: 'Oh, you needn't worry. I enjoyed myself yesterday. I managed things like I used to do. I was able to put my spoke in on three occasions. First, Slim. You'll hear more of this. Oh, yes, he has a hell of a face. Then I saw Gromyko.'[1]

The P.M. grinned.

'One touch of nature makes the whole world kin; my recipe with him, Charles, was a little, but of course not too much, geniality. Thirdly, the amnesty to the deserters. They have been on the run for eight years, have not seen their wives and have been reduced to all kinds of fraud. The Queen was very keen on this. The Government was responsible, the Service Departments were against an amnesty. They all squawked about it.'

This, I think, pleased him most, but he has been generally on the war path; letting some fresh air into stuffy rooms in Whitehall and laying down the law about the coronation arrangements.[2]

'I'm doing some scratching and clawing. They were going to charge everyone in the Abbey – three thousand of them, the elect from all over the place – sixteen shillings for sandwiches. I stepped in and stopped that. The people in the stands at Hyde Park Corner, by Byron's statue, will be there from seven in the morning till five in the evening. They were seeing to their sanitary needs, but doing nothing for them in food and drink.'

A great grin prepared me for a sally:

'Looking after their exports while neglecting their imports. And why?'

A look of withering scorn crossed his face.

[1] Andrei Gromyko, Soviet Ambassador to the Court of St James's 1952–3.
[2] The coronation of Queen Elizabeth II was to take place on June 2, 1953.

'Because alcohol had not been drunk in the royal parks for a hundred years, they were to have nothing to drink. I altered all that. Even the people not in the stands will have booths.

'Then that poor old Florence Horsbrugh[1] has been making all the educational world her enemy. She wanted a reduction of 10 per cent in the grants for adult education. All to save £250,000 out of £2,000 million. Besides, these are the very people who ought to be helped – because they are helping themselves, far more than a stodgy boy of fourteen, sulkily doing his lessons. She would have hit the picked people. . . . I get the most agreeable dreams – the detail is beautifully done. I get the sense of being in a scene or situation.'

He looked once more at the photograph of the Queen.

'Lovely, inspiring. All the film people in the world, if they had scoured the globe, could not have found anyone so suited to the part.'

Then he began singing a hymn. ' "Yet nightly pitch my moving tent a day's march nearer home."[2]

'Do you remember when Monty gathered his staff officers round him in the Desert after El Alamein, I gave them this hymn? But in my dreams it seems to get mixed up with horses.'

March 7, 1953
The P.M. feels that Stalin's death[3] may lead to a relaxation in tension. It is an opportunity that will not recur, and with Anthony away he is sure he can go straight ahead. He seems to think of little else. He is much incensed by the *Daily Mirror*'s remarks about Stalin and describes it as 'dancing on his tomb'. The *Mirror*, for its part, complains of Mr Churchill's 'crocodile tears'.

And yet he will not be sensible and cut out what does not matter. The time has gone when he had the strength and energy to go into every subject in detail. I wish he would get rid of some of the drudgery by devoluting it. For instance, he has just made a speech

---

[1] Miss Florence Horsbrugh, Minister of Education.
[2] Hymns Ancient & Modern (1889), No. 231.
[3] Stalin died on March 6, 1953.

on defence which has taken him a week to prepare, though Head could have done the donkey work for him.

The P.M.'s task might be easier if he had not so many lame ducks. He questioned me today about Leathers, who is the worse for wear and chafing to resign. Leathers dislikes party politics, affirming that war service was different. The truth is that he cuts a poor figure in the Lords, and he knows it.

April 24, 1953
This morning Winston is in good heart.

'I'm really wonderfully well, Charles. Everyone around me is going down. Anthony will be away for months. His doctors are divided, and they are saying that he may have to have another operation. There would not be any danger, but they would like to get him in better condition before anything is done. I have asked him to go to Chequers. Anthony would like to keep an eye on things at the Foreign Office, but I won't let him. I cannot deal with a sick man.'

I knew that this was the P.M.'s way of telling me that he meant to go on with the Foreign Office all the time Anthony was away.

'You could no doubt do this for a short time as an emergency measure,' I told him, 'but to burden yourself with the F.O. for an indefinite period, perhaps for months, is surely not wise.'

'Oh, I like it,' he answered. 'It doesn't add as much work as you think. You see, I've got to keep an eye on foreign affairs at any time. Yes. I have been hunted. I am making my speeches out of my head at present. They seem to go all right.'

But he said this as if he was not at all worried, and there is a general feeling that he is in better fettle, which, of course, gets back to him. Yesterday Swinton said to me:

'What have you done with your man? He is full of energy and doing well too.'

All the same I am not happy about him. To add to the grievous burdens of the First Minister in this fashion is surely folly. I feel certain we are riding for a fall, but when I plead with him all he says is: 'Oh, don't go on like that, Charles.'

He told me he was going down to see the Queen tonight.

'I'll tell you a secret,' he said this like a schoolboy. 'You mustn't tell anyone. She wants me to accept the Garter. I refused it before. But then the Prime Minister had a say in it. Now only the Queen decides.'[1]

April 28, 1953

P.M.: 'This is interesting. We had a hundred and ten Cabinet meetings in the past year; while the Socialists had only eighty-five in a year – and that in a time of great political activity. I am a great believer in bringing things before the Cabinet. If a Minister has got anything on his mind and he has the sense to get it argued by the Cabinet he will have the machine behind him.'

He pushed away the bed-rest, making the breakfast china rattle.

P.M.: 'Anthony is to have another operation tomorrow. Is there any danger, Charles? He is yellow. He pulled up his shirt to show me his incision. I did not want to see it, but it turned out to be quite healed.'

Moran: 'It's not Anthony I'm bothered about. You know I don't fuss, but you are asking for trouble. I don't believe you can go on like this.'

And then, to my surprise, he admitted that he was torpid. That is something new.

'But I'm all right,' he asserted. 'I'm sleeping well. Of course there are plenty of Foreign Office complications. I have lived seventy-eight years without hearing of bloody places like Cambodia.'

With a whimsical look he strung out half a dozen strange-sounding names.

'They have never worried me, and I haven't worried them.'

May 28, 1953

It is a month since my last entry. There are times when I have not had the heart to record the details of his struggle to do his job. He

---

[1] Winston Churchill was made a Knight of the Garter on this day and became Sir Winston.

is, of course, fighting it out inch by inch, but it is a losing game. I asked him this morning how he was weathering the racket.

'Yes, it is a racket,' he allowed, 'and I'm getting older. I miss Anthony. He's going to Boston on the 5th June in a special Canadian aircraft for his operation. Poor fellow.'

He was silent for a time, and when he spoke again he was determined to be cheerful.

'The Cabinet is very helpful. They have confidence in me. Rab is good. I would rather go to the Abbey for the Coronation in a big car with large windows than be hidden away in a box of a carriage. Besides, the 4th Hussars, who are providing an escort for me, have never before escorted a motor vehicle – the two things do not go together. But I must ask the Queen and find out what she wants.'

I told him that his speech in Westminster Hall had gone well. He smiled with pleasure.

'No one else could have done it. It had all to come out of this poor nut. The private office can't help in this kind of thing. I was particularly pleased with the bit about the American constitution. I was bold, too, about the conflict between the Crown and Parliament – a hundred yards from Cromwell's statue; the dirty dog, I never liked him. Oh, the Queen liked my speech. Paul Reynaud was quite right not to try to form a Government in Paris. But it is a pity. He has meddled in great things – though he got the worst of them.'

June 9, 1953

'I wouldn't say this to anyone else,' Christopher said this morning, 'but isn't it strange that as Winston gets older and more entrenched in people's affections, he gets vainer? There is a lot of work at present, and we are often at it till two or three in the morning. And yet he wastes an hour every night in reading the newspapers. He goes through all of them with care to find something about himself.' Christopher hesitated. 'It has become a drug.'

June 16, 1953

'We don't know anything for certain about Bermuda,'[1] the P.M. said. 'My telegram to Ike crossed with one from him. I wanted him to stick to the date fixed for the conference, when the Frogs would come into line. But Ike says we must not hurry them; it will pay good dividends to be patient. Dividends,' he repeated scornfully. 'The bloody Frogs can't make up their minds. With the German elections coming on they are playing party politics in Paris; every little party playing their own game, each with an ideology of their own. They don't care for anything but their own petty intrigues. It is lamentable for poor France. And now the King of Cambodia has bolted on them. Ike only thinks of France. He does not give a thought to our difficulties. The eyes of the world are on us – people are beginning to talk; they wonder what all the delay means. Dulles[2] is a terrible influence. Ike now wants to postpone the conference for a fortnight to give the French a chance to settle down after the election. And every day it's getting hotter in Bermuda.'

Horace Evans tells me the news of Anthony is not too good; his future is uncertain.

June 23, 1953

When I saw the P.M. today he seemed played out – as he was at Cairo before the Carthage illness. I thought his speech was slurred and a little indistinct. Twice I had to ask him to repeat what he had said. He said the Foreign Office was very hard work. I asked him must he really carry the burden of the F.O. until the autumn? He said he must. I told him I was unhappy about the strain, that it was an impossible existence and that I hoped he would find he could do something about it. He grunted and picked up some papers. Before I left No. 10 I sought out Pitblado to tell him that I was worried about things.

[1] Intended three-power conference between Britain, France and the United States at summit level, to discuss the upkeep of military forces in Western Europe. Churchill's illness caused the meeting to be postponed from June to December, 1953.
[2] John Foster Dulles, President Eisenhower's Secretary of State.

CHAPTER TWELVE

Stricken Down

June 24, 1953

About half an hour after midnight the telephone awoke me. It was No. 10: would I go and see the Prime Minister at nine o'clock the following morning? The girl at the No. 10 exchange said no more, and it was not till this morning that I learnt of their failure to get me on the telephone. They had given me up at last and left a message with the girl.

Jock told me that at the dinner for de Gasperi[1] the P.M. had made a brilliant little speech, all about Caesar and the Legions. When the guests were beginning to withdraw Christopher noticed that the P.M. was trying to stand up; before he could go to his assistance Winston suddenly flopped back into his chair. He hurried to him, and, seeing that Clemmie was watching him anxiously some distance away, he told her that Winston was very tired.

'Oh, we must get him to bed then,' she answered.

Christopher interposed: 'We must get the waiters away first; he can't walk.'

While Jock was recounting this, Christopher came into the room. He mentioned that the P.M.'s speech was indistinct; it was difficult to understand what he said. Jock added that others had noticed the P.M.'s plight.

[1] Prime Minister of Italy.

'I think they thought he had had too much to drink.'

Jock was sure his speech was affected; the articulation was only distinct when he made an effort. When I was satisfied that I should get no more out of them, I went to his room.

'Ah, Charles, I thought you would never come.'

I could see that the left side of his mouth sagged; it was more noticeable when he spoke. I got him out of bed to see how he walked. He asked me to open the door of his wardrobe, which is lined with a long mirror; he wanted to see for himself how he got on. He was not very steady on his feet, and once I jumped to his side, thinking he would fall. When he was back in bed he said:

'I would not like to walk to my seat in the House of Commons with members watching. What has happened, Charles? Is it a stroke?'

I told him I would tell him what was wrong when I had examined him. There was no loss of power of the hand or leg that I could detect, even by delicate tests. After I had finished my examination he said, 'I want to know everything.' I explained to him that the circulation in his head was sluggish; there was spasm of a small artery. It belonged to the same family as the incident at Monte Carlo in August, 1949. He said he thought that was the trouble. I asked him if he would like to see Sir Russell Brain. He did not answer. He seemed to be trying to work things out.

'I want to know, Charles, where I stand and what this means.'

I said I would return in the afternoon. After luncheon he telephoned me. I could understand everything that he said.

'You spoke of Russell Brain. Do bring him when you come.'

I advised Brain to be firm, the P.M. might want to do things. There will be lots of people buzzing round, but we must sit tight until we know where we are. In a few days the position will be plainer. When Brain had done, the P.M. questioned him. Then I came to the point. I told him he must not go to the House for Questions. He argued about this, saying he liked Questions. Then he sent for Jock and asked him how many questions there were; which were for him and which were addressed to the Foreign Secretary. Were they important?

'Oh, bring them and let me see.'

While Jock was out of the room I felt I must act before he committed himself. I said I could not guarantee that he would not get up in the House and use the wrong word; he might rise in his place and no words might come. He listened in silence. When Jock came back he read the Questions. 'They are not very important,' Jock added, and the P.M. seemed to agree. Finally, he said abruptly that he would not go to the House.

June 25, 1953

No improvement in his speech, and he is, if anything, more unsteady in his gait.

'I don't feel like managing the world' – there was a long pause – 'and yet never have they looked more like offering me it. I feel, Charles, I could do something that no one else can do. I was at the peak of my opportunities, exchanging friendly messages with Malenkov[1] and Adenauer.'[2]

'You meant to send them messages?'

'No, I have done already. I have stretched out a hand to grasp the paw of the Russian bear. Great things seemed within my grasp. Not perhaps world peace, but world easement. I feel I could have changed the bias of the world. America is very powerful, but very clumsy. Look at this Syngman Rhee[3] business. I could have made her more sensible.'

His speech was becoming blurred and more difficult to follow. He lay back on the pillow as if he were too tired to go on. Once more I pressed him not to attend the Cabinet, and when he became obstinate I said that the left side of his mouth drooped and I did not want him to go among people until he was better. They would notice things, and there would be talk. After I had gone Christopher took up

[1] Chairman of Council of Ministers, USSR.

[2] Chancellor of the Federal Republic of Germany.

[3] President of the South Korean Republic. His objections to the peace terms and demands for the release of anti-Communist North Korean prisoners brought a temporary halt in the Paris Conference, 1953.

the good work; and the P.M. in the end gave up the idea and left about noon for Chartwell. When I dined with Lord Camrose he showed me a letter Jock had sent him explaining, at Winston's request, what had happened. Camrose urged me to get him to Bermuda at any cost. He must rest, and the voyage would cut off his work.

June 26, 1953
'Look, my hand is clumsy,' the P.M. said as I entered his room at Chartwell.

Transferring his cigar to his left hand, he made a wavering attempt to put it to his lips.

'It is so feeble. Hold out your hand, Charles.'

And with that he tried to touch the tips of my fingers with the corresponding fingers of his own hand.

'I'm not afraid of death, but it would be very inconvenient to a lot of people. Rab is very efficient up to a point, but he is narrow and doesn't see beyond his nose. If Anthony were standing by the door there, and I was here, and a telegram was given to him involving a decision, well, in nine cases out of ten we should agree.'

When he had done I examined his left hand and arm. There was some loss of power in the left grip – and this had developed since yesterday, three days after the onset of the trouble. I do not like this, the thrombosis is obviously spreading. He knew that his hand was weaker, and he complained, 'I am having great difficulty in turning over in bed.

'Two days ago,' he reflected, 'I wanted to take the Cabinet. Now I couldn't. I have scratched Bermuda. It will not come out until Ike replies to my telegram.' He handed me the telegram he had sent to Ike.

I drew up a medical bulletin:

For a long time the Prime Minister has had no respite from his arduous duties and a disturbance of the cerebral circulation has developed, resulting in attacks of giddiness. We have therefore advised him to abandon his journey to Bermuda and to take at least a month's rest.

Brain and I signed this. But when we had gone Rab Butler and Lord Salisbury altered it, and persuaded the P.M. to agree to their wording:

> The Prime Minister has had no respite for a long time from his very arduous duties and is in need of a complete rest. We have therefore advised him to abandon his journey to Bermuda and to lighten his duties for at least a month.

They may well be right, that is of course if he comes through. For if he recovers and wants to carry on as Prime Minister, then the less we say about a stroke, the better for him. But will anyone who knows the P.M. credit that he is willing to take a month's rest merely because his doctors thought he was overdoing things? And besides, if he dies in the next few days will Lord Salisbury think his change in the bulletin was wise? It is a gamble.[1]

June 26, 1953

> My dear Prime Minister,
> I am so sorry to hear from Tommy Lascelles that you have not been feeling too well these last few days.
> I do hope it is not serious and that you will be quite recovered in a very short time.
> Our visit here is going very well and Edinburgh is thrilled by all the pageantry. We have been lucky in having fine weather, but I fear that it is now raining after a thunderstorm.
>
> > With all good wishes,
> > Yours very sincerely,
> > Elizabeth R.

The P.M. himself was thrilled by this letter. He showed me his reply, which more than rose to the requirements of the situation.

---

[1] The original notebook reads: 'In the long run it is wisest to be honest with the public.'

Written only five days after his stroke, it seemed to me a remarkable document with its poise, proportion and sense of detachment. I took heart that he could do so much.

In his letter he recalled the circumstances in which he had been stricken down; he spoke of his plight as he lay in bed as if it had happened to someone else; he told Her Majesty that he was not without hope that he might soon be about and able to discharge his duties until the autumn, when he thought that Anthony would be able to take over.

Viscount Waverley has told us that he was able to detect in Winston's composition a streak of humility that had somehow escaped the scrutiny of his friends, and in Winston's approach to the Throne his sense of history invested the Monarch with a certain mystique, so that he always spoke of the Royal House with touching reverence.

June 27, 1953
'I'm getting more helpless. I shall soon be completely paralysed on my left side.'

That was what he said to me this morning.

'I don't mind. But I hope it won't last long. Will the other side be paralysed? Why, it might last for years. Tell me, Charles, is there no operation for this kind of thing? I don't mind being a pioneer. Anyway, it is clear now that we made the right decision in abandoning Bermuda.'

I got him out of bed, but he could hardly stand.

Last night I noticed that he was dragging his left leg. Now it is obvious there is some loss of power, so that the foot drops and the toes catch the carpet. He cannot walk now without two people helping him, though in his wheel-chair he can propel himself from room to room. He paused before his portrait in the blue drawing-room:

'It is the picture of a very unhappy man, painted after the Dardanelles by Orpen. He thought I was finished.'

June 28, 1953

Max Beaverbrook came to lunch. We got the P.M. into his chair at the head of the table before the others appeared. Max was noisy:

'Oh, Winston, you are not as bad as you were in 1949, and you got over that in a very short time. You'll soon be a different man, won't he, Charles? I didn't believe the Trades Union Congress could be managed by any politician, but you've done it. You've got Labour muddled; they've lost the initiative.'

P.M.: 'I think we ought to let the House have a free vote on sponsored television. Are you agin, Max?'

Max: 'Oh, yaas.'

P.M.: 'I'm not taken in by the Russians, but before the British people are committed to another long struggle, I wanted to be sure there was nothing in their recent change of attitude.'

He spoke with tears in his eyes. Then his face lit up and for a little time something of the old vigour of speech came back while Max poured out his soft talk. But I could see the P.M. was getting very tired and that it was time to break up the party. Clemmie had arranged that he should be carried to the swimming pool to see the grandchildren bathe, but he asked me to take him back to bed. He insisted on getting out of his chair, and we helped him to his room; his good foot coming down on the passage with a noisy stump, while the toes of his left foot dragged along the carpet. When we were alone he slumped upon the bed.

'A week ago I was thinking of running the world – and now – ' He shrugged his shoulders. 'When I sit still I feel quite well.'

He looked ruefully at his foot, and then he remembered I had told him that other arteries – what doctors call the collateral circulation – would take on the work of the blocked vessel.

'The blood ought to be getting round the back streets by now. What have you got to say about that, Charles?'

I brought Max to say goodbye, warning him to stay only a few minutes, and then rejoined Clemmie. She told me Winston had said to her: 'I hope I shall either improve or get worse.'

'Even when he is well,' Clemmie went on, 'Winston likes to be surrounded by people petting him and doing things for him.'

I went back to the P.M. His mind wandered to the night when it happened, to No. 10 and the de Gasperi dinner.

'I made quite a good speech impromptu, and then ten minutes after I was like this.'

He turned to Max with a grim smile:

'Today I have knocked Christie[1] off the headlines except in the *Empire News*.'

Max feels all Fleet Street knows what has happened and that it is foolish not to issue bulletins which approximate to the truth. He went away saying he would compose one and telephone me. With all his astuteness, he is obtuse in these matters. If the P.M. is to carry on till October before he hands over to Anthony, I now agree with Salisbury that the less we say about strokes the better. I have a feeling things have taken a turn for the better. It is true that he cannot walk without support, and has little power in his left leg; nor will he admit that there is any real improvement in his hand. But whereas yesterday he sat about doing nothing, as if he had no energy to read or talk or even to think, when I went into his bedroom about six o'clock this evening, he said:

'I have become involved in *Phineas Finn*.'

He is back in his normal mood, and what is left is a physical disability. I was in doubt whether I should stay another night at Chartwell. I could do nothing, but perhaps it might be a comfort to Clemmie if I were on the spot. I thought I would sound her and find out what she wanted. All at once and without warning she shouted:

'You will send me mad if you don't make up your mind. It is a medical matter.'

The strain on her is, of course, mounting.

Tonight Brendan dined with us. He can draw the P.M. out, and has a kind of explosive cheerfulness which seems to help. The

---

[1] John Halliday Christie, responsible for the murder of at least six women.

P.M. said that he had only read one book in the first six months of the war – *Journey to the Western Isles of Scotland*, by Dr Johnson. He admired Johnson. Then Brendan got out of him that he went to the Atlantic Charter Meeting with E. M. Forster's *A Passage to India*.

Winston has learnt to take what Max says with a pinch of salt.

'He poured out floods of optimism as he always does, saying I should soon be in full harness again.'

The P.M. owned that he felt more friendly to the Russians than he had done at some periods of his life. When I pondered on this I remembered a saying of G. M. Young, that there is no better way of bringing a decade or a generation into focus than to ask what they were most afraid of and what they did about it. The fear of another war has occupied men's thoughts since the end of the last war. And in their hearts they feel that the P.M. can do more than anyone else to avert another catastrophe. Winston knows that he is speaking, not for the Tory Party, but for the whole country, and as he watches the slow spread of this creeping paralysis, he is haunted by the lost opportunity. He realizes that little men are tied to their texts, that he alone can break down the wall of suspicion which shuts off Russia from the West.

When Brendan had gone he rang a bell:

'Bring me the Queen's letter and my reply. I want you to see, Charles, what I can still do.'

Jock had told me he had suggested to Tommy Lascelles that the Queen should write to the P.M. in her own handwriting. She did.

June 29, 1953
Camrose came to lunch. He took me aside.

'It's a tragedy, Charles, Beaverbrook being his first visitor. The Conservative Party loathe him so. If it had been Brendan it would-n't have mattered.'

Camrose talked to the P.M. about the final volume of his book; some of the telegrams about the P.M.'s reluctance to give ground to the Russians before Potsdam were, he said, tremendously effective. If only Winston could tell the whole story. But apart from the book, Camrose never seems to have much to say to him. It sometimes appears that he is overawed by the great man. But he sat with him on the lawn for a long time. I left them, and in the rose garden came across Clemmie. She asked if Camrose had gone. I said no; I wished he would, as I thought the P.M. was getting tired. At this Clemmie burst out:

'If you had more courage you'd tell him so.'

June 30, 1953
Still no bulletin. Max rang up and pressed for something. He got excited. The fact is that while Clemmie vehemently asserts that the P.M. should retire now, he wants to carry on until October; and it won't help him if we tell the public that he has had a stroke.

The Prof. to luncheon. He has developed diabetes. When he asked the P.M. how he was, Winston answered with a touch of levity:

'I eats well and sleeps well and drinks well, but when I get along-side any business I go all of a tremble. I could do without smoking but not without my liquor; that would be a sad impoverishment.' His face became grave. 'It is extraordinary between night and morning that I should go like this – a bundle of old rags. To be dif-ferent from other people, and yet I feel quite well. What did you work at last night, Charles, when we went to the film? I only work,' he said, 'when I want to. I must be lured by pleasure, spurred by excitement.'

He spoke of the French with contempt – five years of ignominy, and they have enjoyed every hour of it. With a great effort he turned over in bed.

'I am a hulk – only breathing and excreting.'

He got up for luncheon, but when he had talked for a little with the Prof. he felt weary and, calling for his wheel-chair, went back to bed. Norman Brook came to dinner. Winston likes him, and they talked away for a long time. Jock got the P.M. going about Antwerp[1] – 'a very exciting experience'. Then he told us of the mutiny over demobilization at the end of the First War. They came to him at the War Office and said that this was a serious mutiny. The soldiers were dissatisfied with the regulations for demobilization; they felt it was not being done fairly. They had gathered on the Horse Guards Parade, and things looked ugly. Winston asked: 'How many troops have we to deal with them?' They answered, a battalion of the Guards and three squadrons of the Household Cavalry. 'Are they loyal?' Winston asked. 'We hope they are,' was the doubtful answer. 'Can you arrest the mutineers?' 'We are not certain.' 'Have you any other suggestions?' They had none. 'Then arrest the mutineers.' He stood watching from a window over the parade ground. He expected firing to break out any minute. But the mutineers allowed the Guards to surround them.

We asked the P.M. what he did when the mutineers were under arrest.

P.M.: 'Oh, I changed the system of demobilization overnight: the first to join was the first to be demobilized, and any man with a wound stripe or a decoration could go when he wished. This removed their strong sense of injustice. It was one of the best things I did.'

Brook asked him about Glasgow.

'David Kirkwood[2] asked that they should be given separate machinery to make shells. I arranged this, and soon they were producing shells at a quicker rate than anyone. That was the beginning of my friendship with David.'

Still thinking of mutinies, he said:

---

[1] Early in October 1914 Churchill, then First Lord of the Admiralty, went to Antwerp in an attempt to persuade the Belgian Government to delay their evacuation of the port. Antwerp fell on October 10. It is possible that the five-day prolongation of Antwerp's resistance was a crucial factor in depriving the Germans of a decisive victory that autumn.

[2] Lord Kirkwood, formerly M.P. for East Dunbartonshire.

'Haig wanted to shoot eight or nine of the ring-leaders of the Calais mutiny. [1] But I would not agree in peace-time. They got two years.'

He rambled on, wondering why butterflies were not so numerous as they once were. After the war he would have arranged for clouds of butterflies. The love of flowers and affection for animals were two of the noblest qualities of our race. You did not find gardens in America. You can live a long time with a geranium.

Once more he told how one of our tanks at the end of an engagement had to surrender to the Germans, and how the Germans saluted them and complimented them on their courage in the fight.

'That is how I like war to be conducted,' the P.M. said.

'I'm finished,' he said sadly, 'but a week ago I had big plans. My influence everywhere had never been greater. Nehru and Adenauer were very friendly. Of course I knew that I was taking risks by my advances to the Russians. I might have taken a big toss.'

Alas, he will keep thinking of what might have been. He had given the final volume of the book to Norman Brook to read. He questioned him now about it. Would anything in it cause offence to the Americans?

'If I am going to die, then I can say what I like and take the view that I believe to be right. But if I live and am still Prime Minister, then I must not say things which will anger Ike.'

July 1, 1953
Christopher, finding the P.M. bright-eyed and alert, said encouragingly:

'You are going to get quite well.'

P.M.: 'Yes, but I don't know how much difficulty I'll have in getting back my position.'

'You see,' Christopher added dryly, 'he has not given up hope of a come-back. I don't know what Clemmie will say.'

---

[1] British soldiers mutinied in January, 1919, as a result of slow demobilization.

July 2, 1953

When I saw the P.M. at Chartwell this morning, he said:

'You will look in on your way back from London?'

So I dined there. Harold Macmillan was the only guest. He has curiosity and talked well when the P.M. gave him the chance. Winston spoke of death. He did not believe in another world; only in 'black velvet' – eternal sleep. He kept taking up different subjects and then dropping them, almost at once, as if he could not be bothered to go deeply into anything. He spoke of some African chiefs drinking beer, armed with staves, inflamed with alcohol and inspired by liberal principles – the old love of words – and then of Buddhism, 'a Tory religion'. He used not to believe in rationing or in any other device which would lead to bureaucracy, but Sam Hoare had converted him. He drifted on. Lord Rosebery had written a vivid account of Gladstone's last cabinet.

'By comparison,' Winston concluded, 'my reign has been considerate and reasonable.'

When I took him to his room I asked him the history of a badger's skin hanging on the wall.

'Oh,' he said, 'I was returning one night from the Other Club, rather hilarious, when just outside the gates there was a bump. I got out and saw a badger fighting for breath. I took it in my arms. They said it had killed one of my swans; but there was no proof, and in any case I forgave it.'

When I rose to leave he said, 'Oh don't go, Charles.' He was rather excited and not ready for sleep. I got away half an hour later and was opening the door at Marshalls when I heard the telephone ring. It was the night nurse. The P.M. wanted to speak to me.

'My leg has been twitching for the last hour,' he said, 'the arm too has twitched a little. What does it mean?'

I comforted him, but my mind is ill at ease.

July 3, 1953

The report this morning is reassuring. He had slept well once he got off, and according to Jock, seemed in good spirits. It is strange that no one around the P.M. seems able to grasp what is the exact nature of his disability. This is not an acute illness from which he may recover completely. He will never again be the same man he was before the stroke, because the clot in the artery has cut off some of the blood which went to his brain and was the ultimate source of all his activities. So his brain is always anaemic, and when the circulation flags a little, then he has no zest for work and cannot face detail, or his leg twitches, or something of the kind. He is really living on a volcano, and he may get another stroke at any time.

ıting Back

ollope. I asked him if he had read any-
, 'No.' Clemmie explained that he had
s own plans that he had had no time for

It is the same, she said, with a lot of things. Why, Charles, when Winston took up painting in 1915 he had never up to that moment been in a picture gallery. He went with me – do you remember, dear? – to the National Gallery, and pausing before the first picture, a very ordinary affair, he appeared absorbed in it. For half an hour he studied its technique minutely. Next day he again visited the gallery, but I took him in this time by the left entrance instead of the right, so that I might at least be sure he would not return to the same picture.'

He spoke of the Westminster Election.[1]

[1] Churchill left the Liberal Party because they had combined with Labour to defeat the Baldwin Government. Labour in consequence came into power. In 1924 a by-election occurred in the Abbey division of Westminster, a Tory stronghold. Baldwin was determined to have nothing to do with Churchill. Winston decided to challenge this, and stood as an anti-socialist candidate in opposition to the official Tory. The Tory caucus were furious, and all the resources of the Party were mobilized to ensure his defeat. Churchill lost, but only by forty votes. It was a moral victory. Baldwin saw he could not keep Churchill out, and nine months later, when the Tories were returned to power, he was given the safe seat of Epping, and made Chancellor of the Exchequer.

'At the head of each of my committees was a Conservative, who was helping me in defiance of the orders of the Central Office. Families were divided. It was most exciting.'

Suddenly the P.M.'s voice broke and tears streamed down his face.

'Since this happened I have been very lachrymose. At parts of *Phineas Finn* I became very tearful, though it is not at all a moving story. Will it go on, Charles?'

'What happened at the election?'

'Oh, we were beaten by forty votes, but it did good. Baldwin learnt my hold over the Tory Party. I expected he would give me office in 1935. He had spoken to me in friendly terms before the election.'

Jock: 'Was India the reason?'

P.M.: 'Oh, no. India was over by then. But the war-monger business had begun.'

Jock: 'As far back as that?'

P.M.: 'Yes. Baldwin was receiving Baptists and that sort of person, and he gave a pledge to the Peace Society.'

Jock asked about the eleven years in the wilderness.[1]

P.M.: 'I was quite happy at Chartwell. I was making £20,000 every year by my books and by journalism. I wrote *Marlborough* and finished *The World Crisis*. I think I will go and rest now.'

I went with him to his room. As he got into bed he smiled at me mischievously:

'There will be a bloody row if I get well. And it does not seem impossible.'

Franklin Roosevelt had been dead seven years, he reflected.

'I always looked up to him as an older man, though he was eight years my junior. I am no longer really interested in public affairs. Oh, yes, I mean that. You see, Charles, you must be right in it, or interest flags.'

---

[1] 1929–39. Shortly after the Conservative defeat in 1929, Churchill resigned from the Shadow Cabinet. He was not given office again until the war broke out. Throughout the 1930s he was deeply distrusted by both the major political parties.

He told me a story I had not heard before.

'When I was a subaltern I was sitting on a couch with a girl at a kind of dance hall in Oxford Street; my legs were crossed, and a big fellow, as he went by, caught my toe. I did not move my feet, and next time round the big fellow caught my foot and pulled me round the floor by it. When I got up I rushed at him. I remembered no more till I found my head in a spittoon in a corner of the room. He turned out to be a retired pugilist. That is the only time I remember being knocked out like that. It wasn't painful. Of course, my creed is when a man hits you, you must in honour hit back. Next morning I had a thick head, the only time in my life I have had a headache.'

When he noticed that I was examining a long chart on the wall, depicting the results of the U-boat struggle throughout the war, he said:

'You see, up to Pearl Harbour we had got it in hand; then when America came in her merchant fleet was almost too easy a target. Look how sharply the losses rose.'

Next to the chart there was a print of the great statesmen of the First War.

'It was painted by Sir James Guthrie,' the P.M. explained, 'I never heard of him either before or since, but it is a fine composition. I like it. Arthur Balfour is the key figure. Guthrie has put me in the centre of the picture; it is a little out of focus, for I was in low water then.'

He rose and walked across the room to the picture. There were sixteen men in it.

'I'm the only one left alive,' he reflected.

I glanced at two photographs, one of his father and the other of his mother, with several of Clemmie in many positions, and Mary and Sarah. Over his bed was a painting of a room.

'That is the dining-room of my mother's last house. It was furnished by her – she had a remarkable gift for this. My mother's coffin rested there the night before burial.'

Alongside a print of the Battle of Blenheim was a photograph of the balcony at Buckingham Palace on Victory Day. The King and Queen and the two princesses stood by his side. His old humility where the Royal Family was concerned came out: they had been kind enough to sign the photograph, he said. Stalin's portrait had been replaced by three paintings of his horses in desperate finishes: Colonist, and 'the poor horse' which won a race and then died. I was on the point of asking what happened to Stalin's photograph when, turning round, I saw he was deep in *Phineas Finn*.

July 4, 1953

A good day. Full of spirits. He can walk a short distance and says that each day he will do a little more. During dinner his retirement in October came up.

'I shall do what is best for the country.'

Clemmie: 'Of course, dear, I know you will.'

P.M. (*with a whimsical smile*): 'Circumstances may convince me of my indispensability.'

There it is: he has no intention of retiring if he can help it. All afternoon he has sat on the croquet lawn reading under his sombrero, hardly once did he look up; it was some time before I discovered that he had fallen asleep. During dinner he spouted some verses which he said expressed exactly the Socialist point of view. They were from *Punch*, perhaps fifty years ago. He thought they were called 'Reflections from St James's Park'. Then he quoted from Longfellow – at length. Afterwards there was a film about the siege of Malta, which gave him pleasure.

July 5, 1953

The night nurse reported that his leg had twitched for nearly an hour, but it was not so severe, and he did not mention it to me. He can walk alone now.

Monty came to luncheon and stayed to dinner. He arrived with a theme. If, he argued, Western Germany rearmed, they would be with the West. But this isn't going to happen. Germany, according to Monty, will be united before she is armed, and he wants this united Germany to look to the West and not to the East for allies.

Monty: 'What I fear is an alliance between Russia and this united Germany. Russia would give them back what they have lost. Her change of tone is all propaganda designed to bring this about.'

Moran: 'Is the Foreign Office alive to this?'

Monty: 'I very much doubt it. I know Strang;[1] he is a routine fellow. Prudent no doubt, but without vision. There are too many routine people in the Foreign Office.' Without a moment's thought he strung off the names of three ambassadors who were 'wet, weak and needed a weed-killer. What is needed is vision. The F.O. ought to make an intensive study of the problem. They ought to be ready with a thought-out plan which could be put into operation the moment Germany is united. I think it is most important that a man with a strong personality should be posted as our ambassador in Paris when Oliver Harvey retires. He will retire very soon.'

Monty produced two documents which he gave to the P.M.

'They give my views on this problem.'

The P.M. began skimming through them. When he had done he put them down.

'They are very important papers. My own mind has been moving along the same lines.'

At this point the P.M. rang for a secretary and asked for volume vi of his book, *Triumph and Tragedy*. It was brought to him in chapters. He became immersed in the long galley sheets. At last he extracted one of the chapters.

'Read this,' he said, handing it to Monty. 'That is the most important telegram I have ever sent. It was dated May 12, 1945 and addressed to President Truman, pleading that we should not give up the part of Germany we occupied to the Russians until we had made a firm agreement with them. Truman replied that we had given our word. I argued that this did not hold under the new circumstances, because the Russians had broken their word over Vienna.'

Monty read the telegram and put it down; then he read it again.

---

[1] Permanent Under-Secretary of State, Foreign Office, later Lord Strang.

'That was the first mention of the Iron Curtain? All these telegrams,' he said, 'ought to be published. People think we are winning the cold war. It is not true. We are losing it – thirty love. The Big Three ought to have met earlier; Potsdam was too late.'

P.M.: 'Yes, June, 1945, or May.'

Monty: 'This all began at Casablanca. Unconditional surrender meant that Russian troops would invade Germany, and once that was decided we ought to have made certain we'd be first in Berlin, Vienna and Prague. It could have been done. If Alex's command had not been weakened he would have got to Vienna.'

Moran: 'Wasn't the shortage of landing craft throughout the war a crucial factor – a fatal handicap?'

Monty: 'Yes, that is true.'

P.M.: 'I warned the Americans before Potsdam not to withdraw from any of the part of Germany we occupied until we had a satisfactory understanding. They would not listen. And they will not listen now when I warn them about Germany. At Potsdam I wanted Prussia isolated and Germany divided horizontally and not vertically.

July 6, 1953

A bad day; the P.M. does not feel on the top of things.

P.M.: 'I can understand death or illness, but not this. I had a busy, scheming brain once, and now' – pointing to his head – 'it's empty. Today we should have been at Bermuda. The punch seems to have gone out of the movement. I should have said things to the French no one else could say. They want the best of all worlds – not to fight in the war, but to remain a great power.'

Strang (*mildly*): 'They have, sir, put blood and fortune into Indo-China for better or for worse.'

P.M.: 'Either they must sign E.D.C.[1] or we must adopt punitive measures.'

[1] E.D.C. was the stillborn European Defence Community or European Army. It originated in France and Germany in late 1950 after Mr Churchill had called at Strasbourg in August of that year for 'the immediate creation of

When they had gone, I went with the P.M. to his room. He sat on his bed and began to give me Longfellow's 'King Robert of Sicily.' He went on and on without apparently hesitating for a word. I asked him when last he had read the poem. He answered: 'About fifty years ago.' 'Wait a moment,' I said, and went in search of a copy of Longfellow. When I found it and had taken it to his room, I said:

'I believe your memory is as good as ever it was, but I want to be sure.'

I asked him to repeat the lines while I checked the words from the text. Wanting to come out with credit, he entered into the spirit of the test:

> *Robert of Sicily, brother of Pope Urbane*
> *And Valmond, Emperor of Allemaine,*
> *Apparelled in magnificent attire,*
> *With retinue of many a knight and squire,*
> *On St John's Eve, at vespers, proudly sat*
> *And heard the priests chant the Magnificat.*
> *And as he listened, o'er and o'er again*
> *Repeated, like a burden or refrain,*
> *He caught the 'Deposuit potentes*
> *De sede, et exultavit humiles';*
> *And slowly lifting up his kingly head,*
> *He to a learned clerk beside him said,*
> *'What mean these words,' The clerk made answer meet*
> *'He has put down the mighty from their seat,*
> *And has exalted them of low degree.'*
> *Thereat King Robert muttered scornfully,*
> *''Tis well that such seditious words are sung*

Footnote from page 136 continued
a European Army under a united command in which we should all bear a worthy and honourable part . . . in co-operation with the United States and Canada.' Successive Labour and Conservative Governments in Britain did not feel able to take part, and it was finally killed when it was rejected by the French Assembly in 1954.

Only by priests and in the Latin tongue,
For unto priests and people be it known
There is no power can push me from my throne!'
And leaning back, he yawned and fell asleep,
Lulled by the chant monotonous and deep.

When he awoke it was already night;
The church was empty and there was no light,
Save for the lamps, that glimmered few and faint,
Lighted a little space before some saint.
He started from his seat and gazed around,
But saw no living thing and heard no sound.
He groped towards the door, but it was locked;
He cried aloud, and listened, and then knocked.
And uttered awful threatenings and complaints,
And imprecations upon men and saints.
The sounds re-echoed from the roof and walls
As if dead priests were laughing in their stalls.

This may perhaps give critics pause, if the day should come when he is harshly judged for sticking to his post. Here and there he got a word wrong: priests became monks and lamps candles; perhaps half a dozen words out of three hundred and fifty. The stroke has not touched his memory. I told him so. He brightened and smiled.

He is confiding in no one, but he means to carry on if he is able, and the question whether he will be able is hardly ever out of his head. This is his secret battle. There are moments when he does not want to do anything, when a dreadful apathy settles on him and he nearly loses heart. But he always sets his jaw and hangs on.

July 7, 1953
Lord and Lady Salisbury to dinner at Chartwell. For two hours the P.M. expounded his views on the international situation, until the acting Foreign Secretary was fully briefed for his visit to Washington; and this the P.M. did without obvious fatigue.

July 8, 1953

There is some gain in the strength of the left foot and an obvious improvement in his 'attitude to life', to use his own words. During dinner Winston leant towards Clemmie:

'You will not be angry with me, dear, but you ought not to say "very delicious". "Delicious" alone expresses everything you wish to say. You would not say "very unique".'

Whether Clemmie respected his loving care for language I cannot tell, but she turned his flank, choosing her own field of battle. She began with a disarming air of innocence.

'In *Phineas Finn* you took people *out* to dinner, not *in* to dinner.'

This acted as a preface to a discourse on manners, in which Clemmie did all the talking and Winston took in every word. Men lit a woman's cigarettes, but did not necessarily listen to her conversation. Winston listened with curiosity. The small change of good manners was to him a foreign currency.

He had read three chapters of *Jane Eyre*, and had been 'arrested' by them. He rose and walked to the lift with an occasional lurch. New possibilities were opening up. He would entertain the Jockey Club to dinner at Downing Street. Mr Baldwin had been host to the King and Queen at dinner before he resigned. Mr Churchill would like to follow that precedent. Other engaging adventures passed through his mind. The suspicion of a smile advertised his thoughts.

July 10, 1953

I asked the P.M., while he was waiting for his breakfast, what he made of the dismissal of Beria from the Communist Party,[1] as an enemy of the party and of the Soviet people. We had come to think of the head of the Russian secret police as one of the ruling triumvirate, on the same level as Molotov and Malenkov.

---

[1] After Stalin's death (March 6, 1953) Beria became one of the four Deputy Prime Ministers as well as Minister for Internal Affairs. He was dismissed on July 10, 1953, for 'anti-party and anti-state activities', and executed after his trial for treason on December 23, 1953.

P.M.: 'Beria – Siberia. Strange things are happening there. It is very significant and supports the line I have taken. The Russians were surprisingly patient about the disturbances in East Germany. The aggressive party in the Kremlin must have said: You see what comes of giving in, this is the result of concessions. But they had not the power to arrest Malenkov. At a conference of the Big Four he would have welcomed me particularly.'

The P.M.'s eyes dilated, he spoke eagerly.

'I would have met them more than halfway. It might have meant a real UNO, with Russia working with the rest for the good of Europe. We would have promised them that no more atomic bombs would be made, no more research into their manufacture. Those already made would be locked away. They would have had at their disposal much of the money now spent on armaments to provide better conditions for the Russian people. I trust the opportunity may not slip away. I have not given up hope of attending a Four Power Conference in, say, September. Do you think, Charles, I shall be fit by then?'

I asked him if he had read an article in the *Spectator* on his oratory.

'I am not an orator,' mused Winston. 'An orator is spontaneous. The written word – ah, that's different. You write: "There exists some uncertainty as to his whereabouts." You say: "Where is he? Does he exist?"'

Moran: 'What do you mean when you say that great orators are spontaneous and you are not?'

P.M.: 'Oh, they indulge in a great deal of dramatic art.'

Suddenly he spouted with great feeling a speech by a country-man against towns.

Moran: 'Who said that?'

P.M.: 'I did. I just made it up. A hundred and fifty years ago dramatic art was conspicuous in great orators. It was my ambition, all my life, to be master of the spoken word. That was my only ambition. Of course you learn a lot when you have spoken for fifty years, and as a result of my great experience I no longer fear that I shall say something in the House of Commons which will get me into a hole. In my youth I was always afraid of that. But that is only competent speaking. Oratory is repetition. Lloyd George and Bevan are carried away by their feelings. I'm not. I run short of something to say.'

Moran: 'I suppose that was why Lloyd George criticized your choice of words?'

P.M.: 'What do you mean?'

Moran: 'Lloyd George said you were more concerned with the sound of words than with their effect in influencing a crowd. John noticed that you use unusual, bookish adjectives: that for example, you wrote of Mussolini's invasion of Abyssinia that his conduct was "at once obsolete and reprehensible".'

P.M.: 'Ah, the "bs" in those words, obsolete, reprehensible, you must pay attention to euphony.'

Moran: 'You are very fond of eighteenth-century phrases. I catch the same cadences in your books and in your speeches. They seem to owe something to Gibbon and Macaulay, just as Asquith's style was moulded by the writers of antiquity.'

P.M.: 'Oh, I have not read much, though I have written a lot.'

I read to him Rosebery's description of the way in which Lord Randolph prepared his speeches. But the P.M. had stepped out of the confessional and was now just talking. He grumbled that he did not get forty-eight hours' seclusion in which he could think out what he was going to say.

Moran: 'You are supposed to be a bad patient, but you have behaved very well in the last fortnight.'

P.M.: 'I feel I have done my bit.'

He changed the subject abruptly.

'I find *Jane Eyre* very exciting. It is a wonderful book. I'm so glad I have read it.'

July 11, 1953

I drove over to Chartwell from Marshalls in the late afternoon. When I asked him how he was he lifted his left arm above his head and turned on the switch of the reading lamp.

'I could not do that yesterday. Come, we will walk in the garden and you will see what I can do.'

He insisted on walking without assistance. We picked our way over great stepping stones across a little pond – I felt he must fall, but nothing happened. The detective produced a tin of squirming maggots, and the P.M. fed the goldfish with them. He called for a chair and, flopping into it, said:

'I'm better, but I'm not entirely recovered yet. I get very weary. You must give me some strength, Charles, before I can do anything. At present I keep dropping off to sleep.'

He seems bent on attending a race meeting at Lingfield in a week's time. I explained that he would have to be helped to his box, but he insisted; his mind was set on it. Somehow this must be stopped.

'It does not matter,' he argues, 'what people think of me now; it's what I can do in the autumn that will count. If in two months' time I can do a good broadcast and say something which the others can't say, it will be all right. People will ask: Is the brute competent? If he is, they will prefer me to others. If he isn't – well, that's different.'

Suppose he is obstinate and appears in public now, everyone will know he has had a stroke. He thinks that does not matter. I believe it matters a great deal. When people hear someone has had a stroke they feel that something has happened in the head which leads to paralysis and some deterioration of the mind. The man may perhaps go on living for a while, but for serious things he is finished. When the P.M. wrote to Ike he said he had a stroke, that he was completely paralysed and that his speech was affected. I don't know why he went into all this detail. It was quite unnecessary. When I reasoned with him, trying to persuade him not to talk of a stroke and of paralysis, he repeated the word 'paralysis'.

'But I like the word,' he persisted.

Some sense of the drama and of the poignant part he had to play in it was at the back of his mind. He is so unlike anyone else.

July 12, 1953

The nurse telephoned that the P.M. did not feel so well when he woke this morning. He was much stiffer, particularly in his back muscles. She thought he was worrying about it. I told him it meant nothing; that in his walk in the garden, balancing himself and correcting the weakness of the left side, he had made excessive use of muscles he does not generally use. Thus reassured, he banished it from his mind. But he complains of 'immense fatigue'.

'Can't you give me a tonic, Charles? Something to get rid of this horrible sense of exhaustion?'

I asked him what he could do. He rang for a secretary and asked for a memorandum which he had just dictated for Lord Salisbury, to be sent through the Ambassador in Washington.

'The thought is good, but the words are slovenly. I show it to you not to extract your political views, but in order that you may know what I can do.'

The document began by saying that the Cabinet tomorrow would consider the postponement of E.D.C.

> I do not object to the postponement, though I believe E.D.C. would have made the French less troublesome and Soviet Russia more disposed to work with me. The French want the Four Power talks to be carried out under such conditions that nothing will come of them. They are resolved to prevent German rearmament. And the Americans are behaving like fools. Dulles particularly. They want to make enemies of Russia and to stir up her satellite states. That can only lead to war. Malenkov is, I feel, a good man. I wish I could meet him. If we'd got E.D.C., then we could have spoken to Russia from strength, because German rearmament is the only thing they are afraid of. I want to use Germany and E.D.C. to keep Russia in the mood to be reasonable – to make her play. And I would use Russia to prevent Germany getting out of hand. It sounds cynical. The underlings don't want a Four Power Conference at this highest level; they want a meeting of the Foreign Secretaries. Nothing will come of that. In the war we decided the mood and they worked out the detail. It won't work in any other way.

The document ended with a sympathetic understanding of the difficult task Lord Salisbury had undertaken. 'Try to get a Four Power Conference. It will give great satisfaction.' The P.M. knew we were at a 'turning-point of the world', and as he lay there, half the man he was, I thought of one of his heroes, Nelson, lying mortally wounded, listening to the roar of the cannon on deck and wondering what was happening in this battle that would decide the fate of the world.

'Poor Anthony will be relieved at this,' the P.M. said grimly. 'He must have thought I would go on for ever.'

I wish I had that feeling about Winston. Last night his pulse was rapid, and he gets out of breath with the slightest exertion. That did not happen before. When an old man gets a thrombosis in one artery he often gets a clot in another. Will he end with a coronary thrombosis?

July 13, 1953

P.M. in good form, though his leg twitched for an hour last night. But the problem we have still to face is not the paralysed arm and leg, for it already appears that there will in the long run be no loss of power in his limbs, it is the fatigue on any exertion, whether physical or mental, that may remain as a permanent handicap. There is, too, another disconcerting relic of his illness: he is liable to become emotional, so that without warning, as he is saying something or reading a book, in his own words he 'blubs like a child'. I found him reading Trollope's *The Prime Minister*.

P.M.: 'I find the difference between those days[1] and the present time interesting.'

Moran: 'In what way?'

P.M.: 'Oh, they mixed up society and politics. What happened at the Carlton and Reform Clubs mattered to the Prime Minister then, and the House of Lords had a lot of power. Though the franchise had already been extended, public opinion had less power

---

[1] 1876.

then. The wife of the Prime Minister filled her house with a weekend party of forty-five people, and the talk influenced the course of events. On one occasion the Leader of the House went for a walk with the Prime Minister; he suggested that they ought to have a policy, to bring in two or three measures, instead of just drifting along, and the Prime Minister was affronted. Another time the Leader of the House was not asked to dine with the Prime Minister, and there was a serious bust-up.

'I have loyal friends,' the P.M. reflected, implying that there was little loyalty in Trollope's world.

Moran: 'How is Ike doing?'

P.M.: 'The Americans want to hold a Four Power Conference at a lower level. The Foreign Ministers might meet. Dulles is ambitious to be one of the big figures of the world. And' (sadly) 'I am not in a position to make a fuss. But the Russians may refuse. Bidault's only aim is to prevent the conference doing anything.'

There was a message from Clemmie that she would like to see me before I left. I found her concerned with his progress.

'How long do you think he will have to have two nurses?'

I said it was too early to say. Had Winston any views? Clemmie smiled.

'Winston is a pasha. If he cannot clap his hands for a servant he calls for Walter as he enters the house. If it were left to him he'd have the nurses for the rest of his life. He would like two in his room, two in the passage. He is never so happy, Charles, as he is when one of the nurses is doing something for him while Walter puts on his socks.'

July 14, 1953
Found the P.M. on the croquet lawn. He was weary.

'Talking tires me,' he said.

I was told that Max had come to luncheon and had been shouting at him for two hours. He wanted a General Election. But the P.M. has learnt at last that Max is not a reliable counsellor where elections are concerned. He has no intention of going to the country.

'I am tired of making decisions,' he told me. 'I am taking a holiday. Doodling and reading novels.'

Jock said that he showed the P.M. this morning a number of Foreign Office telegrams, which a month ago would have riveted his attention. Now he hardly glanced at them. He had lost his zest for work. Yet he has not given up hope that he will get well and carry on just where he left off when he was struck down.

'In two weeks,' he said, 'I may be very different, but I do not know if I shall be able to seize power as I exercised it when the Foreign Office was in my hands.'

He had a short waterproof over his greatcoat and a rug drawn over his knees. When he had been reading for some time big snorts came from under the big sombrero, which had tilted forward. Then he awoke, gazed around with a dazed look and, raising himself in his chair, began to talk.

'I dislike weakness, but I do not think anything that has happened in Egypt so far justifies wholesale measures. [1]

'I am disappointed with events in America. They've bitched things up. The Foreign Ministers are to meet in the autumn: Bidault, Dulles and Molotov.'

He lapsed into thought. At length he said:

'I'm turning over in my mind saying something serious to Ike. I want to make clear to him that I reserve the right to see Malenkov alone. It's no good seeing the Russians after the Foreign Ministers have drawn up agreements.'

He went indoors to telephone to Rab, to tell him of his misgivings, but I do not know if Rab was able to console him.

I talked to Jock as we drove from Chartwell to London. I reminded him that Maynard Keynes had written that Churchill went wrong over the Gold Standard, because he lacked instinctive judgement to tell him what was wrong. Jock thought this might be

---

[1] General Mohammed Neguib forced King Farouk of Egypt to abdicate at the beginning of the year. The country was declared a Republic on June 18, 1953, under Neguib's leadership.

true, but that if Keynes had known him better he might have added that from time to time he seemed to recognize instinctively, before others, that some course of action was right. For example, giving South Africa back to the Boers. An opportunity of the kind might soon occur, Jock went on, to give self-government to the Gold Coast. He smiled.

'I am afraid the P.M. will not be interested in the inhabitants of those parts.'

July 15, 1953

There is no noticeable change in the P.M.'s condition. Speaking with a kind of detachment he said:

'I don't think I shall ever get well, but I shall not make any decisions until September. Anthony will mew a good deal.'

He spoke rather irritably to the nurse, and then he added:

'As patients get better they get more ill-tempered. I must warn you of that.'

And he beamed at her. He was troubled often with fluids going down the wrong way. Turning to Clemmie after one of these bouts of coughing, he said:

'You see, dear, we have a turnstile in our throat, and it is so arranged that traffic is bound to go the right way, until things go wrong.'

He showed me a memorandum that he had written on helicopters. When they were 300 feet from the ground or less, if the engine cut out or the propeller came off there was a nasty crash. His memorandum contained suggestions to meet that contingency; the propeller was to be hollow, and in the hollow there was a parachute. He had sent his paper to the Prof. for his comments.

July 16, 1953

Decided to see the P.M. in the morning after breakfast, before he was tired. As I entered his bedroom he was speaking with vigour into the telephone.

'I have never allowed my private communications to the President to be submitted to anyone, in the war or since.'

He paused and listened.

'Oh, I have no objection to Lord Salisbury seeing my message. Yes, show it to him. Tell him I wish him to see it before it goes. Tell him I think he has done very well in the circumstances – no, in face of great difficulties, in face of Bidault and Dulles. Ike ought to know I do not agree – Oh, I agree of course, but that I do not approve of what has been done about the Four Power Conference.'

He put down the telephone. The massage lady, whose ministrations had gone on intermittently throughout the conversation, now made a spirited effort to persuade him that as his left side was weak he must hold the walking-stick in his right hand. He insisted it must be in his left and not his right hand. Christopher joined in and demonstrated the point by walking across the room.

'You see, you swing your arms.'

P.M. (*with a grin*): 'That is optional.' Then impatiently, and with an air of finality: 'I have thought it out.'

There was no more to be said. She was cowed into silence. He turned to me:

'I think I ought to have a new eye lotion. I am a great believer in change.'

Christopher followed me when I left the room.

'How do you think he is? He seems up and down. Yesterday Cox, you know, the fellow who advises about the garden, came to lunch. Winston was tired and uncommunicative. He had a fit of coughing when he was drinking his brandy. When he got his breath he said to Cox, "I am only concerned with changing the guard properly and with dignity. It must all go smoothly. Then I shall live here – I hope not for long." It was,' Christopher continued, 'very embarrassing in the presence of Cox, who had been told nothing. And then tomorrow morning he will be quite perky and absorbed in planning what he will do in the autumn.'

July 17, 1953

I found him struggling with *Wuthering Heights*. He said:

'I find it difficult to follow – rather confused. The narrator . . .'

He is better and has more grasp of things.

July 18, 1953

Found the P.M. in the blue drawing-room at Chartwell engrossed in *Wuthering Heights*. He looked up as if to say: I'm really very interested. Do you think you could find anything to do for a little? What he did say was:

'Charles would like some tea.'

And so I was parked out for a time with Clemmie and Duncan Sandys. When they had gone I went over to his corner, and with an effort he put down the book, holding out his wrist for me to count the pulse.

'I am dominated by this book; fascinated by its confusion. It is altogether exceptional. What is my pulse?'

Ike is in disgrace, and there was scorn in his voice when he said:

'Apparently Ike is like a king; he can't deal with detail. There was no nonsense of that sort about Franklin Roosevelt. Of course, Dulles is at the bottom of this.'

I was told that before I came the P.M. had been very belligerent, and that in disposing of Ike and others he showed something of his old fire.

July 19, 1953

A bad day. Apathetic. When I got to Chartwell about five o'clock Walter told me that he had just woken up.

P.M.: 'My legs feel tired, not refreshed as I had hoped. Is this a recession, Charles?'

His speech was very slurred; more than once I had to ask him to repeat what he had said. Annoyed with this, and determined to correct the slurring, he spat out 'lazy' with great emphasis.

'I could not at present conduct the affairs of the Government of the country. That is obvious. Yet the physical recovery is good.'

He threw his legs out of bed and walked to the bathroom to demonstrate how much better his walking was. In the bathroom a bar had been put by the side of the bath; grasping this, he stepped into the empty bath and then proceeded to lever himself down till he sat in triumph, with only his silk vest on his person: 'I couldn't have done that a week ago.

'I have a horror of a day wasted, when there is nothing at all to show for it, when one has achieved nothing. Even to read a fine book, which one has not had time to read before, is something; or perhaps one does a little work on the book.

'Dulles lied when he said Ike did not want to do detail; when I saw him six months ago it was Ike himself who suggested a conference at Stockholm. Of course the Russians may refuse to attend a conference on these terms. They would like me to visit them, I think, to spite America – not that I would ever split from the Americans.'

Moran: 'Is Ike really fitted for his present job?'

P.M.: 'Well, in the war he had a very genuine gift for friendship and for keeping the peace. But I decided in the States six months ago that he was really a Brigadier.

'I had a nice letter from Augustus John. Yes, I like him; he used to lunch here and keep an eye on my painting.'

July 20, 1953

I was prepared to hear this morning that the P.M. had been in poor form when Rab came to dine with him last night. But nothing of the sort. According to the office he was in excellent spirits. Indeed, Rab said that he was astonished by the progress he had made in the course of a week. It became plain that Rab did not rule out a comeback. The P.M. beamed at me.

'They said I was very good with Rab.' His voice became stronger. 'I am again a forceful animal. I could kick people around this morning.'

He has got back his self-confidence. I asked him what attitude the Party would take in the House of Commons on the debate on foreign affairs.

'Oh,' the P.M. answered, 'they are going to stick by my statement of May 11.'

July 21, 1953

Winston may be confident, but he was all agog to hear about Rab's speech on foreign policy. 'You weren't in the House?' There was a note of reproach in his voice. He wanted to know what Rab had said of him and how he came out of it all. He rang his bell, and when Miss Gilliatt appeared he told her to telephone Christopher. When he could not be found, he demanded a word with Jock. But Jock was on his way home. So in the end the Chief Whip was called to the telephone. His verdict on Butler's speech was that it was rather tame.

'He doesn't seem to have brought it off,' the P.M. murmured.

I don't know why the P.M. is making all this fuss about Rab's speech. He does not usually bother his head about his colleagues' opinions. But now things are somehow different. What the Party is thinking has come to matter. At Margate they will decide his future. 'I must know where I stand,' he grumbled.

Miss Gilliatt came in with a letter from the President.

'A new letter? That is interesting.'

When he had read it he handed it to me:

Dear Winston,

Many thanks for your letter.

In the first place let me say how greatly I rejoice at the report of a great improvement in your health. Your own country, and indeed the whole world, can hardly spare you even in semi-retirement, and I rejoice that you expect to emerge in full vigour in September.

I have a feeling that it is dangerous to talk generalities to the Russians unless and until their proposals for Germany and Austria show that we can depend on them. I like to keep talks informal with those I can trust as friends. That was why I looked forward so much to Bermuda. But I do not like talking informally with those who only wish to entrap and embarrass us. I would prefer, at any rate in the first instance, to leave the initial approach to the Foreign Ministers on limited and specific lines. . . .

There followed a paragraph to the effect that as President it was difficult to leave America.

. . . I greatly look forward to your reappearance in September.
With warmest regards,

                                                                                    Ike.

'A nice letter. He is very friendly. The Russians feel my illness is a put-up job. Christopher sat next to Malik[1] at a dinner. He said: "Mr Churchill knew he would get a rebuff from the Americans, hence his illness." I think I must see Malik sometime. Ike takes a very cautious line about Russia.'

Sat next to Alex lunching at the House of Lords. He said to me in his confiding way:

'Now, Charles, you know Winston better than anyone. Can't you get him to retire?'

I suppose this is in the thoughts of many people.

July 22, 1953
Found the P.M. in poor form. Speech very slurred, and he is walking badly. Camrose, who had come down to see about Volume VI of the book, said to me:

'He will never go back to the House.'

Only once was there a glimpse of the Winston we have known. He began quoting poetry – Pope – and for a little time his manner became animated, his voice strong, his eye alert. Camrose was astonished at his memory. The P.M.'s thoughts went back to his nursery days: he was very happy with his old nurse, till he was sent to 'penal servitude'. That was his description of his life at his prep. school at Brighton, where he was from his eighth to eleventh year. He said that at the school there were volumes of *Punch*, and that he

---

[1] Jacob Malik, Soviet Ambassador to the Court of St James's, 1953–60.

would pore over them and their story of what had happened in recent history. Then his thoughts came back with a jerk to the present. He could not get out of his head the opportunity that had been lost at Moscow. Dulles was 'clever enough to be stupid on a rather large scale'.

He sat brooding; at last he looked up.

'I made an exhibition of myself today. I get maudlin. It seems a feature of this blow. Why am I like this, Charles? I'll have to go. The trouble is, it is easy to go, but it's not so easy when you find them doing things you don't approve of.'

I said the general opinion seemed to be that Rab had not held the House in his speech on foreign affairs.

'Ah,' he said, 'it's easy to hold out bright hopes as I did. It's more difficult to apologize to the House when they do not come to fulfilment. I've not enjoyed July. I've not had much fun. If the rest of my life is to be like this I hope some means may be found of accelerating – '

He stopped short, and abruptly took up a book and began to read.

July 23, 1953
This morning the P.M. handed me a typed message. I read:

> Monsieur Bidault told the Council of Ministers that the P.M. is suffering from complete paralysis, and that though he retains his intellectual lucidity, he is incapable of moving without assistance. Mr Eden is cutting short his convalescence in order to fly home.

Moran: 'Is that in the French Press?'

P.M.: 'Yes, and in all the bloody American papers.' (*Grinning*) 'They are issuing a correction.' (*Fiercely*) 'I don't care what they say. If a month from now I appear and can walk and talk all right, that will shut them up.'

He jumped out of bed and, walking across the room, climbed on to a chair and stood erect without holding on to anything.

'What do you think of that?' he asked defiantly.

Christopher came into the room.

Christopher: 'The Press – even the television people – are going to be at Downing Street in force tomorrow. Why not go direct to Chequers and cut out London?'

P.M. (*a little inconsequently*): 'But I want to sit again in my chair in the Cabinet Room.'

Christopher: 'You can do that on your return from Chequers in a fortnight's time.'

P.M.: 'Very well, we'll go direct if Charles can get Brain to come to Chequers.'

Christopher grinned with pleasure at his unexpected docility.

P.M.: 'I think, Charles, Salisbury was right to alter your bulletin. It was better to say I needed a month's rest than all that business about a disturbance of the cerebral circulation. I didn't like that.'

Moran: 'No, you preferred saying you had a stroke. Salisbury and Butler took a chance, and it came off. But doctors are not there to gamble. They issue bulletins to gain time.'

P.M.: 'I don't follow.'

Moran: 'When a man has a stroke, for two or three days you can't tell what is going to happen. He may go out.'

P.M.: 'What do you mean? Go out?'

Moran: 'Die, of course.'

P.M.: 'Oh, I see.'

Moran: 'If you had perished after we had said a rest was necessary the public might have thought you had got a pretty long rest. In fact, they would not have thought Salisbury's bulletin clever at all. The gamble came off – for the time. But we have not finished with explanations.'

I saw that he was not listening.

Chequers, July 24, 1953

The P.M. moved from Chartwell to Chequers today. He loves Chartwell, though there is nothing there except a rather ordinary house – and the Weald. But Clemmie insisted that the servants must have a rest, or they would leave. The country around Chequers looked enchanting in the evening light, and the long gallery brought back a lot of war memories.

When I went to his room to see if he was tired he began at once about the Russians. He said they had refused to work with us in Europe.

P.M.: 'The Americans were simple-minded to expect them to do anything else. They want the Kremlin to give up the part of Germany they themselves gave up to Stalin.'

Moran: 'What is the next step?'

P.M.: 'Perhaps I may take it if I can learn to walk properly. Would you come with me to Moscow? I knew you would, my dear Charles. We have travelled a good many miles together.'

I wonder where it will end. Sir Russell Brain, a careful, prudent physician, puts the P.M.'s chance of coming back alive from a trip to Moscow as low as fifty–fifty. Excitement might bring on another stroke, or at any rate leave him unable to play his part when he got there. But if he knew the odds I am sure he would take them.

P.M.: 'You look very solemn, Charles. What are your thoughts?'

Without waiting for an answer, he continued:

'My plan for dividing Germany horizontally and not vertically was the right one. Prussia would have been treated politely but severely; there would have been a gathering of states on Vienna – Bavaria and the rest.

'Rab had a bad headache during the Foreign Office debate, poor fellow, he seems to have had only an indifferent day. He made the mistake of telling the House that we had done well at Washington.[1] And now everyone can see we didn't. Lord Salisbury agrees with me. When dealing with powerful allies we have to take the best we can get, not what we want.'

Moran: 'How are you getting on with Trollope? You're reading *The Duke's Children*?'

---

[1] R. A. Butler had accompanied Eden to Washington for talks with the new Eisenhower Administration (March 4–7, 1953).

P.M.: 'Oh, the Duke was a silly man. He objected to his daughter getting married to a perfectly respectable man. His only sin was that he was not a nobleman and had no money. So much in those days depended on whether a man had money.'

During dinner Clemmie told how at a luncheon given by the French Ambassador, she had sat next to Lord Halifax.

'Edward seemed to suggest that Winston was a handicap to the Conservative Party. At last I turned on him. "I don't know what you are getting at," I said rather hotly. "If the country had depended on you we might have lost the war." Edward was furious and demanded an apology.'

As she recalled the scene she laughed aloud.

'Later he talked to Winston, saying I ought to apologize. Winston replied he hoped I'd do nothing of the sort. You see, Charles, Edward Halifax has been spoilt. Baldwin was largely responsible.'

Winston went on to recall an incident in 1911 when he was at the Admiralty.

'A.J.B.[1] called on me. He leant against the mantelpiece' (the P.M. does not often notice that kind of thing) 'while I told him of some of my plans in the event of war, particularly of an expedition into the Baltic. I remember what he said. "Winston, I believe your hour has come." That was 1911,' the P.M. pondered, 'and it wasn't till 1940 that I had a chance.'

Chequers, July 25, 1953

The P.M. has come to no harm from the journey and is in good form. He has put on a special show for Sir Russell Brain.

'When I can walk without a limp, then we can let the movies do their worst.'

Brain thinks he may recover 90 per cent. physically. But he is less certain about his ability to concentrate. He doubts whether he will be alive in a year's time. Winston told Brain:

[1] Arthur James Balfour, then leader of the Conservative Opposition.

'I don't like concentrating, unless I'm excited or irritated.' Then with a gush of hope: 'I don't see why I shouldn't recover as I did at Monte Carlo. Do you see any reason, Charles?'

The P.M. kept his eye on Brain, who had not, of course, transmitted his forebodings, and, when he said nothing, began to question him closely about the prospects of becoming less tearful. Brain said cautiously that the tendency might get less.

'I was always a little blubbery, but now when I read anything, it moves me. I care so much about some things. I have decided to hold a Cabinet when I return to Chartwell in a fortnight's time. All the invalids would be present – Eden, Macmillan and myself.'

Moran: 'Why be in a hurry? I am against an early Cabinet. Someone will make a speech saying how glad they are to have you back, and you may break down.'

I fancy this went home and we may hear no more of this Cabinet.

P.M.: 'Anyway, October 10 is the annual Party meeting at Margate, and I must make a speech then or get out.' Pointing to his forehead: 'I feel there is a small bit of the brain which has been affected by this business and may, if I use it too much, crack. Of course I know it's pure imagination – not scientific medicine,' and he put his hand affectionately on my shoulder. 'Eden is coming on Monday. Perhaps it would be better, Charles, if I saw him alone. It is a delicate business. You might come in the late afternoon and stay to dinner. I don't think I shall commit myself when I see Anthony. I don't like being kicked out till I've had a shot at settling this Russian business.'

He leant towards me:

'You realize, Charles, I'm playing a big hand – the easement of the world, perhaps peace over the world – without of course giving up proper means of defence. If it came off, and there was disarmament,' he lisped in his excitement, 'production might be doubled and we might be able to give to the working man what he has never had – leisure. A four-day week, and then three days' fun. I had my teeth in it. I have become so valuable that they would allow me to do it in my own way. I must be right, of course – but I need not be busy – others would do the work.

'What is happening in Germany is very important. You've not seen it in the papers? It was in the *Telegraph*. The Germans are taking my line. They want a Locarno. America must be ready to attack Germany if she should attack Russia, while if Russia is the aggressor America would declare war on her.'

The thought of this better world, where the United Nations would at last keep the peace, left him in tears. He could not speak for some time. Then with an effort he took refuge in levity:

'I am trying, Charles, to cut down alcohol. I have knocked off brandy' – the coming sally made him smile – 'and take cointreau instead. I disliked whisky at first. It was only when I was a subaltern in India, and there was a choice between drinking dirty water and dirty water with some whisky in it, that I got to like it. I have always, since that time, made a point of keeping in practice.'

But since the stroke he has discovered that alcohol does him no good. It makes his speech more difficult to understand and fuddles what is left of his wits; and yet he does not attempt to control his thirst. 'Is alcohol a food?' he enquires inconsequently.

July 27, 1953
When I dined with the P.M. at Chequers he was full of vigour and talk. I found him in bed, though he was already late for dinner, absorbed in *Candide*, in an English translation. He looked up:

'This is an extraordinary book, Charles, have you read it? "The best of all possible worlds" philosophy is attacked with measureless satire. I'm excited about what will come next. Listen,' he said with a grin, turning to the famous passage on syphilis:

'The next day, as Candide was walking out, he met a beggar all covered with scabs, his eyes were sunk in his head, the end of his nose was eaten off, his mouth drawn on one side, his teeth as black as coal, snuffling and coughing, and every time he attempted to spit, out dropped a tooth.'

Walter came into the room.

'Dinner is ready, sir.'

He took no notice, but went on reading with gurgles in his throat as he savoured Pangloss's explanation to Candide how he had been reduced to this miserable condition.

' "Oh, Pangloss," cried Candide, "is not the devil the root of it?" "Not at all," replied the great man, "it was a thing unavoidable, a necessary ingredient in the best of worlds; for if Columbus had not, in an island of America, caught this disease which contaminates the source of generation, and frequently impedes propagation itself, and is evidently opposite to the great end of nature, we should have had neither chocolate nor cochineal." '

As he put down the book reluctantly he sighed:

'I'm burning to get on with it.'

'Have you never read it before?' I asked.

'No, my life has been too full of things to read much.'

While he was dressing I asked him which of the three Trollope books he liked best. He replied without hesitation, '*The Duke's Children.*

'Why? Oh, because it is a good picture of an extraordinary world that has gone. The Duke is, of course, a poop; a Liberal he calls himself, yet he is so narrow-minded.'

The P.M. was in no hurry and gave me a chunk of the *Ingoldsby Legends* by 'a great rhymster'. After that he recited with gusto:

> *Life is mostly froth and bubble,*
> *Two things stand like stone –*
> *Kindness in another's trouble,*
> *Courage in our own.*

'Yes. Adam Lindsay Gordon. Come, they will be waiting for us.'

After dinner, when we were alone, he went on talking for a long time.

'I had a greater opportunity before the blow than I ever had since I became a Member of the House of Commons – if only, Charles, I had the strength. I'm a sort of survival. Roosevelt and Stalin are both dead. I only am left. People say: "He means us well, all this is within his reach."

'We have had a leisured class. It has vanished. Now we must think of the leisured masses. Why not? It isn't impossible. When there is no longer a risk of war a lot of money will be set free, it will be available to provide leisure for the people.'

It was the old hankering for a romantic role. War had been his hobby. Nothing had been to him so consistently stimulating. But that was gone and done with. And now, with his life running out, it was in his mind to end as a maker of peace among men; in this, his final role, he would appear before the world as, perhaps, the only hope of breaking the cold war.

And this was not just a dramatic curtain to his long life with all its vicissitudes. His generous heart seems, as the days pass, to be flushed with kindly thoughts about all mankind, even about the Germans. He has always admired them, they are a great people. He admired their Army, and would have liked, he once said, to go to Germany to appeal to young Germans to wipe out the disgrace of Hitler and of the cruel murder of the Jews. There is so much to do and time is getting short.

'Before I lead the British people into another and more bloody war, I want to satisfy my conscience and my honour that the Russians are not just play-acting. I believe they do mean something. I believe there has been a change of heart. I have talked with two Popes. What do you think we talked about? Bolshevism!'

I asked him why Roosevelt had been so friendly to Stalin. But he did not answer my question. It is not easy to draw him out. He thought that the hydrogen bomb accounted for a certain arrogance in the Americans. He did not want them to be arrogant.

July 28, 1953
Dined at Arlington House with Max and Brendan. It became obvious that this was planned to pump me; they wanted to find out what I really thought about Winston and what advice I shall give him about his future. Max as a preliminary tried to fill me up with champagne. I asked him point blank how he saw Winston's future.

'Oh, he ought to retire,' he said without any hesitation. 'Attlee will attack him presently; they will say it is a government of invalids, and there will be trouble too in his own party.'

Besides, Max thinks he will break down in the House if he comes back. I let Max do the talking.

I asked the P.M. whether he had discussed with Anthony what was going to happen in October about the succession. Was Anthony in a patient frame of mind?

'Oh, he didn't mention it,' the P.M. answered, 'and I didn't expect he would.'

July 30, 1953

David Maxwell-Fyfe[1] and his wife were at Chequers when I lunched there. David has won the solid goodwill – perhaps I might say the affection – of the House of Commons, by his simple, straight-forward honesty and his kindly nature. They have learnt that when he does a job it is done once and for all. But these are not the particular qualities that make a man congenial to Winston. Today David sat next to the P.M., almost in silence, unless Winston spoke to him.

The P.M. seems to have more energy. Miss Gilliatt says he is clamouring for work. That, of course, is an exaggeration, but it does mean that he is willing to look at some papers which the private office has collected. He himself is sure that he is gaining ground, though he made this cryptic remark:

'I have a feeling I am only half in the world. It is a curious feeling. Adlai Stevenson[2] lunched here yesterday. I like him.'

At times he wonders whether Ike's election was a good thing for us – or for the world. Perhaps, after all, we should have been better off with Stevenson and the Democrats.

---

[1] Home Secretary and Minister for Welsh Affairs, later Lord Kilmuir.
[2] Democratic candidate in the American Presidential election in 1952. Defeated by General Eisenhower.

August 5, 1953

I found the P.M. closeted with Moir, his solicitor, when I arrived at Chequers for luncheon. He told me later that he had learnt from Winston that Randolph was to be his biographer; we agreed it was an unfortunate arrangement. But the P.M. had other things on his mind this morning. We had hardly taken our seats at luncheon when he turned to us (Lennox-Boyd[1] and Leathers were the other guests) and asked if we had read the article in *The Times* on Beria's fall. Leathers thought it sounded well informed.

'Who wrote it?' the P.M. asked.

'Isaac Deutscher.'

He had not heard of him.

'If it is true, I do not want to make Malenkov's acquaintance. It would serve no purpose. In this man there can be no strength and no sense of decency as we understand it.'

To the P.M. this event seemed to blast all his hopes, his castle in the air came clattering down. He had decided that Malenkov was a good man – after all, there must be decent Russians – and now, apart from any question of decency, what was left of his plan? If it was possible to overthrow Beria so easily, what guarantee is there that Malenkov cannot be displaced with just as little effort? What was the good of meeting him if, the day after, he, too, might be swept away?

One thing Winston thought could be salvaged from the wreck.

'If our conciliatory attitude does no good abroad it may help at home.'

He meant that it had convinced the public that his Government was resolved to end the cold war if it was given half a chance. In their mind he had become associated with a determined effort to ease world tension and to avoid at all costs a third world war. The thought of Malenkov came back. What had become now of his plan for meeting the Russians in Moscow? It seemed as if the last excuse for hanging on had been snatched from him.

[1] Minister of Transport and Civil Aviation; later Lord Boyd of Merton.

I went with him to his room. He sat heavily on the bed:

'I did want to last until next year. The party meeting is on October 10; Anthony may not be fit by then. He looked very frail when he was here; and I thought he seemed subdued. It would not be fair to Anthony to let Rab take it. Of course, everything depends on whether I can face October 10. I could not walk up the floor of the House of Commons at present. You must help me, Charles.'

Leathers brought me back to London, talking about himself all the time. In his conversation he cuts a bold figure. He had said to Winston, 'I cannot accept this, or do that.' In fact, he is quite meek and does what Winston tells him.

August 8, 1953

Lunched at Chequers. Rab Butler and Salisbury there. Butler, like an Asquith, is rather too impatient with pedestrian folk. He has more staying power than Anthony, but at present he lacks what people call the 'common touch'. They complain, too, that he will back a horse both ways. He seems none the worse for the grind while the P.M. and Anthony were away ill. He does not get worked up like Anthony. Of course, he is aware of the danger of racing the engine, but he says he has 'a normal family life and does not feel the strain'. After we rose from the table the P.M. stumped on to the lawn.

Butler (*turning to the P.M.*): 'Have you read what Somerset Maugham says about Burke? Burke uses short sentences, so unlike you. I suppose you were influenced by Macaulay.'

P.M.: 'Yes, Macaulay was a great influence in my young days; and Gibbon.'

The P.M. began to recite the opening lines of the fourteenth chapter of the *Decline and Fall*.

P.M.: 'I have been reading Forester's book about 1814. He has the art of narrative; it is only the harmonious arrangement of facts.'

Something was coming. His grin broadened.

'I made an attack once in the House on Arthur Balfour. I made a tremendous onslaught on him.' Here he declaimed, with great vigour in his voice, the climax of his attack, culminating in the accusation, which the P.M. hissed out, 'You hold this House in contempt.' 'A.J.B., speaking very quietly, "No, I have no contempt for the House, only for some of its members." ' Winston chortled at Balfour's hit. 'I have in my life concentrated more on self-expression than on self-denial.'

He likes this aphorism and often repeats it in conversation.

Butler: 'Alex[1] has been very helpful in the reduction of expenditure on the Armed Forces.'

P.M.: 'There will be trouble if the Air Force is weakened.'

Butler: 'It's the Navy that will be cut.'

P.M.: 'If I had been returned in 1945 I would have introduced a constituent assembly for India. Of course, they might have got rid of us anyway, but I'd have liked to try.'

He told how some Indians had been treated with contempt.

'If we had made friends with them and taken them into our lives instead of restricting our intercourse to the political field, things might have been very different.'

August 9, 1953
The nurse telephoned this morning that yesterday, when Sir Winston was playing croquet, he hit the ball hard, and then, hurrying after it, became very short of breath – he was cyanosed, she added. But Jock said he was in fine form at night, hilarious in fact, and kept them up until one o'clock.

August 12, 1953
Arranged with Russell Brain to see the P.M. at No. 10, on his way from Chequers to Chartwell. Winston took us to the Cabinet Room. Smiling, he said:

'Pray take your seats at the Cabinet table.' He went on: 'I am not the man I was, but I have made a great improvement. I can tie my bow now. I couldn't do that a short time ago. And I can feel now if the razor has done its job. Before I couldn't feel the stubble. I am less emotional. Of course at times I still blubber. For instance, when

[1] Earl Alexander of Tunis, then Minister of Defence.

I was told the Germans like me – after all I have done to them. But you would like to examine me. Come to my room.'

Winston lay flat on his bed in nothing but his vest.

'Would you like to take my pulse, Charles?' and he held out his arm.

Russell sat contemplating the P.M. for what seemed a long time. I became a little uncomfortable.

'I'm getting cold,' grumbled the P.M.

When Brain had finished his examination, and pulled up his chair, the P.M. said:

'You haven't tried if I can feel a pinprick.'

Whereupon Russell meekly got up and resumed his examination.

'Well,' said the P.M., looking at Brain, 'what is the position? What do you think? Have I made progress?'

'Yes,' Brain answered dryly.

'But surely, Sir Russell, you do agree I am better?'

This time Brain got as far as admitting 'considerable progress'.

'You really feel I am getting on?'

'Oh, yes, Prime Minister. I am very pleased.'

Brain is not good at patter. He did not seem to discern that the P.M. was seeking reassurance.

P.M.: 'When Walter goes out of the room I want to say something to you. The Queen has asked Clemmie and me to the St Leger on the 12th of September. And then to go on to Balmoral. I'd like to go. Oh, I've accepted. Of course, if anything happened and I am worse, I can get out of it.'

Brain rose and took his leave. When he had gone the P.M. turned to me.

'Sir Russell isn't keeping anything back? I want to know everything. He is at the head of your profession? He doesn't seem to get much fun out of life.'

I was afraid that the P.M. might underrate Brain. It is easy to do that. He has a first-rate intelligence, but it is hidden behind a rather ordinary exterior. And Winston only glances at the shop-window, he doesn't bother to go behind the counter. So far Brain has failed to impress the P.M., just as Wavell failed, and probably for the same reason. When I was searching for this, George Meredith's cautionary words came into my head:

'It is a terrific decree in life that they must act who would prevail.'

As we drove away, Brain said:

'Probably in a month's time he will be as well as he ever will be. I doubt whether he will be able to re-enter public life. If the Prime Minister goes to the Party meeting on October the 10th he might become emotional, or he might get very tired and walk away from the platform very badly, or he might even forget what he meant to say.'

I said I would not be surprised if he died from a heart attack, and not from another stroke. But Brain thought his stiffness and shortness of breath were largely due to his being out of training. I doubted this.

Brain told me that Horace Evans had tackled him about the Prime Minister. Evans had said that his patient, Anthony Eden, complained that he did not know where he was: at first the Prime Minister had written to Mr Eden as if everything was at an end and that he would have to take over; and now he is behaving as if nothing had happened.

August 16, 1953

When I asked the P.M. this morning how he had been since he left Chequers he replied:

'I was very depressed last night. I would have liked to see you. I nearly asked you to come over. I get anxious about myself, though,' he hastened to add, 'I don't mind what happens to me. I was conscious of my heart. How? Oh, just like it feels when you are troubled with wind. Then Oliver Lyttelton came to dinner and he cheered me up – he's an agreeable personality. I was depressed, not only about myself, but about the terrible state of the world. That hydrogen bomb can destroy two million people. It is so awful that I have a feeling it will not happen.'

Winston seems to have put the mishap to Beria out of his mind.

'I am thinking of going over to see Eisenhower. When? Oh, about September 20th. I don't mind if anything does happen to me. I should stay at the Embassy for three days. I have a lot of things I want to say to that man. I can do something with the Russians which no one else can do. That is the only reason why I am clinging to office. But I have no mental zeal. I don't want to do things. I used to wake in the morning wanting to do a lot of things. Perhaps I need a tonic. I can correct proofs, of course; that is no effort.'

He picked up a galley proof from the bed that he had been reading when I came in.

'Read that. We made an arrangement with Stalin in the war about spheres of influence, expressed in percentages. Rumania, Bulgaria, Greece and so on. Here they are in print. Read the last paragraph. It seems rather cynical, I said to Stalin, to barter away the lives of millions of people in this fashion. Perhaps we ought to burn this paper. "Oh, no," said Stalin, "you keep it." We did that, Charles, on the spot in a few minutes. You see, the people at the top can do these things, which others can't do.[1]

'The eye man – what's his name? – yes, King, of course, said to me yesterday, "You are much rested since I last saw you the day before your illness." That means something, Charles. He has been trained for years in the scrutiny of faces. Of course, I have not had a rest like this for a long time. I hope that Anthony and I will both

---

[1] At his meeting with Stalin in Moscow in October, 1944, the Prime Minister said to Stalin; 'Let us settle about our affairs in the Balkans . . . don't let us get at cross-purposes in small ways.' While his words were being translated the P.M. wrote out on a half sheet of paper the predominance of Russia and Britain in percentages.

Rumania	*Greece*	*Bulgaria*	*Yugoslavia and Hungary*
Russia 90%	Great Britain 90%	Russia 75%	Russia 50%
Others 10%	Russia 10%	Others 25%	Others 50%

This Stalin blue-pencilled as a sign of agreement. Winston Churchill, *The Second World War, Volume 6: Triumph and Tragedy* (Cassell reference, 1954), p. 198.

be able to meet the Party Conference on October 10th. We would say, "We two invalids have come here to report to you." '

When I left him I heard that Clemmie wanted to see me.

'How is Winston?' she enquired, and did not wait to hear my answer. 'Of course, he has to make a very great decision in the next month – whether he goes on. He is talking now of going to America to see Ike. But Ike does not want to see him, he was delighted when Bermuda was scratched. If Winston was at his best, then he might be able to fix up something with the President in the course of the next two years, but as it is, Ike is waiting to see which way the cat jumps, and whether Winston will retire. Moreover, Charles, Ike doesn't like his countrymen saying that the Prime Minister of Britain is making up the President's mind. I believe,' she continued, 'when the blow has fallen Winston will settle down to build a new life here at Chartwell.'

She keeps telling me this. She does not realize that he has no future – he must live for a little longer on his glorious past.

CHAPTER FOURTEEN

Struggle for Survival

August 17, 1953

I had arranged to take a small boy to the Test Match at the Oval, when I was summoned to Chartwell to see the P.M. He was apprehensive about stiffness in the back, which has been bothering him off and on for a fortnight. 'Could it,' he asked, 'develop into something which might prevent me appearing at Margate?' There are symptoms which are significant, throwing light on the course and nature of an illness, and others which are never explained, and in retrospect appear irrelevant. Such a distinction has no meaning for Winston. There is no sense, I tell him, in giving different-coloured medicines for symptoms until I know their cause. Yet he goes on demanding action. Anything that is done, however futile, brings him satisfaction. 'But surely you can do something,' he will say petulantly; and when I was driven to suggest that aspirin might relieve his 'stiffness', if it were muscular, he said, 'I'd like that.' At once he became interested and asked how many tablets he must take and at what time.

When we had emerged from this rough and tumble he suddenly said:

'I am taking the Cabinet tomorrow.'

I said I was sorry he had made that decision. He ignored my remark. I want to gain time for him. His plan for meeting Malenkov has so far helped him to face the uncertainty of this wretched, drawn-out illness, but for the moment at any rate he has lost faith in his

Moscow visit, and the real struggle for survival is only beginning. He sees clearly certain tests he must pass if he is to stay in public life.

'Have you read the *Daily Mirror*?' he asked, and rang for a secretary.

As it was handed to me, I read the big headlines on the front page: 'What is the truth about Churchill's illness?' The *New York Herald Tribune*, according to the *Mirror*, had stated that the P.M. had had a stroke in the last week in June, and that although he had made a near-miraculous recovery, those in the best position to judge did not believe he would ever again be able to assume active day-to-day leadership of his country.

> Is there any reason [the *Mirror* went on] why the British people should not be told the facts about the health of their Prime Minister? Is there any reason why they should always be the last to learn what is going on in their own country? Must they always be driven to pick up their information at second hand from tittle-tattle abroad? The public is baffled and worried . . . the nation is rightly concerned. The United Nations Assembly meets today to pave the way to a firm and lasting peace. It is for Britain to save the conference from futility and the United Nations from failure. She must speak with all the strength that comes from firm leadership. So long as the Prime Minister's physical fitness to lead the country is in doubt, she cannot do that. Let us know now whether Sir Winston Churchill is fit enough to lead us.

'Five million people read that,' the P.M. said grimly. 'It's rubbish, of course, but it won't help at Margate.'

This snarling by the Press is something new. So far they have left him to fight it out alone.

'What are your plans for tomorrow?' I enquired.

'I'm having a luncheon party here for my book, and then I shall go up to London for the Cabinet at 5 p.m.'

I disliked the plan, and said so. The luncheon would be convivial and go on till three-thirty, then he would have an hour's drive, arriving at No. 10 tired, and below his best form.

August 18, 1953

The P.M. telephoned. Could I see him at No. 10 at one o'clock? That was how I learnt that he had cancelled the luncheon. I said I would rather see him after the Cabinet to see how he had weathered the discussion. But he persisted, because he wanted me to give him a sedative pill to give him sleep in the afternoon. He was very short tempered and on edge, shouting at a porter when the lift was not ready; and when we got to the bedroom he complained irritably:

'I was very well this morning. Now my head is fuddled. The noise of the car and the traffic and reading the papers on my way here tired me. I am going to have my luncheon in bed while Norman Brook tells me about the agenda for the Cabinet. I must get some sleep this afternoon. What about a red?'

When I said it would only do harm by depressing the circulation, he appeared disappointed. I asked him how long the Cabinet would last. He replied:

'I shan't hurry them; it may take three hours.'

I called again at seven-forty. He was still in the Cabinet Room with a Minister, but the Cabinet itself had only lasted an hour and forty minutes. I waited for him in the bedroom. As he entered the room I knew things had gone well. He thanked me affectionately for coming.

'Well, how did it go?'

'Oh,' he answered cheerfully, 'they say I was better at the end than at the beginning. I had to settle two important things after the Cabinet, so that I was either explaining what I wanted or arguing for nearly three hours. It was very concentrated work, but I was able to dominate the Cabinet and settle things the way I wanted. I made my little jokes. Of course, one oughtn't to be nervous, but I was. I wondered how it would go. I thought about it a lot all day, whereas usually I never give it a thought till I go into the Cabinet Room. After all, it was my first Cabinet since it happened. It will be less of a strain next time.'

Norman Brook told me that he did not think any of the P.M.'s colleagues noticed anything different from an ordinary Cabinet.

'Winston let other people talk more than usual perhaps – he certainly talked less himself. No one noticed anything strange in his speech, and he walked to his seat much as he usually does.' Brook added: 'He has dipped his foot in water, and it wasn't cold; he wants to go on. This isn't the moment to make decisions about retiring.'

The P.M. had arranged to dine with Brendan at his house at eight-fifteen, but at that hour he had not got into his bath. On coming into his room he threw off his clothes, lay back on the bed and seemed disinclined to move.

'I am very tired, Charles; I don't want to do anything.'

As Brook put it, 'Tired but happy.'

Before midnight Brendan telephoned me. Winston had just left. Brendan wanted me to dine with him on Friday. He is against the P.M. going on and wants my views.

August 19, 1953

The P.M., the nurse reported, went to bed at eleven o'clock, but twitchings in both legs kept him awake until one o'clock. I found him suffering from reaction. He was not so well, he said.

'In what way?'

'Oh, I cannot concentrate, and I don't want to do any work; my head was muzzy this morning. I took 7 grains of aspirin. You know, Charles, it is much more effective than 5 grains. If a Cabinet can flatten me out like this, what will Margate do?'

When I had examined him I told him there was no real set-back; it was only reaction after the Cabinet, it would not happen at Margate. At once he became more cheerful and began to tell me about Persia. Mossadeq[1] had received a reverse and his Foreign Minister had been torn to bits by the mob.

---

[1] Dr Mohammed Mossadeq, Prime Minister of Persia, was arrested on August 19, 1953, following a three-day struggle for power by the army, whose right-wing leaders had gained influence with the Shah. Mossadeq was accused of collusion with the Communists and the USSR.

P.M.: 'Gascoigne[1] came to see me this morning; he is just back from Moscow. He said that Beria's fall is a good thing. He and Malenkov were great friends, but Beria was thrown to the wolves without a moment's hesitation. They are like wild beasts. There has been no change of heart in Russia, but she wants peace.'

The P.M. showed me half a dozen numbers of a monthly magazine called *History Today*.

'Brendan tells me they sell thirty thousand copies every month. He is behind it. It is written by young historians for serious people. This is the more serious side of the nation. I find all this very encouraging. It would appear that not everyone in England reads the *Daily Mirror*. These young historians will be very useful to me. Before the war I wrote *A History of the English-speaking Peoples*, in four volumes – a million words. I will get them to check its accuracy.' He smiled. 'I've been living on the *Second World War*. Now I shall live on this history. I shall lay an egg a year – a volume every twelve months should not mean much work. I am reading another of Trollope. I find him very readable.'

Clemmie gave me tea and some advice about Winston. She said he was not so well – he was very white.

'What do you really think of him, Charles? You know about the St Leger and Balmoral? I told him I thought he was crazy to try to do all these things.'

August 21, 1953

The P.M. in poor spirits.

He grumbled: 'I've done nothing today, yet I feel tired. Why should I be like this, Charles?'

I suggested he was paying for Tuesday's Cabinet. He neither agreed nor disagreed.

'I've no zeal, no zest.' He smiled. 'I could never say my sibilants like ordinary people. I can only say zest by giving an expiratory snort. I can't make sibilants by putting my tongue against my

[1] Sir Alvary Gascoigne, British Ambassador in Moscow, 1951–3.

teeth. . . . I am only thinking whether I can do anything to help; not what will be the effect on me – that doesn't matter. . . . My stiffness is less troublesome.'

Moran: 'I'm not worried about that.'

P.M.: 'What are you worried about?'

This question was accompanied by a searching look; he was interested in my answer.

Moran: 'Fatigue – that is our enemy.'

P.M.: 'I think I could make a speech now.'

Moran: 'I'm sure you could. What I'm not sure about is whether you would be up to a difficult job next day if you had to face something of the kind.'

P.M.: 'I had some twitching of one leg last night for a short time.'

Moran: 'Before Tuesday you'd no twitching for a fortnight. This is all part of Tuesday's bill. Now you've done it once I don't think the next Cabinet will take so much out of you.'

P.M.: 'Painting takes a lot out of me. I can't face it. Of course, what it takes is quite different from anything I have been doing. I think things in Persia are a little better.' (*Grinning*) 'Mossadeq's troubled, as I am, with being too emotional.'

Then the smile faded and he said very gravely:

'People think they can settle these obstinate world issues at one stroke. You can't do that. No one can do it. The essence of my policy is to get agreement about bits of a problem – to gain three or four years' easement.'

I asked him whether he intended to go to America to see Ike in September. He thought for a moment.

'I think I'd rather go and see the Russians. The country will be very disappointed if I give up trying to get the Russians in a friendly mood.'

Alan Hodge, a young historian, had lunched with him. Together they had looked through some of his first volume on *A History of the English-speaking Peoples*. He sighed.

'I wish I could write as I did ten years ago. Though they say the sixth volume of my book, which I call *Triumph and Tragedy*, is the best of the lot – more meat in it. Of course, the Americans will like it, because there is a lot about them. They are sometimes too confident. I have to tell them that.'

He took up some photographs taken yesterday for *Life* and handed them to me.

'Could you tell from them,' he asked, 'what had happened?'

August 24, 1953
I have noticed that the P.M. has become very short of breath on any exertion since his stroke two months ago, and though this is plainly due to degenerative changes in the muscle of his heart, associated with old age, I thought he ought to see Parkinson.[1] I went with him today. When Winston had gone into another room to dress, Parkinson said he was shocked by the way he had aged since he saw him four years ago; he felt quite sure he could never again act as Prime Minister. Mindful of 'Honest John's' uncompromising way with patients, I asked him not to be too gloomy. At that moment the P.M. came back into the room dressed. Parkinson told him his heart was years younger than his age, and more in that key, until the P.M. must have wondered why I had taken him to a heart specialist.

The P.M. turned to me: 'Well, Charles, we need not bother about my pump any more.'

Addressing Parkinson, he said: 'I have at the back of my mind whether or not I shall be able to take the Party meeting on October 10th. Everything depends on whether I can appear in public. I think I can, but I shall make no decision till the end of September. I shall carry on for a little,' he went on, as if his doubts had been dispelled by Parkinson's verdict. 'I'm only thinking of my work, my duty. I have nothing to gain from hanging on. I don't mind dying in harness – but I don't think I shall. I believe I shall have some warning.' Then he said: 'Well, Sir John, what can you do for me?'

[1] Sir John Parkinson, Cardiologist to the London Hospital.

August 25, 1953

Russell Brain was hardly more cheerful today than Parkinson had been. He doubts whether the P.M. will ever be able to make speeches in public or to answer questions in the House of Commons.

'Even if I am wrong and he resumes his duties in the House, I believe that in a few weeks the effort would be too much. His walking, which is still unsteady, might get worse, and he might be so fatigued that he could no longer carry on. In any case, probably a month from now his gait will be much the same, at any rate when he is tired.'

I reminded Brain that the P.M. was rather a law to himself. The second day after the stroke he insisted on walking about, where others at a like stage would be lying in bed; his will-power may well have called into play what he calls the back streets, and we doctors term the collateral circulation. Brain agreed this had no doubt helped him. He agreed, too, that if he retired now he would probably be dead within a year. Moreover, that year in retirement must be something of an anticlimax; he would no longer find his name in the papers; he would not be forgotten, but he would have little say in the control of events. On the other hand, if he decides that he can still do a useful job of work for the country it is for his doctors to help if they can, and certainly not to hinder.

Both Parkinson and Brain were so gloomy that I decided to ask Norman Brook how the P.M. had weathered his second Cabinet since the stroke. He is full of good sense, detached, and yet friendly to the P.M. The Cabinet, I was told, lasted two hours and forty minutes, and at the end the P.M. was quite fresh; indeed, he kept bringing up matters for discussion, when it was obvious that his colleagues wanted to get away – were, in fact, leaving one by one. He was animated, spry and had no difficulty apparently in concentrating as long as the discussion lasted. After the Cabinet the P.M. remained in close deliberation with Lord Swinton[1] and Rab until

---

[1] Secretary of State for Commonwealth Relations.

seven o'clock – the delicate task of reorganization of the Government engaged their attention.

'At seven o'clock,' Brook went on, 'I understand the P.M. went to his room and, calling for the proofs of *Triumph and Tragedy*, worked on them until dinner-time. Swinton and Rab dined with him and did not leave him until one o'clock. From three in the afternoon until one o'clock in the morning,' said Brook, summing up, 'the P.M. was in continuous debate on intricate matters of government.'

I told Brook I could add a postscript to his report. I found him at nine o'clock this morning, breakfasting, and right at the top of his form. He looked up brightly as I came into the room.

'I notice I am clear-headed in the mornings now – a great improvement. Even the irritation of my skin vanished when this other business came, as if the Deity felt I could not play with two toys at the same time. I feel 90 per cent. – at any rate 80 per cent. – of what I was.'

Of course, in measuring the strain a great deal depends on the attitude of his colleagues, particularly the senior members of his Cabinet. I asked Brook bluntly:

'Does the Cabinet want him to go on?'

Brook answered that it was difficult to answer my question.

'Some of them are, of course, interested. But when his illness began I was surprised how upset certain members of the Cabinet were – I am thinking of some of his colleagues whom I did not expect to be so friendly – and when it looked as if he might not go on, they were quite nonplussed.'

When Brook had told me this I said to him:

'There are two courses open to the P.M. Which do you think is in his interest?'

Brook confessed he had changed his mind.

'I think now he ought to go on for a while; it would probably be best for the country. As for the P.M.'s personal happiness, I have no doubt about the choice. He talked to me one day before his illness, saying he could not bear to see things mishandled, and might feel angry and frustrated. Besides all this,' Brook ended, 'I am astonished at the speed of his recovery after what had happened. In some ways he seems better than before his stroke.'

Pitblado gave me his view. He was surprised by the P.M.'s grip of things.

'He showed no signs of flagging at one o'clock this morning – indeed, I made up my mind we were going to have a very late night working at papers. At present he seems in pretty good form.'

I talked to the P.M. for a little.

'If I resign,' he said, 'I shall probably go to Barbados for two or three months.'

I asked him about his immediate plans. He answered:

'I'll go to Chequers after luncheon and I shall stay there till September 8. But I have not decided whether to go abroad in September – if my painting at Chequers is a success I shall stay there.'

He had been annoyed with Selwyn Lloyd, who had broken off in the middle of an important conference to join his wife for a holiday abroad.

'He pleaded tonsillitis. Very well: illness is one thing, a holiday is another. I am told that all the preparations for the holiday were made before there was any talk of illness. And this man was unknown the other day – had never held office. It's bad. I'm seeing Lord Salisbury about it.'

Having delivered himself of these strictures, the P.M. said:

'I'm clever at pushing away things and yet keeping an eye' – his eyes dilated – 'on what matters. The political situation is satisfactory. Labour is divided and uncertain of its theme. We are building three hundred thousand houses; but all the time old ones are falling into disrepair, while owners will do nothing as long as rent restriction is in force. It would be cowardly not to face this challenge.'

August 26, 1953

It is now my job to try to persuade the P.M. to be sensible about his health. I do not look forward to the task. He is a poor listener unless you agree with him, and I am conscious that the time is ill-chosen to preach care. For when I entered his room this morning he said that he felt as well as ever he did; as if nothing had happened; that the Cabinet had not tired him; that he had worked without a break for ten hours without ill effects.

'It's pretty good, Charles, I don't think things are too bad.'

He has felt since his stroke that his future depends on clearing a number of hurdles, which begin at Doncaster, where he will make his first appearance in public at the St Leger. He is quite prepared to make elaborate preparations and to have rehearsals of each crucial test. But it is not really as simple as that. I have felt from the first that he would probably rise to a special occasion. What I doubted – what I still doubt – was whether the cumulative fatigue of his onerous duties would in the end bring about defeat. Until he gets this into his head we can hardly expect him to make a deliberate attempt to nurse his dwindling capital. It is, moreover, a task foreign to his nature, for he has always been profligate of his resources.

'You are firing on four cylinders instead of six,' I began.

'Only four?' he asked in some consternation.

I explained that it was a figure of speech; there was no precision in the number.

'Suppose you have to make a journey to the north of Scotland. It isn't a question of whether you can get up the first steep hill on the road, though of course if you can't the whole journey collapses. The crux is, can you finish the journey? In other words, I can see you taking cabinets as well as ever you did, and making speeches as effective as any in the past. But if you do this, say, on a Monday, will you be able, on the Tuesday, to transact important business, or will you be too tired? That is our problem. There can be no certain answer, no definite yes or no. All we can do is to watch the result of a Cabinet, or of the journey to Balmoral, and try to appraise the fatigue so that we can form an opinion of what you can do. That is why seeing you yesterday at noon was little help to me; whereas if I had seen you after the Cabinet I might have learnt something.'

To my surprise, he showed no signs of impatience as I unfolded my theme. On the contrary, he listened attentively to what I said without interrupting me once. So encouraged, I went on to point the moral.

'If you decide not to resign, then you will have to think out how to do your work as Prime Minister without squandering your strength. You will have to learn how to live within your income.'

'If I go on,' he put in, 'I must do the job properly.'

'Yes, but that does not mean that you can take up the reins just where they were taken out of your hands by your illness. If you attempt to conduct the affairs of the nation as you have done before this happened you will probably fail. You would soon find yourself so weary that you yourself would decide you could not carry on. We have taken a good many risks together. But now it's my job as your doctor to warn you bluntly that if you are not willing to think out a new way of being Prime Minister, then you would be wise to resign before October.'

'I've been troubled a good deal, my dear Charles, with this decision. I am not sure the effect of giving up everything all at once would be very good for me.'

Moran: 'I'm not sure either. I must stick to the doctor's part in this business, but I am not certain that some of those I hear giving you advice have thought things out. It is easy to say that you could build up a new life at Chartwell after you retire, writing another book and seeing people you like. But would it work out that way? You might be unhappy with the way in which the Government was conducting the affairs of the nation, feel frustrated and even be tempted to criticize old colleagues in the House. You might even become, a little prematurely, part of history, while still very much alive. This isn't my job, but I hope you will do nothing in a hurry.'

With that I left him before I strayed too far from my brief.

September 1, 1953

It was half-past seven in the evening when I arrived at Chequers and found him in bed correcting proofs.

'I was frightfully well this morning,' he began, 'quite like old times. Now I feel flat. I have had to make a lot of small corrections in the book. I had left out any mention of Bernie Baruch, and I had to correct this and then fit in what I had written to the text. And all the time the bloody telephone kept ringing and I had to break off to talk about the reshuffle I am making of the Government.'

I saw he wanted to finish what he was doing, and was about to leave him, when he said:

'Will you go and get ready for dinner and come back when you have changed?'

On my return he was still in bed. He seemed too tired to make the effort to get up, though dinner was waiting for him. When he did get out of bed his gait was very unsteady. I asked him at what hour he had gone to bed. He admitted he had talked with Harold Macmillan and Anthony till a quarter to two.

'It won't do,' I expostulated.

P.M.: 'Now, Charles, you must not fuss me.'

Moran: 'Well, if you want to be fit by the party meeting you are not going the right way about it. I don't think you have got hold of the way Brain and I are thinking, and (mindful of Clemmie's advice) I'll put it on paper.'

'Oh, don't do that,' he said peevishly. 'I know what's bad for me. I must get into bed by midnight.'

There was no one at dinner except Clemmie and a relative living at Brighton, who had been staying at Chequers for the past week. The P.M. slumped in his chair and made no effort to talk. From time to time he sighed heavily, yawning and opening his mouth very wide, when Clemmie would pick up a fork and tap his knuckles as a rebuke for his bad manners. He took this in good part, but when at last he said something it was about blackamoors and niggers, so that he fell into further disfavour with Clemmie. She rose, saying, 'We will get the cards ready; don't be too long.'

He brooded for a while over his brandy and then, pulling himself heavily out of his chair, shuffled into the drawing-room, where he stood gazing rather stupidly at the card table.

'I'm very tired,' he said, 'I think I will go to bed.'

And without waiting for Clemmie's comment he trudged off to the private office. When he had gone, Clemmie put down her cards, and looking up at me said:

'How do you think he is?'

'Well,' I replied, 'I'd be happier if he'd give up Doncaster.'

'Why don't you tell him so?' she retorted sharply. 'Winston,' she went on, 'played a little croquet this afternoon, he played quite well – he has a good eye – but I thought he looked used up after it.'

When the P.M. did not come back, I went after him and found him dictating to a secretary. I told him that he was overtired and ought to go to bed. In a few minutes he rose wearily, swayed as if he might fall and walked unsteadily to his room. There he plopped down on his bed and rang for Walter.

'I'm going to bed,' he grunted.

Walter took off his slippers, and when with an effort the P.M. had disengaged his arms from his boiler suit, Walter tugged at his trousers till the garment peeled off. When he had discarded all his clothes he lay on his back, naked and breathing heavily. Walter then handed him his eye drops. The P.M., holding the drop bottle above each eye in turn, performed a ritual he had carried out for fifty years. Then he called for his hair-brushes, and lifting his head a little from the pillow, he brushed his head as carefully as if he had hair; and when he had done, and all the rites were completed, Walter pulled the clothes over him as he settled low in the bed, mumbling words and grunting with contentment.

September 2, 1953

The P.M. is rested after nine hours – beautiful sleep, but is a little subdued.

'I am sad,' he owned. 'The world is in a terrible state. Germany is rapidly regaining strength and will soon be reunited, while Russia and America and Britain outbid each other for her favour. Read that,' he said, handing me the *Daily Mirror*. 'No, not now, take it away when you go. The Americans are very angry with us. They have lost more than a hundred thousand men in Korea, and all they hear is the Socialists bleating about China.'[1]

The *Mirror* printed a number of extracts from the American Press, all about the increasing friction between Great Britain and the United States.

'There is no hope for civilization if we drift apart,' he said to himself.

Then he began questioning me about electricity. Was it nationalized?[2]

'I don't like this strike. It seems more like a conspiracy than a strike. It is surely a new technique. Certain key electricians are called out, while the rest go on working; they pay the wages of those on strike.'

He rang for a secretary.

'Is electricity nationalized?' he demanded.

Pitblado thought it was.

'Make certain,' he said impatiently. 'Find out the exact position.'

I asked him whether the strike would hold up everything.

'Oh, no, it can't go on for long. It would cause too much annoyance and interference with people's lives. I mean to take a hand,' he said, setting his jaw. 'Walter Monckton has gone for a holiday.'

A wide grin told me that something was coming. 'He is worn out giving way. His deputy is coming down after luncheon. Walter told me he used to make sixty thousand pounds in a year till he came into the Government.'

'You get no peace,' I interposed.

'No, but I don't dislike it. I wouldn't do it if I did.' He corrected himself. 'I do it because I believe I can be useful.

'Do you know anything about dreams, Charles, and their meaning? I have curious, elaborate, complicated dreams. I wake, but

[1] Total number of US troops in Korea 2,834,000.

Killed in action	27,704
Wounded	77,596
Deaths other than in action	9,429

[2] Electricity was nationalized April 1, 1948.

when I go to sleep again they go on. They are too complicated to explain. Yes, they are enjoyable. Sometimes they are not at all involved. For instance, last night I dreamt of a large woman of the Eleanor Roosevelt type, and this woman was President of the United States. It was all extremely vivid, but I want to know what it means. Yes, tell me about them. I was too tired last night. It is all the detail that worries me. I can't deal with it as I did, but I am all right this morning.'

He got out of bed to demonstrate how well he could walk when he gave his mind to it; he had nothing on but a silk vest, so that, as I followed him along the passage and out into the great hall, I could see how much more steadily he walked now that he was rested.

'Pretty good, I call it. But why was I so unsteady last night? Can you explain that, Charles?'

'Probably a combination of fatigue and alcohol.'

I told him why alcohol affected his gait since his stroke. When he was tired it made his walk very unsteady. He did not think there was much in this – but perhaps my warning may bear fruit.

'Come and see how I get into my bath.'

It was waiting for him, filled almost to the brim. He stepped in, and grasping both sides of the bath, slowly sat down.

He sat back and in a few moments called, 'Walter, put in some more warm.' And then he found he could turn the tap with his foot – even with the left foot. He held a big sponge to his face while he held his head under water. All the time the water overflowed on to the floor with a slapping sound.

'Parkinson tells me that baths are bad for the circulation. What nonsense! Why, I've had two every day for fifty years. I really feel very well now.'

I asked him, when he felt like that, if he noticed any difference since the stroke. He hesitated, and then said:

'Yes, my memory is not so good. I sat between two people last night during dinner and I could not remember their names, though I knew them quite well. I find it very embarrassing. I've just finished a minor reshuffle of the Government – quite important as far as it goes. The Overlords[1] are going. Leathers has wanted to resign for a long time. I only kept him by calling him a deserter. I hope there will be no leak. It is difficult to discuss it on the telephone with colleagues when they are all over the place, and keep it secret. But I like to carry them with me, and anyway it will all come out on Friday. You cannot imagine how complicated it all is – little details. Amory said he did not think he had done anything to deserve being made a Privy Councillor. I have told Anthony that he can be Foreign Minister again or lead the House; that I shall not decide anything about myself until I see how I get on, but that at present I feel able to carry on.'

He sent for a secretary.

'Has Mr Eden had time to reply yet?' he asked.

Nothing had come from him up to date, was the answer. Mr Eden has been too long in diplomacy to be precipitate in the expression of his feelings.

'Salter[2] will be here in a few minutes. I put him in to strengthen the economic side. I'm sure he has done his work well, but he isn't a House of Commons man. Now I've got to tell him that he will not be required after the reshuffle. I hope he'll soon join you in the other House. They are all very good about it,' he mused ' – not all. It appears that Sir Anthony Nutting goes about saying I am much slower since the stroke.' He smiled grimly. 'When you, Charles, and Dunhill persuaded me to have my operation in 1947, Nutting said: "Perhaps the doctors will do what the 1922 Committee could not do – remove the Prime Minister." Yet I promoted him,' he reflected, 'in spite of what he said about me.

'And there is another uncertainty. On October 23 my book will appear. It will have a great effect on the Americans. They will learn

[1] Ministers appointed in 1951 to supervise groups of ministries, i.e.: Lord Woolton, Food and Agriculture; Lord Leathers, Fuel and Power; Lord Cherwell, Scientific Research and Atomic Energy.
[2] Minister of State for Economic Affairs, 1951–2; Minister of Materials, 1952–3.

what I tried to prevent and how far Truman is responsible; how far he botched things. Have you read my Iron Curtain telegram, Charles? It may be said that the British Prime Minister should not have said things offensive to the Russians, while he is trying to bring them into line with America. Of course, my decision at the end of September may settle this. If I go, I can say what I like, what I believe to be history. It is this uncertainty whether I go or stay which is trying, particularly when it is my own decision which will decide it.'

I wanted to make my attitude clear.

'I am not against you going on in certain circumstances, for a short time. But I am against a premature appearance in public. When you do appear, I want you to bring it off. I'm not happy about this Doncaster programme.'

He listened glumly, protesting that Doncaster would do him no harm; he would only have to walk four yards to the Royal Box; after that he would be sitting until they drove to the train.

'I have never been on a Royal train. The last time I travelled with the Sovereign was in 1915, when I went with the King to inspect a division that was going to the Dardanelles. I remember we had a very good dinner. I shall fly back from Balmoral. There's nothing in it. You need not worry.'

I said nothing and we sat in silence for a long time. Then he rang for Pitblado.

'Don't telephone Lascelles till I tell you,' he said. 'If the strike goes on, it might seem like levity to go to a race meeting. I may decide to fly direct to Balmoral.'

From Pitblado I learnt that Lascelles was only waiting for a word from the Prime Minister to send out the announcement. Winston was still undecided about Doncaster. As I was leaving he called me back.

'Have you written your name in the Visitors' Book? Do. I would like you to. I may never come back here.'

He mumbled something about: '"Why am I loth to leave this earthly scene?" – yes, Burns.'

September 8, 1953

'I have taken a step forward, Charles. This morning's Cabinet was a considerable advance on the first two.'

That was how he greeted me when I called at No. 10 about three o'clock. 'Of course,' he went on, 'I am tired now.'

I warned him to be careful about alcohol when he went north. He smiled:

'I promise I'll be on my best behaviour. Come,' he said, 'and see the Chancellor.'

We found him waiting in the Cabinet Room. The P.M. addressed him cheerfully:

'I thought that I was all right this morning. Did you think so?'

Rab agreed in such a way that I felt the P.M. had really done the Cabinet well.

When I left them I had a few words with Pitblado. I asked him whether the P.M. had made a good impression on his week-end visitors. Pitblado pondered for a little.

'I think,' he said, 'Head and Macmillan left probably without making up their minds. The P.M. was older, but, on the other hand, I don't think they felt he must necessarily give up. Of course, the Chief Whip is different;[1] he sees so much of him.'

'Do his colleagues want him to carry on?' I asked.

Pitblado hesitated:

'I think Eden would be happy if he knew when the P.M. was going to retire, even if it was April. Something definite, that's what he wants. Rab is probably quite happy; he may be in a better position now than he would be if the P.M. resigned, and he has demonstrated that he is of Prime Ministerial timber.

'I have an idea, gathered from little things, that the P.M. is not certain himself what to do, but that his present intention is to carry on. Of course, this trip north may help; if anything goes wrong he may decide not to go on.

---

[1] P. G. T. Buchan-Hepburn (1st Lord Hailes, 1957), Conservative Chief Whip, 1948–55.

'As for his colleagues, they are bound to be influenced by what happens. If he can sail through the party meeting on October 10 and carry on in the House as before I don't think anyone will stir a finger. It is, after all,' Pitblado added, 'because he has so obviously been master of the House of Commons and has dealt so effectively with the Opposition since he became Prime Minister that the Party has been so docile.'

Is the P.M. really uncertain what to do? If Pitblado means that he is turning over in his mind yet once more whether he must go, no doubt he is right. But if he means that the P.M. is faltering in his resolve to stay on if he is physically able, then I am sure he is wrong.

There are times when I wonder if he is wrestling with still deeper uncertainties. For five years he has tried to justify to posterity in the six volumes of his book all that he did in the war. But have there been black hours when he has not been so sure? There was the sinking of the *Prince of Wales* and the *Repulse* and the lives of the English sailors lost in that unhappy affair. And there was— But the mind of the man of action does not work like that. When he has taken a decision on which thousands of lives depend, he puts it away from him. How otherwise could he keep sane? He may do it crudely, so that it jars on our senses, like Stalin when he demanded: 'What is one generation?' Or he may do it by thinking at another level, like Winston when he said, 'It pays us in the air to exchange machine for machine with the Germans.' And yet, when all this is said, my doubts remain. Does the artist, for that is what Winston is, really escape so lightly?

September 11, 1953
The P.M. goes by train this afternoon to Doncaster for the St Leger. This is his first public appearance since the stroke, and he is keyed up about it, though he may make a show of taking it in his stride. I found him in good form.

'I'll give you an exhibition,' he said cheerfully, as he threw off the bedclothes and swung his legs out of bed.

In his vest and reading jacket he proceeded to walk very carefully across the room, with a determined, concentrated expression on his face. In turning he swayed, and impatiently repeated the movement. When he reached the bed he stood on his right leg like a stork, and then on his left, when he was a little unsteady. Then he bent both knees, dropping down till he nearly sat on the floor.

'I'm pretty steady, don't you think, Charles? There is a longish walk at the station, but I think I can manage it.'

He got back into bed, and then he had another idea. Sitting on the edge of the bed and balancing his left foot above his bedroom slippers, embroidered with the letters WSC in red, he picked up a slipper between his big toe and the next.

'Not everyone could do that, even if they were all right,' he said with a touch of pride. 'Camrose came yesterday. He saw a great improvement. He particularly noticed that I was less emotional. Bill was afraid the enthusiasm of the Yorkshire crowd might move me, but' – rather scornfully – 'that's not what makes me emotional. It's when I read about something – I am rescuing Joan of Arc or something of the kind. When I was looking at my *History of the English-speaking Peoples* yesterday I twice became lugubrious. Camrose went so far as to say that I'm quite all right again. He is sure no one would dream of turning me out if I wanted to go on. But I will on no account carry on if I cannot do my work properly.

'I've had some very vivid dreams, the detail is quite extraordinary. And it's all reasonable. I dreamed last night that we were on a train in Russia with all the Russian Bolsheviks, Molotov, Malenkov, Zhukov, Voroshilov; the relationship between us was so vivid and so correct. There was a counter-revolution. We had some special bombs, none of them larger than a matchbox, with a very local effect. With them we destroyed the Russians, all of them. There was no one left. The counter-revolution was entirely successful. The dream went on for a long time. Can these dreams do any harm, Charles?

'They say we ought to have more young men in the House and in office. I answer: "Give me their names and I will at once see them personally." Of course, the truth is there isn't a large stock of the kind we want. Neville Duke[1] lunched with me yesterday. He is very able. I should be quite happy to have him in the Cabinet. But he might not be able to get a seat, and' – with a smirk – 'he mightn't turn out to be a Conservative. I don't think we are doing too badly in the House. Of course,' he ruminated, 'there is the cost of living. I am going to have an enquiry into the amounts of the common foods that are consumed – and see how the figures compare with those of twelve years ago and six years ago. This ought to tell us something.

'I've finished the book and I've started another one which will give me occupation for another three or four years, if I live. The *History* will be a standby if I don't go on in politics.'

He was silent for a little. 'Anthony is getting better, Horace Evans reported to me. But he has to stick to a strict diet, and this prevents him putting on weight. He is still very thin.'

He rang for Walter.

'Bring me the new cigars – the Filipinos. They are very mild,' he explained, 'you hardly know you are smoking, which, of course, is the object of smoking.'

I asked him about his movements.

'In a few moments the income-tax man is coming to take away most of what I have. It is all very complicated; you have to go back before last April – and then the surtax is for another year. That hit some of the Labour people. They had to come down from £5,000 to £1,000, and then, out of their reduced incomes pay their out-of-date supertax.

'I come back on Tuesday – it only takes two and a quarter hours. Do you think you could see me between five and six o'clock? I would like that very much. Then on Wednesday there will be a Cabinet and de Valera[2] is lunching with me. I am glad it has been possible to arrange this. He is nearly blind, I am told. They'd give

[1] A fighter-pilot who destroyed 28 enemy aircraft in the Second World War.
[2] Eamon de Valera, head of Government of the Republic of Ireland.

me a great reception if I went over to Dublin. On Thursday I go to Max for nine or ten days. Mary will come with me, but Christopher will have to come in another plane. Man and wife ought not to travel in the same plane when they have young children.'

September 15, 1953
'I have been worrying quite a lot about my problem – whether to give up my task. I have had a full mind. I don't want to. I'm quite clear about that. Why, in the morning I feel the same as I always did. In the last ten days I am more myself. I am better,' he went on with conviction.

'How do you know that?' I asked.

'I've got a different outlook on life now.'

I asked him what he meant. He held up his hand.

'Before, I did not coincide with myself: one hand didn't cover the other.'

Seeing I did not understand, he leant over the bed, and, taking a pencil, drew the outline of a man, very roughly, in red pencil. And then he drew another figure in blue.

'You see, Charles, one wasn't on the top of the other. My self-confidence has come back. I am more determined to go on.'

He got out of bed and walked across the room, a little unsteadily.

'You see, I am a little shaky, but I am tired now; I have done a very long day. I think in the north they felt that I was all right. I walked in the heather yesterday for three-quarters of a mile, and when I got out of the aircraft this afternoon I inspected the guard of honour and shook hands with everyone. You see I am not behaving like an invalid. I am doing everything I should normally do.

'Oh, no, I shan't overdo things in France. I shall not do anything there except my speech – thirty-five minutes perhaps. I feel now I could take on anyone who wanted to get me out. But I don't think they want me to go. I am really very popular. At Doncaster, when the Queen appeared in the box, I kept back, but when she came out and said to me, "They want you," I went into the box, and when I appeared I got as much cheering as she did.'

Winston talks like this to still the nagging fear that he is no longer fit to carry on.

'I went to church at Balmoral. It is forty-five years since I was there. Now there were long avenues of people, and they raised their hands, waving and cheering, which I was told had never happened before. I think I shall be all right on the 10th. I have important things to say that concern the country.'

'I'm not bothered about your speech to the party meeting. That isn't the trouble.'

'What is the trouble?' he demanded abruptly.

'You were a rich man once, physically, but you've gone through a fortune.'

'How I appear in public,' the P.M. persisted, 'is what matters. I am improving. Don't you think so? And I shall have a good story to tell them. They talked of a million unemployed and there aren't any. They foretold strikes in every industry, and there is a small strike in only one. Of course there is the cost of living. I don't believe in percentages, in protein and that kind of rubbish. I believe in tons of food consumed. Three hundred thousand tons more meat are consumed than when Labour was in office. That is a solid fact. Two years ago there was a sense of crisis. People felt anything might happen. That's gone. Of course there's plenty of criticism, but it's well meaning. I don't think the Russians want trouble.'

When he made his quip that he went to Crathie church forty-five years ago I remembered that the morning papers had a photograph of the young Winston outside the same church just forty-five years ago. He was President of the Board of Trade then. What an innings he has had!

September 16, 1953
The P.M. leaves for Monte Carlo tomorrow. I found him rested after the long Cabinet yesterday.

'I was on top of the Cabinet business. We discussed the housing programme. It was clear we could not go into it all again in detail, and they took the course I advised, and were quite happy about it. Most of the time was taken over Egypt. I can follow an argument as well as ever, and I made them laugh a lot. Didn't they say anything about it in the private office, Charles? They must have heard it. When the challenge to my position is over I shall take things quietly,' he said reassuringly. 'I don't want to hand in. I am better and I shall go on. Not for long. Perhaps a year. I don't want to go to the country. It would be trading on my popularity. I have been working quite hard. No, I have done no reading. There has been no time. I have had to see a lot of people. I don't see many people as a rule – and those I see are usually the same people. I don't like seeing a lot of strangers. De Valera lunched here. A very agreeable occasion. I like the man. They talk of my taking a holiday in France. It is absurd. I don't take holidays,' he said scornfully, 'coconut shies and that sort of thing. I shall work all morning and paint all afternoon. I've finished my book.'

'The history?'

'Oh, I haven't to do much writing. The first volume is practically done. All I have to do is to gather together a team of experts to correct it.'

When he had gone to his bath I sought out Christopher. He told me that the family felt that Winston ought to retire, but he had told them that it was selfish of them to want him to resign if he could help the country. Christopher questioned me about the P.M.'s future.

'I sit just behind him in the House of Commons, and I keep watching him, expecting that any moment I may have to carry him out. But I see quite clearly,' he continued, 'that he will do what he wants to do. You have more influence with him than anyone, but of course that's not very much.' And Christopher smiled on me benignly.

'You remember, Charles, when he was in bed, and it was uncertain whether he would come through, he used Anthony's illness as an excuse when he said he would have to carry on. I told you then, you remember, that if he hadn't this excuse he would find another. Well, now that Anthony's quite well enough to lead he just says: "I'm not going to retire. I shall carry on."'

'The Queen told Miss Gilliatt that the improvement he had made since she last saw him was astonishing.'

CHAPTER FIFTEEN

Ordeal of Margate

October 2, 1953

The P.M. returned from Monte Carlo yesterday, and I saw him this morning. Miss Gilliatt was not very cheerful about him. He had been in low spirits, and she thought his walking had not improved. Walter said that he had been very irritable. They spoke of him as abstracted and moody; he seemed to be brooding over Margate. Winston told me that he had done 4,000 words, enough for an hour's speech. I suggested that fifty minutes would do, and he did not demur. I gave him the political gossip. I do not think he took it in; his mind was on the conference.

October 6, 1953

'I am more myself,' he said this morning. 'Do you know what is the best cure for me? Sleep. Soon, I hope, I shall have a long sleep. They have taken things lying down.'

'You mean Anthony and the Cabinet?'

'Yes. There is going to be a bloody row in Guiana.[1] You must give me something to take before my speech at Margate. Rab has an idea. He thinks I might sit on a very high stool while speaking.'

---

[1] British Guiana was given its constitution along with adult suffrage in 1953. In April the left-wing Dr Cheddi Jagan came to power after the elections. Fears that Communism would be allowed to spread caused the British Government to suspend the constitution and reintroduce military government.

'Good God,' I ejaculated.

I discouraged him from experiments of that kind. The more everything is the same as usual the better.

'Well,' he said, 'I must try the speech out. If you could come on Thursday at three o'clock I would do everything just as it will happen on Saturday. I shall have a very light luncheon, perhaps pâté and a dozen oysters. Then I would stand for forty minutes and say my piece and see what happens. I don't even know if I can stand that time. I haven't been on my feet for more than a few minutes on end since it happened.'

Then he gave me the peroration.

'It is a good ending, I think. Oh, yes, the speech is finished.'

For weeks now, whenever an idea came to him he would try it out on us. Yesterday when it was all in type he began to ask if they would notice anything wrong with his articulation.

'It's not at all noticeable, Charles? Of course, you must not judge me now when I am only half awake.'

He was silent for a time.

'I am going to practise my speech in front of a looking-glass, watching myself speak as I did in bygone days, long ago.'

He is resolved that nothing shall be left to chance. C. P. Wilson, his throat surgeon, will be at Margate in order to spray his throat before he speaks, while I hope to redeem my rather negative reputation as a vendor of nostrums by inventing a pill which he will take an hour before he rises to address the meeting.

When I left him I sought out Jock. I found him with Pitblado. I told them that I was sure he would bring off the speech.

'What worries me is what is going to happen then?'

'Yes,' said Jock. 'If it is a terrific success he will throw caution to the winds. "I haven't felt so well for years," he will say.'

October 9, 1953

I came back from Truro by the night train to see if the dress rehearsal had gone all right and if he was in good fettle for tomorrow. He told me all about it:

'I did everything precisely as it will be done tomorrow. The speech is now timed for two o'clock, so I had a dozen oysters, exactly two mouthfuls of steak and half a glass of champagne at noon. Then I took your pill at one o'clock. It was a great success. It cleared my head and gave me great confidence. Then promptly at two o'clock I got on my feet and went through my speech in thirty-six and a half minutes. I made no allowance for applause. Clemmie sat behind me, so I had not the stimulus of an audience. But I know now that I can stand that time. I feel it is all right.'

I left him happy and confident, and returned to the West Country.

October 10, 1953

In the train returning from Bath I could not get Winston out of my head. I could not help fretting over him, though I knew there was no sense in moping, because I could not change anything. But sometimes his terrific concentration on his immediate purpose frightens me. He is like a gambler who doubles, then trebles, his stake until all that he has depends on the turn of the dice. The P.M. has put his shirt on this speech.

'Never before,' he said as I left him, 'has so much depended on a single bloody speech. You think it will be all right, Charles?'

The Cabinet did not matter, he could deal with them. It was the Party that would decide. I tried to reassure him, but he persisted. If he could hold the meeting all would be well. If he failed in that, life for him was over.

This is something more than the old panic before an important speech. He has been living with this speech almost from the start of his illness. Only a week after his stroke – now nearly four months ago – even before the paralysis cleared up, when most people would be thinking nervously of their chance of coming through, he was turning over in his mind how he could get back to No. 10.

There were black moods, of course, especially at first, when the uncertainty preyed on his spirits. But not for a moment did he allow these moods to deflect his purpose. His mind was irrevocably set.

The bother is that Winston has made me as windy as himself about this infernal speech. I have myself spoken in that hall at Margate, and I can picture the sea of faces peering up at him. Will they notice anything different in him? Will they see that his mouth droops at the left side, that he does not swing his left arm, that his walk is unsteady when he's tired? Will they hear that his articulation is not so clear when he comes to the end of his speech?

The train was late, and it was after ten o'clock when I called at No. 10. I found the P.M. with Clemmie, Diana, Duncan Sandys and Jock Colville, listening on the wireless to the account of the day's events at Margate. A glance at the P.M.'s face told me that it had come off. Flushed, a little fuddled perhaps, he was ticking over happily. There was about him an air of complete relaxation, which one does not associate with him. He greeted me affectionately.

'The pill was marvellous,' he said, putting his hand on my arm. 'What was in it? Did you invent it? Now, Charles, I know you don't like medicines, but you see what good they can do. You must have given a lot of thought to this pill. I won't ask for it often, I promise. Perhaps once a month when I have a difficult speech in the House. Anyway, Charles, what harm would it do if I took it more often?'

When I did not answer, he went on:

'Of course if I had not tried the pill out on Thursday I should not have dared to take it, because I remember Edwin Montagu took a stimulant before a debate in the House and everything went wrong. But on Thursday it completely cleared away the muzzy feeling in my head. I felt just as I did before the stroke. It gave me great confidence at Margate. I knew I could get through without breaking down. I owe a great deal to you, my dear Charles.'

He turned to Clemmie.

'Who is that speaking?'

Duncan answered for her:

'John Strachey.[1] He is debating with Ted Leather about your speech.'

[1] Secretary of State for War in Labour Government, 1950–1.

'Oh, switch it off.'

Clemmie took up the wireless and carried it under her arm into the next room. When they had gone, he said:

'Now I can sit back and get others to do the work. I shall ease off. I need only make occasional speeches. I shall not take part in the Guiana debate. I'll get Harold Macmillan to help Anthony. I may have to say something in the Suez debate, but I shall put Anthony in front. It's his business. If he likes this policy of scuttle in Egypt he must defend it.' The P.M. repeated: 'It's his affair.' He spoke with distaste.

Does Winston really mean to take things easily? He is always saying that you must attend the House of Commons regularly or you lose the atmosphere.

'I think it went very well,' he continued; 'they all said so. I have never, Charles, taken so much trouble over a speech before. I fussed over it all the time I was in France. I knew from the beginning this was the hurdle I had to surmount. It is an immense relief to have it behind me.'

A pile of Sunday papers lay in front of him.

'They are very good to me,' he murmured. 'Have you seen this in the *Sunday Pictorial*?'

'There appears,' I read, 'to be a slight twist on the right side of his face, which became more marked as his speech progressed.'

'It is not very noticeable, Charles?'

'If it were, they would have got it on the side affected,' I answered.

He picked up the *Observer* and gave me the *Sunday Times*. After a little he said:

'Shall we exchange?'

While he was absorbed in the *Sunday Times* I slipped out of the room. I wanted to find out from the office if they knew how the speech had gone down. The reports were reassuring. When his speech was at an end, the members of the conference gathered, I was told, in little groups in the passages and in the streets. There had been all kinds of rumours in the country. They wanted to know if they were true. Was it a fact that he had had a stroke? Was he finished? They went to Margate to settle finally whether he was fit to go on. Now they could see for themselves and hear for themselves. And there could be no doubt about the answer. 'He is not a bit changed, after all; he is still in good shape,' said one. 'I guess the Old Man will be with us next year,' said another.

What he said to them did not seem to matter. The points he made were familiar to me, he had tried them out on us more than once. But it seems that they were hardly mentioned in the talk outside the hall at Margate. And yet his central theme is surely a fitting curtain to the drama of his long life. For three score years he had been fascinated by war and all its ways; even in the last election his Party lost many votes because Labour had called him a warmonger. And now this astonishing man, who is about to enter his eightieth year, wants to be accepted over the world as the apostle of peace:

'If I stay on for the time being, bearing the burden at my age, it is not because of love of power or office. I have had an ample feast of both. If I stay it is because I have the feeling that I may, through things that have happened, have an influence on what I care about above all else – the building of a sure and lasting peace.'

He still has the power to express what everybody is thinking in words men remember:

'My prime thought is to simplify. The vast majority of all the peoples desire above all things to earn their daily bread in peace. The world needs a period of calm rather than vehement attempts to produce clear-cut solutions. . . . Five months ago, on May 11th, I made a speech in the House of Commons. I have not spoken since. This is the first time in my political life that I have been quiet for so long. I thought that friendly, informal, personal talks between the leading figures in the countries mainly involved might do good and could not easily do much harm.'

His plan is not dead. As Prime Minister he may still be of service to the Party as the embodiment of the common yearning for peace and for security. He will stay on 'for the time being'. It was noticed that he did not tell the conference how long that might be. But tonight, with the ordeal over and his mind at rest, he began to think aloud:

'I am interested in the scene, but I shall not make use of Margate to stay for long. Anthony has accepted the position, and there is no fuss in the Cabinet. But I shall go some time next year, perhaps when the Queen returns.'[1]

Perhaps it will not be left to him to decide. What I fear is the burden of his long day. I believe that it is the House of Commons which will in the end get him down.

He had put away the papers and was, I think, going all over Margate once more, when Diana came into the room.

'Papa, you are coming over very clearly. Do come and listen.'

He pulled himself wearily out of his chair and shuffled towards the door. Clemmie beckoned me to sit beside her on the sofa.

'Who is that speaking now? Cannot I have it louder?'

Duncan explained:

'It is Ted Leather.'

'And who is that now? I cannot hear very well what he is saying.'

'That's you, Papa, speaking,' Diana answered, smiling.

He leant forward, cupping his ears.

'In the first two years of Tory Government the British nation has actually eaten four thousand tons more meat than it did in the last two years of Socialist administration.'

A broad grin greeted this.

'I ought to have said four hundred thousand. I got out of that by saying how lucky I was that I was not complicating it with percentages. Personally, I like short words and vulgar fractions.

'What's that about Germany?'

Duncan repeated the words:

'It is nearly four years ago since I said that Western Europe could never be defended against Soviet Russia without German military aid.'

[1] The Queen was leaving on November 23 for her Commonwealth tour, lasting six months.

'They didn't like that, but they took it,' Winston mused.

The applause went on for a long time. The way he speaks, his little tricks and mannerisms, bring back to them the war and all they owe to him. And, of course, Winston's personality dwarfs those around him. Eden and Butler fall into place and seem to grow visibly smaller when he is about.

Jock brought in a message:

'It's from the President. It came from the American Ambassador.'

The P.M. seemed to wake up as they switched off the wireless.

'Give it to me.'

Jock grinned at his impatience, adding:

'Ike doesn't know Foster Dulles's commitments, but he is sure he will be sympathetic when he gets your invitation.'

'We asked Dulles to come over to see Eden,' the P.M. explained. 'I have given up the idea of meeting Ike at the Azores.'

This was evidently news to Duncan.

'What about the Azores?' he asked.

'Oh,' said the P.M., 'I gave it up because it meant asking Ike a favour.'

'You're tired, dear,' Clemmie put in.

'I'm not in the least tired,' he protested vigorously, 'I don't feel like going to bed for a long time. I shouldn't sleep if I did.'

A small black kitten jumped on to his knee. It was found on the steps of No. 10 and had been taken in.

'It has brought me luck,' he said, stroking the purring cat.

He had assumed proprietorship.

'It shall be called Margate.'

Rufus, the P.M.'s poodle, had gone to bed in a sulk. The P.M. soon tired of the debate on the wireless. There was too much Strachey and Leather. Long before these inventions, he said, pushing the wireless away, the people received a broad and pretty accurate impression of what was happening, soon after it had happened. Richard III governed the country quite well, but the people had got it into their heads that he had murdered the two princes in the Tower, and so in the end he was killed at Bosworth. Winston talked for a time about Henry VIII and his wives. No one had minded them, because of the importance of an heir.

'I've sent Rab away for a week – he is very tired.' He said this as if he could not help being sorry for his Cabinet, who were always going away sick. It was time for bed.

CHAPTER SIXTEEN

The P.M. Relaxes

October 11, 1953

Called on the P.M. to see if he was the worse for wear. Found the black kitten licking itself on his bed. He was reading *The Dynasts*; as far as he had got he did not like it.

He hates the policy of 'scuttle' which the Foreign Office and Anthony have persuaded him to accept about the Suez Canal,[1] but tries to console himself with the fact that the eighty thousand troops can be used elsewhere, and that it will mean a substantial economy. The Foreign Office, he thinks, 'is an excellent institution for explaining us to other countries, but when its head is weak it seems to spend its time seeking agreements abroad at our expense.'

I asked the P.M. if he would have a more peaceful time with Margate behind him.

'Oh,' he answered, 'things sound less alarming around the Cabinet table than in the Press.'

Things were, indeed, very quiet. Eden, back at the Foreign Office, wasn't allowing much to go beyond him, and the P.M. is not accepting any engagements – he will not even go to Guildhall for the Queen Mother's Freedom.[2]

---

[1] The Anglo-Egyptian Agreement was eventually signed on July 27, 1954. All British troops were to be evacuated from the Canal Zone within twenty months.
[2] The Queen Mother received the Freedom of the City of London on October 28, 1953.

But it is only a lull. Jock says it is not true that they have taken things lying down. Anyway, it is not true of Eden. He is by nature not given to being disloyal. But his role as heir apparent is like that of the Prince of Wales in the last years of Queen Victoria's reign when she would not let him see official papers. I asked Jock what was likely to happen.

'Oh,' Jock answered, 'nothing much for six or eight weeks. Then if the P.M. isn't in control of the House there would be murmuring, and the Chief Whip would have to tell him that the Party was not happy. At that point Anthony might force a showdown, or he might even resign – history might repeat itself,' Jock mused.

Anthony might strike. Somehow it is not a word we associate with Eden, but I am told that he is being pushed from behind. Presently the Party will take charge.

It appears that Rab Butler is sitting on the fence with one leg dangling on each side. He likes cricket similes. He is trying to keep a straight bat, he says. He is not trying to make runs.

'The Queen's going away from the country complicates things. The P.M. says that if he is going to retire he will do so soon, so as to give the new P.M. time to settle in before the Queen leaves the country. But he won't,' said Jock smiling.

October 20, 1953

If there is going to be a tussle with Anthony I must patch up the P.M. It is not going to be easy to put him on his feet. Yesterday he telephoned to me three times within an hour; the third time to ask if he could take a tablet of aspirin at dinner-time. He was 'so stupid'. I was in bed with a feverish cold, and he was plainly torn between the fear of picking up my cold and an urge to talk about his troubles. He said he had felt sickly all day, but when I asked him whether that was the whole trouble he admitted that it was not, that he would like to go into things with me. He does not usually say that sort of thing, and I was not very happy about him, particularly when he told me that the Cabinet would probably go on for four hours. So this morning

I got a mask from Bell and Croyden, and muzzled in this fashion I called at No. 10.

Jock told me that he had been worried about him yesterday. He had been reading *The Dynasts* and kept getting fiction and reality mixed up. He was expecting Queen Charlotte to come in through the door.

'You know, Charles, I was like that,' Jock said, 'after the war when I got a kind of delayed shell-shock. The P.M. kept repeating himself. He talks about his hurdles. Margate was one, and his first appearance in the House of Commons this afternoon, to answer questions, is another. I felt he would do Margate all right, and I am sure he will get through this afternoon with credit.

'But I am not too happy about him. He was not in very good form at the Cabinet.'

Jock thought for a moment.

'You know, he is always acting a part, but I am sure he was not acting last night after dinner when he suddenly said: "I think, Jock, we are near the end of the road." Before dinner he said that if he retired he would still have his seat below the gangway and his *History of the English-speaking Peoples* to keep him occupied. But I sometimes think,' Jock mused, 'it would be better for him to go out in harness.'

I found the P.M. reading *The Times*, while the black kitten, lying on its back, pawed the fluttering edges of the paper.

'I'm not frightened of the House of course, any more than a child is frightened of its nursery.'

October 21, 1953

As I entered No. 10 Pitblado was in the hall. He told me that he found the P.M. reading *The Dynasts* after breakfast; it would be about ten o'clock, he thought. That was quite new. He supposed it was a sign that the P.M. wasn't brimming over with energy. He had a long day before him, but it was no use trying to persuade him to give up the Trinity House[1] meeting when the Queen was going. Last night he came back from an Audience overflowing with her praises.

[1] The general lighthouse and principal pilotage authority. Both the Sovereign and Churchill were Elder Brethren of Trinity House.

Walter explained that the tailors were in his room preparing his uniform for the meeting.

If the P.M. was an ordinary mortal one would say that the game is up. But he will not admit that he was unduly tired on Monday, and now that they were over the P.M. said he hadn't been really worried about his first Questions in the House.

'You see, Charles, I have been so long at the game that it has become almost automatic. Besides, I am stronger. Why, I walked the whole length of the corridor to the Smoking Room and no one, I think, noticed anything.'

That is one of the difficulties in dealing with him, he won't put all his cards on the table for anyone. Perhaps he talks like this to comfort himself that he is still up to the job. To persuade others is, by comparison, a simple task.

There appears to be general agreement that the P.M. was quite himself in the way in which he handled Questions. Harvie Watt, who was his parliamentary secretary during the war, thought he had done it very well: 'much better than I expected'; while the lobby correspondent of the *Manchester Guardian*, whose sharp eyes do not miss much, was satisfied that Mr Churchill had not suffered any change since he was last on view at Westminster. And when he announced that he had gone back on a firm pledge to the House of Commons – the pledge to restore the University seats – it seemed to be merely the recording of an act of statesmanship.

I asked him: 'Did it tire you jumping up and down for nearly a quarter of an hour answering Supplementaries?'

'Oh, no, not at all; but it did make me rather short of breath.'

He picked up the *Guardian*, but when I rose to go he half put it down as he said:

'Thank you, Charles, I hope you got no harm yesterday coming out to see me. You hit the bull's eye with the pill.'

October 23, 1953

Clemmie telephoned that if my cold was really better she would like to talk to me about Winston. She had picked up influenza when she was staying with the Harveys in Paris and she was not right yet. Winston had been very glad to see her back, and then for two days he had sat at meals huddled up, without a word for anyone.

She hesitated. 'He promised me that he would retire when Anthony was fit to carry on, and now when Anthony is perfectly fit he just goes on as before. Monsieur Bidault will not come to London because he cannot get a word in edgeways. The Harveys told me that.'

A smile flickered over her tired features. She became grave again:

'You know, Christopher is very fond of Winston, and he has promised to tell me if his stock falls in the House of Commons. He has given me his word that I shall be told if they want to get rid of him. But the trouble is, Charles, that his stock has actually risen, until they say it has not been so high for a long time. Do you know what I mean by the 1922 Committee? They are very Right. Well, when they met to discuss Egypt the Chief Whip wanted Winston to open the discussion. But he refused. Anthony ought to open, Winston insisted. And then at the end he got up and gave them a tremendous wigging. They knew that he was not a Little Englander, but he told them bluntly we simply could not afford to stay in Egypt. He looked to them for support in a difficult situation, not for that kind of carping. They were tremendously impressed. The old lion could still issue from his den, and when he did his growl was as frightening as ever.'

She laughed at the thought.

'They cannot make it out at all, Charles. They have heard all kinds of rumours about a stroke and paralysis, and now he seems in better form than ever. They described how he strode up a long corridor in the House of Commons, swinging his arms as if he was twenty.'

Her pride in Winston struggled through the clouds of irritation.

'Of course he has worries. But what really upset Winston was that Walter has given a month's notice. He was very hurt about it. You see, Walter has been with him for four years, and we have been very kind to him. I am scouring London for someone to take his place. Valeting Winston is not very easy.'

And then she came to business.

'How is he really, Charles?'

I answered that I was not very happy about him.

'Then why do you not tell him so?' she rapped out sharply. 'Cannot you do something? You will wait until he gets another stroke.'

Her manner softened.

'It may not be a bad time to get him to retire. He won't let them push him out, but when all his colleagues are saying nice things about him he is much more likely to think it is time to go.' She smiled. 'Winston sent for Dr Barnett and told him: "My wife wants me to resign, but I am not going to." Dr Barnett thought perhaps the seed had been sown. You know, I don't want to hound him into resigning.'

October 27, 1953

When I called at No. 10 he had just finished breakfast and was reading a book. He put it down reluctantly. He had to master a difficult problem before the Cabinet met. Then perhaps two and a half hours with the Cabinet; then half a dozen questions in the House; then an audience with the Queen, and after that a deputation had come from Leeds to give him the Freedom of their City. It was going to be a long day. He gave a great yawn.

'I have been reading *Quentin Durward.* I like it very much, as much as *Ivanhoe.*'

Christopher came in.

'Have you read the paper on meat yet?'

The P.M. grunted that he was about to do so. Christopher joined me a few moments later in the secretaries' room. With his mixture of good humour and outspokenness he said:

'Considering how much a Prime Minister has to do, and how little Winston does, I think we are rather clever. I have been trying to get him to read this document on meat, but he keeps saying, "I must read another chapter [of *Quentin Durward*]." He is alert enough when he brings himself to do anything and he has been in a good mood, but, Charles, he has no zest for work. He does not want to be bothered with anything. I do not know where this will end. I cannot get him to read important papers. Of course we must remember his health isn't everything.'

Moran: 'You know, Clemmie tackled me.'

Christopher: 'To get him to retire?'

Moran: 'Yes, she said I would wait till he had another stroke before I did anything.'

Moran: 'If you and Jock and Norman Brook agree at any time that he is doing himself no good in his job, then I will try to get him to retire.'

Christopher: 'That time has not come yet.'

I saw Jock before I left.

Moran: 'I don't think he will be happy if he retires.'

Jock: 'No, I'm sure he won't. I love him dearly, but if he goes out in harness, it's probably the best thing.' (And then half to himself): 'I don't know what happens when a Prime Minister is lazy, but I suppose he can carry on like that for a bit.'

CHAPTER SEVENTEEN

A New Winston Sees Visions

November 3, 1953

Called at No. 10 to find out if the P.M. was happy about the speech he is making today on the address. He said there had been a dispute. Anthony did not want him to talk about a change of heart in Russia. He and the Foreign Office do not believe that there is any evidence that anything of the kind has happened there. The P.M. reached for the small sheets on which his speech was written out.

'This is what I was going to say.'

He read a page of his speech.

'I shall tone it down. I don't want any difference or any unpleasantness.' There was a smirk. 'The F.O. has a gift for saying that something is neither better nor worse. There is no evidence, they argue, that it is better; on the other hand, no one could say it was worse. I shall speak for fifty minutes. You will listen to me? I shall look up to the gallery.'

It was a placid Winston I left, sitting up in bed, turning over the sheets of his speech, loosely held together by a green thread. He was cheerful, and when he is in good heart before a speech I have few qualms. I met Miss Portal on my way down. She said that this is the first speech that Winston has made in the House of Commons since his stroke, but that it had taken much less out of him than the Margate address. He had taken trouble over it, of course, but he did not get worked up preparing it, and seemed happier about the way it would be received. Even Anthony's intervention was no more than a pin-prick. In the old days there would have been an explosion.

The fact is that he has greatly changed since his illness.

'Winston is positively good tempered these days,' Lord Woolton exclaimed.

Even his secretaries can relax, for when things go wrong they can tell him without a scene. 'He is not easily put out,' they say with an affectionate smile, as if it had always been so with him. Last week a Labour Member of the House of Commons came up to me: 'What have you done to Winston?' he asked. 'There is something serene about him.'

A discerning friend of Winston's answered for me: 'Of course he has mellowed. Thrust a man out of political life into the wilderness for eleven years and then let him be taken into men's hearts wherever they are free and what do you expect to happen? It is difficult to think ill of a world that is so friendly and so anxious to sing hosannas.'

House of Commons, November 3, 1953

In his speech in the House today we were listening to a man chastened, I had almost said cleansed, by a grim experience. What he had to say he resolved to put, as far as he was able, in the most persuasive way possible. He did not believe the nation was so divided as some people would like to make out. There were a great many things on which most people agreed. Fourteen million vote Tory, and about another fourteen million vote Socialist, and it was not really credible that one of these two masses of voters possessed all the virtues and all the wisdom, while the other lot were dupes and fools. It seemed to him nonsense to draw such sharp contrasts between them. It was difficult for specialists in faction to prevent members getting very friendly with each other. His course was clear:

'We have to help our respective parties, but we have also to make sure that we help our country and its people. There can be no doubt where our duty lies between these two.'

His party, it is true, was opposed to the nationalization of industry, but where they were preserving it, as in the coal mines, the railways, air traffic, gas and electricity, they were doing their utmost to make a success of it, even though (and here he beamed on the House) this might somewhat mar the symmetry of party recrimination. When he came to speak of the highly controversial subject of the repair of houses and their rents the Opposition could hardly find the heart to differ from the 'old man'.

'We have to face the fact that two and a quarter million houses were built a hundred years ago, and another two million are between sixty-five and a hundred years old. Surely this is a matter which ought to interest the whole House. If the Opposition has a counter-proposal, let them put it forward, and we shall give it our earnest attention. Would it be very wrong if I suggested that we might look into this together, with the desire to have more decent homes for the people counting much higher in our minds than ordinary partisan political gain?'

It was impossible to resist this reasonable way of looking at things. Never had his authority over the House been so obvious.

Only when the House was in this mood did he begin to unfold the great theme which he himself regarded as his valedictory message to his country. It seemed as if he was brooding on the future of the world, which he knew he must soon leave. The death of Stalin had led to the assumption of power by a different régime in the Kremlin. Might the end of the Stalin epoch lead to a change in Soviet policy, a change of heart?

'Have there been far-reaching changes in the temper and outlook of all the Russians? I do not find it unreasonable or dangerous' (though he would not say so too positively because of Anthony) 'to conclude that internal prosperity rather than external conquest is not only the deep desire of the Russian people but also the long-term interest of their rulers. It was in this state of mind that six months ago I thought it would be a good thing if the heads of the principal States and governments concerned met the new leaders of Russia to establish personal acquaintance.'

And then the thought of Anthony returned, and he warned the House that there was a risk that such a conference might end in a still worse deadlock than existed at present. Yet he could not pretend to the House that he thought it a great risk; even the hydrogen bomb made war improbable:

'The rapid and ceaseless developments of atomic warfare and the hydrogen bomb – these fearful scientific discoveries cast their shadow on every thoughtful mind, and yet the probabilities of another world war have become more remote. Indeed, I have sometimes the odd thought that the annihilating character of these agencies may bring an utterly unforeseeable security to mankind. When I was a schoolboy I was not good at arithmetic, but I have since heard it said that certain mathematical quantities, when they pass through infinity, change their signs from plus to minus or the other way round. It may be that this rule may have a novel application, and that when the advance of destructive weapons enables everyone to kill everybody else, nobody will want to kill anyone at all.'

If the bomb had convinced men that war had become impossible the resources set free could be used to enlarge the well-being of the people. The time had come to spread before the House his own splendid vision of an alternative to mass-destruction, the swiftest expansion of material well-being that had ever been within their reach or even within their dreams:

'By material well-being I mean not only abundance, but a degree of leisure for the masses such as has never before been possible in our mortal struggle for life. . . . We and all nations stand at this hour of human history upon the portals of supreme catastrophe and of measureless reward. My faith is that in God's mercy we shall choose aright.'

As I left the Chamber I was stopped by a Labour Member. His eyes were full of tears.

'He is a very great man,' he murmured. 'Can't you take him away and let him have a good long rest? The country needs him.'

I found the P.M. in his room, tired but in good heart.

'That's the last bloody hurdle. Now, Charles, we can think of Moscow.'

He gave a great yawn, opening his mouth very wide.

'Your pill cleared my head. Now I can turn my mind to other things. You do not realize, Charles, how much depends on the Russians. I must see Malenkov. Then I can depart in peace.'

His face was grey. I wanted him to go back to No. 10 to rest. But he was worked up and was all agog to hear what they were saying in the lobbies about his speech.

'The House liked it, I think. That mathematical bit was my own; it will go round the world.'

He emptied his glass and, rising with an effort from his chair, tottered out into the Lobby.

CHAPTER EIGHTEEN

Now for Moscow

November 4, 1953

This speech is a step forward. Winston has been profoundly shaken by this illness, and it will be some time before he can build up his old self-confidence. But every time he goes over what he calls 'one of these hurdles' he gains in assurance. His first appearance in public at Doncaster, his first Cabinet, the speech at Margate, the first occasion when he answered Questions in the House, and this speech, which is the first he has made in the House since his illness, each has been an ordeal which he has met without flinching. I have never felt so near to him. Most people, after a stroke, are only concerned with keeping alive. He never for a moment seems to give a thought to this. I love his guts. I believe that he is quite invincible.

It is single combat. No one, it seems, is with him in his valiant fight to seize this last opportunity of bringing about world easement. Camrose declared that Winston would never return to the House of Commons, Max said he was finished, Alex blurted out, 'Cannot you make him resign?' Indeed, I sometimes feel as if I were aiding and abetting him in a foolish course of action which must end in disaster. Then at other times he himself gets the path he has chosen in its true perspective.

'What does it matter if anything does happen to me?' he exclaimed. 'There is no disgrace in going out trying to do one's job.'

When I saw him this morning he seemed rested. He was devouring the morning papers, which were full of his speech.

'I am getting better every day, Charles. Don't you think it is a remarkable recovery? Have you ever seen any similar case? I take things for granted now which even a fortnight ago worried me. I still become lachrymose at times, and if some of the thoughts in my speech had occurred to me for the first time in the House I should have been tearful. But I'd been over it all before, so I wasn't troubled.'

This is the first time he has spoken of this affliction with detachment.

'I am thinking of substituting port for brandy. You wouldn't be against that?'

I answered that it was the lesser of two evils, whereat he grinned broadly. The smile vanished.

'Before I can go to see Malenkov the President must agree. This is very secret. I may go to the Azores. It would take Ike ten hours to fly there – or perhaps to Heaven. Only six hours for us. The *Vanguard* would be waiting for us there to provide accommodation. Of course it depends on Ike's other commitments. There will be a deadlock with the Russians, and Dulles will not be against the Azores once he sees no possibility of himself meeting Molotov.'

'When would you go?'

'Oh, perhaps in the middle of December. I might go by sea. I don't want to go to Washington as long as there is a waddle in my walk. I have decided to walk a thousand yards every day, in the garden or in the Park. I think if my muscles were toned up I might walk better. I couldn't deal at present with all the reporters at Washington.'

He caught sight of the Queen's photograph in a paper.

'The country is so lucky,' he murmured.

He held out his hand. He wanted to read the papers.

November 10, 1953
The P.M. has fixed up with the President to meet at Bermuda on December 4. He is quite excited about it.

'I put out my paw to Ike, and it was fixed up at once. My stock is very high. There is a feeling that I am the only person who could do anything with Russia. I believe in Moscow they think that too.'

What an asset his optimism is! It keeps out the facts. He has set his heart on Moscow, but Ike thinks it can do no good, while Anthony is as certain it will do harm. So Winston has a difficult hand to play.

'I shall go by air. It costs £30,000 if we go by *Vanguard*, and only £3,000 by air. Besides, at this time of year we might be battened down for most of the voyage. Ike wanted to keep it quiet till he was ready, but the French leaked. I have been bothered with indigestion, and have started my exercises again. I have eleven Questions today, with Supplementaries it means twenty.'

I asked him would they bother him? He made a contemptuous little gesture. Then he grinned.

'I have only to tell one man to mind his own business.'

November 12, 1953

Jock is not very happy about Bermuda. Aldrich[1] was very frank about things. He admitted that Winston's stock had fallen in the States. They don't like his views on Moscow. Nor does it help that Ike has been found out; he is no politician, he is a soldier. This means that Dulles is in charge. I feared that very little might come of Bermuda. Aldrich was afraid that this might be true.

He knows what many Americans forget: that Winston's prestige in the world is a wasting asset, in the sense that he will not be in public life much longer. When America is ready to do something he may be gone. Ben-Gurion[2] told Black Rod[3] recently that the only statesman he trusted was Winston Churchill, and Horrocks said that it was the same everywhere in the Middle East.

November 18, 1953

The P.M. looked up as I entered his room this morning.

'I'm not sure I'm getting any better,' he said, 'I am very stiff, and

[1] Winthrop Aldrich, American Ambassador in London, 1953–7.
[2] Prime Minister of Israel.
[3] Lieut.-General Sir Brian Horrocks.

my walk is very tottery, and my body feels tired. And when I do any work my head gets tired. I am at my worst from one o'clock till about half-past three, just when Questions come up. I'm confused, so that I don't want to talk to anyone when I am lunching. From five o'clock on I am all right, especially if I get in an hour's sleep. It would have been easy to retire after Margate when I had made my speech; now I must carry on until the Queen returns in May.'

His condition is unlikely to change, and I have told him this in the plainest terms.

'I am bewildered by the world; the confusion is terrible,' he complains. 'There is the news from Egypt, and now the F.O. wants a war with Israel. Ernie Bevin apparently made a treaty with Jordan. I don't want war.

'There were some old fellows here last night, when the Jockey Club dined here. General Baird, who is ninety-four, got up the stairs all right and made a short speech.'

The P.M. said there would be no 'Parl.' for a month at Christmas. He looked out of the window at the fog.

'I hate the winter,' he said. 'I may go to Max's house at Cap d'Ail when Parl. rises. I would like to win this by-election,[1] but I don't think we shall.'

He jerked out unconnected sentences as if it were too much trouble to pursue anything for long.

November 23, 1953
Last night, after I had gone to bed, the telephone rang. The P.M. thought he was getting a cold and would like to see me in the morning. When I arrived at No. 10 I knew from the air of expectancy in the hall that he might arrive at any moment. He elbowed himself out of the car awkwardly and shuffled down the passage to the lift. The journey from Chartwell had tired him. He said he felt chilly and got into bed, though the Cabinet was due to start in ten minutes' time. I told him he didn't give himself a chance

[1] Holborn, won for Labour by Mrs Lena Jeger in November, 1953.

coming up from Chartwell like this at the last moment. He grumbled something under his breath – he doesn't like criticism. But I stuck to my point. Two hours in the Cabinet would not help matters, and by the time he got to the airport to bid farewell to the Queen he would be unsteady on his feet – I explained that I was afraid of the Press. He gave me a look: Must you really go on like this? it seemed to say.

Canopus, *December 2, 1953*

This may be my last journey with Winston. We began life humbly enough, in an unheated Lancaster bomber, and end it, twelve years later, in high state in the strato-cruiser *Canopus*. Messages no longer pass to the captain asking at what height we are flying; 18,000 feet or 11,000 feet (both were recorded last night), it is all one to us, pressurized at 5,000 feet. Most of the seniors and quite a number of the juniors came to me last night for sleeping pills – this weak-kneed generation that needs dope for a few hours in the air.

Lunched at a table for four; the Prof. and the P.M. on one side, Anthony and I opposite. After greeting Anthony cheerfully, Winston took up his book, *Death to the French*, by C. S. Forester, and kept his nose in it throughout the meal. The Prof., who is getting deaf, could not hear what we said, so giving up the attempt to bring him in, I talked to Anthony.

The P.M., he said, was very anti-Frog. 'The French are pretty hopeless,' Anthony went on, 'but France is a geographical necessity. As for the Americans, he thought "they mistake movement for action"; as long as something is happening they are quite happy. They still loved Ike, but were beginning to have doubts about him.'

Everything Anthony said was sensible, and his judgement of men was discerning. For instance he liked Monty, but there was one thing about him he did not like – he was jealous. What he said of Gott and others was rather ungenerous. 'Alex,' he went on, 'had no brains.'

When I found that out for myself during the war I spoke of it to no one, I had a feeling I must be wrong, it seemed so improbable.

And then one day Alanbrooke blurted it out, and after the war Freyberg, of all people, who had seen much of Alex in the Desert in Italy, said the same thing in almost the same words as Anthony. Alanbrooke was quite sure that Alex and Sir John Harding, his Chief-of-Staff in Italy [*sic*], were too dangerous a combination and must be separated, and here they were ten years later hand in glove. Anthony said Robertson should have been C.I.G.S. instead of Harding who was very weak, but he didn't hear of the appointment till it was made. Winston would consult him about some platoon commander, and then appoint Harding without a word. Anthony isn't like Winston, he looks behind the façade. He isn't taken in by Pug's little ways as most people seem to be. Pug went about saying he must resign from N.A.T.O. but, said Anthony smiling, 'he's there for life. Nothing will get him out. He put it about that he couldn't get away to go to Bermuda and then he moved heaven and earth to get an invitation. But it doesn't alter my affection for Pug.' Looking across at the P.M. buried in his book, he said:

'They say to him exactly what they said to Neville Chamberlain, that he is the only man who can save the situation. And,' Anthony added, 'the people who are saying this to Winston are the same who said it to Neville.' He went on: 'I wanted to give up the F.O. and take some office in the Cabinet which would give me experience of the home front, but' (*smiling*) 'Winston has got used to me; he said Salisbury could not be Foreign Secretary because he was in the Lords. He was so much against my leaving the F.O. that I gave in.'

There it is in a sentence: the essential difference between the two men is exposed. If the roles were reversed it is impossible to picture Winston meekly accepting such a handicap in the climb to power. Once, it is true, Anthony brought himself to the point of resigning from the Cabinet, but day in, day out, he lacks the hard core which in Winston is hidden by his emotional nature and by his magnanimity.

Where people are concerned Winston Churchill exists in an imaginary world of his own making. Sometimes his ideas, too, have no roots in reality; the supposed change of heart in Russia may be one of them. Both as a judge of men and as a cool appraiser of events, Anthony is much sounder and more discriminating than Winston, but the personality of the P.M. and his power over words raise him into another world, which will always be closed to Anthony, who was born, and will remain, a secondary figure.

I was roused from my thoughts when Christopher appeared. He wanted the P.M. to read some briefs for the Conference, but Winston did not seem at all keen on work. We were bumping on the edge of a storm, and possibly his mind went back to the night in February, 1943, when we were crossing the Atlantic and were struck by lightning. His flying memories are not at all happy, and however he may hide it, he is full of apprehension.

The P.M. looked down. We were crossing the coast of Newfoundland, and were flying over a desolate expanse of rocks and great pools. 'Bloody country,' he ejaculated, picking up his book, while Anthony retreated into Turgenev's *A Sportsman's Sketches.* He held it so that I could read the title. 'It's Clarissa's,' he told me.

CHAPTER NINETEEN

Bermuda – Hope Deferred

Bermuda, December 3, 1953

A few steps lead from the balcony of the Mid-Ocean Club to the golf links. At the top I stopped to pass the time of day with a Welsh Fusilier on guard, who apparently knew me. At the bottom I found that I had forgotten my golf balls, but before I could re-enter the building I had to produce my pass to the Fusilier. When the President leaves, all these precautions will disappear.

Archie Compston was in command on the first tee. He had prospered as the professional to the Coombe Hill Golf Club. Now he winters in Bermuda as the local instructor. His flattery is as grooved as his swing. He promised Christopher, the merest beginner in the game, that if he put himself in his hands in the summer he would undertake that he emerged the winner of White's handicap.

The Americans have taken over the first floor, the French have the second and the third belongs to us. I went to the P.M.'s room to see if he was ready for dinner.

'There will be great difficulties arranging things here,' he began.

'You mean the agenda?'

'I don't like the word.'

He had been turning over in his mind the question of an atomic war. At dinner he took up the theme:

P.M.: 'There was a time when the Western Powers could have used the atomic bomb without any reply by Russia. That time has gone. How many atomic bombs do you think the Russians have?'

Prof.: 'Oh, between three hundred and four hundred. The Americans may have three thousand or four thousand.'

P.M.: 'If there were war, Europe would be shattered and subjugated; Britain shattered, but, I hope, not subjugated. Russia would be left without a central government and incapable of carrying on a modern war.'

There was a long silence while the P.M. brooded over his dinner plate, which he held between the forefinger and thumb of both hands. It was one of his black days, when his imagination conjures up what might happen to mankind if he fails with Malenkov.

P.M.: 'We have been living in a time when at any moment London, men, women and children, might be destroyed overnight.'

I was glad to turn the conversation.

'But does Russia want war?'

P.M.: 'I believe it is not in her interest to make war. When I meet Malenkov we can build for peace.'

Moran: 'Then who is making difficulties?'

P.M.: 'Ike. He doesn't think any good can come from talks with the Russians. But it will pay him to come along with us. I shall do what I can to persuade him. I might stay longer here than I meant, at any rate if I could persuade Ike to stay too. He is the key man in this business.'

Moran: 'I thought Dulles was.'

He took no notice of my remark.

P.M.: 'I would not hesitate to go on to Washington if that was necessary. I think, Charles, I could manage it. I don't feel old, though I have some of the disabilities of old age. My outlook on things has not changed. It is exactly what it was. In the mornings I feel the same as I always did, but I have become torpid in the middle of the day. You ought to be able to think out some line of action which would help me. This old carcass of mine is a bloody nuisance.'

He changed the conversation abruptly.

'There are some interesting people in the party – Bob Dixon,[1] for example.'

Such a remark was so alien to his usual way of thinking that I had the curiosity later to trace it to its source. Anthony had put it into his head. The P.M. does not notice whether people are interesting or uninteresting; as long as they are good listeners and are congenial to him he is content.

'The French are going to be very difficult. They will want everything and give nothing.' The P.M. grinned broadly. 'I have been reading *Death to the French.* I must get Christopher to put it away before they come. I have had a good talk with Anthony; we have clarified things.'

December 4, 1953

At the dinner at Government House my neighbour, a member of one of the old families who governed Bermuda, Butterfield by name, who was at Oxford with Anthony and had dined with him the night before, said that Anthony spoke of Winston as a 'sick man', and was worried about him. But it was Anthony who looked tired and bored during dinner. He listened with a feeble smile to the P.M., who was in great form, exchanging old memories with Ike. Anthony has behaved very well, but the role of heir apparent does not become easier. The P.M. made an adroit, unprepared, speech about America and Ike. She was out to serve, not to dominate or rule. The French Prime Minister, who was sitting opposite to me, looked as abstracted and bored as Anthony; he appeared to be dining off E.D.C.

On our return I went with the P.M. to his room, where we were soon joined by Christopher. He told us that the Press had got a full account of the first meeting and were making a great story of the division of opinion between the P.M. and the President about Russia. The P.M. seemed put out; he did not know that the Press would be informed in this way. But when Christopher went on in his loud voice about the harm it would do, Winston became impatient:

---

[1] Sir Pierson Dixon, Deputy Under-Secretary of State, Foreign Office.

'It is foolish to exaggerate. Everything I have said will do good in England. It was all very carefully considered. I believe that I am going to be master in the discussions. Ike is a pal on the same level.'

December 5, 1953

The P.M. is less sure about things today. It appears that when he pleaded with Ike that Russia was changed, Ike spoke of her as a whore, who might have changed her dress, but who should be chased from the streets. Russia, according to Ike, was out to destroy the civilized world.

'Of course,' said the P.M. pacing up and down the room, 'anyone could say the Russians are evil minded and mean to destroy the free countries. Well, if we really feel like that, perhaps we ought to take action before they get as many atomic bombs as America has. I made that point to Ike, who said, perhaps logically, that it ought to be considered. But,' said Winston, resuming his seat, 'if one did not believe that such a large fraction of the world was evil it could do no harm to try and be friendly as long as we did not relax our defensive preparations.'

I asked him how Ike had managed to retreat from his attitude towards Russia.

'Oh, he hasn't,' the P.M. put in, 'but when we came out of the meeting he said there was a lot in what I said. Most people, when beaten in argument, become sulky. Ike is so selfless.'

I asked him what the French thought about all this. The P.M., shortly:

'I take no account of them, they are harmless.'

I lunched with the Governor. Hood[1] is a full-blooded red-faced Scot with no neck to speak of, as if he had stepped down from a Raeburn portrait for our correction. He has a fine record as an administrator, and the islanders do not want to part with him.

On my return I went straight to the P.M.'s room. When I told him where I had been he said, 'I like Hood. Would you like to be

[1] Lieut.-General Sir Alexander Hood.

a Governor, Charles? I believe you would do it very well.' Winston
does not waste much time speculating on the possibilities of those
around him. It only occurred to him that I could hold an adminis-
trative post when he saw another doctor doing work of this kind and
doing it well.

The P.M. complained that he was muddled and stupid. I asked
him how long he had before his next Conference. He looked at his
watch. 'It is at five o'clock, just an hour from now.' He said he would
not bother to take off his clothes; then he changed his mind for 'even
half an hour next to the sheets seems to do a lot of good.' He got out
of his clothes lazily, and plopped into the bed naked, as his habit.
He lay for a time as if it was too much trouble to turn over. Then,
when the curtains were drawn and he had put on his black eye-
shade, he settled to sleep.

As I left the room a message came from the French Prime
Minister.[1] He did not feel well; he had pain when he coughed and
his temperature was nearly 105°. I doubt whether he will take any
more part in the conference.

December 6, 1953
This morning, as I sat beside the P.M.'s bed, he said slowly: 'The
world is in an awful state, I cannot cope with it.'

I saw him again after the five-o'clock meeting.

'The presence of the French means that every word has to be
translated, and in any case they cannot do anything,' Winston grumbled. 'Bidault[2] talked for an hour and a half about four villages in the
Saar. I went for him, telling him plainly that if American troops were
withdrawn from Europe British troops would leave too. Bidault said
to me, "Do not be so unkind." I did not say to him what I ought to
have said: it is because of my love for France that I am unkind.'

I asked him what part Ike had played. He answered:

'Things are very easy between us. I think he trusts me. I have
now had eleven hours' private talks with him. He is going to make

[1] Joseph Laniel.
[2] Georges Bidault, French Foreign Minister.

a speech in New York on atomic bombs, which will mean that all this Bermuda business will be forgotten as unimportant.'

The P.M. has been trying to persuade himself that Ike will give way over Moscow. But he is less certain about things. He got up as if it were a great effort and went off to dine with the French, while Pug and I were the guests of Ike, supported by half a dozen of his party. After dinner Ike said:

'No one has treated me so well as Winston Churchill. He knows I love him; sometimes he takes advantage of that.'

We broke up early and I went to the P.M.'s room to wait for him. After a time he stumbled in and threw himself in his evening clothes across the bed. 'Do you mind ringing the bell, Charles?' When his servant came he appeared for a moment alarmed by the complete relaxation of the prostrate figure. 'I am very tired,' Winston groaned.

When I left the P.M. I found Norman Brook smoking his black pipe as if he had time for anything. I value his opinion because he gets hold of the facts and does not exaggerate what can be learnt from them. He knows my only concern is to keep the P.M. on his feet; he is very cautious and discreet – as Secretary of the Cabinet he must be; besides it is part of his temperament.

'During the war,' he said, 'the Prime Minister had a gift for picking out two or three things and getting them up in detail – that was his strength. He made no attempt in those days to keep up with lots of things. Now, of course, he is a lazy Prime Minister; he reads novels after breakfast. But it is much better from the country's point of view that he should stay on.'

Norman was not delivering a moral stricture, he was merely recording that the P.M.'s faculties were not what they used to be. But he did not think people noticed that the P.M. was easing off. He was doing the Cabinets all right.

December 7, 1953
It is not like Winston, when he has a fixed purpose, to admit that he is not up to the job. After a morning meeting he told me that they

were discussing Egypt when an argument had suddenly occurred to him which completely changed the American view. There were other matters of a domestic nature in which his will prevailed. 'You ought not to think, Charles, that I am too tired to do my work.'

It had been arranged that the *Canopus* would return on Wednesday, but during luncheon the P.M., without any warning, announced that he would like to stay another day in Bermuda. Christopher interposed that Anthony had lunch and dinner engagements in London which he would have to cancel, whereat the P.M. blew up:

'To hell with his engagements. He's not running this show.'

When we were alone his mood changed.

'When I had a chance to speak to the President he told me he did not need converting. We ought not to pay any more attention to McCarthy than they did to Aneurin Bevan. I cannot make it out. I am bewildered. It seems that everything is left to Dulles. It appears that the President is no more than a ventriloquist's doll.'

He said no more for a time. Then he said:

'This fellow preaches like a Methodist Minister, and his bloody text is always the same: That nothing but evil can come out of meeting with Malenkov.'

There was a long pause.

'Dulles is a terrible handicap.' His voice rose. 'Ten years ago I could have dealt with him. Even as it is I have not been defeated by this bastard. I have been humiliated by my own decay. Ah, no, Charles, you have done all that could be done to slow things down.'

When I turned round he was in tears. That was the last I heard of Moscow while we were at Bermuda.

Winston seems to have lost interest in the Conference. He grunted under his breath that he did not want to talk with the 'Bloody Frogs'. That was Anthony's job. He is nearly played out, and I was relieved when he said he would get a little sleep before the conference. When he woke he noticed that the fingers of his right hand were numb. He thought he must have slept on them. I could see no purpose in disillusioning him, but I shall be glad when we get him safely home. At that moment there was a knock on the door. It was a message for the P.M. from the conference of Foreign Ministers. Could they have another half-hour?

When Anthony eventually came up to the P.M.'s room I noticed how thin and drawn his face is these days.

'We have had a hell of a time. The communiqué is giving a lot of trouble. Oh, the French are making all sorts of difficulties about E.D.C.' Anthony spoke in a tired and rather petulant voice.

The conference had met at half-past five and went on till the P.M. broke it up by sending for them for dinner. The French were led to his room, silent and self-conscious. The P.M. had done enough talking, and during dinner he sat abstracted. The conference was resumed about ten o'clock, and it was after one o'clock when the P.M. came upstairs. I did not like this drawn-out meeting, which had gone on for seven hours, but he did not appear jaded, depressed, or sluggish. He was in fact bright and good-humoured.

'Your pill worked wonders. Anthony failed to get anything out of Bidault, so he has gone to Laniel's room to see what he can do with him. It will do his pneumonia good,' he said grimly.

When Anthony appeared he collapsed into a chair. The communiqué, though weak, did, he argued, represent what had happened. Winston grunted:

'It is obvious there was no agreement between us, and that the French would not accept E.D.C. The Americans talk about pulling out, but when it comes to the time I think they will draw back from this.'

No one made a move; it was as if they were too weary to get up and go to bed. I thought it was time I saw my other patient, Laniel. His room was full of excited Frenchmen. Laniel seemed upset, as far as a stolid Norman shows any emotion. I gave him a stiff sedative, and packed the rest of them off to bed.

December 8, 1953
The P.M. is surprisingly well after yesterday's performance.

P.M.: 'The communiqué was a flop. In refusing E.D.C. the French may have thrown away the last chance of saving France.'

Moran: 'The Americans will take it badly?'

P.M.: 'Oh, very badly. They may pull out, and if they do we shall follow.'

Moran: 'What will happen then?'

P.M.: 'Oh, France may become a kind of Czecho-Slovakia, a satellite of Russia.'

Moran: 'And where does Adenauer come in?'

P.M.: 'The Germans would form a secret army, but the Russians will attack them before they can do anything. But my view is that the Russians are afraid. They may listen to reason.'

Moran: 'What kind of defence could we put up if things go like that?'

P.M. *(shrugging his shoulders)*: 'What the Americans call peripheral defence: Iceland, Spain, Turkey, wherever there are bases. Bidault is prepared to sacrifice his career for E.D.C. He knows it is necessary. I would like you, Charles, to go to Laniel and invite him to return in the *Canopus*.' He grinned. 'It would have the additional advantage that it would provide a reason why we took another day away from the House of Commons. Will he be well enough to travel with us?'

Moran: 'He is taking a chance. If he didn't, he could not be a candidate for the Presidential Election.'

P.M.: 'Anthony is very good with other people. His voice is so smooth and his manner so quiet, so persuasive.'

December 9, 1953

When I saw the P.M. after breakfast he told me he had had some twitching in his foot. He said he would have an easy day. The Governor would drive him round the island in the morning, and he had promised to inspect the Bermuda troops in the afternoon.

Dinner began dismally. After the soup there was steak. The P.M. blew up.

'Is there no fish? Who ordered the dinner? Christopher?'

He had never heard of such a thing. However, the efficient Henri, who had been imported specially from Calgary to look after the

Prime Minister, somehow produced whitebait, almost as if it had been ordered with the dinner, and the P.M., who likes this particular dish, was placated.

There followed a long discussion about our defences against a Russian attack. Pug felt the strength of the Russians had been exaggerated. In the event of war they would have long lines of communication, and would always be looking back over their shoulders at Poland and the other satellite countries. The P.M. agreed they were probably not so strong as people thought, but even if they were only a third as strong we had no real defences in Europe to hold them back.

As long as this discussion went on the P.M. remained alert and interested. He was particularly scornful of the lack of proportion shown in the allocation of the House's time for debate – two days for TV and only one day for foreign affairs and atomic war. He might be out of date, but to him it sounded fantastic. He decided he would send a letter now to Rab about these matters and tell him when he and Anthony would speak. He rang for a secretary to take it down. But there was no one in the private office and no one in the Foreign Secretary's office. Everyone, it appeared, had gone bathing by moonlight. The P.M. became very irritable. He would never again bring only two private secretaries to a conference. At this point Anthony volunteered to take down the P.M.'s words, and it was in this manner that the letter took shape. The P.M. turned to Christopher and asked him how he thought something would go with the Party. Christopher answered at some length.

P.M. (*interrupting*): 'Oh, do please let me get on with my letter.'

Christopher (*in injured tones*): 'I thought you wanted my opinion.'

As he finished, Miss Portal put her head in, and the tension was relieved.

The talk grew thin. Pug exchanged a look of understanding with Anthony, who wanted to go to bed, but Pug was in time to agree with Winston's views on Germany. When the P.M. retired at last to his room he picked up a paper, though it was one o'clock and he was now very tired.

December 10, 1953

This is the first conference that the P.M. has attended where the Press has got hold of everything and printed it full of partisan colouring. That, anyway, is his complaint. Yesterday, while Clemmie was in the air on her way to Stockholm to receive Winston's Nobel Prize,[1] he was jumpy and worried. Then a message came. As he read it his face cleared.

'They have arrived. I hate to have people I love in the air – unless I am with them.'

After lunch a car took him to the beach, where, leaning on his stick and on a detective, he descended a steep sand dune. At the bottom there was a rock, about twice a man's height. Up this, to everybody's amazement and consternation, he proceeded to crawl. We got him down eventually and pulled and pushed him up the dune. At the top he stood getting his breath, perspiring profusely.

'I have not sweated like this since my illness,' he said. 'Take my pulse, Charles.'

There were people all round, and I got out of it somehow.

'Are you very angry with me,' he asked, looking at me like a naughty child.

He insisted on driving to the aquarium, eight miles distant.

Christopher said that I was against it. The P.M. had done enough. Winston dismissed such counsels of weakness and climbed into his car, while I trudged back to the Club. When I got there I found he had changed his mind and had gone to his room. I found him lying on his bed. He wondered if the sweating had done him harm. I gave him a vigorous rub-down with a rough towel and bundled him into bed. He was quite pleased with himself.

'It is a lovely spot,' he said. 'I must come here for a holiday.'

He picked up *Royal Flush*.[2]

'I think it is very good indeed,' he said, quite unaware that I had given it to him.

---

[1] Sir Winston Churchill had been awarded the 1953 Nobel Prize for Literature.
[2] An historical novel by Margaret Irwin.

Soon he became absorbed in the story and I left him. I marvel at his spirits. It is a long way to come for so little.

December 17, 1953
The P.M. was still sleeping when I arrived at No. 10. He had slept nine and a half hours at a stretch, with the help of a red and a green. When his breakfast came he began to wake up.

'We had a good day yesterday,' he began, 'with good majorities. A good many decisions were taken – the bloody TV business is settled at last. Of course not all of them went the way I wanted. It was decided to ask Alex to talk to the Foreign Affairs Committee. I didn't want that. He isn't good at this kind of thing. Anthony and I generally seem to come to the same conclusions. We sent telegrams to each other, which crossed, approving Dulles's warning to France. He was quite right to tell them bluntly that if they don't swallow E.D.C. soon there will be a drastic change in American policy. Dulles,' the P.M. added, 'was better at Bermuda than we expected.

'I shall go to the Other Club tonight. I must dine somewhere. I shall only have three-quarters of an hour there, because I must get back to the House to hear Anthony's speech.

'I may go in a month's time, or wait till the Queen returns. Probably I shall wait.'

When I left his room I met Christopher. He told me Winston had said the same to him. Christopher gave a great laugh: 'I told Winston: "You will wait till the Queen returns and then you will find a reason why you must carry on – perhaps Anthony's health." '

'What did the P.M. say to that?' I asked.

'Oh, he smiled and said: "I don't know why you should say that." '

I listened to the P.M.'s speech from the gallery of the House of Commons. He had nothing new to tell them, but it was done with verve and vigour; he explained that he must leave Mr Bevan time to explain his journalistic exploits in Cairo. Winston's amusement was not shared by Aneurin; the venom in his thoughts disfigured his countenance while the P.M. was speaking. It was Winston in a genial mood (though his main theme was a warning to France of the consequences of rejecting E.D.C.); in Mr Attlee's apt phrase, he was dressed up as Father Christmas, without the presents. That was what the House missed.

On my way home I called on Brendan. He took quite a different line from Christopher. He believed that Winston was seriously considering going. I asked him why he thought that.

'Well, Charles – er, er – I think Winston is – yum, yum – stung with the – er, er – idea of bringing out his *History of the English-speaking Peoples* in – er, er – three or four volumes.'

When Brendan said this I remembered that the P.M. told me that *Life* had offered him 50,000 dollars for each of four volumes to appear every year for the next four years.

'You see, Charles,' Brendan went on, 'Cassells hold the serial rights of the *History*, but – er, er yum – because they felt the terms arranged before the war were no longer er, er – fair to Winston under the altered circumstances, they have surrendered them.'

I told Brendan that I doubted whether the P.M. would resign just to write another book.

'Er, er – probably you are right, Charles.'

December 18, 1953

'I was naughty last week,' Winston began. 'I went back to the Other Club after Anthony's speech, and did not go to bed until after one o'clock.'

He put down the *Manchester Guardian* glumly.

'They complain I have nothing new to tell the House. They cannot expect me to make the speech of my life every day. A speech is a serious undertaking these days. I am not as fertile as I was. Of course I do better when I am worked up, but I am not so easily annoyed as I used to be; my reactions are not so quick. But after all, Charles, I have not really had a let-up since Margate. I want to keep my influence with the Americans. I think that is very important. They don't share my views about Russia.'

I said that the French were not likely to change their policy over E.D.C.

'Impotence isn't a policy,' the P.M. retorted. 'What do you think of Anthony?' he asked, and without waiting for an answer continued: 'He seems fitter. He made a good speech in the House last night. He hates the Tory rebels more than the Egyptians. I may go soon. I am bored. I don't like some of the things which are happening.'

For three days in succession Winston has played with the idea of resignation, but I do not now believe that he will give up office until he has to.

In the early afternoon the P.M. telephoned that he had burnt his hand. I said I would bring Sir Thomas Dunhill. He asked if he was well versed in the modern treatment of burns. The P.M. had been lunching at Trinity House, where Anthony was elected one of the Elder Brethren, when he put down his cigar on his plate so that a box of matches burst into flame. He had some big blisters on his left hand. I explained that Dunhill would see him before he went to Chartwell, as I was going to Wales. He asked me the object of my journey, and I told him: to watch a rugger match between Wales and the New Zealanders. He did not appear to think that it was a very good reason.

December 20, 1953

On my return from Wales I went with Dunhill to see the P.M. at No. 10. While Sir Thomas was preparing the dressings I was told that it had not been a very peaceful day at Chartwell. Christopher had been shooting pheasants when a bird came over very low and the gun on the other side of him wheeled round. Christopher saw what was happening and ducked, but the man next to him was hit in the face. Then two foals had got loose and had galloped over Clemmie's new croquet lawn, but the damage would be put right before she heard of it. A new black swan had arrived.

'If I retire, and I am seriously thinking of it, I shall be looking round for a convenient disease which will carry me off.'

At this point Dunhill said he was ready. There followed an extra-ordinary performance. Everything Dunhill did the P.M. criticized, advancing his own views of the manner in which the hand should be dressed and bandaged. It began when Dunhill's deft fingers were stripping off the dressings and plaster.

'Let me do it. I'm getting to know about it all.'

He gazed at the big blisters exposed.

'That shows how well my skin responds to injury.'

When the dressings were replaced he pointed out a spot which he did not think had been properly covered with gauze. Then he complained because the bandage came too far down his fingers; it made so much difference if he could move his fingers freely.

'This is the boundary line, the bandage must not come below that. Give me the scissors. I can cut away the part which comes too low.'

At last I intervened.

'You ought not to speak to the man at the wheel.'

'I'm the bloody wheel,' and the P.M. gave me a great grin. 'I really think it's still not right. Couldn't this part be done again?'

Whereupon the patient Dunhill undid much of what he had just done and started again.

'I want to wash the tips of my fingers. They are sticky.'

Dunhill said mildly: 'I washed them a few moments ago.'

When the P.M. persisted I had come to Dunhill's assistance. 'You've got water on the brain,' I told him.

He knew he was being perverse and smiled broadly.

'When I get to Chequers, what shall I do?' Dunhill suggested that when the dressing had to be changed the P.M. should go to Stoke Mandeville, but he replied that he could not think of going to the surgeon; the surgeon must come to him.

'I hope,' Winston added, 'he will accept my assistance.'

Kipling, Dunhill reminded him, wrote of the toad beneath the harrow which knows where every point goes.

'Yes, that is the point,' the P.M. said.

He lay back on the bed, closing his eyes.

'I am so sleepy. I don't know why,' he muttered.

December 30, 1953

I went into his room with his breakfast. Before I could say good morning he barked out what was in his mind. Government, he grumbled, had become more complicated than it used to be.

'You mean Labour is difficult and has more say in things?'

'Oh, no, it's worse than that, we have to consider intricate matters, valuations and that kind of thing, which never came before the Cabinets I can remember. For example, some agricultural land was requisitioned during the war as a bombing range. Now for some reason they no longer want it as a range.'

'You mean Crichel Down?'[1]

'Yes. It would seem proper in the circumstances to return it to its owner, who is asking that his ancestral acres be returned to him, with of course such compensation as may be agreed. But not at all – the government department concerned wants to take it over as Crown lands, though nationalization of land is against Tory policy. It seems to me all wrong. The land was taken for military purposes in a national emergency; it is no longer needed, and cannot be retained for some other purpose.'

He yawned noisily. 'I get very tired when I do anything. My back aches, and I don't want to tackle a difficult job. No zest. No energy.'

I said that when I last saw him he had some thoughts of retiring.

'Oh,' he answered in an offhand way, 'I'm not thinking of that. I don't want you to think I'm in a bad way. Yesterday I was as clear-headed at the end of the Cabinet as I was when it began. I sleep well;

[1] Crichel Down was compulsorily purchased by the Air Ministry in 1937. It was transferred to the Ministry of Agriculture in 1950, and at large public expense the land was used for the setting up of an experimental farm. A Public Enquiry reported in June, 1954, that civil servants had been high-handed in their dealings with the original owners and that undue public funds had been spent on the experimental project. The affair led to the resignation of Sir Thomas Dugdale, Minister for Agriculture.

it is a great blessing. Nature ought to make some provision that as we get older we sleep more and more. A time would come when we might sleep eighteen out of the twenty-four hours, though when we were awake we should be nearly as good as ever.' He gave a great grin. 'And then we would sleep all the time. I have just slept eight hours, and I could go off again now.' (Miss Portal told me that he had dropped off to sleep in the middle of the morning while actually dictating – more than once this had happened.)

'You haven't taken my pulse.' I felt it.

At that moment Mowlem, the plastic surgeon, who had been looking after his hand while he was at Chequers, came into the room. Winston had already related how Mowlem had told him: 'The recuperative powers shown by your hand are those of a much younger man.' That is the kind of patter Winston likes. It showed, on Mowlem's part, a good working knowledge of psychology. I had not met him before, but I knew without asking that the P.M. liked him and had confidence in his skill, so that he did not suggest that Dunhill should see him again; in the field of surgery Winston can usually spot a master craftsman. His answers to Winston's questions were clear and decisive. There were no doubts in his mind; his manner was full of easy assurance.

When we left the room Mowlem recalled the first time he saw the P.M. at Chequers; how he sat on his bed for nearly an hour while Winston talked about Omdurman. It took me about a year to reach that stage with Winston. I left Mowlem and returned to the P.M. He kept yawning, opening his mouth very wide, without putting up his hand. 'I'm not properly awake yet,' he said. 'My memory for names, Charles, is very bad; it seems to be getting worse. I shall soon forget my own name. Oh, no, my memory for details is quite all right.'

I asked him if he had read anything in the Christmas holidays.

'No,' he answered reflectively, 'I have done very little; often I did nothing at all. A man I his eightieth year' – he smiled – 'does not want to do things.'

PART FOUR

Winston and Anthony

CHAPTER TWENTY

First He Said He Wouldn't

January 12, 1954

'Winston,' Jock said this morning, 'was always a procrastinator, a waster of time. In the war he was not so bad, but now he wastes whole days. I don't mean that he has been in bad form. Sometimes he is almost as good as ever, but these occasions are rarer, and last a shorter time.' He has told Jock he would like to wait until the Queen returns. I fancy that when the time comes he will find some other reason for going on, but I believe he'll go in July.

I told Jock that I gave Winston a pill before the last Cabinet because he did not seem able to concentrate; when I said something to him there was a long pause before he answered. With a suspicion of a smile, Jock said that this might be due to inattention; they all suffered from this. 'Sometimes at meals,' he went on, 'Winston is very apathetic. Then Clemmie gives him a rebuke, and he'll pull himself together and be quite normal.'

January 21, 1954

He showed me a scar on his right arm.

'That's where I gave some skin for grafting to Dick Molyneux after the battle of Omdurman – it hurt like the devil. His death is in today's paper.'

The P.M. grinned.

'He will take my skin with him, a kind of advance guard, into the next world.'

January 26, 1954

Winston is very subdued this morning.

'I wish, Charles, I had more energy. Can't you do anything for me? I must do something for my living. The *Mirror* is suggesting I am past it, and that I ought to resign. Read it,' he growled, passing me the paper. 'Why do I waste my time over this rag? I am being bloody tame. I defer too much to other people's opinions.'

February 4, 1954

When I was in the north of England Christopher telephoned. He was worried about Winston. This was his story: 'While Winston was answering questions in the House he had to keep bobbing up and down, perhaps as many as twenty times in all, and I noticed he got very short of breath. I tried to count his respirations from my seat just behind where he sits on the Front Bench. I made them fifty in a minute. What ought they to be? What does it mean, Charles? Can anything be done?'

I explained that his shortness of breath was due to degeneration of his heart muscle associated with old age, and that very little could be done for it.

'I'd like you,' Christopher continued, 'to put a call through to Winston. Ask him how he is, and he'll tell you all about it.'

When I telephoned, the P.M.'s voice was quite clear. 'Are you in London, Charles? Leeds – oh, you're still in the north.' His voice fell. He repeated what Christopher had told me. Then he said a little abruptly: 'When are you coming back?' I knew that he was not happy about things. I went straight from the station at King's Cross to No. 10, where I found him in the pillared room, playing bezique with Clemmie. When he saw me he said: 'Here's Charles,' and putting down his hand, rose from the table and came over to an arm-chair. Rising with difficulty from its depths, he proceeded to illustrate how bobbing up to answer questions had been an effort.

'Now, I oughtn't to have done that just before you take my pulse,' he murmured. 'I don't think I've been so well, Charles, the last two days. I must go without lunch, or be content with something light about noon.' He paced up and down the room a little unsteadily. Then he collapsed into his chair with a deep sigh.

The P.M. rose, went over to a table and, opening *Punch*, handed it to me.

'They have been attacking me. It isn't really a proper cartoon. You have seen it?'

'Yes, there's malice in it. The *Mirror* has had nothing so hostile. Look at my hands – I have beautiful hands.'

It was true. Those podgy, shapeless hands, peering out from a great expanse of white cuff, were not his. I was shocked by this vicious cartoon; there was something un-English in this savage attack on his failing powers. The eyes were dull and lifeless. There was no tone in the flaccid muscles; the jowl sagged. It was the expressionless mask of extreme old age. Under this venomous drawing was inscribed this caption:

Man goeth forth unto his work and to his labour until the evening.

On the opposite page the editor of *Punch*, Malcolm Muggeridge, supported this attack on Churchill's decline in an effusion entitled: 'A Story without an Ending'. It was full of spleen. Writing ostensibly of a Byzantine ruler, Bellarius, he wrote:

By this time he had reached an advanced age. . . . His splendid faculties . . . began to falter. The spectacle of him thus clutching wearily at all the appurtenances and responsibilities of an authority he could no longer fully exercise was to his admirers infinitely sorrowful, and to his enemies infinitely derisory.

So it had come to this. Winston was hurt. Then, with an effort, he seemed to pull himself together.

'*Punch* goes everywhere. I shall have to retire if this sort of thing goes on. I must make a speech in a fortnight's time,' Winston continued; 'it is necessary when things like this happen.'

I said what I could. While I talked he sat feeling his pulse.

'Without taking it I can feel it isn't right. It keeps missing a beat, one–two–pause, one–two–pause.' And then with a touch of impatience: 'Well, I don't care. One day there will be no pulse to be felt.'

I noticed that when he rose to get a glass of whisky he lurched to one side as if he might fall. 'Are you going, Charles?' When he thanked me for my visit he made a little affectionate gesture, though I'd done nothing. He appeared to be on the point of breaking down. 'Clemmie,' he said, 'Charles is going.' And Clemmie put down her cards and thanked me too.

February 7, 1954

On my arrival at Chequers, before I went to Winston's room, Christopher took me aside. 'You know, Charles, I have noticed a marked deterioration in Winston in the past month. He is much deafer – keeps turning to his neighbour, asking what is he saying? People can't help noticing it. Besides, he made a box of his speech about the rifle. He must pull out. He mustn't meet the new Parliament as Prime Minister. You are the only person who can persuade him he ought to go. It ought to be his friends and not his enemies who persuade him to resign.

'You can't compete with him,' Christopher laughed. 'Why, he said to me today, supposing I did retire, and two months later some world event happened, and I wanted to take a hand in it, I might be very sorry I'd pulled out. It might well be a course of events which I could have directed and perhaps guided the country safely through.'

Christopher gave a great guffaw, and his untidy features were stretched with glee. 'Well, Clemmie wants to see you before you go to Winston. If you don't agree about his retiring you'd better have it out with her.'

I found him in bed, coughing, sneezing and damning everyone. When I had gone over his chest I asked him would he like me to stay the night? 'If,' he answered, 'that is not very inconvenient. It would be nice if you would see me out of this.'

I enquired about his plans.

'I shall do some work this morning. I like to feel I am doing something no one else can do. I don't think we've done badly in the last two years. The Government has been sensible if not brilliant. Doing nothing is often very important in the art of government. You see, I have influence and a store of experience which no one else has, and I can decide things at a meeting as well as ever I could.'

In these times he is for ever grappling with his conscience, trying to persuade himself that he is fit to do his job and that the country will gain if he carries on.

Is he fit to be Prime Minister? The framework is everywhere giving way, but in his outlook he seems to have aged little.

February 8, 1954
Winston said: 'Christopher wrote to that awful fellow, Muggeridge, you know the editor of *Punch*. He knows him, lives in his neighbourhood. Muggeridge wrote back saying that he was a journalist and must do his duty as a journalist. If he held opinions he must express them; said that he was one of my greatest admirers, but that I was no longer up to the job. He instanced the scuttle from the Sudan.'

There was a long pause.

'Many people in the country may feel as he does. I never liked it. But he isn't very logical. If I went, Anthony would succeed, and he is passionately for our getting out of the Sudan.

'Most people feel that the Prime Minister is always responsible; he should insist on getting his own way. That is not my idea. I don't think he should be an autocrat. I never was, even in the war. Of course I had great powers, my relations with Roosevelt and things like that ensured this. But the Cabinet ought to have their say. There are a few occasions, of course, when the Prime Minister must have his own way or resign.'

There was another long pause.

'There are always a lot of bloody rows in politics – that's what politics is for. A lot of fires blaze up, and it's my job to put them out. You get habituated to the heat.'

February 23, 1954

Winston had thought of publishing the Mau-Mau oath,[1] but it was not really fit for publication, so it was decided to put it in the House of Commons in a place where Members could read it.

'It is very long. No one could have made it up if he had tried. It is incredibly filthy.' Smiling grimly. 'It was certainly calculated to impress the recipient.'

I spoke to Oates[2] before I left, suggesting that perhaps I saw the P.M. at his worst, usually in the early morning. Oates thought there might be something in this.

'Last night the P.M. worked on his speech from ten-thirty until midnight, with a Foreign Office expert, making some very good points and directing the argument. Then he went over questions for today and finally read the early editions of the morning papers. He went to bed about a quarter to one. He was really as alert as before his illness. He is generally like that in the evenings.'

March 4, 1954

I found him breakfasting. He was wide awake and positively cheerful. Well, Christopher's right after all. The P.M. hasn't waited for the Queen's return to fish up an excuse for hanging on.

'I shall stay to the end of the Session – the last days of July. You see, the Ministers have most of them got Bills – they're up to the eyes in the details, and if I went when the Queen returns it would be very inconvenient for them. Harold Macmillan[3] told me a change in the Government would affect his plans. Besides, I've got back a great deal of my activity, physical and mental. I was struck by my vigour in winding up the debate – so was the House. A good deal of it had to be extempore. I had to pick up and answer points in the debate. I was doubtful before the speech how far I could do this.

[1] The Mau Mau revolt began in 1952 among the Kikuyu tribe of Kenya. The leaders administered oaths of a revolting and obscene nature, often by force, upon tribesmen, who were then obliged to kill or harm Europeans or loyal Kikuyus if so ordered. Appalling attrocities here committed.
[2] One of the Prime Minister's private secretaries.
[3] Minister of Housing and Local Government at this time.

But,' he said reflectively, 'I've been at it so long. It is almost second nature. Of course, it is a great exertion, and next day I don't feel like doing anything.'

He rang me up in the evening after the Cabinet. He had taken a pill which he called the 'Lord Moran' in the morning; did this mean he could not take my 'special' pill in the afternoon? Would they clash? Not being able to get hold of me, he had taken a chance. 'You see, I had five hours on end.' I asked him if he was very weary. 'Not at all. Now I am going out to dinner with the American Ambassador.' This astonishing creature obeys no laws, recognizes no rules. He goes his own way, and I am left to pick up the bits.

March 12, 1954

Jock said this morning that the P.M. had not been in such good form for years, and I went to his room expecting to find the sun shining. But he looked up at me without a smile and said sadly: 'It casts a shadow over your work when you are going to give it up soon.'

As I left the room, Christopher met me. He told me that Winston had read out something he had said during the war, and had added demurely, 'I was very modest then.' I told him it was a very different story now, and he was much amused.

March 19, 1954

'I'm going to resign at the end of June. They have all been so nice. That's what gets me. If they had attacked me I could have snarled back. I don't want to be selfish.'

He turned round and looked at me with interest. I knew something was coming. 'I don't suppose many people have survived two strokes?' Without waiting for an answer he continued: 'Of course, any day I may get another.' He grinned. 'That would solve a lot of problems.'

March 26, 1954

I found Winston quite perky, to use Jane Portal's words.

'It seems to be widely felt that I ought to be able to bring things to a head over the Bomb. I don't know when I shall retire,' he went on. 'I have to think of other people. It may sound egotistical, but

I don't know what the boys will do when I go. So far they have only produced television and the muddle over Egypt and the Sudan. I am more worried by the hydrogen bomb[1] than by all the rest of my troubles put together. I may speak on it next week.

'My book comes out in this country on April 26. The American edition led to no ill-feeling. On the contrary, there are a good many people in the States, according to Henry Luce, who said that I was right and they were wrong about the Russians. The Americans don't mind admitting when they are wrong.

'Max is very busy with his Lloyd George book. He bought his letters for a song – he has a thousand which Lloyd George and I wrote to each other. One, dated January 19, 1918, warns him very plainly that the Germans will probably attack us – that was two months before the March offensive. I advised Lloyd George not to weaken the army. The book was written for Max by Frank Owen. My label for him Charles, would not be in your diagnostic vocabulary. I never liked him.

'Max and Brendan have given up smoking and drinking.' He grinned. 'They must want to live very much.'

'I can't get excited about television. I can't make out what all the fuss is about. I have never given my mind to it as I did to the hydrogen bomb, but I feel this bloody invention will do harm to society and to the race.'

'You'll speak when they debate it?'

'I suppose so,' he grunted, sighing deeply.

March 31, 1954

W.C. was reading about the hydrogen bomb debate in the morning papers when I entered his bedroom. He looked up.

'They are asking what has happened to the old warrior. As if I can do anything,' he said impatiently. 'If the Americans don't want to give us details, we can't make them. They wouldn't part with this bomb for anything in the world. It is not fair to blame me. I had an agreement

[1] The first H-bomb was exploded by the United States on March 1, 1954, in the Marshall Islands and was equivalent to 14 million tons of TNT. Russia exploded her first device in the following September.

with F.D.R. that neither America nor Britain would use the bomb without the consent of the other. But Attlee gave it all away. When I told MacMahon about the agreement, he said at once: "If we had known about this at the time, there would not have been an Atomic Secrets Act in its present form. Attlee said nothing to us about an agreement." You were present during the conversation, Charles? You heard what MacMahon said?' He pondered. 'I may have to call you as a witness. MacMahon is dead. I may have to tell the House about this. Attlee lay doggo, he was very quiet during the debate.'

When I left the room, Miss Gilliatt asked me how he was. She said:

'He is thinking a lot about this bomb, and he is worried about Lady Churchill. He is giving hell to everyone.'

April 1, 1954

My cook from Ayrshire takes her political views from the *Mirror*, and when it is particularly venomous about Mr Churchill she brings me her copy. It was half-past nine by Big Ben as I made for No. 10 to see for myself whether the *Daily Mirror*'s attack had got under his skin. When I went upstairs his valet said he had not gone to bed until one o'clock and was still asleep. Outside his bedroom there was a pile of morning papers. I settled down to get the hang of things.

On the back page, under the caption, 'What America says about Churchill now', the *Mirror* quoted the *New York Times*: 'For the first time since Parliament reconvened last autumn, Sir Winston appeared unsure of himself and tired. This wasn't the Churchill of two years ago and was only the shadow of the great figure of 1940 . . . In his replies to questions Sir Winston contradicted himself.'

I turned to the leader in the *Daily Mirror*, 'Twilight of a Giant', to find what the Editor was about. He dotted the i's and crossed the t's.

The exposure of the myth of Winston as a post-war leader is now complete. . . . There are demands in Parliament that Britain should give a lead to the world in facing the horror-bomb problem. . . . That we should talk straighter and harder to America. What is Churchill's reply?. . . Old and tired, he mouthed comfortless words in the twilight of his career. His battles are past. . . . This is the Giant in Decay.

I turned to the *Daily Worker* and the *Daily Herald.* They made poor reading. The Left had made up its mind to get rid of the Prime Minister. His great influence stood between them and power.

When Winston rang his bell I tidied up the papers and went in. It was some time before I could get anything out of him. 'I woke at five,' he told me, 'and could not get to sleep again. I began thinking of my speech for Monday, and my brain became active.' 'Have you much to do today?' 'Everything in the world,' he replied gloomily.

I made up my mind to call on Norman Brook. He would know how the P.M. was shaping under the stress of events. Brook took his pipe out of his mouth and began: 'I've seen a good deal of the P.M. in the last few days, and he seemed to be in good form, storming at the Americans and at our Ambassador, and generally rampaging; but,' said Norman smiling, 'we take that as normal. He thinks he will put Attlee on his back on Monday, and I daresay he will.'

Jock thinks there'll be a row if the P.M. doesn't retire in July. I asked Brook if he agreed. There was a long pause. 'Yes, I think I do,' he said at last. 'They are thinking of a General Election in the autumn of 1955. If the P.M. pulled out in July that would give Anthony nearly a year and a half before the election to reform the Government and to give the country a chance of seeing how the new Prime Minister and his government are shaping. They want younger men, full of energy and drive. Of course, Winston's colleagues may not say as much. They feel an affection for him, as we all do. But I think this is the state of feeling. The one thing that is definite and fixed is the P.M.'s declaration that he will not lead the party in another election.'

I repeated my doubts whether Winston would be happy in his retirement. He had so often said to me: 'I must have something to look forward to. I can't do nothing for the rest of my days.' Brook had his doubts too, but he hoped the novel-reading habit would grow. 'Though of course,' he added smiling, 'zip may go out of it when it's no longer forbidden fruit – when he can read without feeling he ought to be working – the cigarette behind the bush business.' Norman Brook is a good friend of the P.M., loyal, yet missing nothing.

CHAPTER TWENTY-ONE

The Prime Minister Loses Ground

April 5, 1954

As I made my way to the House of Commons to listen to the debate on the hydrogen bomb, the idea that the P.M. was in for a rough time never entered my head.

The discussion began quietly. It was in no party spirit, Attlee argued, that the Opposition had raised the issue. They believed that mankind had, for the first time, realized what it was to live in the world of the hydrogen bomb, and that this had brought disarmament within the reach of practical politics. It had made possible a British initiative, and the Opposition was eager for a meeting of the three Heads of State in the new atmosphere to reconsider the reduction and control of armaments.

Mr Attlee, in his speech, rose to the level of his grave theme, and the P.M. himself, when he replied, called it a 'thoughtful and inspiring speech'. He seemed prepared to carry on the high argument where the leader of the Opposition had left it: 'These stupendous facts,' he said, 'glare upon the human race,' but in 'the universality of potential destruction' he found hope. And then, when the whole House was still and silent, seemingly numbed by the tragic issue confronting the world, he shocked Tory and Socialist alike by making it a party matter, a fight to be won on points.

The P.M. did not see why the Government should be blamed because the Americans could use the bomb without consulting us.

When in 1945 he quitted office our position was very different. He then told the House for the first time of the agreement which he made in 1943 at Quebec with President Roosevelt. These were the facts: America and Britain agreed that they would not use the atomic bomb against third parties without each other's consent; and they agreed that there would be a constant exchange of information. That, he said, looking at the Members opposite, was how things stood when the Socialist Government came into office. It was unfair to blame him because Mr Attlee had abandoned this agreement.

Mr Attlee sprang to his feet, while a wave of anger and astonish-- ment swept over his supporters. He did not understand why the Prime Minister should say the Labour Government had abandoned the agreement; they had abandoned nothing. It was the McMahon Act, passed in 1946, which prevented the American Government from carrying out the Quebec agreement. (Here Mr Attlee's memory was at fault. The Act did not touch America's obligation to consult and inform us. That was not lost until 1948, when, as Mr Attlee himself admitted to the House in 1951, the Quebec agreement was 'changed and altered' and a new agreement drawn up by Mr Attlee's Government.)

At this point the P.M. could have risen and told Mr Attlee that he protested too much, that his recollection of the sequence of events was not in fact accurate. There would have been nothing more to say. But unhappily the P.M.'s memory served him no better than Mr Attlee's: they were both equally vague about the McMahon Act; they had both forgotten the debate of 1951. So it happened that when Mr Attlee spoke of the McMahon Act the P.M.'s mind went off at a tangent. Instead of pointing out that the Act had nothing to do with the issue before the House, he argued that if Mr Attlee had shown the Senator the Quebec agreement there would have been no Act. The Senator himself had told him that two years ago.[1] This seemed to raise the temperature on the Opposition benches. Mr Attlee leapt to the box. He was flushed and spluttering with rage.

[1] See pp. 66–7.

It was not his job, he protested, to tell the Senator; that was the business of his own Government. I quote from Hansard:

> The Prime Minister: I did not intend – (Hon. Members: 'What? Did not intend what?') I did not intend – (Interruption.) I have no doubt whatever that before the McMahon Act was passed he [Mr Attlee] ought to have confronted the people of the United States with the declaration. That is what I believe will be the view of history.

When Mr Churchill had charged Mr Attlee with abandoning the Quebec agreement there had begun a disorderly scene in the House, and now the shouts of 'Withdraw' and 'Resign' made it difficult to hear what was said. 'The Right Honourable Gentleman is dragging us down to the gutter,' the member for Cardiff shouted. 'This is disgraceful,' another member bawled. Mrs Braddock advised the Prime Minister to 'get out.' The P.M. floundered on, and the Deputy Speaker complained that there was so much noise that he could not hear what the Prime Minister was saying. Each time the P.M. had to give way to an interrupter, he half sat down, keeping his hand on the table and using it to pull himself to his feet, slowly and with increasing difficulty, so that he might resume his speech. Lord Layton whispered to me: 'This will bring his resignation nearer.'

The Prime Minister struggled on: 'Now let me say only–' Mrs Braddock: 'You have said too much. The Right Honourable Gentleman should look at the faces behind him.' And indeed the Tories were in poor shape: they could not manage a single cheer for their leader; they sat mute. Sir Robert Boothby, white-faced, rose from the Tory benches and walked out of the Chamber. The Opposition cheered wildly this apparent mark of dissatisfaction with his leader.

I viewed the turn of events with growing concern. I marvelled that this man, in his eightieth year, and only half recovered from a stroke, could stand at the box for a full hour in all that uproar and tumult, in the face of such bitter hostility, and yet remain apparently unmoved. He had bungled the business. All the same, it made me very miserable to sit there watching him without being able to help. I wondered how it might affect him in the Party. Would he have another stroke? And then, as if the House was spent, its venom exhausted, the cries of 'Resign' and 'Withdraw' died down and in the lull the P.M. meandered on. When they allowed him to finish his speech in silence, in some strange way it seemed to increase my fears. All expression had gone from his voice, which quavered into the high-pitched speech of a very old man; he had somehow to get through a set piece before he sat down, and he gabbled through it as if his only purpose was now to get to the end.

When he left the Chamber I followed him to his room. He was flushed, and now that I was near to him it was apparent he was controlling his excitement. But he stoutly denied that he was tired, brushing aside my questions. He felt very well, he lisped rather defiantly. That his speech had miscarried did not seem to occur to him. 'It will be all right in the morning papers,' he said. A secretary brought the Prime Minister whisky, and he said obstinately that he would go back to the Chamber. Christopher was rushing about, asking everyone for Hansard. And when the volume he wanted was put into his hands he began fumbling in its pages. 'Give it to me,' the P.M. said impatiently. 'Give it to me. I know where to find it.' As his eye skimmed the debate of 1951 his face fell, he realized the opportunity that had been lost. 'I have been too tethered to my notes,' he said sadly. When I left him I ran into Norman Brook hurrying along the passage and looking as composed as usual. Attlee had sent for him. He, too, wanted Hansard. The two old gentlemen were documenting their speeches after the event.

In the Lobby I met Lady Tweedsmuir, a friend of Winston's. She was sad. 'Yes,' she said, 'he lost the House.' Some of his supporters were talking in groups. They had long faces, and looked at me as I passed. In the House of Lords I found the Lord Chancellor having tea with Lord Salisbury and Lord Swinton; they had been in the gallery and were very grave as they conversed in low voices. At another table sat Lord Woolton with some Tory peers. When I joined them their conversation stopped. After an awkward silence

Woolton said: 'I was glad to see you in the gallery; it must have been a great strain on Winston in his state of health. It must have upset him; at least I know it would have upset me.'

I went back to the Lobby, wondering if Winston was all right. Members were asking why the P.M. took a party line. I held my peace, but the answer is not in doubt: he was going to knock Mr Attlee through the ropes. Carefully coached by Lord Cherwell, he had come to the House in that mood. Lord Cherwell's influence with the P.M. should not be underrated. Winston says he has a 'lovely mind', and in such matters listens to his advice. The Prof. is an intriguing figure: entirely disinterested (he did not want to be a member of the Cabinet) and without any political ambitions, this old Alsatian is a man of iron; his logic seems to rule out counsels of moderation.

But I must not lay all the blame on Lord Cherwell. If he led Winston astray it was because the P.M. wanted to go that way. Even now, at the end of his life, when the nation, regardless of party, insists on looking to him as the sagacious world statesman, brooding over the incalculable future and thinking only of broad horizons and world events, his tastes lie in the rough and tumble of the House of Commons. He loves a fight. He looks forward to the 'tu quoque' of Questions in the House, enjoying every minute of the back-chat. In short, he is still at heart the red-haired urchin, cocking a snook at anybody who gets in the way. Why should anyone be surprised that he loves bickering? When he was in opposition those around him were always praying that he would leave Morrison alone and not indulge in dog-fights, which hardly befitted the world figure of the war years. And last week, when he was preparing his speech, those who serve him at No. 10 were hoping that he would leave Attlee alone.

April 6, 1954

Winston's second thoughts this morning were sober and penitent.

'Things didn't go as well as I expected. When one gets old one lives too much in the past. I ought to have told the House that I was

very happy the Opposition had come round to my view that the
Heads of the three States ought to meet, instead of . . .'

He was silent for a little, lost in thought.

'You see, Charles, I felt it was an extraordinary act of folly on the
part of Labour to throw away the Quebec agreement. For years I
have wanted it published. I was irritated that we had been relegated
to a position where we had no say in things. Besides, I thought that
what I said might have some effect on America. But there is truth in
what the *Manchester Guardian* says this morning, that it's no use
crying over spilt milk.'

I asked him if he had been upset by the hostility of the Labour
benches. 'Oh, no,' he answered at once, 'I felt very well. After my
speech I went to the Smoke Room and had a nice talk.' He pondered
a while. 'I can see I must leave it alone,' he said sadly. 'Anthony did
extremely well. It gives me confidence that he can control things so
well. It was his best speech since his illness.'

He got out of bed and shuffled into the bathroom. I picked up
The Times and read that the Prime Minister's 'sense of occasion had
deserted him sadly' yesterday; he was responsible that 'the proceedings had degenerated into a sterile, angry, and pitiful party
wrangle.' There was a feeling, not confined to the Labour Press, that
by his inept handling of the debate he had played into the hands of
those who insist that he is no longer fit to be First Minister of the
Crown.

CHAPTER TWENTY-TWO

A Tired Mind

April 8, 1954

I was settling for a night's work when the P.M. telephoned: 'Charles? Are you in London? I would like to see you. I have had a very hard day.'

I found him in his dark-blue velvet boiler suit, drinking brandy with Duncan and Diana. It was ten o'clock, but they had only just finished dinner. He had slumped into his chair, and appeared to have difficulty in keeping awake.

He began to tell me of his talk with the 1922 Committee.

'I met them at seven o'clock. I did not feel well. When I looked at them – it was a record attendance – I had a sense of helplessness. I felt very bad. I was tottering about. And then will-power came to my rescue. I spoke to them for twenty-five minutes. They cheered me warmly when I began, and again when I sat down, treating me with great respect. The meeting was about the pay of Members of the House. They believe the public will be restive if the House votes itself a rise in wages. But I told them Tory democracy must make a gesture. It was for the good of Parliament in the long run that the salaries of members should be raised.'

Duncan Sandys, who unlike Christopher cannot follow the old man's moods, launched out into an argument that it would do the Government a lot of harm if it was thought they had brought in higher salaries of their own accord. They ought to be careful that

the Opposition was made plainly responsible for the rise. The P.M.
did not seem impressed by all these tactics. But if Duncan had
noticed that the P.M. was restless, he did not allow it to affect
his purpose. He knew his facts – if need be he would stay up all
night to master them – and he thought the P.M. ought to know
them too.

As Minister of Supply he had become convinced of the necessity
of economy in money spent on defence. Winston interrupted
impatiently: it was folly to spend eighteen millions on a carrier and
then a few months later to put it in moth-balls; it created a very bad
impression.

The P.M. made little pretence of following Duncan's argument,
though it was clear, cogent and forcibly put. There is good stuff in
this fellow – great industry and guts – and it makes me sad that
Winston is only bored by his son-in-law. Of course it has always
been like that with him. If a man is not congenial nothing happens.
In such circumstances he will obstinately shut his eyes to unusual
merit.

Diana looked at me meaningly, as if to say, 'Cannot you get him
to go to bed.' When I did nothing she whispered: 'Papa is very
weary.'

And then Malenkov's name came up. Mary and Christopher had
lunched with the Soviet Chargé d'Affaires and they gathered that
Malenkov would welcome a meeting with the Prime Minister.
Winston seemed to wake up.

'I feel better. I feel quite different.'

He began to talk with vigour.

'They will say, of course, that I may get a snub. I don't care. What
does a snub matter if you save the world.'

Then he said with an air of finality:

'I shall not relinquish office until I meet Malenkov.'

'Where,' I broke in, 'would you see him?'

'Oh, there would be no difficulty. Ike said once that he would like
to meet Malenkov at Stockholm. I could join the Russians there. It
would be a great thing if he came out of Russia to meet me.'

He did not think the Russians would object to a meeting outside Russia on grounds of *amour propre*:

'At my age, with death at my shoulder, the Kremlin cannot speak of jealousy. They know I have nothing to gain. I would pop over to America first, to make it all right with them. I know them so well, they would not think I was up to dirty work.'

His eyes became more prominent.

'The Americans know I am the greatest anti-Communist of all time. Besides,' with a mischievous grin, 'they would see I was going in any case.'

Of course, the Cabinet might try to prevent him going. It would not be easy, but he thought that public opinion would be on his side. Duncan heard all this for the first time; he warmly welcomed the plan. Could it be set in motion quickly? Everything seemed ripe for it. That could not last. Winston snapped out impatiently that nothing could be done until after Geneva.

'If the conference fails, I shall pick up the bits. If it triumphs, I shall go to meet Malenkov to exploit the victory. You will come with me, Charles?'

His voice grew stronger as he thought of what might come from such a meeting.

'I would ask for something in return for being an intermediary – Vienna perhaps. Austria might be set free.'

Christopher was getting into his car as I left No. 10. He said 'good night', but Mary got out and bustled me into the seat beside Christopher. 'We will take you home,' she said.

Christopher was certain that he had seen a steady deterioration in Winston during the past two months. 'He knows he is not up to it. He must pull out.' Christopher thought Whitsuntide was the time for him to go. 'You know, Charles, you are the only person who can persuade him he ought to go.'

April 9, 1954

When I saw Winston this morning he said:

'It is sad about the loss of the Comet.[1] So much of our reputation abroad seems to depend on them.

'The result of the by-election[2] is disappointing. It is bad; we thought we might win.'

He grinned.

'It distresses me more than the Comet.'

He came back to Bevan and his friends, who were saying that America, unless she changed her tune, would have to 'go it alone'. He became very grave. Bevan's line was full of danger.

'I think she might retire from Europe, and rely on peripheral defence, or she might declare war on Russia and blow her to pieces. It will be two years before Russia will be able to take her bombs to America.'

I asked the P.M. what would happen to Germany if there was war between Russia and the United States.

'Poor lambs, they would be over-run and our neutrality would not save us. I wanted America to have a show-down with the Soviet Republic before the Russians had the bomb.'

April 12, 1954

The big idea still quickens Winston's pulse. He said today:

'I am told that if a thousand hydrogen bombs were exploded the cumulative effect on the atmosphere might be such that the health, and even the lives, of the whole human race would be affected. I would like to know if that is true. I want it investigated. If it proved true there might be in the world a new common interest in preventing these explosions.'

---

[1] The loss of two Comet airliners in rapid succession during the early months of 1954 dashed hopes for the ascendancy of the British aircraft industry. The whole fleet was grounded, and a special enquiry showed that metal fatigue was the cause of the disasters.

[2] On April 8 Labour held Edinburgh East with an increased majority.

April 14, 1954

He lit a match and held his cigar over the flame.

'Poor Boothby, everyone is attacking him because he walked out while I was speaking.'

The P.M. can afford to be generous. It appears that there has been a sharp reaction in his favour. The *Observer*, for instance, puts down the explosiveness of the debate to strained nerves. The Old Man seems to have nine lives.

He stopped rambling and became very solemn.

'I am thinking again about the question of retiring. I don't see why I should go. Yesterday I developed great strength. I talked more than anyone else in the Cabinet. I guided, collected opinions and expressed my views. It went on for three hours, and at the end I was fresher than most of them.'

April 28, 1954

After Anthony had flown to London from Geneva on Sunday, the Cabinet on his advice said 'no' to Dulles, who wanted to intervene in Indo-China. The P.M. said to me this morning:

'It is no good putting in troops to control the situation in the jungle. Besides, I don't see why we should fight for France in Indo-China when we have given away India. It would have given me pleasure to fight for Britain in India. We think we can hold Malaya even if Indo-China falls.'

He became more vehement.

'The French want us to look after France in Europe while America watches over her Empire. It just won't do. They are making E.D.C. impossible.'

He told me how he had prepared his speech for the House.

'The F.O. sent a mass of verbiage, Foreign Office clichés. It would have shocked the House. They only wanted to hear that we had no commitments.'

'It was woolly stuff?'

'No, not woolly, but they think they can hide behind a cloud of words. I tore it all to pieces. I took an hour and a half over it.

I am slower than I was. But it is all in my head, I have a grip on the whole situation. I told the House that we must not let the Dien Bien Phu[1] battle mar the sense of world proportion. They liked that. We have the confidence of the House. I was going to make a ten minutes' speech at the Albert Hall on May 1st. Now I shall make it half an hour and deal with this situation.'

As he said this he jutted out his jaw.

'When I go I shall be bored doing nothing. I don't think it will do my health any good, but—'

He stopped. He looked very sad, as if life were over.

'This is a secret which you must tell to no human being. It might increase the danger to the Queen. I am going out to Gibraltar to meet her. I shall come with her in the yacht across the Bay. I am an experienced sailor. Then I shall go to America, perhaps ten days later. It's not yet fixed up. Ike can't fix anything till he is certain that Dulles will be there to hold his hand.'

He told me how Bevan had driven into a van and had then driven off; how a man in a car, with his wife, saw what happened and hopped out, taking Bevan's number as he drove off. The police came up and questioned this man, and he gave the number of the car, without knowing that Bevan was in it. It turns out that the man was a relation of Attlee – a chance in a million. The P.M. grinned broadly.

'If only I had been at Chequers that week-end it might have been the beginning of a coalition!'

I suggested that it was a poor way of doing things, to drive off.

'Oh, no,' Winston said; 'it might have happened to anybody.'

A handsome saying, bearing in mind what he thinks of Bevan.

'Did the Cabinet tire you?'

'No,' he answered. 'It amuses me.'

I walked across to the House, where I met the Lord Chancellor. I spoke of days when there was more leisure to think things out.

[1] Situated in Thai country west of Hanoi. The post was occupied by French paratroops during the Indo-China war. After a fifty-five-day siege, it fell to the Vietminh on May 7 and led indirectly to the end of the war (July 21, 1954).

'Yes,' the Chancellor agreed. 'How true that is. I am a new boy in politics. After a lifetime in the Law seeking justice and truth, if that doesn't sound priggish, I have a feeling all the time that we are doing things looking over our shoulder at the voter.'

May 4, 1954
Winston said this morning with an air of finality:

'I shall go in July, unless of course more unexpected developments occur which makes me indispensable. I no longer find life attractive. There is no fun in it. People,' he added gloomily, 'are too base or too stupid to master the new ways of the modern world.'

If he had little or no say in things was it worth while to go on? He had never seen foreign affairs so complicated.

'Have you read, Charles, Stirling Cole's speech in the *Manchester Guardian*? You know, he succeeded McMahon as Chairman of the Atomic Energy Committee. He says that one plane on one mission can today carry more destruction than all the bombs carried by all the Air Forces of all the Allies and all the Axis nations during the six years of the war. We cannot at present defend ourselves against an atomic attack. We should not even have time to evacuate the great cities. Cole says that there is worse to come, that in three or four years from now Russia will be able to launch a saturation attack against us which will make retaliation impossible.'

Winston pondered for a little, his voice became stronger.

'There is one gleam of hope: revolutionary changes are taking place in the science of defence.

'Two high-ranking officers in the American Army told me yesterday that they had not read Cole's speech. If a man reads nothing else he should read that.'

The P.M. went on to speak with concern of the tension between the United States and Britain.

'The danger is that the Americans may become impatient. I know their people – they may get in a rage and say: Bevan is right. Why should we not go it alone? Why wait until Russia overtakes us? They could go to the Kremlin and say: "These are our demands.

Our fellows have been alerted. You must agree or we shall attack you." I think it would be all right. There is fear in the Kremlin. If I were an American I'd do this. Six years ago in my Llandudno speech I advocated a show-down. They had no bombs then.'

He spoke of Dulles.

'He is a dull, unimaginative, uncomprehending, insensitive man; so clumsy. I hope he will disappear.'

To change his thoughts I asked him about the book.

'Ah, more copies have been sold of it than of any other book except the Bible.'

He smiled.

'I am not competing.'

May 7, 1954

'I am not going to Gibraltar,' Winston began this morning. 'There is too much work to do. Our majority was down to three. So many of the Party seem to be ill. I shall meet the Queen on Friday in a destroyer.'

May 8, 1954

Winston telephoned after dinner: 'I am streaming and I am having no treatment. Are there no quack remedies for a cold, Charles? I would like to try them. Is there no new spray I could use? What about another Dover's powder tonight?'

I advised him to go to bed. 'No,' he retorted with vigour, 'I am not going to bed. I want to go to a film. I feel quite well, I have no temperature. Why should I go to bed?'

I asked him if he would like to see me.

'Yes,' he replied, 'I'd like that.'

The visit was not really necessary. No fever, no cough. Just apprehension.

May 9, 1954

Saw the P.M. at Chartwell in the middle of the afternoon. 'Well, what about your cold?' Winston deliberately made some wheezing sounds for my benefit. 'Listen with your stethoscope – if you have brought it,' he added with a smirk. I listened to his chest and reassured him.

He said he was worried about the Queen at Gibraltar, he would not be happy till he heard that she had left for England. It was probably nerves on his part, but there might be demonstrations and even explosions.

'I was,' he continued, 'reading Hans Andersen's fairy-tales when Pitblado came into the room, and I gave a hell of a jump. Why do I do that? I never used to start like this.'

As I was leaving him I stopped to look at a small head of Napoleon. 'Ah, that was the most beautiful countenance from which genius ever looked upon mankind.' 'Someone said that,' Winston mused.

May 10, 1954

Exactly an hour was spent this morning in deciding whether he would go to London to answer a question by Bevan in the House on the proposed Security Pact for South-East Asia.[1] He sent for Pitblado, who handed him a paper. 'It is the Foreign Secretary's advice about dealing with this question; he sent it from Geneva.' At last I said: 'If you do not take care of your cold you will infect the Queen on Friday.' That went home, and he decided that he would not go to London. 'I get nothing out of Anthony. I don't know what is happening,' the P.M. murmured. This is a new tune.

May 14, 1954

To No. 10 today to see if the P.M. was fit to meet the Queen. At least that was my purpose. But it soon became clear that his mind was made up already. 'I am going to carry out the plans I have made,' he said. 'At my age it can do no harm to be in the open in this warm weather. It would be different if it were cold and boisterous. Besides, I have a lot of important business with the Queen.'

---

[1] The South-East Asia Defence Treaty was signed on September 8, 1954, and set up S.E.A.T.O. as an Asian complement to N.A.T.O..

But he had his own doubts. He asked me if his cold was still infectious? Would he give it to the Queen? He did not appear to be interested in my answer. Then he shot at me quickly: 'If I did get more harm, what would happen? Would my cold go down into the smaller tubes?' He became more cheerful. He would be back at No. 10 at half-past one tomorrow. He asked me to lunch with him. 'You shall give me medical advice, and I will give you some nourishment.

'You are not pleased with me, Charles?'

'Oh, I don't know about that; there is a risk that this cold will settle on your chest. But it isn't a great risk, and I'm not going to waste time by presenting a minority report.'

He grinned broadly.

'My dear Charles, you know I always listen to your advice.

'I woke very early. I'm not sleeping as well as I did. Perhaps providence, in view of the long sleep into which I must soon fall, does not deem it worth while to trouble over details. After all, does it matter so much whether I sleep six or eight hours? I fancy my mind is too active, it will not be put to sleep. There are so many grave matters calling for decisions. The French are dreadful – Laniel with his majority of two. If they had extended the period of conscription to two years the war in Indo-China might now be over. As it is, the real fighting was done by the Germans in the Foreign Legion. They were magnificent.'

As I left his room, Jane Portal said Chequers wanted me on the telephone. It was Clemmie. 'Is that Charles? Have you seen Winston? Do you approve of his going to meet the Queen? The Royal Family do not like picking up colds. They always keep their engagements. The Queen is very fond of Winston, but she will not be at all pleased if she catches his cold. Besides, there is the danger to himself. What do you think about that?' I saw no purpose in nagging. He knew the risks – such as they were – to the Queen and himself. He himself must make the decision. Clemmie did not seem to agree.

May 15, 1954

Mary, Christopher and their son, Nicholas, were in the middle of luncheon when I arrived at No. 10. Mary explained that they had to be at Buckingham Palace by 2.30 p.m. I decided to wait for Winston. He arrived late.

'How is your cold, Papa?' Mary asked at once. I was relieved when he said: 'Certainly no worse; on the whole I should say it is better. You were right, Charles, to oppose my going. I ought not to have gone.' He grinned. 'My behaviour was wrong, but your predictions were wrong too. I was on the bridge for an hour and a half, and it was pretty draughty most of the time, but I have an idea sea air does a cold good.' 'Did you stand all that time?' asked Christopher. 'Oh, no, the Queen was kind enough to direct a chair to be brought for me.'

'Is she well? How did she look? Has she really enjoyed the trip?'

'I could not detect,' Winston answered, 'the slightest evidence of strain. When I came from the bridge to the saloon I did not at once recognize a masculine figure in khaki trousers. It was the Queen, who had taken off her coat. Prince Philip came in. "Come and meet your mother," he said to her. She laughed. "How can I, like this?" She is so completely natural.'

'Did you do much work with her?' Christopher enquired.

'There was no opportunity. We had a film, a very poor film, called *Maggie*. The cinema was very cold. I held a cushion to my chest like this, I was so chilled. I had never been up the river before. The Duke knew all about its history. I must get Lord Ivanhoe' – he paused – 'yes, Viscount Waverley, to take Clemmie.'

'Lord Moran will have port,' he said to the butler. 'Oh, yes, Charles, Stilton is wedded to port; let no man put them asunder. That terrible fellow has given you water,' he said contemptuously.

Winston handed me a letter from the President. He wants the P.M. to go to America on June 18. The letter ended: 'With warm regards, as ever, Ike.' 'You see, Charles, he wants a discussion between the two of us. He is very friendly.'

Christopher had spent the morning at Epsom and was full of the promise of one of Winston's horses. It had put up a great gallop.

'We have had nothing like it since the days of Colonist.[1] I put on £10 each way for you. It's running today.'

I said that a horse's legs were poorly adapted to meet wear and tear. Winston broke in:

'I don't know why, Charles, you, who know so much about Nature, should attack her so unfairly. When she designed a horse she never meant her to carry a man. You say a horse never lasts any time in a campaign. The unfortunate beast carries, besides a trooper, his saddle, and equipment and arms, a matter perhaps of fifteen stones.

'You did not think of that,' he said slyly, as he put his hand on mine in a disarming way.

Montague Browne[2] came in. 'It's time, sir, you went. You are due at the pier at two fifty-five.' The P.M. looked at his watch. 'Oh, there's plenty of time,' he said, pouring out another glass of port.

May 21, 1954

Yesterday, Winston admitted, was a rough day: a long Cabinet with some difficult problems. He grinned broadly, and I waited for what was to come.

'I was determined that the Committee should agree to a free vote in the House on Members' pay. They were then certain to lose.'

He became serious.

'It is all wrong when members go about scratching a meal here and a meal there. Do you know, Charles, that a large number, perhaps as many as a hundred and twenty, of the Members of the House have less to live on than a coal-miner? Some of them, poor devils, are not sure of a square meal. When I think of the power and grandeur of their situation I am certain that it is most dangerous to keep them in poverty; it is just asking for trouble.

'They are very decent people when you know them. Of course, they are tiresome at times. One of them rose and proposed the

---

[1] 'Colonist II' – winner of the Jockey Club Cup, the Winston Churchill Stakes, the White Rose Stakes and second in the Ascot Gold Cup (1950).
[2] Anthony Montague Browne, Private Secretary on secondment from the Foreign Office.

motion that there should be no increase in the payment of Members until Old Age Pensions were put on a satisfactory basis. I said, "What clap-trap." As if the two questions had anything in common.'

His voice rose till he was half shouting.

'How absurd to link them together. The cost of increasing Members' pay would amount, at most, to £250,000, while the Pensions would mop up forty or fifty millions. Besides, if things go well we might get both. I got my way in the end; I am not afraid of them, and they know it.'

He contemplated his breakfast.

'I mastered them, though I was not very good. But they were very friendly after the meeting.'

Montague Browne, when I saw him, put the matter rather differently. The meeting of the 1922 Committee had not gone very well.

'The P.M. left here,' Montague Browne continued, 'with a definite idea in his head as to how he would run the meeting, and the speech he was going to make to them. But the meeting in fact went quite differently, and when the P.M. worked off on them the speech he had prepared it wasn't really to the point. You know, Lord Moran, he will play bezique, instead of mugging up whatever is coming up. Yesterday, for example, he knew that the Chancellor was going to the Committee, and he ought to have talked it over with him, but he gets absorbed in cards.'

Winston, on the other hand, had a good word for bezique:

'It is strange, you have to use your brain, but it is a different part. I find it restful. It takes my mind away from things. I lunched the Home Secretary. You know, I don't like seeing people I don't know well.'

'They tire you?'

He grinned.

'No, they bore me. I like familiar faces round me. Christopher, for example. He is very good.'

While he talked to me he bound round his cigar a ribbon of what appeared to be brown paper. 'It's an anti-slobber device invented by one of the jewellers. I cannot use it in public, or they would ask me what it was for.' A broad smile lit up his face.

'Anthony has had no experience at all of Home Affairs. He has always done the Foreign Office, and done it well. But I don't know how he will get on with all the Home stuff.'

May 25, 1954
'I am near the end,' he said.

I had nothing to say, and he went on:

'I am glad now it is the end.'

I could not let this pass.

'But you aren't in bad shape?'

'Ah, Charles, when you see me in the morning I feel strong and capable. Though even now my back aches as if I had had a hard day's hunting yesterday. And I have a tired mind.'

He yawned, opening his mouth very wide.

'I have got to make a speech to those bloody women in the Albert Hall on Thursday. It will take me four or five hours to knock together, though I shall only be on my feet for twenty-five minutes. I have cut it down to that. Of course, I can still do administration; my great experience helps me in that. I can force myself to do anything. It is the lack of desire, Charles, which worries me.'

We sat for a time in silence, Winston staring gloomily into space.

'There is no let-up at all; everyone wants to see me. I am a specimen, a kind of survival. I wish things were quieter in the House and that the world was more at rest. I hardly walk at all now. I have not been out for a month, except to go to the House or to Chequers.'

He pushed away his bed-rest, stretching his arms and yawning again.

CHAPTER TWENTY-THREE

Anthony Had Better Accept

May 27, 1954

'There is a good deal of depression.'

'But surely the debate on Members' pay went as you wished?'

'Yes, I got my way, but I am depressed at the general bloodiness of things. I cannot see why anyone should want to quarrel with America. She stands alone in the world against Communism. The difficulty is how far we ought to go in restraining her from taking risks which we cannot share.'

His face lit up. 'I am seeing Billy Graham at noon and the Duke of Windsor at twelve-thirty.'

When I called at No. 10 this afternoon, to see if Winston was very tired after his speech at the Albert Hall, I was told that he had gone direct to the House of Commons. There I found him in his room in a cheerful frame of mind. The speech had gone well, he said.

'I was in command. My voice was hoarse yesterday – you know, I still bring up a lot of phlegm – but your namesake is very good; he did his job well.[1] After he had sprayed my throat my voice was loud, resonant and commanding.'

Winston said this with great vigour and verve, as if to say: that was how I did it.

---

[1] C. P. Wilson, ear, nose and throat surgeon to the Middlesex Hospital.

'They had passed a resolution the day before against the payment of Members but I talked to them very straight, telling them they'd got to have it.'

He seemed lost in thought for a little.

'Anthony would not have liked it if he had been present. I was in the saddle; there was no sign of inferiority or failure. I can still make a great speech.'

I asked him whether Anthony was becoming impatient. 'Oh, of course,' Winston replied. 'He'd like me to go.' Then he added quickly: 'I don't mean he'd like me to come to any harm.'

He grinned: something was coming. 'Woolton was down to make a short speech, but the lady who was in the Chair doesn't like him, and she had arranged with the organist that immediately I sat down he was to play "God Save the Queen". Oh, no, I'm not tired. I could have gone on for an hour; I spoke for thirty-eight minutes. But what is wrong is that I should make such a bloody fuss over this speech.' I suggested that he had had a worrying week. He mused. 'My relations with Anthony – ' he began and stopped short. 'The President and I consider Dulles and Anthony as a junior grade.' He said nothing for some time. 'Yes, Anthony would like me to go.'

June 2, 1954

As I approached Winston's bed he threw away the *Daily Express* with a sharp gesture of impatience. 'Max's paper attacks me in one column about the payment of Members, and on another page prays me to banish the idea of retiring.

'Stanley Baldwin, just before he resigned, proposed that members should be given an additional £200 every year, a sum equivalent to £500 now – and the unemployed could be counted in thousands then.'

His mind went back to the House of Commons.

'I despise these people's shifts and turns. The world deserves all it gets if it acts from fear. What else could I do?' he demanded hotly. 'Thirty Tory Members were determined to vote for the increase in pay, whatever happened.'

He mused for a time.

'I think they would be hard put to it if I go. My experience enables me to make a great many decisions quickly. You don't want me, Charles, to retire on health grounds?

'Anthony tells me nothing. He keeps me out of foreign affairs, treats them as a private preserve of his own. Now he doesn't want me to go to America. I don't mind. I'm ready to go alone.

'I shan't get a sleep this afternoon. I have a pretty full day. Two Cabinets with the Derby in between. A friend of Clemmie's dreamed some time ago that Lavengro would win the Derby. She put two pounds on this horse when it was forty to one. I think I shall back Lavengro. After all, a dream is a great thing. No one had heard of this horse then, while lately it has become more and more prominent in the betting.'

Pitblado met me in the passage. He told me that the P.M. had had a letter from Anthony which irked him. Pitblado smiled. 'They irk each other. Of course,' he continued. 'I can see the Foreign Secretary's point of view; when you are struggling against odds at Geneva[1] it is a nuisance to have a fixed engagement in Washington.'

June 4, 1954

Pulvertaft took a swab of the P.M.'s eye, which looked red and angry. When he had gone, Winston passed me the *Daily Mirror*. 'There is a serious row in the Party about this payment of Members. It is a crisis.'

'What will happen?'

'I can't tell. It depends on what attitude we take – whether we give way. The Cabinet has been in on everything. Nothing has been done without consulting them. Of course, Anthony has been absent a good deal, but he agreed with the line we took.'

His voice rose in anger: 'If they do nothing for Members who are worried about their income, I shall resign. I'm not going to run

---

[1] The conference met on April 26, 1954, to discuss the peaceful settlement of the Korean question and to restore peace in Indo-China.

away. I don't mind a row with some of the bloody fools among the Tories. They didn't care a bloody damn about Old Age Pensions before this came up. Now it serves their purpose to think of them in connection with the pay of Members. I had made up my mind to go at Whitsuntide, until Harold Macmillan said it would be very inconvenient for members who had Bills to put through the House. Then I decided to resign at the end of the session. If I stay longer it will be because of this controversy over pay,' and he jutted out his jaw and looked very fierce.

I asked him if all this affected his visit to America. 'I shall know more about that after I've seen Anthony,' he replied. 'I could go alone, of course. Anthony doesn't want that.' He thought for some time. 'I may not go.' I said I wished he could have a short let-up; a little peace. He said grimly: 'We've had our peaceful time. Now there is going to be trouble. Geneva is hotting up. Things are not looking well. It appears to be a crisis. We can do nothing,' he said sadly. 'We have no weapons. We can only bleat: "Please do not harm us. We are powerless." '

'If nothing comes out of Geneva,' I said, 'it will not do Anthony any good.'

'Oh,' Winston said quickly, 'it's not his fault. He has made a tremendous effort.'

June 10, 1954
I found a message from the P.M. by the telephone: 'The Prime Minister would be grateful if Mr Edgar King[1] and Lord Moran could call at 3 p.m.' We found him in his bedroom.

'My eyes are very troublesome,' he grumbled, 'worse than they have ever been.' He lay down in his frock coat on the bed (he had been at the Trooping the Colour in the morning). When King went to the bathroom Winston fixed me with a keen look. 'This will mean more work for me. Everything had been arranged. I was to go at the end of July. I was very happy about things. It was just

---

[1] Ophthalmic surgeon to Moorfields Eye Hospital.

a case of transferring the burden to Anthony's shoulders as smoothly as possible.' His voice became strong and resonant. 'Now it's a case of a world crisis. I could not leave the Government in an emergency such as this. It is not,' he added quickly, 'that I want to hang on to office for a few weeks more. But I have a gift to make to the country; a duty to perform. It would be cowardly to run away from such a situation. It would be wrong to think of the convenience of the Party now, to do something just to make it easy for Anthony to succeed, something which would allow him to get into the saddle before the Tories meet in the autumn. The Tories themselves would not wish it.' He paused. 'I don't know, of course, what view Anthony will take of this.' His jowl protruded as he said in firm tones: 'I'm in office, I'm master. I cannot plead that my health is so bad I ought to resign. My duty is plain. I shall postpone my visit to America for a week. Anthony would probably be able to go on the 17th, but he can't be sure, and the President himself suggested a postponement.'

June 15, 1954
Went to No. 10 to see if the P.M. was any the worse for the Garter ceremony at Windsor. He looked up and began turning over a pile of the morning papers. 'There is a very good picture of me in the *Yorkshire Post*. You haven't seen it? I can't put my hand on it. Oh,' he said, leaning over the bed, 'it's there on the floor. I haven't looked so dignified for a long time. The scene in the chapel was lovely.'

It had been a long day. 'I began at eight o'clock,' he continued, 'and went on till after midnight. I had to climb a great many stairs up to the Chapel and afterwards in the Castle; and there was a lot of standing, and I'm no good at that. In addition, I had an audience with the Queen. There were some very important matters I had to tell her. Of course I was weary – physically tired – at the end of the day, but my head was quite clear. I could have gone on working when I went to bed. I'm sure I have more vigour than I had, Charles. There is no doubt in my mind about that.

'I'm not thinking of retiring, at any rate till September. I have written to Anthony that I do not intend to resign at present. I don't know if he has accepted it. He'd better.' The P.M. looked very grim. 'Could I tell them,' he added as an afterthought, 'that you thought I was as well as before the stroke?'

I advised him not to use the expression 'stroke'.

'But I like the word,' he said obstinately. 'Of course I know that I'm nearly eighty and that I may get another stroke any day. My heart may stop at any time, but my health is certainly no excuse for evading all these great issues, just because one doesn't know the answers. I'm not going to quit. It would be cowardice to run away at such a time. No,' he said with great emphasis, 'I shall certainly not retire when any day anything might happen.

'It is not' – and his voice rose – 'as if I were making way for a strong young man. Anthony seems to be very tired. I detect strain in his telegrams. Sometimes he sends three thousand words in one day – and there is nothing in them. For instance, he wanted to change all the arrangements that have been made with Ike. He said Dulles had been very difficult and had attacked him. They showed me the account of what had happened, but it had to be pointed out to me how it could be taken as an attack on Anthony. Why, one of the incidents,' the P.M. said scornfully, 'happened a quarter of a century ago. I said I would not change my plans.' There was a pause and then the P.M. said quietly: 'He submitted. Look up my May 11 speech, Charles, and you'll see how I gave a warning that nothing can come of these talks at a lower level. They go on, day after day, endlessly. The Foreign Office keeps on splitting hairs. There is no one to say: "Bloody well go and do it." When I read what had happened at Geneva I felt a great sense of defiance. It was just like the war.'

June 17, 1954
The P.M. seemed in great heart this morning. 'The idea of a visit is a great success,' he began. 'It has been very well received. You saw what Ike said about the bridge over the Potomac river?' He picked up the *Daily Express* and read:

The existence of a bridge over which thousands of persons travel daily isn't news. But if the bridge falls it is instantly news. We are trying to keep the bridge between this country and Britain strong.

'I like that. And *The Times* is very friendly. I'm in control of the machine again. There is no one who has the cheek to suggest that I should go at the present time.'

His eyes were much better. King was in high favour. 'The bug has been been knocked on the head. I make my own defences quickly against infections.' As I was leaving he said: 'I'm glad you are coming, Charles. It will be very hot in Washington – it's over 100° there now, but I'll see you are comfortable and I'll insure you in case anything happens while we are in the air.'

CHAPTER TWENTY-FOUR

The One Consuming Purpose

June 24, 1954

Soon after we left Heathrow in the strato-cruiser *Canopus* I dined with Winston, Anthony and the Prof. Anthony did most of the talking. He was critical of the present administration in the United States. Speaking generally, they were not so intelligent as Truman's administration; this lack of *nous* was particularly noticeable in the State Department. Foster Dulles acted foolishly when he walked out of the conference at Geneva; it was a miscalculation on his part; at any rate it failed to produce the effect he anticipated. It was stupid of the Americans to hold aloof; they hardly exchanged a word with the Russians, and never spoke to the Chinese. 'You cannot expect,' Anthony continued, 'to get anything out of people if you won't speak to them.' Winston grunted approval. 'I say "Good morning" to the member for Ebbw Vale,[1] but I cannot claim that I feel very friendly to him.'

Anthony believes that the Russians and the Chinese could be separated if only the Americans would not insist on boycotting the Chinese. At present, it is true, the Russians and the Chinese work together, and Anthony gave us an amusing illustration of this.

'Molotov came to me one day and insisted that he must open the discussion. I was in the chair and said to him: "You can't be the first

[1] Aneurin Bevan.

speaker, for I have already got a name down." Molotov obstinately refused to give way. At last I said to him: "The name of the first speaker is Chou En-lai."[1] Molotov appeared very surprised; he had no idea, he said, that Chou En-lai intended to speak; he would certainly not stand in his way.'

'China is a more formidable power than you will admit, Winston. Unlike the Russians the Chinese do not seem to be frightened by the hydrogen bomb. Perhaps they don't know much about it.'

It was difficult to tell how far Winston was following this dissertation. He has always been sceptical of China as a great power, and when Roosevelt used to say that it was better to be friends than enemies with a country of four hundred million souls, he would listen in silence, but later he spoke scornfully of 'little yellow men'. It would seem that he has scarcely moved an inch from his attitude towards China since the day of the Boxer Rebellion.[2] In truth he is not interested. What matters to him is the situation in Washington. 'How,' he asks, 'can we expect them to see our point of view if we start nagging?' He was disturbed by Anthony's conversation, though he was resolved not to get into an argument with him.

The P.M. bottled up his misgivings, so that I could not detect a vestige of ill-feeling between the two men as they talked during dinner; they were gay and communicative. Winston was particularly cheerful, looking incredibly young, his face pink and unlined, his manner boyish and mischievous. Anthony had been to Wimbledon, and his face was reddened by the sun, but he looked tired. He told us that he had found the six-hour sessions at Geneva very fatiguing, especially when he was in the chair. Winston did not appear much interested in his account of Geneva. Perhaps, in the plane, he had difficulty in hearing what Anthony was saying.

The P.M. always claims that Anthony and he agree on most things in the field of foreign affairs, though it is not often very

[1] Chinese Minister for Foreign Affairs.
[2] The Chinese attempt to oust foreign influence from their country (1899–1900). After the massacre of many Europeans and Chinese Christians an international relief force re-established law and order.

noticeable; they don't seem, for instance, to have much in common about Suez, or China, or in their approach to Americans. It is true that Winston has appointed Anthony as his heir – after all, someone has to follow him – but he still regards him as a young man, and is not much influenced by his views.

Besides, when Winston's mind is set on something he can think of little else. He has always felt that the future of the world is bound up with the union of the English-speaking races. Now, at the end of the long day, nothing else seems to matter. He is going to America – he thinks it may be his last visit to his mother's native land – to see if anything can be done to narrow the rift about Moscow that is opening up between the two countries, and here was the Foreign Secretary bleating about what was wrong with the Americans. Later he confessed to me his misgivings. 'I hope Anthony won't upset them; they are so kind and generous to their friends.' He changed the subject rather abruptly.

Picking up my book, General Spears's *Prelude to Dunkirk*, he began:

'Hell knows no fury like a woman scorned. Spears used to love France; now he hates her. Some while ago I stipulated that he should not publish anything for a certain time. The time is up. I haven't read the book, but I expect he has made up for lost time.'

Winston was gazing out of the window at the clouds below.

'I wish flying had never been invented. The world has shrunk since the Wrights got into the air; it was an evil hour for poor England.'

He sighed heavily and turned from the window. He was tired now, and when he spoke his remarks were of a desultory and personal nature, as if he no longer felt equal to connected discourse; calling the steward, he demanded caviare. He grinned broadly.

'Do you remember, Charles, when Joe offered it to Stafford Cripps and he wanted to know whether it was eggs or fish? He said he could take it if it was eggs. Stalin didn't know which it was; he said he didn't worry about such questions.'

At last the P.M. called for his servant and prepared for bed.

June 25, 1954

No one, save Winston, seems to think that much will come out of this visit to Washington. Christopher says the Americans are hopping mad with us. There will be some straight talk, and Winston will be disappointed: he won't get what he expects to get. But surely, I tried to argue, Ike is friendly? 'He doesn't count,' Christopher rapped out. Winston, for his part, has never been a Doubting Thomas. He seems to have taken a new lease of life since we left London. At ten o'clock this morning by English time he called the steward and ordered him to take away the whisky and to bring champagne. Then he proceeded to make a meal off caviare and toast, though he had had a hearty breakfast only an hour before.

Four hours later the *Canopus* made a bumpy landing. We all waited for Winston. Presently he appeared, shuffling down the space between the seats of the aircraft. Christopher reminded him that he was wearing his spectacles, whereupon he stuffed them in his pocket without putting them in a case. Then Christopher said something in his ear, and he took the unlighted cigar from his mouth and handed it to the detective, while Anthony watched, with a grim smile, all these preliminaries to taking a curtain.

Before we landed, the P.M. handed me a sheet of notepaper: 'You might like to read it. That's what I shall broadcast. It's simple and clear,' he said. When he left the microphone on the airfield a way was made for him through a throng of photographers. Then the procession of cars began to move, and gathering speed rushed down the road, all the police sirens wailing, so that there was a great screeching sound. Every car on the road, when it heard the summons, pulled up obediently to the side while the high priests of democracy passed by.

When the evening came I made a point of arriving at the White House before the P.M. began to dress for dinner. He was with Anthony. Christopher came out with an important air and admonished me in his loud voice: 'You know, Charles, Winston has been in conference without a break since he left the airfield at nine o'clock this morning.' He said this as if I were personally responsible.

However, when I saw the P.M. my doubts were at once dispelled. His eyes were full of life and he was in tremendous spirits. He turned to me solemnly:

'The day has been an incredible success. It is astounding how well things have gone. Whatever cropped up, we seemed at once to agree on the principle which ought to guide us in seeking a solution.'

There was a long pause, then the whites of his eyes began to show between the pupil and the upper lid, and speaking with suppressed excitement he said:

'This may lead to results which will be received by the world with a gasp of relief and amazement.'

He appeared to believe that Ike liked his idea of meeting the Russians. He would go with Anthony. 'It's my show entirely. I have been working for this for a long time.' I asked him when he would go to Russia. 'It might be in July,' he answered, as if he were parting with the information reluctantly. He asked me not to discuss this with anyone. 'I tell my young people,' he explained, 'they must not talk about it, and I don't want to set a bad example.' He asked the hour. 'Oh, I've plenty of time.' Then he lay on his bed, and Kirkwood, his valet, brought him hot packs, which he held to his eyes, that were red and watering. As last he got into his bath, holding an enormous sponge as a fig leaf. 'Kirkwood,' he shouted, and without waiting called out in more peremptory tones, 'Kirkwood, turn on the hot tap.' He dressed very slowly, trying on one or two white coats in turn. While he was still deliberating which to wear, Anthony came in and commended his smart appearance. 'We ought to go,' he said mildly; 'the President will be there before us.'

Marshall invited me, when dinner was over, to sit beside him. The strain of the war on soldiers in high places had been grievous; it had taxed his strength until, as he told me at Quebec in the summer of 1943, his heart was 'all over the place'. What happened to him after he came back from China[1] I do not know, but it appears

---

[1] Marshall visited China from December 1945 to February 1946.

that some time ago he had a serious operation, and I was told that he could no longer concentrate for long on anything.

Now he lives in the past, so that we talked of the war for some time. He spoke of Winston with a kind of affectionate pride, telling me how he had been against the invasion of Normandy, though in the end he had animated and inspired the whole venture. Marshall affirmed, with an indulgent smile, that it had been part of the task of the Chiefs of Staff to wean Winston from wrong strategic conceptions – a point Alanbrooke made more than once. He did not tell how by the force of his character he himself dominated the Combined Chiefs of Staff during the war and prevented Winston getting his way with Franklin Roosevelt.

Great men are two a penny in wartime. It is not that there are more of them about: just that the public is in the mood for the grand epithet. And so, as far as I can follow military history, the admirals and generals have always been allowed to bask in the sun, that is if they won their battles. Their characters hardly seem to count; small busts of Napoleon and Nelson keep Winston company in his bedroom. And yet in this war no one, I suppose, thinks of a general as a military genius dictating the course of events by his craft. It is what Marshall was, and not what he did, that lingers in the mind – his goodness seemed to put ambition out of countenance.

The President came over and sat down and talked to Marshall about the war. It seemed to be his lot in life to do jobs that he did not care for, and he made no secret of the fact that his duties as President came under that heading.

June 26, 1954
Why Winston was so cock-a-hoop yesterday I cannot tell, unless he has come to some understanding with Ike about meeting the Russians. I can think of nothing else that will explain his mood. If he can only talk with Malenkov he is sure things will happen. This idea has completely taken possession of him. It has indeed become an article of faith and is never out of his head for long.

To hold off the threat of war until it is no longer worth while for anyone to break the peace – that is the only thing left to him now, his one consuming purpose. Without it there is little meaning in life. In his heart he has a great fear: he dreads another war, for he does not believe that England could survive.

He was talking to me yesterday of the war:

'They were terrific times, and yet I am more anxious now than I was then. My thoughts are almost entirely thermo-nuclear. I spend a lot of time thinking over deterrents.'

It is his belief – and this he holds with a fierce, almost religious, intensity – that he, and he alone, can save the world from a frightful war which will be the end of everything in the civilized globe that man had known and valued. And, he keeps saying, time is short.

No doubt there are other instincts at work. For one thing, Winston's mind is practical; he is, as he will say, a political animal. He knows that to bring about a lasting peace with Russia is now the only plausible reason for hanging on to the leadership of the Party. If there was no change of heart in the Kremlin, if a policy of peaceful co-existence was only a myth, it would be difficult to justify his holding on to power in his eightieth year, when he has not completely recovered from his stroke.

He has not forgotten the Socialist taunt of 'War-monger'. It hurt him then, it hurts him now. They had to admit that he had been a great war Minister. He would show them that he was as great a peace-maker. He would like, he once owned to me, to end his days with that final, resounding triumph, which would round off his story in war and in peace. And yet, when the P.M. presses for a meeting with Malenkov, he is not altogether thinking of himself. It is not just the old craving for personal distinction. I have learnt, where Winston's motives are concerned, to keep repeating to myself: 'Winston is not worldly.'

An idea that stirs his imagination can still drive that crumbling frame to surprising exertions. He knows that the longing for peace represents the deepest feelings of the country. Only yesterday he confessed that he would like once more, before he went, to speak for England as he had done in the trough of the war, if that would avert another war. He stopped and I saw that he was in tears.

But before he can do anything with Moscow it is necessary to bring the President into line with his plan for pacifying the world. That is really why he has come to Washington. He does not underrate the difficulties of his task. America does not trust the Soviet Union. She cannot forget Stalin's duplicity; she cannot believe that a Russian promise is worth the paper it is written on.

I had tossed about in bed piecing together what Winston had told me, so that when I went to the White House this morning I somehow expected to find him worried and irritable. He was reading Spears's book and looked up with a smile: 'It was two o'clock before I went to bed,' he confessed. 'You were then twenty-four hours out of bed,' I put in.

'I do not feel at all tired. There is something in the magnetism of this great portion of the earth's surface which always makes me feel buoyant. Take my pulse. I don't think I am any the worse for two of the most strenuous days I can remember.'

June 27, 1954
When I had changed I went to the White House and found the P.M. in his room. He began at once about the need for more time in order to tidy up what had been done during the Conference. He would like to come back to Washington after Ottawa, work for a couple of days and then return to England by air. It would be much better than wasting the time at sea. Christopher argued that the P.M. had still a day and a half before he must leave for Canada. But Winston blew up. 'It's not enough. Great things hang on what we do here.' He stumped off to the bathroom. 'Charles!' he called out, 'Christopher!' He was lying flat in his bath, with only his nose and mouth out of the water. 'I don't want you to think I'm ungrateful. I know you arranged the sea trip for my good. But I have to think of more important things than my health.'

Winston came into the room in his bath towel. 'Is Mr Eden back yet?' he demanded of his servant. He went on talking of what he would gain if he had more time in Washington. Then he shouted: 'Kirkwood! Mr Eden must be back. Oh, go and see. Christ! I hope they haven't quarrelled and killed each other,' he added with a grim smile. But he was not really amused at all; he was on edge about the result of Anthony's meeting with Dulles.

The door opened. 'Can I come in?' It was Anthony's voice. Winston jumped up and advanced towards him with outstretched arms. 'Anthony, my dear, tell me what happened.' Before I withdrew I heard enough to know that the interview had gone well. 'We talked about a number of things,' Anthony began, 'E.D.C., Egypt, with I think very good results.' Winston relaxed, and subsided heavily into a chair.

Ottawa, June 30, 1954

Washington took a good deal out of Winston, and he was already tired when he arrived last night at Ottawa. After his wonderful *tour de force* at Washington we had expected great things, but when faced by a string of questions at the Press conference at noon today he was listless and appeared jaded. At the end he got very sentimental over Canada and her connection with England, but there was more strength and life in his voice when he went on to speak of Canada's future and her boundless resources. She was the master link of Anglo-Saxon unity. This phrase was hammered out in the air on the way to Ottawa.

When he had done, the spark died out as suddenly as it had come to life, and it was in a very subdued mood that he sat down to luncheon with the High Commissioner. And then, as he put it later, 'with the help of some liquor I came to.' He did not talk a great deal, but seemed at peace. When, however, we returned to the hotel he struck a very bad patch, one of his black moods, sombre and full of dark thoughts. His voice had become querulous. He snapped at Jock, and bit the head off anyone who came near him. He would be glad when this bloody broadcast was over. He has always got worked up before an important speech, and now to his fears and apprehension was added a rather alarming degree of exhaustion. He seemed all in. He told me he had tingling in his cheeks. Did it mean anything? He asked me to take his temperature. 'I sat in the sitting-room between two fans half an hour ago. If I caught a chill, is it too soon to produce a pain in my chest?' He decided to play bezique, and then got very fussed when they told him there was only half an hour left and he had not yet finished his broadcast.

I left him; there was nothing I could do. The corridors of the hotel were lined with excited people, and from the steps of the hotel a great crowd swelled out into the streets beyond. Washington likes Winston, but it takes him very calmly. These Canadians were different. They were wildly excited. He belonged to them, and they had a feeling that they might never see him again, that he had descended into Ottawa out of history to say 'goodbye' to them. I went to his car, which was open, and put up the windows, and as I was doing this there was a burst of cheering. He was flushed and perspiring freely as he came down the steps after his broadcast; he paused to wave to the crowd and then clambered clumsily into the big Cadillac.

All the way to the Country Club, where he was to dine as the guest of the Canadian Prime Minister, crowds lined the road, waving frantically and smiling their affection. As his car drove off there was loud cheering, and I could see that Winston was greatly moved. I ran back to my car, and as the cheering grew in volume Winston levered himself out of his seat in the well of the car and with some difficulty perched himself on the body behind. There, with his hat in one hand, he held up the fingers of the other in the victory sign. Anthony had followed his example, and from my car some way behind they had the appearance of two marionettes acknowledging the cheers of the people with sharp, jerky movements of their arms. When the crowd thinned and the cheering died down Winston felt the chill night air, and putting on his hat subsided into the well of the car. Then as the car passed through a village there was more cheering and more crowds, and once again he hoisted himself, so painfully, on to the body of the car.

During dinner Winston became very happy. The broadcast was over, and he had not broken down. That had always been at the back of his mind. He had dreaded it, feeling that it would be something of a disgrace. Anyhow, he had got through and now he could relax. Mr St Laurent,[1] who sat on his right, looked a very tired man and made little attempt to talk to the P.M. But Winston was full of life and fun and beamed on everyone. The chicken broth particularly pleased him; he could not get it made like that at home, and they had paid him the compliment of providing the particular brand of champagne he likes – Pol Roger. At times he seemed to sit in a kind of stupor. Then he would wake up and raise his glass to Howe,[2] and talk with great animation. He said he did not want the party to break up; he was very happy. Anthony leant over; they were getting late, he said, they must set out for the airfield soon. Winston took no notice. It was a quarter-past eleven before we left the ground at Ottawa. In the air Winston kept talking of the kindly greeting the people of Ottawa had given him. 'I purred like a cat,' he said, 'I liked it very much.'

R.M.S. Queen Elizabeth, *July 1, 1954*

It was an immense relief last night to get Winston safely on board. I felt all day as if I were watching a patient with high fever which was only kept in bounds by cold sponging. Nowadays one does not ask whether a speech went well, but only, 'Is he all right?' It has come to that. Just to get through is an achievement in itself. A trip like this, though he loves every minute of it, makes great calls on a person of his temperament, it taxes his resources – and they are no longer there.

The Prof. and I decided to go to the veranda restaurant on the sun deck to keep a table for the P.M. We waited for some time, and then the buzz of conversation stopped suddenly as the P.M. came through the door. He appeared, very small and stooped and all huddled up as he walked, not very steadily, towards the table where we were seated. There, collapsing into a seat, he said contentedly, 'It's good to have nothing to do.'

---

[1] Prime Minister of Canada.
[2] C. D. Howe, Canadian Minister of Trade and Commerce.

But presently his brow clouded. 'It's abominably hot here,' he exploded. 'I don't know why I was persuaded to come by sea. We should have been at Chartwell now if we had gone by air as I wanted. Is there no fan?' he demanded in angry tones. 'Cannot you open a window? They are fixed. Good God! The sun is beating on me through the glass. It is quite intolerable. I shall never come here again.' By this time everyone in the small restaurant was looking at him and listening, for his voice carries. 'This is very embarrassing,' Christopher said. Jock appeared uncomfortable. The P.M. got up and stalked to another table, and when this proved to be no better he rose and moved to a third, where he slumped down, in the sulks. 'He seems very apprehensive about himself,' I said to Jock, 'all on edge.' Jock answered that he was not surprised. 'Things with Anthony are coming to a head. Anthony is on edge too; he does not know how to put it to Winston.'

July 2, 1954
This morning, after eight hours' sleep, his pulse is 72, and soft like that of a young man; he is positively benign and, incredible as it will seem to those who know him, lazily content. When I asked him if he had any speeches on the stocks he replied that he was not going to do anything for the present, except, of course, urgent telegrams. 'After all, Charles, that is why I came by sea, to get some rest. I do not think I shall retire at the end of the month. I don't think Anthony expects me to. He is contemplating a holiday – poor Anthony, he needs a change.' Winston said this as if it would be very inconsiderate to interfere with the Foreign Secretary's plans by resigning prematurely.

'I'm planning to go to meet the Russians, if they would like it. I shall draft a telegram to Molotov this morning. Anthony is not against it. He would come with me.' Speaking more quickly he went on: 'Ike has crossed a gulf of thought. He has taken a very important step. He has made up his mind that Communism is not something which we must at all costs wipe out, but rather something we have got to learn to live with, and alongside – peaceful co-existence.'

I told him of a saying of Pitcairn – a great physician in his time – that the last thing a doctor learns is when to do nothing and to leave things to nature. His eyes lit up. 'Yes, exactly.'

At that moment Jock came in, and when he saw me made to withdraw. 'Don't go,' Winston said. 'I want you. You haven't shown my Molotov letter to Anthony?' Winston did not catch Jock's answer. 'You say you have not?' he reiterated. 'I have not,' Jock repeated, almost shouting the 'not'. 'Good,' said Winston, 'I will show it to him myself. Come back, Charles, and lunch with me.'

Everyone appeared to be in high spirits when we began luncheon and there was a hum of animated conversation, a rare event at Winston's table. The P.M., it is true, did not apparently hear much that was said, and from time to time he turned to Anthony for enlightenment. But he seemed in good heart, and was amused when he was told a joke. 'I'm going on deck,' Anthony said at length. Winston then said something to him which I could not hear. The rest of the conversation was not at all difficult to follow.

Anthony: 'Oughtn't you to consult your colleagues before sending a letter to Molotov? I think you should tell them before taking this important step.'

Winston: 'Oh, during the war I always claimed the right to send messages to the President without any censorship. I put a communication to Molotov on the same level.'

Anthony: 'But it is a new principle.'

Winston: 'Is it? I am only asking Molotov if the Russians would like me to visit them. If they say "No," well the matter is finished, and I need not bother the Cabinet.'

Anthony: 'And if they say "Yes"?'

Winston: 'Well, in that event, if my colleagues do not approve, I can easily get out of it by telling Molotov that they do not agree.'

Anthony: 'That would be rather rough on the Russians. Besides, if it should get about before Geneva finishes the Americans would feel annoyed.'

Winston: 'It need not get about. The Russians are able to keep secrets.'

Anthony: 'They are certainly able, but will they be willing? That is quite another matter.'

Among those who went with Winston on his wartime travels, none ventured to argue with him in this fashion, and as Anthony and Bob Dixon were often in his company then, it means, I fear, that people no longer speak under their breath in the great man's presence. While this was passing through my head I became conscious that Christopher was making signals that we should leave them alone to fight it out.

July 3, 1954
'It is difficult,' said Winston as he stepped into his zip-suit, 'to find new interests at the end of one's life.' Not that he tries very hard to overcome the difficulty. The effective use of words and the exercise of power make up his life now, as they have done for more than half a century. He asked me if I had read Harold Nicolson's *Public Faces*. 'A very remarkable book,' he said, 'because, written in 1932, it is all about the atomic bomb.'

During dinner and afterwards until he went to bed at midnight Winston kept reverting to the prospect of a meeting with the Russians. Turning to Anthony, he enquired, 'Do you think they will answer "Yes"?' Anthony thought they would agree, unless there were internal difficulties. At Geneva he had seen Molotov every day; usually, it was true, about procedure, what should go on the agenda and things of that kind; not perhaps, Anthony conceded, about matters of high statecraft. But he had been very agreeable; he might help. Anthony thought that there was no doubt that Molotov had mellowed since the war. He discussed things as if he wanted to smooth over difficulties, not to make them. Winston said:

'I am counting on the Russians wanting a better time; they want butter, not bombs, more food, more comfort. For forty years they have had a pretty rough life. They may have given up dreams of world conquest, and be ready for peaceful co-existence. Anyway, Ike has crossed the gulf which separates a mission to destroy Bolshevism from living side by side in peace. I must admit that

I myself have crossed that gulf. I would like to visit Russia once more before I die.'

July 4, 1954
'I've had a lovely sleep,' Winston began while waiting for his break-fast. 'Eight hours is my proper ration. I took two reds; the drugged feeling they leave is very agreeable. I had dreams, but I cannot remember them. They soon faded.

'I shall retire on September 18th. I would have liked to go on, because I have everything at my finger-tips. They are fools,' he said impatiently; 'I can do it all so much better than anyone else.'

He changed the subject abruptly.

'Have you read the *Ocean Times*? Adenauer is demanding that France should ratify the European Defence Treaty. I am glad he has spoken out. The French are a disgrace. When they gave up in 1940 they wanted us to surrender too. We picked them out of the gutter, and now they think of nothing but themselves all the time; living in a welter of intrigue, they never seem to think of their country.'

'Will you go to Moscow before September?' I asked.

He picked me up. 'Vienna is the place I have in mind. I shall try and persuade the Russians to sign an Austrian treaty. If that came off people would whoop with joy. I might pay a courtesy visit to Moscow after Vienna – perhaps staying forty-eight hours. It has been my most strenuous week for many years. I did not know whether I could stand up to a strain of this kind, but I set my will to work. Coming at the end of this trip, I felt the broadcast at Ottawa most. I consider that my answers to questions at the Press luncheon at Washington – all spontaneous, without any preparation – was the greatest triumph of my career.'

I thought the P.M. seemed silent and preoccupied during dinner; he made no attempt to join in the conversation. But gradually he thawed and began to talk of the First War; of Plug Street[1] and the

---

[1] British nickname for Ploegsteert village in Flanders. Churchill commanded the 6th Royal Scots Fusiliers when holding the line which ran through Ploegsteert.

Battle of the Somme; and then, skipping a quarter of a century, how he had asked Bernard Freyberg the number of his wounds, how he answered 'thirty-three,' and had stripped and shown Winston the scars; and how he had bathed from Monty's caravan in the desert. This exchange of memories led to a very friendly atmosphere; it was difficult to believe that Anthony and the P.M. had any differences. Even when a telegram was given to Winston which brought up the projected visit to Russia, the discussion was mild and harmonious.

'After all,' said the P.M., 'both Ike and Foster Dulles have given their approval; they put it on paper in April of last year. They said that if the Prime Minister wished to make a "solitary pilgrimage" to Moscow, though they would not advise it, it was all right by them. Do you remember the message ended: "Of course you have the right to go whenever you wish." '

Anthony, who all along has been strongly opposed to such a visit to the Russians, once more bowed to Winston's tenacity and strength of will. He put it like this: 'When, Winston, you saw the President in Washington only a week ago you discussed everything but the date of this visit. You spoke to him then of a reconnoitring patrol, and you could send a message now to Ike saying that you proposed to go to Moscow as part of the patrol and would keep him informed of what happened.'

Winston is glad now that he took Anthony's advice and consulted the Cabinet about the visit to Molotov. The Government had agreed, with a few minor modifications, and a telegram had been sent to Molotov; he was now waiting for an answer. Anthony thought the odds on the Russians agreeing to a visit by Winston were 6–4 on, and perhaps 10–1 against a later meeting of Molotov, Eisenhower and the P.M. 'It may fail,' said Winston. 'If it does, then with a clear conscience and an easy mind I can go to my Maker.'

At that moment Miss Gilliatt appeared and handed the Foreign Secretary a telegram. He read it twice. Then, putting down his cigar on a plate, and half turning in his seat as if he wanted to concentrate more on the telegram, he began reading it again. It was from Roger Makins. The Ambassador was worried by the storm suddenly raised in the United States by a speech of Senator Knowland,[1] who appeared to insinuate that the Prime Minister and the Foreign Secretary had gone to Washington to get Communist China admitted to the United Nations against American wishes. The Ambassador pleaded for a disclaimer. He wanted the Foreign Secretary to say that it had hardly been mentioned in the discussions in Washington, and that there was general agreement that this was not the moment for China's admission to be considered.

Anthony handed the telegram to Winston without a word. When he had read it he looked up and said to Anthony: 'It is curious that only this afternoon, after I had read the Press extracts, I got out of bed and went to you with exactly the same point as the Ambassador makes. I agree with Roger,' Winston said.

'I don't,' Anthony retorted with some warmth. 'It would be an intolerable position if the F.O. had to make a statement every time Senator Knowland attacked Britain.'

'Roger's telegram is too long, of course,' Winston put in, in his most accommodating manner. 'Why not, in six lines, say that you do not propose to support China's application for membership of the United Nations at this moment while they are still at war, and in fact the aggressor nation? Then when the whole question comes up it can be judged according to the circumstances existing at the time.'

Anthony thought this point was too technical and too subtle.

Neither the P.M. nor the Foreign Secretary would give an inch; they kept on reiterating the same points. At last Jock intervened: 'Why not ask Ike to say at his Press conference that the matter to which Senator Knowland referred had hardly been mentioned at the Washington meeting?' The argument became so sharp that Christopher beckoned to us, and we rose and left the room. Almost at once Winston came into his bedroom, where we had retreated. He mumbled that it made things very difficult when Anthony could not distinguish between a big and a small issue. It was a row over

---

[1] Republican Senator for California.

nothing. The P.M. was worried. After all, the ambassador is Anthony's man. Jock repeated his suggestion of Ike and the Press conference. But when the P.M. went on mumbling as he paced his cabin Jock saw that nothing was to be gained by argument and slipped away.

Christopher, however, began the argument all over again. I whispered to him that it would be better to adjourn the discussion, whereupon, taking my hint, he said: 'Wow! I'm going to bed.'

The P.M. lay flat on his back, mumbling away. I kept silent. He said again that he was very worried, though I could not see why he should get into a stew if it was a small issue. 'You can go into this in the morning,' I said mildly. 'It is nearly two o'clock.' The P.M. on such occasions is like an alarm clock; you must let him run down before there is quiet. The voyage had been doing him good; it was a complete rest. He had admitted as much, and had said this morning that he was reconciled to a ship, and here we were, having a pitched battle in the small hours of the morning. How could he expect to get to sleep when he was upset like this? I left him still mumbling.

July 5, 1954

I was late in waking, and went at once to the P.M.'s room, not without some trepidation. Vaguely – it did not come down to details – I had a feeling that last night's fracas could have done him no good. I found him placidly reading a novel. He had had a beautiful night. How many hours' sleep? 'Oh, I went off when you left the room, and did not wake till half an hour ago.' Winston seems, to a doctor's eyes, to be designed on lines quite different from the rest of mankind. Part of the difference I ascribe to some kind of shock absorber which is not included in the make-up of most men. As for Anthony, he confessed to me that he had taken aspirin 'for the strain'.

Lunched with Anthony and Tony Rumbold;[1] Winston was not mentioned once.

[1] Sir Anthony Rumbold, Principal Private Secretary to the Foreign Secretary.

For our last dinner on board Christopher had taken counsel with the chef, and between them they had planned a tremendous feast; but it was not the unusual repast so much as the change in the climate that pleased me. Last night I lay awake going all over the unpleasant altercation between Winston and Anthony, and it was with some apprehension that I had looked forward to another uncomfortable sitting. But tonight everything was different. Winston was in his most benign mood. He did not avoid delicate subjects; he seemed to be able to talk about them with Anthony's full approval. A topic, which last night was full of perils, was now touched so lightly that it was seen, as it were, in retrospect in a spirit of amused detachment. His words, to be sure, were not very different from those he used last night, but he seemed to have now only one purpose in his mind – to smooth over the changing of the guard.

To Anthony Winston talked as father to son, as if he were only concerned for his future happiness. Speaking very earnestly, he implored him not to quarrel with America, whether China was or was not a member of the United Nations. He spoke of himself as a link with Queen Victoria, and it was surely the historian who impressed on Anthony that influence depends on power.

'Up to July 1944 England had a considerable say in things; after that I was conscious that it was America who made the big decisions. She will make the big decisions now.'

Winston said this with an air of finality.

'We do not yet realize her immeasurable power. She could conquer Russia without any help. In a month the Kremlin would be unable to move troops. The Americans would become enraged – violent. I know them very well. They might decide to go it alone. That was what Dulles meant when he talked about an agonizing reappraisal of policy. Without their help, England would be isolated; she might become, with France, a satellite of Russia.'

Winston's voice broke, and his eyes filled with tears. And then someone mentioned Roger Makins's telegram. It seemed possible now, among friends, to discuss any subject quietly and without heat. Anthony said good humouredly that he paid a good deal of attention to ambassadors' opinions and that Roger was a very good ambassador, but he had found that the man on the spot was inclined to take local events and issues too much to heart. Winston thought we were inclined to take China too seriously; her strength had been exaggerated; she only produced two million tons of steel in a year, and steel was everything in war. Anthony revealed how he had ragged Chou En-lai about his wish to be in the United Nations. Chou became embarrassed; it was obvious that he was most anxious that China should be recognized as a member.

The storm had passed and the smell as of a garden after rain made everyone happy. We sat back and watched the P.M. pick his way, light-footed as a cat, among the pools. We were relieved, of course, by his tact, but not perhaps altogether surprised. After all, he has spent his life putting things to people and waiting to see how they take it. When he has a mind to make the effort no one can be more adroit, more skilful in a difficult situation. But Winston's dexterity in dancing a verbal minuet is nothing new to those of us who have been with him since the war began.

Tonight there was something more. As the banquet unfolded and one delicacy followed another we all sensed that something unusual had happened and that Winston was in a strange expansive mood, in which he was taking notice of his guests. He had become conscious that those who served him and waited upon his wishes had been part of his life for a long time, that they were human beings and that they were devoted to his service. This might be the last time that he would travel as Prime Minister and some of those with him now had gone wherever he had gone since 1940.

It was late now, but Winston's gaiety and good humour had spread to his guests, and there was no thought of bed. The old man bubbled merriment. Then he went back to the First War – always a sign with Winston that the weather is set fair. Anthony began reciting Persian poetry, rather shyly and without confidence. Winston was astonished and excited. 'But Anthony, I did not know you could speak Persian. I had no idea you had this gift. It is extraordinary. When did you learn this language?' I reminded

Winston that Anthony had taken his Final Schools at Oxford in Oriental languages, and got a First in them. Winston knew nothing of this. Why should he? He had nominated Anthony to succeed him, but that did not mean that before he did so he had ferreted out all the facts of his life. Anthony began writing in Persian the names of those round the table, but Winston's interest in Persian poets soon began to flag. He beamed round the table; the dinner, he said, had been very agreeable, he hoped a year tonight the same people might meet and dine together. 'You, Anthony, will be able to give the party at No. 10.' 'No,' said Anthony. 'Whatever happens I will be your guest.'

I went with Winston to his cabin. When he had nothing on but a vest he suddenly remembered some lines of Pope which he could not recall when round the table. Waddling quickly across the room, he disappeared into Anthony's cabin, and through the open door I heard him say, 'I must recite to you the words I could not remember just now.'

CHAPTER TWENTY-FIVE

The Prime Minister
and the Suez Rebels

London, July 14, 1954
I found the P.M. a little deflated this morning after a long and tiring day. Following a tough Cabinet, he had to wind up the debate on Suez.

'It was Anthony's policy, but I had to bear the odium of it. Nobody hates getting out of Egypt more than I do. But it's no use to us in the present circumstances. Not a single soldier is in favour of staying there. Why don't Waterhouse and the rebels see that?'

Winston turned on me:

'Oh, I'm glad somebody has some spirit left. They are right to make their protest.'

He was not angry with them. He went on:

'Mary is a fortnight overdue. It's an extraordinary business this way of bringing babies into the world. I don't know how God thought of it.'

July 20, 1954
Summoned to No. 10, I was about to go into his room when a secretary came out and said would I mind waiting a few minutes; the Prime Minister was just dictating a telegram. Pitblado, Oates and Miss Gilliatt were all bobbing in and out of his room; something unusual was afoot. As I entered his room he held out his hand in an absent-minded way, and without taking his eyes from a document in front of him said:

'There is a crisis – a political crisis – this bloody Suez business. I can't tell what will happen. I don't know. I may get my way.'

He seemed to have forgotten that he had sent for me, and went on studying the document. After a time he looked up and held out his hand: 'Thank you, my dear.'

When there is trouble brewing I like to keep an eye on him, and after dinner I called at No. 10. He was, they told me, at the House of Commons. I found him in his room. 'It is an extraordinary business, Charles, getting old.' Until a year or two ago it appears that he had not heard the 'inaudible and noiseless foot of time'. I asked him what he noticed. He shrugged his shoulders. 'Everything.' He does not watch the onset of old age with detachment; he regards it as a stab in the back when he is fighting to keep his power. With a gesture of impatience he set his jaw, if he lost he would find things to do when he resigned.

'I have my book, *A History of the English-speaking Peoples*. It is an important book. People will lap it up. I shall not give up politics. If there is an election and we are defeated, as we may be, I would seek re-election and sit on the front Opposition bench.'

Christopher wanted him to fly to Ulster to see his horse run. I think we scotched that.

'I must see Anthony tomorrow,' he said gloomily.

July 28, 1954

I found a pile of morning papers outside his room, and a notice 'Do not disturb' hanging on the handle of his bedroom door. He was still asleep. There wasn't a sign of a secretary or of Kirkwood. I took the *Daily Mirror* and the *Daily Herald* from the pile and waited. At half-past nine the buzzer went. No one answered it. It went again, this time without stopping. I went into his room. He looked sleepily at his clock. 'I went to bed at half-past one, so I have had eight hours sleep.' He picked up a green pill from his table. 'I put it in my mouth when I woke at seven o'clock, and then I took it out again.' He plainly felt that he deserved a good mark for his self-discipline. 'There is another crisis,' he said wearily. 'Read this,' and he gave me the *Daily Express*. 'No, read the Leader; it's unpleasant.' I turned the page. 'A Day of Sorrow, a Day of Shame.' Beneath these headlines I read: 'Under our very eyes, by the hand of a Tory Government, the greatest surrender is taking place since the Socialists and Mountbatten engineered the scuttle from India.'

'Fancy ending my career with clearing out of Egypt. I wish I hadn't had to do it. The Opposition are dying to get at me. They were terribly keen on evacuating the Canal, but they may combine with the rebels just to get us out. We might be defeated. In that case we'd have a vote of confidence in the House on Friday. We might go to the country. I might lead. It would have to be put to the Party. I don't know what they would do. They'd have to choose between a doddering old man and a young, brilliant –'

He stopped short and rang his bell. When Montague Browne appeared he said: 'Will the Queen hold the Council at Arundel? Go and find out.' They brought his breakfast. He slashed across a fried egg and pushed the plate away. He picked up a paper, though he had read them all before he went to bed, and almost at once he put it down again. 'It's the dream of Anthony's life,' he murmured.

July 29, 1954

The P.M. has complained lately that his eye is no better, and it has been arranged that he should see Sir Stewart Duke-Elder and Mr Davenport in consultation. Winston said he would like that. His dislike of strangers does not apply to doctors. Then this Suez debate threatened to upset our plans. However, a message came through from No. 10 that the Prime Minister would see us in his room at the House of Commons at four o'clock. We found him in a reasonable mood. If he was on the verge of defeat in the House of Commons it did not seem to worry him. I decided, however, to be at hand in case things went wrong, and when the doctors had gone I made my way to the Gallery of the House to wait for Anthony Head to open the debate. He was the ablest of the young soldiers on Winston's staff during the war, and I knew he would

talk sense. He surely did. Speaking without a note, he told the
House that there was no alternative to evacuating the base. The
hydrogen bomb had changed the whole situation. This weapon
would be used in the next war, and used too on Britain. In such circumstances our ability to send large armies overseas would be
'severely strained'. Apart from the bomb, the base would be of little
use to us in peace or war if Egypt was hostile. Finally, he drew attention to Turkey's admission to N.A.T.O. and claimed that this had
completely altered the position in the Middle East.

Attlee, who replied for the Opposition, had a simple task. The
arguments the Government were advancing to justify the evacuation of Suez were precisely those which Mr Churchill had repudi-
ated so vehemently and so scornfully when in opposition in 1946.
He had only to give chapter and verse. When the plan to withdraw
our troops was announced by the head of the Labour Government
Mr Churchill said that 'it was a most painful blow.' 'He must have
been in acute pain yesterday,' said Mr Attlee, thrusting forward his
hatchet face as if he was about to cleave the Prime Minister's skull.
Mr Churchill had spoken with derision of a policy of scuttle – the
rest of Mr Attlee's sentence was lost in a tumult of Labour cheers.
In the spring of 1946 Mr Churchill had said, 'Things are built up
with great labour and cast away with great shame and folly.' What,
asked Mr Attlee, would the Right Honourable Gentleman have said
if the Labour Government had brought forward the present proposals? If, Mr Attlee concluded, the Prime Minister had stood up to
his own back benchers a better settlement could have been arranged
than was possible now. He had refrained from doing what was right,
and had now to eat humble pie.

When Mr Attlee sat down bedlam broke loose among his supporters; for a full minute they bellowed their approval. It had indeed
been a savage and damaging attack; so effective that I found my
heart thumping. I hated every minute of it. Winston's face was grey
and expressionless, as if he no longer knew what was happening; he
was so still he might have been frozen to the bench. He was hurt,
but there was worse to come.

Captain Waterhouse rose. He was the leader of the Tory rebels. The agreement[1] had been signed: 'There it is,' he exclaimed, waving a piece of paper, 'and in this piece of paper we have got all that is left of eighty years of British endeavour, thought and forethought.' He turned towards the P.M. 'It must be grave indeed for him now, to have to take this decision.' Winston, who had been sitting with his head bowed, turned round quickly and looked at him. Did this rebel really know how he hated the whole miserable business?

If Winston has believed in anything at all in the course of his long life it has been in the British Empire and all that it stands for. Some of his happiest hours as a young subaltern were spent in India – and India was gone. Now this rebel was reminding him of 'The River War'. It must have brought back a flood of memories of Omdurman and the 21st Lancers and the dervish spearmen and the wild gallop in the desert; and Egypt, too, was gone. His heart was with the rebels.

'If,' said their leader, 'the electorate of this country had seen or foreseen this paper in 1951, we should not now be sitting on this side of the House.' He had to pause until the storm of Opposition cheering died away. Happily the P.M. did not seem to hear. His mind was a long way off. 'If,' Captain Waterhouse went on, 'the hydrogen bomb is making our position in the Suez Canal completely untenable, why have we been fiercely arguing for six, eight or ten months about the power of re-entry?' He did not believe these were the real reasons at all. We were becoming weary of our responsibilities, we were losing our will to rule.

That was the fear that was gnawing at Winston's peace of mind. He was not thinking at all of the defeat of the Government; did that, after all, really matter? When Captain Waterhouse had done, the P.M. rose with difficulty and, stumbling along the Front Bench, left the Chamber. I did not follow him, because I felt he would not throw up the sponge. In a few minutes he came back. He had changed his mind. I knew that he was going to speak.

[1] On July 27, 1954, an agreement was signed in Cairo providing for the withdrawal of British troops from the Suez Canal Zone.

An opportunity to intervene soon came. The Socialist Member for Northampton, who had risen when Captain Waterhouse sat down, made a strange charge; he roundly affirmed that an agreement to get out of Egypt had been held up by a back-bench cabal in the Conservative Party, encouraged under the table by the Prime Minister himself. The P.M. pulled himself to his feet. 'That is an absolute untruth.' Mr Paget persisted that Mr Churchill had let it be known that he was against evacuation. Greatly moved, the P.M. rose. He had not concealed in public speech how much he regretted the course of events in Egypt (and indeed in the privacy of his home his lamentations were loud and often repeated). But he had changed his mind because the hydrogen bomb had changed the whole strategic position in the world, making thoughts which were well founded and well knit together a year ago obsolete – utterly obsolete, he repeated. It had changed the opinion of every competent soldier he had been able to meet.

Winston had spoken for four minutes – two hundred and fifty words – and I have given the substance of his speech. But in truth the Secretary of State for War had said as much in opening the debate. Why, then, was the P.M.'s intervention so effective? The answer is to be found, I think, in the fact that Winston is a poet. And it is because he is a poet that he could do what Head, with his logic, had failed to do. He could open the eyes of the House to the appalling spectacle of the first few weeks of the next war. When hydrogen bombs were falling on London, what happened at a base at Suez would not, he thought, matter a great deal. Before he sat down he had restored to the House a sense of proportion, so that they were able to measure the importance of Suez against the incredible calamities of a war of annihilation.

July 30, 1954
The P.M. was in good heart this morning. I said to him that the debate had not ended badly. He corrected me:

'It was a triumph. If I never speak again in the House I can say I have done nothing better. I dominated the House. And,' he continued, 'it was without preparation of any kind. I said they must keep a sense of proportion. If ten million are killed in London by a hydrogen bomb, Suez will not seem of much importance to those who are left alive. When I sat down I was trembling all over. I was very excited. My pulse was over a hundred for a long time after my speech. Take it now, Charles. I don't think it did me any harm. Anthony was good; he got a great reception when he sat down.'

When I left the P.M. I met the Lord Chancellor. He is a friendly soul, but was very critical of Winston's recent achievements. 'At Wednesday's Cabinet Winston didn't seem to take things in. It was painful. I said something to him,' the Lord Chancellor went on, 'which he entirely misunderstood. Oh, yes, he heard what I said all right. Then yesterday he was as lively as a cricket. Perhaps the subjects that came up were less difficult, or he found them more interesting. I am sorry for Anthony and Rab; they don't know where they are. Of course, Moran, you know more about this than I do, but surely things can't go on like this?'

Coming from the Lord Chancellor, this was disturbing. However, though he is an able lawyer, as a politician he is very inexperienced, and I wondered if Anthony had been opening his heart to him. I decided to have a word with Norman Brook. As Secretary of the Cabinet he would know if the P.M. was no longer in control; besides, they all seem to go to him when in trouble. Norman agreed that Winston made no effort at preparation; he was definitely lazy. He instanced a review of Defence policy. 'Why, it used to be his pet subject, but now when it came up he seemed to take no interest in it.' But Brook thought he still did the Cabinet 'all right'. 'It's really a *tour de force*. He picks it up as he goes along. He doesn't bother to master anything in advance. Plays bezique instead,' and Norman smiled. 'It's really this business of meeting the Russians that keeps him from going. Anthony knows this. He ought to go before Parliament meets. There might be real trouble if he hangs on beyond that. He is trying Anthony and Rab very high. Anthony is either very sweet or very angry, he can't be quiet and firm.'

I said that I had noticed for some time that Winston tended to exaggerate things. The first day at Washington, for example, was an 'incredible' success; and he is always telling me how he had dominated the House of Commons or the Cabinet. 'Yes,' said Brook, 'he exaggerates the public success of his visit to Washington, keeps talking about it.' He agreed with me that this was compensatory; the P.M. did it because he wanted to justify to himself his conduct in hanging on to office. It wasn't vanity – he never did this kind of thing during the war – but only an over-mastering desire to make out a case for remaining Prime Minister.

August 3, 1954

Last night Winston telephoned from Chartwell that he had started a cold in the head. He wasn't coughing and had no temperature. What could I do for him? Could he take penicillin? And what about a Dover's powder? This morning a message came that he was streaming and thought he would have to ask the Queen to cancel his audience. He would like to see me as soon as it was convenient for me to come. When I saw him he kept closing his eyes, and then, when he opened them again, he seemed for a moment not to know what was happening. 'I am tired and torpid,' he said.

I asked Jock how he thought Winston had been since Parliament rose.

He answered: 'Last night we were talking, when he said, "I'm sorry, Jock, to harp on this, only I've got to make the most difficult decision of my life." Until he makes up his mind whether to go or not he will be on edge.'

'When will he decide?'

'When?' Jock repeated, as if he was half thinking of something else. 'Well, he's supposed to have made up his mind already. Now he seems busy unmaking it,' and Jock smiled.

CHAPTER TWENTY-SIX

One Man's Will

August 6, 1954

'I don't know what to do,' Winston mused. 'For half of the day I am determined to stay and see the business through, and then for the other half my resignation seems inevitable. I think Anthony would be well advised to be Leader of the House and Deputy Prime Minister.'

There was a long pause.

'But of course Anthony might want to be Prime Minister. I know my theme, and I don't want to give it up. I can do it better than anyone else.'

Then, apparently on the impulse of the moment, he rang a bell.

'Bring that paper,' he said to Miss Gilliatt when she appeared. 'I'm going to show you something which is deadly secret. No one except the Cabinet has seen it. I show it to you, not to get your opinion on high policy, but we have been very close together for a long time and I want you to see what I can still do.'

He handed me a paper folded like a letter, but perhaps twice the size. In the centre of the first page was a heading: 'Two Power Talks – for the consideration of my colleagues'.

On the two inner sides was his argument. There seemed nothing particularly secret in this; it was just the case for a meeting with Malenkov. The United States of America, the argument ran, knows that at present she is well on top in thermo-nuclear weapons, and that this may not always be so. She may feel that it would be foolish to wait until this advantage has slipped away and Russia, in addition to her immense army, is as well armed with atomic weapons as America. She may feel tempted to have a show-down while Russia cannot match her in the possession of these awful weapons of destruction. There is a very real risk in these circumstances of a third world war. Would it not be prudent to give his plan a trial?

I was still in the middle of his argument when he rose, saying that he was going to sleep. 'Bring it to me when you have done.' I was reading it a second time when Kirkwood appeared. 'The Prime Minister would like to see you, sir,' he said. I found him lying flat on his bed, with his eye-shade, though the curtains were drawn. 'You like it? I think the argument is very tight and clear. It took me two hours. Of course, I could have done it quicker once.'

I went off to find Montague Browne to return the document. 'It is remarkable that he should do this in two hours,' I said. Montague Browne explained that the P.M. had said all this to him at different times in snippets. He had just joined the bits together. I asked in the office if the Cabinet had been impressed. 'Impressed but not convinced. The F.O. dislikes it. They say if we seem to appease Russia, other countries, like France, will say let us all hasten and make our own peace with her, and we shall see the break-up of N.A.T.O. Lord Salisbury and Crookshank were very much against.'

Will Winston go in September? No one can tell. They say that the country would like him to go on. As for the Party, no two reports agree. The Tories could, of course, get him out, but I doubt if they have the nerve. They are afraid he might say: 'I wanted to go on, but they wouldn't let me. I wanted to meet the Russians, but they wouldn't have it.' The Tories are afraid that if this got about they might lose the next election. They know that the P.M. won't say this, but they instinctively don't like being exposed to such a contingency. I wondered about the Cabinet. It seems that there is a small clique which is more and more getting up against the P.M. I hear that one of them at least is bloody-minded. Most people feel that it depends on how the P.M. shapes. They find him up and down. He will do something very badly indeed, and then when everyone is saying that he ought to go, he will astonish them by some *tour de force*. And then Montague Browne added as an afterthought: 'If Eden does become Prime Minister I am afraid the people he will get round him will just echo his opinions. He's like that.'

August 12, 1954

I found Winston sitting over the luncheon table with Wheeler-Bennett,[1] who soon took his leave. I brought up Attlee's visit to Moscow. Usually you cannot start him off if you try, but now he gave a grunt of disgust.

'It will lose the Tories a lot of votes. I had the initiative. Now we have lost it. I might have pushed on and done something. As it is, people will think it very sensible on Attlee's part.'

He blamed Salisbury and 'that impudent Crookshank'.

'We had planned our visit to meet the Russians at the end of September as a grand climax for Anthony.'

I asked him would Attlee's visit affect this.

'Well, it has taken the bloom off the peach. There would have been an outburst of joy if I'd seen Malenkov. Now Attlee has done it.'

He said to me: 'I must take half a red and get an hour's sleep.' I refused point blank to be a party to this. 'I don't want to rebel against you,' he said affectionately, and then proceeded to cut a capsule in half, putting his wet finger in the powder. He made a grimace. 'What a horrible, taste. Retribution, Charles.'

August 16, 1954

3.15 p.m. Winston was playing bezique with Jock.

'Last night I woke at three o'clock and lay awake for three hours. My mind was marvellously clear; more efficient and smooth working than it has been for a long time. Almost as it used to be. I saw plainly outlined the most important and burdensome problem

[1] Sir John Wheeler-Bennett, historian and Fellow of St Anthony's College, Oxford.

I have to solve – my relations with Anthony. I don't see why he wants to take over the dregs at the fag end of Parliament – only one more session before the election – when nothing can be done. I suppose he sees himself as the brilliant young leader who will change everything. But there's no money, and without money, believe me, you cannot do anything. I have told them that I am quite willing to go on for another year if they would like me to. There may be an election in May. I'd not go on after that.

August 18, 1954

Winston was sitting up in bed at Chartwell, dictating. 'Don't go away,' he said to the secretary. 'Stay in the dining-room.' He did not hold out his wrist for me to take his pulse; he had other things to think of besides his health. I had the impression that he was seething with suppressed excitement, he talked to me with vehemence, and in a loud voice, as if he were seeking to convince someone.

'I thought of sending a message to Mendès-France[1] that I would like to see him in Paris, but it occurred to me that this might look as if I was trying to put pressure on him. Then yesterday of his own accord he asked if he could come to Chartwell to see me. He's going to Brussels for the meeting of the Six Powers about E.D.C. and would come here on his way back. I'd like that. It would be a good thing if he came to England. I shall say terrible things to him – of course within the limits of hospitality. I shall arrange for a guard of honour at the airfield. I shall wrap up what I am going to say in a lot of flattery. I shall tell him that the world is not going to be ruled by the French Chamber. I shall warn him that if the Chamber rejects E.D.C. France will be alone in the world. I shall tell him bluntly that we shall go on without them. Never was such obstinacy founded on such impotence.

'I shall tell them America may pull out and fall back on peripheral defence bases in the Pyrenees, in Norfolk, in Iceland and

[1] French Prime Minister and Minister of Foreign Affairs, June 1954– February 1955.

Turkey, so that if Russia gets nasty the Americans can drop a few bombs on her. Peripheral defence.' His voice was filled with scorn. 'It means that we shall be in the target without a say in what is in dispute. I don't like that at all. I want to prevent Ike falling back on this kind of defence.'

He smiled grimly.

'It appears that the Kremlin and our Foreign Office are at one; they do not want Malenkov to meet me.'

Moran: 'But why?'

'Oh, they don't know what might come out of such a meeting. I would have kept the Russians firmly in contact with reality; there would have been no swilling champagne,' he said bitterly. 'Of course, they might have refused to meet me outside Russia, and I couldn't have gone to them, but at least I'd have made a gesture. I'd have offered to meet them, and people would have known that it wasn't our fault if there was no meeting. It is a great relief to have charge of the F.O. instead of having to argue with Anthony. I can get something done. Anthony works very hard and is most conscientious, plugging away at routine. But that's not what is wanted at the Foreign Office, where you must take up the big issues and deal with them.'

He glowered at his papers. Then he looked at me.

'I want you to help me. In the afternoon I can neither keep awake nor go to sleep. Lennox-Boyd came to luncheon, and he was haranguing us when I dropped off to sleep, sitting at the table. I hate not being able to do one thing or the other. When I rise from luncheon I have seventy-five per cent of sleep in me; what I need is something to tilt the balance in my favour. All I ask for is an hour of oblivion – unconsciousness. I love the sensation of going to sleep. I love sleep. I don't get the kind I did forty years ago when I was at the Admiralty in the First War.'

He shut his teeth together as if he were biting something very hard.

'I've made up my mind. I shan't go. At any rate till Christmas. There may be a bloody row. I don't mind. I don't think they will gain anything by knocking me about. You must not conclude that

I am just sitting still and doing nothing. Osbert Peake[1] is coming down tomorrow about Old Age Pensions. Nearly all the Ministers are away on holiday, but I shall go on working.'

'The P.M. is determined to stay,' Jane Portal said, 'and he is taking steps to see those who can affect the issue. Christopher has been very good. He knows the House of Commons and tells the P.M. what he thinks will happen. But he does not try to bully him. That's no good. It only makes him more obstinate.'

'I don't know where we are going,' I said as I left her.

'Nobody does,' she replied.

August 24, 1954

When I arrived at Chartwell I was told that the P.M. was still at the luncheon table with Harold Macmillan. Pitblado looked at his watch. It was four-fifteen. 'I think,' he said, 'we might send up a message that Lord Moran is here.' Macmillan soon took his leave. When the P.M. came into the office he appeared flushed and rather excited. 'Come, let us go to my room,' he said.

'We were talking about important matters,' he began. 'I dare say you can guess their nature. Harold is very able and will have a say in things if it comes to a row.'

Winston denied that he was tired.

'We must have talked for three hours, but I feel full of vigour. I ought to write to Anthony. I have written him two letters already; I tore them up, they were try-outs. Can I say, Charles, that you think I am able to bear the burden? It won't do Anthony any good if a rumour goes about that he got me out.'

It had come to that. He did not speak for a little, then he said:

'I don't think I'm selfish, but it seems foolish' – and here his voice rose and he spoke with great animation and vigour – 'to throw away all that I have to give. I can bring Dulles here tomorrow. He says he is ready to come. They need my flair. You saw my message to Eisenhower?'

---

[1] Minister of Pensions and National Insurance.

I suppose I looked puzzled. 'You mean Adenauer?'

'Yes, Adenauer. I mustn't confuse the two names,' he added, smiling. 'Well, my message eased the situation. When Adenauer received it he agreed to see Mendès-France and they got on quite well together. Both of them can see the realities of the situation. Why, if there were war tomorrow we would all fight under General Gruenther.'[1]

He sat down with a flop into a chair.

'I don't know why I am such a bloody fool as to want to go on.'

August 28, 1954

This morning I found Winston more at peace about things than he has been for some time.

'I had a very agreeable conversation with Anthony.'

'You don't mean he gave in without a fight?' I blurted out.

Winston ignored my interruption.

'I should resist and resent it if they tried to push me out. But everybody has been very nice. I would like to play the game,' he said after a pause. 'I want to be magnanimous and broad-minded. I shall go a year from now. I shall not lead in another election. They need my influence. Look at Mendès-France's visit. He came of his own free will. I did not ask him. Of course, the best thing would be if I could die during that year. Like poor Cys. – you know, Cyril Asquith – he said he would have his dinner in bed, and his wife went to make arrangements. When she came back he was dead.'

[1] Supreme Allied Commander, Europe.

CHAPTER TWENTY-SEVEN

The Burden of Life

August 29, 1954

'All the members of the Cabinet have accepted my staying on. There won't be any trouble, I think.' Winston smiled mischievously. 'They don't know what they can do about it.' He became grave again. 'But I'm not so sure about things.'

That Winston has got the better of Anthony is, I fear, no more than a Pyrrhic victory. It is not Anthony we have to fear, but Winston's advancing decrepitude. The fact is that he is in poor shape.

'Of course, I don't attempt to work after dinner as I used to. I play bezique instead. And after lunch I sleep. It is dreadful. I shall not go on if I don't feel up to it. I don't look forward to this session.'

He sighed deeply.

He is depressed by his inability to think things out. He realizes that the discovery of the hydrogen bomb has made drastic changes in our defence policy inevitable. Ten or fifteen years ago his imagination would have been stirred by such a challenge. Now he no longer has the energy of mind to think out a new policy. He does not want to be bothered. He can see the size of the job. He can see that he is no longer up to it. He is tormented by the thought that he might let the country down; it is eating away at his peace of mind.

'I have become so stupid, Charles. Cannot you do anything for me?'

September 2, 1954

When, about four o'clock, Winston woke from an hour's sleep he could not stop yawning.

'The world,' he began, 'is in a terrible condition. The throwing out of E.D.C. is a great score for the Russians.'

Then, waking up, his voice rose:

'The French have behaved in an unspeakable way, execrable. No thought at all for others, ingratitude, conceit,' he spat them out with intense distaste. 'I cannot feel the same about them in the future.'

I asked him if he had been surprised by the majority[1] in the French Chamber against E.D.C.

'No,' he answered, 'Mendès-France said there was no chance of getting it through.' Then, with more animation: 'But look at the swine, wasting three vital years. It was their own invention. They made us do it. My very pleasant relations with Anthony make things more difficult. I would have liked to control this business, but if I did I would be taking the bread out of Anthony's mouth after denying him the square meal he so much wanted.' He grinned broadly.

The Germans, the P.M. says, will take advantage of France's weakness. He had written to Adenauer; the letter had crossed one from him.

'I would like you to see the difference in tone between his letter and mine.'

He rang for a secretary. When the letter was brought he handed it to me.

'It doesn't need concentrated thought, it's the tone I wanted you to note. Generosity is always' – he hesitated for the word – 'wise. If Adenauer had said: "We are not going to take advantage of this situation, we shall not ask for anything more than we should have got if the voting in the French Chamber had gone differently," the effect in this country and in America would have been very great. But,' he went on sadly, 'he's going to get all he can out of France's stupidity.'

---

[1] 319 to 264 with abstentions.

He struggled into his zip-suit with Kirkwood's help.

He paused at the pond and rapped his stick against the stone pavement, when golden carp darted out of the shadows to gobble the maggots.

'They are twenty years old and will see me out; probably they will see you out too.'

He looked across the pond at the blue hydrangeas reflected in the clear water, saying half to himself:

'That pine tree would make a good background. I like its red bark. I shall paint this. I would have done it yesterday but for the Cabinet. It's a different period of the year today,' and he turned up the collar of his coat.

September 7, 1954

Calling on Winston in the middle of the morning at Chartwell, I found him working with Miss Gilliatt. She gathered up her papers and left the room. The P.M. went on talking and seemed in no hurry to call his secretary back.

'I'm very useful,' he said simply.

Ike had sent him a 'lovely letter'.

'He says my letter to Adenauer was exactly right. The Chancellor has been more moderate since I wrote to him; he sent me a gushing reply. I think Ike may come to London. I believe I can wheedle him. Then I shall be ready for the Russians. Of course the throwing out of E.D.C. rather bitched things. We have done badly in the Gallup poll in the *News Chronicle*: lost six points.'

I asked him if he thought that the Labour visit to China was responsible.

'Oh, no,' he answered gloomily. 'Rising prices and rents.'

And then he said more cheerfully:

'But there won't be an election this year. If the Socialists come in war will be nearer. There will be a coolness with America.'

He spoke of the trade-union vote reaffirming its belief in German rearmament with some emotion.

'They are fine fellows. That is the element which has been the strength of England for a thousand years; responsibility, constancy. "Death," Schiller said, "is so universal, it must be good!" We make too much of it,' Winston added. 'All religions do.' Then he grinned. 'Of course, I may alter my views.'

September 14, 1954
Called at No. 10 about six o'clock. The P.M. was still in the Defence Committee which began at three o'clock. I called because Winston telephoned me before lunch saying he was very muzzy and could he take another minor. When I saw him I found out why he had telephoned. He saw Lennox Boyd before lunch, when his head was full of defence matters, and he began talking to him about Admiralty matters as if he were Jim Thomas. 'I always think of them together. They are rather alike,' he said by way of extenuation.

I said to Montague Browne that I could not understand how Eden took Winston's decision not to resign lying down, and that it seemed possible now that he would never be Prime Minister. 'That would be no disaster,' Browne put in. He thought Eden had seen that this would happen for a long time. Winston had played his cards very well. He began by getting all the people who counted on his side, and then those members of the Cabinet who were in the opposite camp helped – oh, yes, quite unintentionally. Lord Salisbury had burst out that if the Prime Minister went to Moscow to see Malenkov it would break up the Anglo-American alliance. And then Ike said he had no objection to the visit. After this Lord Salisbury lay very low.

'You remember the hydrogen bomb debate when Winston made a mess of things, and we were all sitting on the edge of our chairs. Crookshank said to Eden, "Don't get up. Let the old man stew in his own juice. Don't speak. Leave him to get out of the mess. He made it." Eden ignored his advice and made a most useful speech. Within twenty-four hours Winston had heard the whole story.'

September 26, 1954

Winston was struggling with his speech for the Party Conference at Blackpool when I saw him at Chartwell this morning. He looked up at me as if he were carrying the burden of the world.

'Bloody,' he ejaculated.

'When is it?'

'October 7. I shall go up the night before and get to bed early.'

'Anyway, it isn't a formidable hurdle like Margate last October, and you've started in good time.'

'Oh, I don't know,' he grumbled. 'I'm not looking forward to it, I've nothing to say.'

As Miss Gilliatt was collecting her papers before leaving the room, he took up a sheet of paper and gave it to me to read. It was in his own writing.

'I haven't written out a speech in my own hand for forty years. I did it because I was determined to make myself compose – I won't be beaten.'

His voice became stronger and more vehement.

'I'll write out the whole bloody speech if necessary. I do all my work in the mornings now – though, of course, I can preside over meetings at any time.'

While I was reading, he said in a vigorous voice:

'We must learn the lessons of the past. We must not remember today the hatreds of yesterday.'

I knew he was trying it out on me, not so much to discover what I thought about the words but rather to get an impression how they sounded to him.

'If millions of people in one country learn to hate millions in another trouble is bound to come. This fellow Aneurin Bevan is deliberately stirring up anger and passion by bringing up Germany's sins in the war. It is very wrong. My right foot feels cold.'

He threw back the bed-clothes, and taking my hand, directed it to the offending limb.

'Of course I take no exercise; I get tired at once.'

I asked him how much he could do before he felt fatigue. 'Nothing,' he answered.

I tried to hearten him by reminding him that only last week he had come through a fifteen-hour day.

'I was very depressed next day,' he said grudgingly. 'I don't know why I get depressed as I do. They gave me Lord Russell's book on German war crimes.[1] A terrible book. Have you read the *Conspiracy of Silence*? It's by an Austrian,[2] who is in Paris now, and has a preface by the man[3] who wrote *Darkness at Noon*. Yes, the Russians questioned this poor fellow for eighteen hours at a time, and if he showed any signs of exhaustion they hit him in the face. It is a terrible world.

'You know, Charles,' he said sadly, 'I have come to think Stalin very culpable. Eight million lives were lost in the famine and another seven million in the collectivization of the farms. I did not realize this.'

'Don't you remember Stalin saying "What is one generation?"'

I had caught his attention by this remark.

'Did he say that? When?'

He said nothing for some time, brooding. Then he quoted Stalin:

'"A single death is an incident of consequence and pathos, but the death of a million is a matter of statistics."'

'I want,' said the P.M., 'to leave the conference to Anthony as much as I can. He likes doing it very much and does it very well.'

In the car on the way to Chartwell Mrs Romilly[4] told me how she had dined with Winston the night the First War broke out. 'Clemmie seemed crushed, but Winston was elated' – she hesitated – 'perhaps elated is the wrong word. Anyway, he was bursting with energy and excitement.' She thought Clemmie would want to play croquet if the rain held off. I told her about Monty and his croquet tactics. 'Oh, yes,' she laughed. 'You know Mrs Attlee is almost a professional

---

[1] *The Scourge of the Swastika* (Cassell, 1954).
[2] M. Blizowd.
[3] Arthur Koestler.
[4] Lady Churchill's sister.

player, but Monty kept giving her instructions. At last she put down her mallet. "I know a great deal about croquet," she said. "Please do not order me about. It is quite intolerable." Monty seemed rather confused, but after a little he again began directing the game. He cannot help it. But Clemmie is very fond of him, though they have sharp tiffs at times. I suppose,' Mrs Romilly added inconsequently, 'he is a very fine soldier.'

October 1, 1954

The P.M.'s fear that America might withdraw from Europe and 'go it alone' was not without reason. When the Nine Power Conference met on Wednesday Mr Dulles spoke of a great wave of disillusionment which had swept over America after E.D.C. had been rejected; there was a feeling, he said, that 'the situation in Europe is pretty hopeless.' It was in this bleak atmosphere that the delegates were asked to find some means of rearming Germany that would be accepted by a majority of the French Assembly. Round the table they sat, doodling, mumbling, despairing.

Then Mr Eden rose and told the representatives of the Nine Powers that if the conference was successful Britain would undertake to keep on the Continent the forces now stationed there; that she would not withdraw them without the consent of the majority of the Brussels Treaty Powers, including West Germany and Italy, as well as France and the Low Countries. Mr Eden called this 'a very formidable step to take', since it committed Britain to the defence of Western Europe. The delegates sat dumbfounded. The silence was at length broken by M. Spaak, who, turning to M. Mendès-France, said, 'You've won.' Everyone felt that the situation had been transformed and that Mr Eden's pledge saved the conference when it seemed bound to end in a fiasco.

It was accordingly with a light heart that I entered the P.M.'s bedroom this morning, as Kirkwood backed out with the breakfast tray. But somehow the P.M. did not seem particularly elated; indeed, he seemed to take more interest in the result of the East Croydon by-election, and what the papers said about it, than in the conference. He was frankly delighted with the figures. 'Why, Charles, in proportion they are better than in the last three by-elections.' He spoke of Bevan's performance at the Labour Conference at Scarborough with distaste. 'That fellow is a gold-mine to us,' he said cheerfully. 'Such a cad.'

I brought him back to Anthony's pledge. 'It can be cancelled at any time,' he went on with a mischievous smile. 'It does not mean anything. All words. Of course I shall not say that,' he added hastily. 'But what is all the fuss about? No one in their senses thought we could bring our troops home from the Continent. No one imagined that if Russia decided to march to the West we could sit still and do nothing; if there is war we are bound to fight. We have always been better than our word. Now they are going to do exactly what I suggested at Strasbourg in August, 1950. Never,' he said, smiling broadly, 'was the leadership of Europe so cheaply won.'

I wondered why the P.M. had taken Anthony's historic declaration at the London Conference so coolly. After all, President Eisenhower called it 'one of the greatest diplomatic achievements of our time', and Mendès-France spoke of the historic importance of Anthony's words. Is it because the idea came from Anthony? I banished the unworthy thought. The P.M. feels that the pledge at the conference has not changed anything. The French wanted our troops on the spot. It is the effect of the pledge on feeling in the Cabinet and in America that is new.

'Adenauer wants me to do what I can to strengthen and arm France.' The P.M.'s eyes opened wider. 'Germany wants a strong France,' he repeated; he did not wish me to miss the significance of Adenauer's attitude. 'I can go to Germany now. Oh, I haven't been into dates yet. All the credit is due to Anthony. He arranged everything.'

He sighed deeply. 'Now I have got this Blackpool speech on my hands. I wish it was in shape. I shall not take you to Blackpool, Charles; it would only draw attention to my health. It's different, of course, when I go abroad.'

October 5, 1954

When I asked Montague Browne how the P.M. had been, he said at once, 'I wouldn't say he was in his best form. Up and then down.' I asked him why he was like this when things seem to be going so well. Anthony hesitated. 'Well', he said, 'he has the Blackpool speech on his mind. You know the more important the speech the more he worries. And there have been strains and stresses.'

'You mean with Eden?'

'Yes.'

'I thought all that had settled down and that Anthony had accepted the situation?' I put this half as a question.

Browne smiled: 'When you work here at No.10 it is for a great historic personage; over there,' and he jerked his head in the direction of the Foreign Office, 'you are working for a great hysterical figure.'

October 9, 1954

The P.M. was abstracted, grave and uncommunicative. He was due to leave the house for Blackpool in an hour, and was going over his speech in his head. I said that it was not like last year; he would take it in his stride. He smiled doubtfully. 'I think I can harangue the bastards for fifty minutes.' He did not want to talk, and I left him.

October 10, 1954

A year ago the delegates went to Margate to find out the truth about 'The Old Man'. There had been talk about a stroke. Would he be able to carry on? they had wondered; while we in London sat on tenter-hooks dreading that he might break down in the middle of his speech. This morning, however, when I picked up the *Observer* I did not turn at once to the P.M.'s speech. When I did what I read put me in good heart. The reporter knew all about Mr Churchill; he had got him in focus even down to the delighted little crows before the jokes. He recalled how at Margate last year the conference had bidden goodbye to Sir Winston – some of the delegates had felt a lump in the throat as they took part in an historic, a unique occasion – and here he was once more as if nothing had happened. Was the Party impatiently crying out for a change? The *Observer* was quite sure of the answer. 'The conference was endlessly delighted with him.'

Certainly it did not enter the Prime Minister's head that he was at Blackpool on approval. There was, indeed, a suggestion that as he slowly climbed the stairs to the platform he was chuckling over something. Would the delegates really like to know when he was going to retire? Well, he was not going to tell them. That was his secret. He seemed, in his own impish way, to be enjoying their bewilderment. 'At any rate, for the moment,' the paper concluded, 'the rank and file seem content that he should go in his own time and how he pleases.' After all, he seemed, strange to relate, in far better shape than a year ago.

But when I got to Chartwell and asked Jane Portal how it had gone she did not seem so sure. Opinions were mixed. Anyway, judging by the applause, it went well with the delegates. Jane smiled affectionately. 'He was as quick as ever to cover his mistakes; he said "sovereignty" when he meant "solvency", and then in the same breath added: "Quite a natural mistake to make, for the two go together very well." Of course, he fumbled for a word at times. I suppose,' she said, 'we've got used to that and hardly notice when he hesitates for his words.'

However, Jock and Christopher were 'disappointed'. Jock thought it was one of his worst speeches. 'Why?' I asked. 'Because,' Jock said, 'his delivery was so bad.' Christopher had gone down among the delegates and sensed that it was not what the P.M.'s hearers wanted. There was an election, not too far off now, and the Party was frankly worried; the public-opinion polls showed them to be doing none too well. And here was the leader of the Party singling out Mr Attlee and Mr Morrison, praising them because they had been consistent in foreign policy. That, of course, was magnanimous and all that, but it wasn't going to help the Conservatives at the hustings. All this highbrow stuff was, they thought, out of place at a Party conference. The P.M. was, no doubt, a very great man, but he seemed to have lost touch with the rank and file; he did not know what they were thinking.

They had gone to Blackpool hoping for news; what they wanted to hear from the Prime Minister was when he intended to retire. This uncertainty about the leadership was not doing the Conservatives as a party much good. And all they were told was that there was quite enough for both Mr Churchill and Mr Eden to do at the present time. In this mood what more natural than that the delegates should look for signs in the old man that would confirm their feeling that the time had come for him to go. Someone had noticed that he said 1850 when he meant 1950 (he had made the same mistake in the Cabinet), while others thought he looked tired and that his delivery was a little slow and rather halting at times. As long as he made the Opposition look small the Party would be quiet and let him carry on, but he ought to know that only success could justify his lingering on the stage.

However, if those who listened to the Prime Minister had doubts, he himself had none. 'The Tories as a party,' he once complained to me, 'aren't responsive,' but he did not feel like that at Blackpool. When I went to his room and asked him what had happened, he replied:

'Oh, it was a huge success. I was not at all tired at the end. The pill was wonderful. I felt exactly as I did twenty years ago when I could work the whole bloody day like any other man. Tell me, Charles, does it do very much harm to the constitution? It gives me great confidence.' For a time he seemed a long way off, and then he looked up: 'While Anthony has this French business on his hands how could he give it all up and take on my job?'

I did not attempt to answer this conundrum. He continued:

'There may be a strike tonight among the printers, and no morning papers, so that no one will read my speech. I hope very much that at the last minute it will be called off.'

October 14, 1954

I was taken aback when I found the P.M. in an explosive mood. He spoke bitterly of the folly of the Tories in rashly throwing away all he had to give. Something has happened. I suspect that Christopher has told him of the feeling in the Party that he ought to go. My guess was on the target. The delegates might have made up their minds, but the P.M. has no intention of bowing to their will. 'If they try to get me out I will resist.' He stopped short in the middle of a sentence. He had said, I suppose, more than he meant.

With an expression of weariness he went on: 'I have got to go to the station to meet that man from Ethiopia.' So this voice out of the eighteenth century spoke of an enlightened ruler. When I repeated this ebullition to Jock he greeted it with a wan smile. 'Haile Selassie is a great man,' he said; 'one of the few friends we have got in the world.'

*

It was, no doubt, a shock to Winston when he found out that the Party as a whole wanted him to resign. But this is guess-work, for I can find no reference in my diary during the next fortnight to the political situation, apart from a grouse at the work involved in reconstructing the Government.[1] For the time being he was out of conceit with politics.

October 21, 1954

Winston was correcting proofs of his *History of the English-speaking Peoples*. He looked glumly at me, grunting: 'I have been very tired the last few days. I must not let these personal issues rattle me; reconstructing the Cabinet is like solving a kaleidoscopic jig-saw puzzle. It was all so personal, and you know how much I hate hurting people's feelings. The Lord Chancellor wasn't happy about going; did you see the ceremony when David[2] was introduced?'

He did not listen to my answer, but when he asked me whether the House of Lords thought it was a change for the better he turned

---

[1] A major Cabinet reshuffle took place in October. Eight senior ministers were involved.

[2] David Maxwell-Fyfe, Viscount Kilmuir (1954). Succeeded Lord Simonds as Lord Chancellor on October 18, 1954.

and looked straight at me, waiting for my reply. The P.M.'s conscience seems to prick him about this change.

'Simonds,' he continued, 'had no political experience, though he may have been a good lawyer. Lord Salisbury wanted help; he wanted someone in the House who understood politics.' There was a long pause, and I thought the P.M. had done, when he observed: 'David always wanted it. He wanted it when Simonds got it, but I could not spare him then; he was so useful in the House of Commons, where he was most industrious.' David had worked his passage, and had first claim.

Norman Brook took up the story; he told me how the P.M. dislikes telling people they are not wanted any longer. 'He gets out of it whenever he can. All the juniors, for instance, who were discharged had to be seen by the Chief Whip. "You see them and explain," the P.M. said, "and I will write to them after you have done that." Salisbury was given the task of breaking to Simonds that his services as Lord Chancellor were no longer required.'

As for Lord Salisbury needing help, I said that David would not find his new job in the Lords very exacting. There are few peers who speak without notes; most of them just read their pieces. The P.M. interrupted: 'There is no one in the Commons who can get along without his script.' I asked him if the speaking in the Commons had deteriorated in the last thirty years. 'You mean the quality of the speeches?' he asked, and thought for a moment. 'Fewer spoke then. Yes, they had more personality in those days.

'Anthony was very happy about the Garter. It was the Queen's suggestion.' A broad grin appeared as he told me of a cartoon by Low in yesterday's *Manchester Guardian*. Winston thought it a good idea that at eighty a man should get younger every year. The smile vanished. 'But it won't happen,' he muttered glumly.

October 26, 1954
The P.M. handed me a paper with photographs of the Queen receiving the Italian film-stars. 'She knocks 'em all endways. Lovely she is,' and he held the picture away from him to see it better. He picked

up the *Daily Worker* from the bed. 'Poison, hatred for the existing order,' he said sadly.

'The House is giving me a book for my birthday.[1] It is wonderfully got up – the College of Arms is helping – and will cost £400. But I am worried about it. There is a space for every constituency in the House of Commons, so that every Member can sign. Some may not want to sign. Of course, I haven't read it, but I know the general trend. It is full of flattering things; things no man ought to hear in his lifetime; things I should blush to read. Bunyan is brought in. I'm compared to him.

'One of the papers is getting up a subscription for a birthday present. If it's for me, so that I can do what I want with it, I would like it very much. But I don't want them to raise a sum for charity just to bring home some coloured gentleman from Jamaica to complete his education. I'd rather they did nothing. Of course, I might give some of the money subscribed to a charity that I was connected with. But I'm not a rich man. I got nothing out of those six volumes' – he jerked his head towards a shelf on the wall – 'and Clemmie got nothing, except a few shillings. The children, of course, will benefit. The four volumes of my *History of the English-speaking Peoples* will bring me a great income, but the Treasury will take it all.

'I am not in favour of the present rate of taxation on earned incomes. It will destroy all incentive. People will not work as hard. Everything has become so expensive, servants, every single thing. I lunched yesterday at the House of Commons.'

'Anyway, that would be reasonable enough,' I put in.

'I paid £1 14s.,' Winston retorted. 'Oh, I had a brandy and half a bottle of hock. It is not that I have expensive tastes. I stay in bed too much to spend a lot of money. I'm not extravagant. Racing practically pays for itself. If I retired I could make a lot of money, perhaps £50,000 a year, but it would be only 50,000 shillings. If people want to subscribe to give me a birthday present I don't mind.

[1] Winston's eightieth birthday was on November 30, 1954.

'I have accepted an invitation to address the Scottish National Union of Conservatives – where? Oh, somewhere in Scotland.'

He answered as if his mind were elsewhere. Thinking he meant in the immediate future, I asked innocently, 'What date?' He hesitated. Then he grinned. 'May 20th.'

He looked at me as if he was curious to see how I would take it. 'It is some time off,' I said. 'Six months in fact.'

CHAPTER TWENTY-EIGHT

The Woodford Blunder

November 28, 1954

'I used to be frightened in the old days,' Winston once told me, 'that I should say something in the House of Commons and wake up and find it had landed me in trouble. That doesn't happen now. I've learnt a lot; after all, I've had fifty years of it.' But Clemmie only shook her head; she is still terrified that he will put his foot in things, and will never be happy until he resigns. I suppose she is right, from her point of view. Anyway, we're in trouble again. Winston, speaking to his constituents in a girls' school at Woodford on November 23, went out of his way to give them some secret history:

'Even before the war had ended, and while the Germans were surrendering by hundreds of thousands. . . . I telegraphed to Lord Montgomery directing him to be careful in collecting the German arms, to stack them so that they could easily be issued again to the German soldiers whom we should have to work with if the Soviet advance continued.'

What on earth made him say it? *The Times* begins a critical leader with these words, and no one is sure about the answer. Why did he want to tell his constituents about the telegram? It seems that he found everyone at Woodford full of the birthday; there was a lot of celebrating and drinking of toasts, his foresight was extolled. Then someone asked him about the Russians, and

Fulton[1] was mentioned. It was good to recall that he was alive then
to the threat to Western Europe. The rest is guesswork, but I think
I can follow his thoughts. These kind folk spoke of Fulton, but long
before Fulton he was alive to the Russian menace; that wanted
bringing home to people. For only one thing mattered now – it was
often in his mind – when his record came before posterity they must
be fair to him. All this talk about the war having been fought in vain
made him angry. At any rate, he was not to blame. To get that quite
clear he had added a sixth volume to his book and called it *Triumph
and Tragedy*. He would remember then how Camrose and his publishers tried to persuade him that it was a mistake to bring out
another volume. But he would not listen to them. For he was
resolved to make it known that he wanted to take precautions
against some rather ugly possibilities as early as the spring of 1945,
at a time when the Americans were still busy making friends with
Stalin and had not woken up to the danger of Communism.

That, no doubt, was why the P.M. wanted to tell his constituents
about his foresight in the spring of 1945, but why did he blurt it all
out now? He had not, after all, given up hope of talks with the
Russians, and this surely would not help matters. In plain fact,
Winston had no idea at Woodford that he was laying up trouble for
himself. Though he studies the papers morning and evening with
some care, he never seems to know in what way the public will react
to anything that he may do or say. Like Mr Gladstone,[2] he has no
gift for getting into other people's minds; sometimes he does not
even appear to be interested.

It was this that used to puzzle President Roosevelt; that any politician could exist like this in a vacuum was incomprehensible to
him. He himself had spent a lot of time pondering on what his countrymen were thinking – he was in the habit of trying out his speeches

[1] In Fulton, Missouri, on March 5, 1946, Churchill pleaded for Great Britain
and the United States to unite as guardians of the peace, and he set out frankly
the menace of Soviet policies.
[2] G. M. Young, in *To-day and Yesterday*, writes: 'But of those roving explorations
of other men's minds. . . . Mr Gladstone was by temperament incapable.'

on experienced politicians before they were delivered. Whereas when Winston made a speech it was a kind of one-way traffic that owed nothing to the audience.

I turned instinctively to Norman Brook to check whether Winston's detachment was as complete as I have depicted. He is so full of horse-sense that he has no time for fancy reasoning. He agreed that Winston's mind works in this way.

'He is the king-pin, of course, and he will do the job. He thinks of those around him only as menials, they do not really count. Oh, no, he is not in the least interested in any of us, or in our future. As long as we are devoted to him, and do not make bad mistakes, Winston will not think of anyone else. One man at a time has always been his motto.'

With this in mind we can now follow Mr Churchill's thoughts in 1945. True, we are still taken aback by his ignorance of what the ordinary man was then thinking. We still find it difficult to understand how anyone can live so cut off from other people, but what he told us at Woodford no longer surprises us. Did he imagine, for a moment, *The Times* asked scornfully, that the western peoples, hating the Hitler régime with a hatred greater than anything they had known, would understand and accept the use of Hitler's defeated soldiers to set a military barrier against the forces they still welcomed as victorious allies? Did he expect memories and emotions to fade overnight? The plain answer is that he did. Nor will he admit, even now, that what he had in mind would have split opinion in Britain and America.

However, it is no good crying over spilt milk. What everyone wants to know now is whether the Prime Minister is in real trouble or whether this is just another false alarm like the hydrogen bomb debate. Moscow, no doubt, will make a song and dance and hint that talks with Russia are not likely to come to anything while Mr Churchill is Prime Minister. But unless this feeling is at all common in this country nothing will happen. The House of Commons will not give him much trouble unless the country takes it seriously. For it is already obvious that Attlee will not sponsor an attack on the Prime Minister on this issue unless a section of his Party forces his hand. The *Manchester Guardian* has spoken for sober opinion; it does not take the P.M.'s slip at all seriously. Sir Winston, it dryly remarks, could hardly have foreseen, when he told his constituents this little anecdote, that he would be denounced by the oddest of Press choruses – *The Times*, the *Daily Herald*, the *Daily Mirror* and the *Daily Worker*. Their common link, the *Guardian* observes, seems to be the wish to force him out of office.

What does the P.M. himself make of it all? I have not seen him since the speech, but from what I hear at No. 10 he does not seem to have taken it to heart. Anyway he went off to Bristol in good shape, and appears to be having high jinks there. Saturated with gifts, as he has been, there was a break in his voice when he thanked the students for giving him an eighteenth-century salver, 'on a day when, if you look at the papers, I am supposed to be in a bit of a scrape'. For their part they had no feeling that he was an old man; on the contrary, he seemed to be one of themselves, and two thousand young voices shouted their joy and approval. The same puckish humour marked his approach to their seniors. 'I always enjoy coming here, and I may say that I rather like wearing this robe. It was my father's robe as Chancellor of the Exchequer in 1886, and was most carefully preserved by my mother until I had the opportunity of wearing it as Chancellor of the Exchequer myself.'

Oliver Franks happened to be at Bristol that day, and he was puzzled because Winston's physical condition seems to change as quickly as his moods. 'I saw him at Buckingham Palace a few days before,' he told me, 'sitting on a sofa, apparently too weary to listen to anybody; his face was white and like a mask, his body had flopped, he seemed a very old man who had not long to live. But at Bristol he was pink, his expression was full of animation and his eyes twinkled. Perhaps you doctors can explain what happens?'

November 29, 1954
About five o'clock Jane Portal telephoned: 'Could you see the Prime Minister at seven-thirty? The Cabinet ought to be over by then. He

has been sitting taking his pulse with his thumb,' she added. 'He's worrying over Woodford, and he's not happy about tomorrow.' The last of the Cabinet were leaving as I entered No. 10. I found him in the Cabinet Room, and as he came towards me his gait was very unsteady and his face was dull and without expression. 'I'm worried about this stupid mistake of mine. I was quite certain it was in my book, otherwise I would never have said what I did. And now it seems there wasn't a telegram, after all. Anyway, no trace can be found of it. I must have thought better of it. My speech ought, of course, to have been checked.' He sat for some time glowering at his feet. 'If my slip has done harm with the Russians I may pull out sooner than I intended. Take my pulse, Charles.' It was 82. When I had reassured him he brightened up a little. 'The *Daily Mirror* has declared a truce for tomorrow. They have sent £1,000 to my birthday fund. I am to be given a cheque for £140,000 tomorrow. All this leaves me very humble; it is more than I deserve.'

Montague Browne told me that the P.M. was worried about the Russians; he would like to be sure that his speech has done no harm at the Kremlin. 'That's all he cares about. He didn't seem at all depressed by the criticisms of his speech until he read what appeared in *Pravda* yesterday.' I asked Montague Browne about the telegram. It appears that Pownall[1] was asked three years ago to check this telegram to Monty for the P.M.'s book. He could find no trace of any telegram and concluded the P.M. must have decided at the last moment not to send it. I asked if Labour would be able to make capital out of the speech. 'They can and will,' he replied. Christopher added cheerfully: 'It was very stupid of Winston to say it.' As I left, the doorway of No. 10 was blocked by an immense birthday cake which two men were trying to lever into the hall without injuring any of the eighty white candles.

[1] Lieut.-General Sir Henry Pownall. Assisted Churchill in the preparation of *The Second World War*.

CHAPTER TWENTY-NINE

Harmony and Discord

November 30, 1954

Winston Churchill is eighty years of age today – a remarkable achievement for a man of his habits. A fine disregard for common sense has marked his earthly pilgrimage. What he wanted to do he has always done without a thought for the consequences. And now he can say that he has his cake and has eaten it too. To account for his survival it is generally supposed that he has a wonderful constitution. Indeed he is unusual in the way in which he can adapt himself to circumstances; he is indifferent, for instance, to heat and cold; fatigue of mind or body he hardly knew until he was seventy; while whatever may happen overnight in the way of revelry, he wakes with a song in his heart and a zest for breakfast.

On the other hand, he is often in the hands of the doctor. It is now fifteen years since I first saw him, and in that time he has had:

(i) a heart attack in Washington just after Pearl Harbour;

(ii) three attacks of pneumonia, one of which at any rate was a 'damned nice thing';

(iii) two strokes, in 1949 and 1953;

(iv) two operations, one of which found the abdomen full of adhesions and lasted two hours;

(v) senile pruritis, perhaps the most intractable of all skin troubles;

(vi) a form of conjunctivitis unlikely to clear up without a small operation.

(I have not mentioned dyspepsia or diverticulitis, because they have never really caused worry.) To this catalogue of woe I should add that for ten years he has not had natural sleep apart from sedatives. Looking back, he seems to have been in the wars a great deal, but I treasure my battle honours: it has been possible, save for two attacks of pneumonia and some gossip about his stroke in June, 1953, to keep all this from the public, and for that matter from the political world.

When I had written so far I made my way to No. 10, bearing my small gift, Lord David Cecil's two volumes on Melbourne, bound in leather by two Poles who work in Hampstead, and one of the Duke of Marlborough's letters in French from my boys. The room was full of presents of every kind. When I had greeted him he said: 'You've played a big part in this.' He told me very simply that when he read the quotation from John Bunyan on the title page of the book of commemoration he felt very humble, and when he tried to repeat the words to me his voice broke and he could not go on.

Christopher came into the room. 'Charles has given me this book. I wanted to read it.' But Christopher took no notice of Winston's kindly gesture. The P.M. gave me his speech to read, and I was charmed by its airy grace. In the office Jane Portal told me that the P.M. had talked to Mr Attlee about the Woodford speech and has been comforted by what he said. I went back to tell him to wear a greatcoat in Westminster Hall, a gaunt, chilly place. But he said that the Ministry of Works had fitted electric pads to the back of his chair.

When the Queen had opened Parliament I lost no time in making my way to Westminster Hall, where I had the good fortune to find an empty chair. About noon there was a sudden hush, and, shading my eyes against the sun that was streaming through the great window on to the stone stairs, I could see a little party round the Prime Minister. I stood up and looked again. Yes, Aneurin Bevan and Jennie Lee were there. The man next to me, in his excitement, caught hold of my coat sleeve.

All but twenty-six members of the House of Commons had signed the Book and had contributed to a portrait of him by Graham

Sutherland; it had given him pleasure that all parties were taking part in the celebration. For it was not always so. When Gladstone became eighty the Tories held aloof. Indeed, this gathering would not have been possible before the war. Winston's part then made the House more kindly, more tolerant. To mark the universal harmony *The Times* and the *Manchester Guardian* had contrived to hit on the same heading for their leading articles: 'Eighty Years On'.

Then the drums beat out the opening bar of Beethoven's Fifth Symphony – the three shorts and a long which make V in the Morse code – V for victory, the war signal in the occupied countries that the B.B.C. was about to bring them news from the outer world – and, as the Prime Minister turned to the great gathering, the Guards Band played Elgar's 'Pomp and Circumstance'. Winston was in his old frock-coat. He came forward, and as he began to descend the stairs his right leg shot out in the air before it came down on the step; he was not very steady. I held my breath, but nothing happened; he took his seat, sitting bolt upright, his hands laid flat on his knees, while wide-eyed he searched all around him.

When Winston is touched by kindness he expands to his full size, and he can no more hide the underlying goodness that is in him. Now as he faced his friends from both Houses and from all parties he was resolved to keep a grip on his emotions. He told them that they were very kind 'to a party politician who had not yet retired'. Then he uttered a note of warning:

'This ceremony, with all its charm and splendour, may well be found to have seriously affected my controversial value as a party politician. However, perhaps with suitable assistance I shall get over this reaction and come round after a bit.'

At the end of his journey he was in a mood to speak well of all men. Even Graham Sutherland was forgiven. Besides, 'You can't look a gift horse in the mouth,' he said rather sadly.

'The portrait is a remarkable example of modern art. It certainly combines force and candour.'

It had to be said; they must make what they could of it. There was a little pause, and then a gust of laughter swept the hall.

The ending explains better than I can why men love him. 'I have never accepted what many people have kindly said – namely that I inspired the nation. Their will was resolute and remorseless, and as it proved, unconquerable. It fell to me to express it, and if I found the right words you must remember that I have always earned my living by my pen and by my tongue. It was the nation and the race dwelling all round the globe that had the lion's heart. I had the luck to be called upon to give the roar.'

Mr Attlee, who must know a good deal about Churchill by now, found exactly the right words to give him pleasure: 'You had the conception of the Dardanelles campaign, the only imaginative strategic idea of the war. I wish that you had had full power to carry it to success. You urged the adoption of the tank, the only new tactical weapon of first importance in that war.' When the P.M. heard this he looked up at Mr Attlee as if he had only half understood, then a wry smile appeared and he suddenly nodded his head. He had done his part manfully – he had promised me he would not let his emotion get on top – but now as he stumbled through the North door into the winter day he could no longer keep back his tears.

December 1, 1954
When I got out of the lift at No. 10 they told me that Pug Ismay, Norman Brook and Jock were closeted with the P.M. They were concocting the P.M.'s reply to Shinwell for the debate on the Address this afternoon. I sent in a note that I had only called to see if all was well after yesterday's excitement, and that I would not bother him unless he wanted anything. But in a moment they all came trooping out of his bedroom. 'The P.M. would like to see you,' Jock said.

As I entered the room he pushed away the bed-rest, and when I came to his assistance I saw vol. vi, *Triumph and Tragedy*, open at page 498 – the Iron Curtain telegram to Truman. The P.M. asked me to take his pulse. I told him everything was all right, though he looked weary and dispirited. He glanced up at me and said impulsively: 'You have been a great comfort to me.' I promised to call again later, and with that I got up and left him.

There was no venom in Shinwell's attack on the Woodford speech this afternoon, but the P.M. was in poor form when he came to reply. Yesterday was an unusual drain on his ebbing strength; besides, he is out of conceit with himself. He knew, too, that he had not much of a case. What exactly had happened about the telegram was not clear in his own mind. His voice was tired, often he hesitated for a word, and twice I feared that he would break down. Yesterday he was at his best, today he was nearly at his worst.

However, when I was worrying about his poor showing the Speaker reassured me. 'Winston,' he said, 'knows the House of Commons, and the Shinwell business went much better than I anticipated. The Prime Minister was wise enough at once to acknowledge his sins, and the House will always forgive anyone who does this. He was very adroit.' The Speaker added that he was sure it would all die down. Norman Brook was not quite so hopeful.

The P.M.'s speech had been in three parts. The first was ragged and unkempt. 'I made a goose of myself at Woodford, forgetting what I'd done,' he confessed to me. All he had to do in apologizing to the House was to translate this briefly into parliamentary language, but he havered on until it took up a page of Hansard.

The body of the speech, on the other hand, was effective and impressed the House. It was adroit, as the Speaker said, to put beside that ill-timed disclosure the evidence of the Prime Minister's foresight in 1945, which was, after all, the cause of all the bother. Norman Brook had spent the whole morning on the speech, and I can see him saying, 'We must get this thing in perspective.' No doubt it was an indiscretion on the Prime Minister's part, but how insignificant the offence seemed when set against his prescience at that time. The Prime Minister read out to the House the Iron Curtain telegram to President Truman, bearing the date May 12, 1945, to remind Members of the situation then. Our armed power on the Continent was dwindling away, so that there was nothing to prevent the Russians, if they so wished, marching to the waters of the North Sea and the Atlantic. And all this hubbub was because the Prime Minister had foreseen the peril we were in and was trying to take steps to meet it. After all, was there any other way of stopping the Russians except by arming the Germans? At any rate the House was satisfied that the menace was real enough; once more they gave him full credit for his quick sense of danger; he was awake when the Americans were still asleep. No doubt it would have been better if he had left all this to the historian, but as the Speaker put it to me: 'If Winston had always been cautious we should have lost a lot.'

At this point the P.M. should have sat down. Instead he began meandering.

There were about two hundred people at his birthday party at No. 10. All Winston's world was there, with a few thrown in for the sake of political expediency, the 'impudent' Crookshank, for example.

December 3, 1954
Found the P.M. reading the *Daily Worker* and spluttering with rage. He threw it down in disgust. While he was searching the *Manchester Guardian* for approbation, I picked it up. On the front page there was a report of a meeting of the Parliamentary Labour Party. Attlee, opening the discussion, spoke of the 'abject apology' which the Prime Minister had made to the House; he did not think it was good tactics after that to continue the argument. Some of the back benchers were dissatisfied with this course. How, they asked, could the Soviet Union trust Churchill after his duplicity in 1945? How could the Party continue to press for Four Power talks if he was to represent Britain? In the end, Attlee had had to change his mind; he had undertaken to refer to the telegram in the debate on Monday.

'Take my pulse, Charles.' As I put down the *Daily Worker* he said angrily: 'Though I don't care if it isn't good. I'm going to fight this out whatever happens. Abject indeed.' He spat out the offending epithet. 'The only thing I apologized for' – the P.M. was shouting now – 'was that I said I had sent the telegram without checking the facts. Anthony wants to follow Attlee. Now I shall. There might be an election if they press things. World events look worse. I might go and see Ike. A night in the air is nothing to me.' When? 'Oh,' he cried impatiently, 'I can't foresee events. There might be a crisis. There might be war. Mendès-France is only thinking of keeping in office. All my sympathies are with the Germans. Adenauer has sent a big silver goblet for my birthday. You saw Stansgate[1] came out strongly on my side.' He sighed deeply and said no more.

I began to check the supply of pills, cachets and capsules on the table by his bed: Disprins and 'Lord Morans', majors and minors, reds and greens, babies and midgets, to drop into his own vocabulary. He watched me for a time, then he said: 'I have found this fortnight more exhausting than any period since the Government was formed. I shall need your help.' He had not got over the excitement of the Woodford slip, which came on the top of the birthday celebrations, and when he had put Attlee out of his head he became sluggish and uncommunicative.

December 16, 1954

'I think,' said Winston this morning, 'I shall die quickly once I retire. There would be no purpose in living when there is nothing to do. I don't mind dying.' He could not refrain from that little bit of bravado; he would have trotted it out whoever happened to be listening.

Then he went on to tell me what he could still do. 'I made a very good speech on atomics. I didn't need any technical advice, though I checked it with the Prof. afterwards. I can do this kind of thing as well as ever. I can think as well as ever. But of course I get very tired.' I asked him how long his atomic speech took to prepare. He replied: 'Two spells of an hour and a half, two separate mornings. Besides, of course, a lot of arguing about it.' He told me the Speaker had given a very agreeable dinner to the members of the wartime coalition. 'It could have happened in no other country,' he reflected.

---

[1] Lord Stansgate, a Labour peer, said in the House of Lords: 'I believe, and I think the great bulk of the people in this country believe, that the greatest measure of defence we can have is that the Prime Minister should retain his position until his meeting with the Russians takes place.'

He had been given a budgerigar, but they had not yet been introduced. The empty cage was on the floor. He confessed that he had had to 'drive himself' in the past three weeks.

December 22, 1954

Winston had sent away his breakfast things. There was a birdcage on his bed and a budgerigar on his shoulder. I said to him he ought to teach Toby his telephone number in case the bird got lost. Winston received this suggestion with some throaty sounds. 'Oom, Oom, Oom, I don't know my telephone number.'

He was leaving for Chequers tomorrow and would stay there until the New Year. The nine grandchildren would be gathered under one roof. There would be no more Cabinets until the Feast of the Epiphany.

'When is that? And you call yourself an Episcopalian!'

CHAPTER THIRTY

Et tu, Brute

January 5, 1955

The P.M. telephoned to tell me that one of his Ministers had discovered a marvellous pill – his wife had given him one, and he had had a lovely sleep.

'And you know, Charles, all his friends are using it. You really don't keep up to date. It is quite harmless. The French chemists' shops sell it without a doctor's prescription. What is it called? Wait a moment and I can tell you – supponeryl.'

He spelt it out letter by letter.

'Now, what about it? Can I take one?'

I said I could not answer his question until I knew what was in it, but I would find out and let him know later.

About eight o'clock the P.M. telephoned again.

'You haven't let me know as you promised,' he said reproachfully.

I replied with a touch of irritation: 'You have been getting good nights for a long time with the reds, and without any ill-effects. Why do you want to change?'

'Oh,' said Winston, 'I believe in trying a variant now and then.'

'You mean you like to change for the sake of changing.'

'Now, Charles, you mustn't be angry with me. I'd like to try one. It can't really do any harm.'

January 7, 1955

Found the P.M. very sluggish. When I asked him what had happened he did not answer at once. I was not sure he had heard what I said. Then he looked up and began: 'I took one of those things on Wednesday. I had six and a half hours' lovely sleep – it was the quality of the sleep that I liked.' He looked at me rather sheepishly and then observed half defiantly: 'So last night I took two.'

'And today,' I butted in, 'you can hardly keep your eyes open.'

'Well,' he said petulantly, 'I must have sleep.'

'It is quite unnecessary to take two of those pills – they are the equivalent of four reds. No wonder you complain that your foot twitched and that you feel too torpid to do any work today.'

'But,' he argued, 'my pulse is all right – take it. Well, what is it?'

'Eighty-six.'

The P.M. roused himself and made a gesture of impatience. 'Do you realize our anxieties during the last few days? The Cabinet waited for nine hours to get news. Why, if there had been a strike on the railways' – he was shouting now – 'Ministers would have hurtled off to Sandringham to get the Great Seal on the Royal Proclamation; forty thousand troops would have been sent to various points; four trains would have run somehow from Wales to bring milk; coal production would have fallen from six million to one million tons, and with that many factories would have closed down and the production of electricity would have stopped. Do you realize all the things that were bound to happen, the change in the nation's life?'

January 9, 1955

Lunched with Harold Macmillan. He has been one of Winston's intimate counsellors since his resignation became an issue, but he is not at all happy about things. He took me into the garden and talked so freely about Winston and Anthony that I began to wonder if he had lunched with me for that purpose. For fifteen years, according to Harold, Winston has harried Anthony unmercifully, lectured him and butted in on his work, until poor Anthony is afraid to make a decision on his own. Anthony apparently has taken this a good deal to heart, and has been very nervy lately. I suggested that it was Clarissa, his wife, and not Winston who was to blame for this. And, anyway, surely Anthony was very weak to allow Winston to trample on him.

'Oh,' said Macmillan, 'of course Lloyd George would have had Winston out of it in no time. But there it is. Anthony is not strong; look at his lower jaw.'

I said that was why I was doubtful about his future as a leader. However Macmillan thought that Butler and he could bolster him up for a while. Rab was terribly upset by his wife's death, but he was finding distraction by plunging into work.

'It ought to pan out all right. Rab is so much younger, he isn't really a competitor, and I am too old to be Prime Minister.'

Then Harold defended Anthony. He has been very loyal to Winston, and he is a brilliant negotiator, so quiet, so wise, so persuasive. He gave me a sample of Anthony's prowess at the F.O. 'The other day Dulles brought forward a plan that was totally unacceptable to us. I wondered for a moment how Anthony would handle the situation. But he was quite wonderful. I thought his patience would never give out. An hour went by, and gradually I discovered Dulles was changing his position. At last he brought forward another scheme, which was about the exact opposite of the first, and incidentally just what we wanted. Anthony did not rush at him and say: that's what we wanted all along. He murmured that there were parts of this plan he didn't like, and then he appeared to give way to Dulles a little reluctantly.' Harold laughed into his moustache at Anthony's guile. And then he came to the point.

'You know, Moran,' he said, as he picked up a stray spade, 'Winston ought to resign. He didn't interfere in my housing, just left it all to me. But since I became Minister of Defence I have found that he can no longer handle these complicated matters properly. He can't do his job as Prime Minister as it ought to be done. He does not direct. Of course he is still tough and he isn't bothered with principles like Salisbury.' Harold chortled as he stopped to remove a fallen branch from the path. 'When the moment comes Winston will have to decide how he goes; he has missed so many curtains, when he could have gone with everyone applauding, that it won't be as easy now.'

All this was not at all what I had expected. I have looked on Harold lately as an ally of the old man. Tory Prime Ministers have been overthrown by palace revolutions before, and the P.M., since he became aware that something of the kind was brewing, has taken counsel with his supporters – with Harold Macmillan more than with anyone else.

Perhaps Jane Portal was right; Macmillan, she thinks, likes to be on the winning side; he must see Anthony's time is coming, and that it can only be a matter of months before Winston goes. She doesn't like Harold, doesn't trust him, and thinks he is disloyal to the P.M. Anyway he is very indiscreet and talks too much. In politics at the top there is no quarter. All the same I do not bother my head about Macmillan's fidelity. Indeed I sometimes think that Winston's ignorance of what other people are thinking is a source of strength.

*

It transpired that when Harold Macmillan failed to get anything out of me he had gone to Clemmie. He said to her that Winston ought to resign, that he was no longer up to his job. Clemmie, according to Brendan Bracken, listened to what Macmillan had to say and then coldly retorted that he ought to say this to the Prime Minister and not to her. When Harold had gone Clemmie told Winston what had happened. The P.M. sent for Macmillan and told him shortly:

'If in the future you have anything to say that you deem of importance, pray say it to me,' and then dismissed the embarrassed Minister.

These clever people are always getting themselves into a mess.

January 20, 1955
The P.M. was in the Cabinet Room reading papers. When he looked up his eyes were full of tears.

'I did not think it would happen like this,' he said sadly.

'I hate politics,' I blurted out impulsively.

'Ah, no, Charles, it's not as bad as that.'

Harold's intervention has left a bruise. The P.M. had come to depend on him and counted on his support if it came to a row. After all, it was Harold who had encouraged him to hang on. Winston called him the Captain of the Praetorian Guard. And now he has gone over to the other camp.

The P.M. changed the subject abruptly.

'I've read the book you gave me. It was interesting, but Melbourne was attached to no great cause, he just pottered along.'

I said that Melbourne had been clever at holding his Cabinet together. The P.M. thought that this could not have been very difficult. I persisted that Durham and the Lord Chancellor were difficult people to have in a Cabinet.

'Yes, Brougham perhaps,' he reflected. 'The last chapter was . . .'

I pricked up my ears. What did he think of that devastating picture of the loneliness of old age?

'I have been reading Rosebery's *Pitt*,' the P.M. went on. 'It's not very good.'

I asked him whether he thought Rosebery's *Chatham* was a better book, and whether he liked the chapter on his oratory. He answered absent-mindedly:

'Rosebery wrote about Chatham before he became interesting and about Napoleon after he had ceased to be interesting.'

January 24, 1955

Plainly there is a growing feeling among Winston's friends that the time has come for him to go. But only Harold Macmillan has had the guts to say so. I am beginning to have second thoughts. If I did not dread the future I might agree with Macmillan. Anyway he did what he thought was right, and he must have hated doing it.

I asked the P.M. if he had been doing much work.

'I do nothing,' he answered with a grin, 'that I can get out of. I am pretty skilful now at avoiding things. I don't mind dying,' he remarked a little irrelevantly. 'I have seen all there is to be seen.'

Jock had been troubled with indigestion, and the P.M. had given him my white medicine. It soothed him.

'It won't do him any harm?' he enquired a little anxiously. 'I think I must show him my breathing exercises. Before I met you I used to get a sharp pain before meals, and then afterwards a great feeling of discomfort and oppression under the heart, as if I had heart disease. I kept thinking about it. It rather got on my mind. At that time I was under a Portuguese doctor, I cannot remember his name. Yes, Lopez. He used to give me most wonderful prescriptions. There were a large number of drugs in each of them. They did me good. Then the poor fellow died. I went to his funeral and came away with' – he hesitated – 'Taplow. Yes, Ettie Desborough. "What are we to do now?" I said to her. She told me of a man who taught his patients marvellous breathing exercises which helped them a lot. Courtland MacMahon was his name. You must have known him. He wasn't a doctor, but doctors thought very well of him – a dignified man. Let me show you, Charles, what happens when I get indigestion.'

He picked up a blue pencil and began drawing on a piece of red blotting paper.

'My stomach is usually a platform like this, but at times it sags and becomes a saucer like that.'

His drawing was more like the pocket of a billiard table.

'Then poisonous liquids collect in the saucer and give off foetid gases.'

These he depicted as two columns of smoke rising from the edges of the saucer.

'At that moment I do my breathing exercises. My abdominal muscles contract like this' – and he put his hands on his round belly and began breathing deeply – 'so that they squeeze out all the poisonous liquids.'

The blue pencil became very active, crossing out the saucer.

'Your white medicine is a great relief, but of course my indigestion is not as bad now as it was then.' He looked up and waited for my comments.

I reached for his drawing which he seemed reluctant to give up. I took the pencil. 'As a work of art it's not bad, but it's not good physiology.'

He appeared rather crestfallen, but said nothing. He took the blotting paper from me and tore it into small pieces. He is always careful not to leave incriminating documents about. Then he waited for me to explain, if I could, where he had gone wrong. I had just drawn his stomach on the blotting paper when the door opened and Christopher put in an appearance with a handful of papers. The P.M.'s face fell. It was not that he was particularly interested in my views of his dyspepsia, but he knew that when I went he must begin work. I think that was why he talked about Jock's indigestion.

January 27, 1955
The P.M. had made a speech on Tuesday evening to the National Federation of Building Trade Employers.

'We have built a million houses. A very sensible easement of the life of the nation. I showed them my trade-union card as a bricklayer. I went on for about a quarter of an hour – it took me three or four hours to prepare, but it went like hot cakes.'

February 3, 1955
I shall be glad when this Conference is over. Winston is finding it very hard work, he owned to me today, and it's not like him to say that.

'This meeting of the Commonwealth Prime Ministers is a hell of a business. It is not at all like the old gatherings of the Dominions.'

Of course, when I said he must have been very weary after the Palace he protested at once that he was not. He does not want anyone to think that he is not up to it. Then in a few minutes he seemed to forget what he had said.

'The work is unceasing, two meetings every day, five hours altogether, and I am in the Chair the whole time. I get very weary, but I recover. Your "minors" have been my salvation.'

How is he really wearing, and is he doing the job as it ought to be done? He himself has no doubts.

'I'm taking a big part in the Conference. I have held my own, and more than held my own. You must have heard, Charles, stories of my part in the Conference?' When I was not forthcoming, he went on: 'I have led the discussions, made little jokes, given them ideas, and engaged in arguments.

'Some of the others are not lasting as well as I am; they are feeling the strain and show it. Last night Attlee came up to me at the Palace. I could see he was quivering, and then he fainted in my arms. I'm not very strong, but with Mrs Attlee's help I got him on to a couch. Poor Attlee, he is getting old; he is seventy-two. A lot of people saw it happen. But don't mention this. Yes, it will get about, but I don't want to be the someone spreading it. I would not go but for my liking for Anthony. They will be weaker when I am gone. Anthony's foreign policy has not been very successful.'

The Commonwealth Prime Ministers are agreed that Winston is a fantastic old man. Those who saw him at the Coronation think he is in better form now. Brook, Pitblado and the office tell me that when he was saying a set piece to a big assembly, sitting down, he mumbled and havered, but on the less formal occasions he was wonderfully impressive.

I asked the P.M. about Nehru. He said to me: 'I get on very well with him. I tell him he has a great role to play as the leader of Free Asia against Communism.' I was curious to know how Nehru took this. 'Oh, he wants to do it – and I want him to do it. He has a feeling that the Communists are against him, and that,' Winston added with a grin, 'is apt to change people's opinions.

'I told the Prime Ministers,' Winston continued, 'that there were fifty thousand Chinese characters in their alphabet; six thousand of them are used by their Civil Service; three thousand by ordinary people. So the Civil Servant has to be educated for eight years. That is why, for five thousand years, the proletariat in China has been kept out of the Civil Service. They roared with laughter. It had not occurred to them in that way.'

Winston held out his finger as a perch for the bird.

'When I play with it, Rufus walks out.' As if he were addressing the bird, Winston said:

'Molotov attacked me yesterday. I hope he's as wrong about atomic bombs as he is in his facts in what he said about me. Our private information is that they haven't really got a hydrogen bomb. If they had, they would have treated us quite differently.'

Christopher had telephoned to me about Winston's health when I was out, and I asked Jane Portal what was in his mind. She answered: 'He has a fixed idea in his head about the P.M. He wants him to retire.' It has taken a long time, but he has got his way. The P.M. will go in April. Or is this, I wonder, Harold's doing?

CHAPTER THIRTY-ONE

Swan-song

February 16, 1955

'I'm earning my screw in these closing minutes,' was Winston's greeting this morning. 'I work all day. I've made up my mind I shall go in April. But I'm not telling anyone. I want it to come as a surprise. So I'm spreading the gospel the other way that there is no reason why I should not carry on. I think I shall go to Sicily and work north as it gets hotter.

'What is my expectation of life, Charles?' When I did not answer he went on: 'Of course I know I may get another stroke at any moment. I'm still muzzy in the middle of the day. If I can get an hour's sleep it helps. Eddie Marsh used to go to sleep every day after lunch. However, he died quite young; he was only eighty,' said Winston with a smirk.

'When I retire I think I shall take up riding again. It would not tire me. I ride by balance. I would get a quiet horse. Of course I shan't resign if there is a war. Chiang and Chou, bloody stinkers, are shouting at each other and making war possible.' He spoke with great disgust. 'As for the Frogs, they are hopeless, quite hopeless.'

February 21, 1955

Winston was in the Cabinet Room, talking to the Chancellor, when I arrived at No. 10. After a time Jock said: 'How late can you leave here and catch your train?' As he said this the P.M.'s bell rang.

He looked up at me. 'I would have stayed longer if they had pressed me not to give up my office. I shall leave things very unsettled, and my relations with the President have never been closer – fourteen years' friendship. That will vanish, and then it will be Anthony and Dulles.' He sighed deeply. 'But I have given Anthony a date when I shall go. I shall not go back on that now, barring, of course, a war.

'A week tomorrow I have to make a very important speech in the Defence debate. I shall need a "major", because I want it to be one of my best speeches. Before I quit office I shall make it clear to the world that I am still fit to govern. I am going not because I can no longer carry the burden, but because I wish to give a younger man his chance.'

The idea of a valedictory message to the House of Commons has been at the back of his mind since he decided – and this time his decision is, I think, final – that he would go after the Budget. He wants to make it one of his great utterances, something the House would long remember. He wishes to demonstrate to them before he resigns that he is still able to advise the country in great matters.

'After all, I took the decision to make a hydrogen bomb, and, as I told Harold Macmillan, that is what they will concentrate on in the House.'

Miss Gilliatt appeared. 'Lady Churchill wants you to know that a carpet has arrived from the Shah and is spread out for you to see.'

'The Shah of Persia,' Winston explained, 'is lunching here today.'

March 1, 1955

I get anxious now when I am out of touch with Winston. For a week I have been making speeches in the north of England, and even when I was waiting to speak he would come into my head; I wanted to slip out to telephone to No. 10 to find out what was happening. Was he really all right? However, this morning he did not seem as tired as I had expected.

'I've taken a hell of a lot of trouble over this speech,' he began, 'twenty hours over its preparation and eight hours checking the facts. Besides, it was built on what I had already said to the Commonwealth Prime Ministers.'

He was so taken up with his script that he made no attempt to read the morning papers, which were neatly piled on his bed-rest as Kirkwood had left them. He picked up one of the typed sheets and began to try out on me some of his turns of phrase. After a little he appeared to forget my presence; he would take up one of the sheets, glance at it and then put it down again.

When Winston is cooking a speech it is never finished until it is delivered; he goes on fiddling with it, altering a word here, cutting out a sentence there, adding something that has just come into his head. I could not help him; he will be unhappy until it is over.

In the office I found Montague Browne busy preparing chapter headings for the speech. 'The Prime Minister wants them,' he explained, 'though the speech does not lend itself to them.'

'How will it go?' I asked.

Montague Browne hesitated. 'I suppose there is not much that has not been said before.'

'Why then,' I asked, 'is he so worked up about it?'

'Oh,' said Montague Browne, 'it's his swan-song.'

When I left him I walked through the Green Park to Hyde Park Corner; I wanted to straighten things out. This hydrogen bomb has got Winston down. When at Potsdam he told me about the explosion of the first atomic bomb he saw the scene as an artist, but I remember that he had not yet grasped what it meant to the world. It had not occurred to him then that it might in the long run mean the end of everything on which he sets store. The hydrogen bomb is another matter. His mind is full of foreboding, his mood dark and sombre. 'The entire foundation of human affairs,' he said in his speech, 'has been revolutionized by the hydrogen bomb.' This nagging pain is always in his head, robbing him of all peace of mind. I come upon him brooding so that he does not seem to know I am there.

'You are unhappy about the hydrogen bomb?'

'Terrible, terrible,' he repeated, half to himself. 'Nothing so menacing to our civilization since the Mongols.'

I am beginning to piece things together. Until Malenkov[1] fell he believed that he, and he alone, could help to make the Russians see reason. He would make them see that their self-interest would be served by an understanding with the West. When Malenkov went, the bottom fell out of Winston's plans.

'If we had been able to go to Bermuda, where *Vanguard* was waiting, I might have been able to persuade the President that a meeting with Malenkov would be useful. I think Malenkov would have played. Our visit might have strengthened his position and turned the scale in his struggle with his enemies. But the opportunity was missed.'

He brooded over the bed-rest on what might have been.

'Ike got into his "royal" mood and said he could not leave the country, and that sort of stuff, though his predecessors did not feel like that. And there is a new wind blowing from Russia.'

'A cold blast?'

'Yes, they are isolating Malenkov and then they will strangle him. No, my usefulness, where Russia is concerned, is gone. I wanted to give Malenkov a chance, and he has vanished.'

I had come to think that Winston's thoughts had settled into a mould. I certainly did not believe that an old man could change his way of thinking almost overnight as it were, and I was not at all pre-pared for the new note of urgency which the bomb had brought into his thoughts. It had not been there before, even in the war.

But this is not all. For it is no accident that he is choosing the debate on defence for his final pronouncement. It is his duty to tell the House and the nation what must be done if Britain is to survive. He is responsible. He appointed Alex Minister of Defence, partly because he liked having him about the place, but more because he was of a mind to be his own Minister of Defence, as he had been in the war. As Winston puts it in his kindly way, Alex is a soldier and he knows nothing of politics. Not that this matters, for the P.M. keeps assuring himself that he at any rate is on top of the problem. More than once in the last few months he has said to me:

[1] Malenkov resigned as Prime Minister on February 8, 1955.

'I have got it all in my head, I have got a firm grip on it. I know what must be done.'

There are, it is true, moments when he is not so sure, when he is tormented by his vision of the future. Winston is a proud man, and it hurts him to think how vulnerable, in the atomic age, a small, densely populated island like Britain has become. In these dark moments I believe he questions if he is still fit to lead and advise in these matters. At any rate, he keeps telling me that no one in the Cabinet has the same grip on the overall picture of the hydrogen bomb as he has. Sometimes it seems that he protests too much, that he is trying to square his conscience, for, of course, he knows what he can do and what is now beyond his powers. It has been very painful to watch his once confident personality now in liquidation. I hate to think he knows what is happening.

*

I was glad that I had gone to the Peers' Gallery in good time, for the House was crowded. Looking round, I saw Mountbatten in the second row rise as if he were about to leave the Chamber, and then push past me into the middle of the front row, though he could see and hear as well where he was. Winston came into the House in time to answer his Questions. Walking very carefully, he picked his way along the front bench; once he seemed to lose his balance, but recovered himself in time, and as Butler made way for him he flopped into his seat. He spoke for three-quarters of an hour, and his voice at the end was as strong as at the beginning. The speech held the House, though he seemed more concerned with his theme than with its effect on Members. To Winston these occasions, when the House plans for the future, are part of English history.

'We live in a period, happily unique in human history, when the whole world is divided intellectually and to a large extent geographically between the creeds of Communist discipline and individual freedom.'

His voice sank to a whisper as he reminded the House that both sides possessed obliterating weapons of the nuclear age. He went on:

'We have antagonisms now as deep as those of the Reformation and its reactions which led to the Thirty Years' War. But now they are spread over the whole world instead of only over a small part of Europe. We have, to some extent, the geographical division of the Mongol invasion in the thirteenth century, only more ruthless and more thorough. We have force and science, hitherto the servants of man, now threatening to become his master . . .

'What ought we to do? Which way shall we turn to save our lives and the future of the world? It does not matter so much to old people; they are going soon anyway, but I find it poignant to look at youth in all its activity and ardour and, most of all, to watch little children playing their merry games, and wonder what would lie before them if God wearied of mankind.'

A great speech, Winston has himself laid down, must have a single theme. His theme was simple. For safety Britain must rely on deterrents. That was why the Government had decided to make the hydrogen bomb. He was so absorbed in his argument that his words came without study, as he gave out his message, like some ancient clock tolling out the hours of the night over the silent town. However, the habits of a lifetime are not easily put aside. Once he found relief from the solemnity of his argument in words coined at leisure. All the countries of the world might feel so vulnerable that, cowed by fear, they might at last be content to live in peace.

'Then it may well be that we shall by a process of sublime irony have reached a stage in this story where safety will be the sturdy child of terror, and survival the twin brother of annihilation.'

It was at that moment that talks at the highest level might bring results. The mood quickly passed; once more the gravity of his theme weighed upon him. The P.M. was drawn back to the dreadful details. The House knew that if there was war Britain must be destroyed; it measured and accepted the cost. Winston Churchill, who knew that his own days were numbered, took heart that before he went he had given back to his country the leadership of the free world. When he sat down he had done what he set out to do.

What ought we to do if God wearied of mankind? That was the question that tormented him as he came towards the end of his journey. His life had been a series of gay sorties from an inviolable home into the political arena to win personal distinction; looking back, he had enjoyed every minute of the game. Here at the end was something that transcended individual combat.

Winston sat for a time listening to Shinwell. When he rose to leave the Chamber I followed him to his room. The door opened and O'Brien came in; he keeps the P.M. in touch with political opinion and with the Press. Winston turned to him eagerly:

'How did they take it? Good. I thought they might like what I said.'

He was still all agog to find out the response of the House. He seemed to be bottling up his excitement, and I noticed that he was out of breath. 'If you never made another speech,' said Christopher – and he seemed just as excited as the P.M. – 'that was a very fine swan-song.' Winston's face fell.

'I may not make many more speeches in the House,' he said gloomily.

He turned to Jock and told him to have his frock-coat sent over from No. 10; he was going to see the Queen.

He caught my eye.

'It's all right, Charles, of course I'm tired, but not too tired. In fact, I'm very well. I had to do it alone; no one could do it for me. Shinwell said there was nothing original in my speech. I don't know why he should say that,' Winston complained in an injured voice. 'I couldn't—'

At that moment Clemmie came into the room and I slipped away.

March 2, 1955

When the debate was resumed today Aneurin Bevan made a clever, provocative speech. He wanted talks with Russia, but complained that at a time when the existence of this country was at stake these talks were ruled out because the United States would not allow them. The P.M. rose:

'It is absolutely wrong,' he said, 'to suggest that the course that we have followed here has been at the dictation of the United States. It is quite true that I would have liked to see a top-level conference with the three powers, and I would have liked to see it shortly after Mr Malenkov took power – as I said at the time – to see, "Is there a new look?" . . . I prepared in every way to go over to see the President. However, I was struck down by a very sudden illness which paralysed me completely, physically. That is why I had to put it all off.'

March 3, 1955

'You saw what I said in the House about my illness?' Winston began immediately I entered the room.

'Why did you say it?' I asked.

'Oh,' he answered, 'it was impromptu. I was stung to say it by Bevan. But I do not regret it. It put me right with the Party opposite, and it will do no harm in the long run, when my actions will be seen to be simple and straightforward.'

He has always wanted to tell people about his stroke. The drama of his illness appealed to him, and at the time I had great difficulty in persuading him that people in this country, when they hear that a man has had a stroke, are inclined to write him off as no longer a going concern.

The P.M. looked up from *The Times*.

'I've never had such a Press. I like what they say about the way my speech was received in America. They welcome us as a partner in defence'.

I picked up the *Daily Worker*.

'Ah, there it's all abuse and hatred,' he sighed. 'The majority was a hundred and seven and our working figure is sixteen.'

He spat out these words with tremendous contempt.

To change the subject I asked Winston what would happen in the quarrel between Attlee and Bevan.

'Attlee,' he replied, 'has been very upset, but he has come out of it with no discredit; he has shown great courage. Bevan is eructating bitterness. There will be a split; some of them may come over to us. There might be a coalition. If I had been a younger man I might have led it. But I shall not go back on my date with Anthony,' he grinned. 'I am not thinking of a come-back. At least not yet.

'Your "minors" have enabled me to do my work,' though he hastened to add: 'I got well on my own after the stroke. I never lost my sense of direction where public business was concerned. It is less than a month now before I go. At any rate, by my speech I have swept away all thought that I was not competent to do my job. It will make it clear that the sacrifice I am making is a genuine one.'

CHAPTER THIRTY-TWO

Depression

It would be fitting at this point to bring to an end my account of Winston's second term of office, for when he is troubled about England's survival he appears to take on another dimension. But his struggle for his own survival was in fact not fought out at that level. Perhaps his swan-song brought home to him that he was finished and done with, a mere pawn in the great game in which he had been a maestro. Or it may be that his thoughts were turned inwards by all this talk that he was not fit for his job, so that he became conscious of his own frailty. At any rate, my diary for the next two or three weeks makes sad reading:

March 8, 1955
Last night, just before midnight, Winston telephoned. His cold had come back.

'Are you in bed?' I asked sleepily.

'No.'

'Well you ought to be.'

He had started the penicillin spray.

This morning the cold appeared to have gone, but he said:

'Would you like to warm your paws in the bathroom? I would like you to listen to my chest. I have an idea there might be something there. I took my temperature twice last night. I kept it in my mouth for five minutes on both occasions, but it was two degrees below normal. Isn't that dangerous? I have been using the menthol and cocaine spray. I let it trickle down Adenoid Avenue; it does a lot of good.'

I listened patiently to the measures he had taken, and then advised him to stay indoors. He reached for his board containing his appointments. He thought he might take my advice. It would obviously be sensible. I could see that he did not want to lunch at the Mansion House.

'There will have to be something in the Press. We must get Jock.'

He rang his bell. Jock was ready with the words: 'The Prime Minister has a cold and has been advised by Lord Moran to stay indoors.'

'Go away and put something on paper,' the P.M. said.

Jock returned in a minute.

'Directed, not advised,' the P.M. said with a mischievous grin.

'Yes,' said Jock, entering into the spirit of the thing, 'His Lordship is a very masterful personality.'

'Get on to Michael Adeane,[1]' said the P.M., 'I have an audience with the Queen and I ought not to give her the infection.'

March 17, 1955

Monty, in pyjamas, came out of Winston's room as I spoke to Kirkwood. He had not transmitted his good spirits to the P.M., who, poor devil, seemed in an ill humour: he hates going. 'There is a time to be old,' said the sage, 'a time to take in sail.' But Winston is not a sage, he has no liking for the part.

In the office I found Mary. She was concerned about her father. 'From his own point of view it would have been better,' she said, 'if he had gone on till he dropped in his tracks, but his colleagues would not agree to that. He is terribly flat, but when he resigns I think his "lust for life" will keep him going. If his big speech on the hydrogen bomb had been made a hundred years ago nothing more would have been expected of him for a long time. Now it's

[1] Private Secretary to the Queen.

different. Something else blows up without warning; there is no
respite. It's the detail that gets Papa down.'

March 21, 1955

'You will find the P.M. very depressed,' said Jane Portal this
morning. 'He has given up reading the newspapers and sits about
staring into space. They are really kicking him out.' Jane felt indig-
nant. 'The P.M. is so kind and loyal. He doesn't think evil of
anyone.' I turned this over in my mind and decided that it was the
truth. It is quite astonishing after fifty years in politics.

I found him in the Cabinet Room, abstracted. He appeared to
come back to the present with a jerk. 'Look at this,' he said, throwing me the *Star*. A heading gave May 26 as the date of the General
Election.

'They are telling me the day I shall have to go. I wonder who
gave them the date? I suppose the Party. They wanted to fix a date
once and for all for the election. The Central Office must have let it
out,' he ruminated. 'I don't care,' he said impatiently.

Jock asked him if he had liked Randolph's book.[1] 'It can't do any
harm,' the P.M. replied. 'My vanity led me to spend two hours
looking through it – I didn't go to bed until one forty-five. Perhaps,'
he added with a grim smile, 'the public will not be as interested in
it as I was.'

March 23, 1955

'Did you see that shocking affair in the *Manchester Guardian*?'
Winston looked at me as if he thought I could help. I knew what
was in his mind. In this morning's issue there were two big headlines: 'Cabinet urging Premier to resign. His health said to be retard-
ing its work.'

'But Winston,' I butted in, 'they are usually so friendly.'

'Oh, this was not their Parliamentary correspondent, he is very
sound; it was their Lobby correspondent,' and it appears that it was

---

[1] Randolph Churchill, *Churchill: His Life in Pictures*.

all based on the conversation with one Conservative M.P. 'One,' he repeated scornfully.

'If I dug in I don't think they could make me go. But I like Anthony so much and I have worked with him so long. And he wants to be Prime Minister terribly. Several times he has tried to bring on an election because he thought it would get me out.' A wry smirk spread over the P.M.'s face. 'He might succeed in getting me out and fail to get himself in.' He spoke in a kindly way of Anthony, and then suddenly said sharply: 'But he has no business –' He stopped short. For some time he was silent. Then he spoke very sadly of political life. He had been hurt by the things Anthony had said lately. He had always liked him. After all, he chose him to succeed at a time when no one seemed to think of Anthony as a possible Prime Minister. He could not understand why he was so changed, nor what was in his mind. He had not been like this in the old days.

At times one caught a glimpse of the old truculence. He might have to go, but he would not let them trample on him. It was absurd to say he was not fit to carry on. He said hotly: 'I don't know why I am going. I feel very strong. I am really very well.' As Christopher says: 'He is terribly anxious no one should think that he is resigning on grounds of health. He has been deeply hurt by all this talk that he is not up to his job. That's why,' said Christopher with a grin, 'he has made up his mind he will go to Sicily without his doctor. He will show them he is in the best of health and does not need looking after.' His ways are indeed unpredictable, as they have always been. He went about telling everyone that he had suffered from paralysis, and now, a few weeks later, he is intensely anxious to persuade the country that he is in robust health. 'Do you find anything wrong with me?' he demanded, as if he were challenging me to produce evidence of his frailty.

It made him angry when it came to his ear that there was talk of Eden kicking him out. 'I have not just been drifting, doddering along, unable to decide when to go. It has been all design. Months ago I made up my mind when I would go.' He wants it to appear that he chose this particular moment to resign with only one thing in his mind: to make it easy for Anthony to climb into the saddle.

'Of course, I know when I retire I may have a reaction. For nearly sixty years I have been in political life, and I don't know what will happen when it comes to an end suddenly. But I don't mind if I die,' he added half defiantly. 'I have had a good life. I know Clemmie wants me to get out.'

March 24, 1955

Winston seems more reconciled to the course of events this morning. After all, if he himself fixed the date of his resignation it was not for him to complain. All the same, I dread the weeks that lie immediately ahead. Will he decide that there is no purpose in living when there is nothing to do? Will he hand in? Jock admits that the Cabinets will depress him until he gets out of it all. Decisions in the future will not lie with him, and in fact, all power will have gone, but Jock thinks he has been accustoming himself to this thought for a long time. I want him to take Alan Hodge[1] to Sicily to help him with his book. Winston must have something to do.

'You know, Charles, they would be wise to keep me at the top where I did very little, but where they could get my advice, which has proved very sound in practical matters lately. It has prevented some foolish, some very unwise things, being done and said. I have a feeling this would strengthen their position in the country. But these fellows – I mean my colleagues – want to get things into their own hands. And, of course, Anthony would like very much to be Prime Minister. It is natural, I suppose.'

I picked up a paper with a photograph of a smiling Anthony Eden with Nehru. Winston feels that Anthony ought to be graver, more weighty.

'Have you seen the *News Chronicle* poll? The Tories are in a stronger position than they were.'

---

[1] Historian, Joint Editor of *History Today*.

The P.M. himself is much concerned about the Party. He keeps wondering how they will get on without him. He telephoned me before dinner: 'I thought you would like to know that Questions were a terrific success today. There were shouts of laughter, and at the end one of the Opposition Front Bench rose and said that he was puzzled why the Tories wanted to turn out the Prime Minister. I thought you would be interested in what happened in the House.'

April 1, 1955
A letter from Winston. He has made up his mind to go to Sicily without me. He wrote on March 30: 'As I mentioned to you the other day, it would in my opinion be a mistake for me to inflict upon you the burden of coming out with me to Sicily. At this particular time it would give the appearance that I have resigned through ill-health, which is not true.'

As I entered his room this morning, he began to tell me about his plans.

'I shall see the Queen on Tuesday, then on Wednesday, after saying good-bye to the servants, I shall get out of here. I shall go to Chartwell. I love the place. I shall not go abroad until the 12th. I want to go into my private affairs, though they are not in bad shape.'

A report in the *Manchester Guardian* that he would not retire until the end of the Press strike, because he could not bear to go out of office in complete silence, had made him angry.

'It is absurd,' he said with some heat. 'As if I would alter the date of the election because there are no papers; as if I cared a tinker's cuss what they say when I go.'

The wind dropped and he said simply: 'I don't want to go, but Anthony wants it so much.'

This evening there was a party at No. 10 for Clemmie's birthday. Winston looked tired and old. Attlee went into a long rigmarole about his trials when he was host at No. 10, how he was always sitting down with a Frenchman opposite a painting of Wellington or Nelson. The French have long memories. Curious how ill at ease Attlee is at the end of his life; when you speak to him he makes little quick, nervous movements as if he were not sure of himself. Anyway, it is pleasant to see the Attlees at the most intimate family parties at No. 10 and Clemmie kissing Mrs Attlee. I find it comforting after Bevan and Dalton. Harold Macmillan as usual was full of good talk. It appears that he and Rab have had a pretty lively time with the two prima donnas. It seemed at times that the scenery might come down on their heads. The situation was saved by the sound sense of the stage hands.

April 4, 1955

Jock told me that the P.M. was in good spirits last night and seemed reconciled to the change. Winston soon confirmed this. 'You know, Charles, how I dislike half measures. I've had enough responsibility these last few weeks to worry me and not enough to be able to take decisions. Yesterday after luncheon I felt better. I found the thought of throwing off all responsibility agreeable. I felt I didn't care a damn.' For some time he was silent, then he said in a detached way: 'Things are not very friendly – it is difficult to be friendly at the top. There is a clash of interests. I think I ought to take a minor this afternoon. I don't want to be tired when the Queen comes to dinner.'

And then, without any warning, Winston began firing questions at me:

Winston: 'As my doctor, do you think I ought to have gone before?'

Moran: 'I sometimes wonder how I shall come out of this in fifty years' time.'

Winston: 'You have not answered my question.'

Moran: 'Well, last year when Max and Camrose came to Chartwell after your stroke, they asked me what was going to happen. I told them it was guesswork.'

Winston: 'What do you mean by guesswork?'

Moran: 'How long it would be before you had another stroke. They both said you would never again appear in the House of Commons. I told them I had seen patients more paralysed than you were get quite well. We must wait and see.'

Winston: 'Do many people get over two strokes?'

Moran: 'They took it for granted that you were finished as a politician. I felt from the first you were more likely to snuff out if you retired.'

Winston: 'Yes, I felt like that.'

Moran: 'But Clemmie, Christopher, Max and Camrose didn't. They did their damnedest to get me to agree with them. They were afraid you would collapse in the House of Commons or blunder in the Cabinet, or make some gaffe in public. They were thinking of your reputation, while I was concerned with your health and your peace of mind.'

Winston: 'Perhaps – you were both right.'

April 5, 1955

It had been arranged that Winston's carbuncle should be treated with X-rays at MacKenna's house at half-past six, but it was seven o'clock before the P.M. turned up. He seemed in good form, said he had been petted a lot and subsided contentedly into a chair. 'All my plans,' he began, 'depend on the date of the election.'

'Haven't they decided that yet?' I asked him in surprise.

'They? It isn't *they*. I am responsible until my successor kisses hands. Not,' he added with a smirk, 'that this confers on me auto-cratic powers.' While he was taking off his clothes he asked MacKenna whether any microbes had grown in the culture he had taken from the carbuncle.

'Yes, plenty.'

'What were they like?' persisted Winston.

'Virulent,' answered MacKenna.

'Virulent,' repeated Winston, 'but I trust not malignant. We must use terms with precision. Tell me when you begin the X-rays.'

'They have begun,' responded MacKenna reassuringly.

While this was going on Christopher said to me: 'He's taking it very well so far; morale really quite good.' Then Winston, still smoking his cigar, shuffled to a seat with his trousers round his ankles.

PART FIVE

A Long Farewell

CHAPTER THIRTY-THREE

Good Intentions

April 6, 1955

It has come at last. This afternoon Winston leaves No. 10 for good. To him it seems the end of everything. I could think of nothing to say. He threw off the bed-clothes and went to the window, where he stood looking out at the Horse Guards Parade.

'I am going to bury myself at Chartwell. I shall see no one. I have to deal with an immense correspondence. I am in a good frame of mind, unjealous.'

He grinned broadly.

'There is no doubt it does me good to be petted. I don't know what it would have been like if there had been newspapers.[1] I might live two or three years. I have been blessed with good health. My nerves are good. I don't worry about things and I don't get upset, though occasionally I may become bad-tempered.'

He fell silent; after a little he looked up.

'If it were painless, swift, unexpected . . . .' He did not finish the sentence. As long as he can do things, he keeps cheerful. Tomorrow he will go into his finances; then on Saturday he goes to Epsom. Whenever Winston is deeply stirred he instinctively turns to action.

In the hall I met Norman Brook. He said the last few days had

[1] There was a newspaper strike from March 26 to April 20, 1955.

been rather sad – Winston imputing wrong motives to everyone. 'What about Anthony?' 'Oh,' Brook answered, 'on the whole he has behaved well under considerable provocation.'

This is the end of Winston's long struggle to keep his place in politics. I suppose it had to come. But I dread the next few months. I fear he will pull down the blinds. He may read by candle-light for a while. Yet for my part it was without any particular sense of sadness that I left No. 10 for the last time. For three years and six months I have made my way to his bedroom, sometimes once in a week, sometimes twice, always going before the beginning of his day, and often he would tell me what was in his mind. It has been a great effort for him to keep going; a drawn-out struggle with failing powers. He wanted help, and he saw that I must know what he could do and what he could not do, that he ought not to keep back any of the facts. He seemed at times to open his heart, and feel the better for his candour.

And yet I wonder. Even with his doctor the habit of a lifetime was still strong, the habit of dramatizing himself. It may be that I am altogether too sceptical. Certainly at nine o'clock in the morning Winston is at his most factual. If he ever says outright what is in his mind, that is the time. When I think of all the months during which I have listened to him, and of all the things that he has said to me, it seems that this particular bedroom should have a place in my memory.

All the same, when Winston has left No. 10 I shall not associate him with that house. He does not leave his mark on his homes. After all, unless there is a Cabinet he does not get out of bed till luncheon, and unless he has Questions in the House it may be half-past three before he rises from the table. At five o'clock perhaps, or six, he will, if he can, return to his bed for his rest. Take away another two hours at the dinner-table, and what is left of the day? Why should he be interested in the furniture and fittings of rooms he hardly enters? Besides, what has seemed to matter most in his life, as far as I have had any part in it, has happened elsewhere; when he has been right up against things, it has not been at No. 10.

Before Winston left for Chartwell he said to Christopher: 'I would like to go down and see the Cabinet Room for the last time.' Perhaps his mind had gone back to the blackest days of 1940, when in that room he had told them the truth. The room was in darkness. When the light was switched on it appeared in disarray, ready for the cleaners, the chairs, shrouded in their covers, pushed to one side, the ink-pots gone. Winston looked for a moment in bewilderment on the scene, then he turned on his heel and stumbled out into the hall.

April 8, 1955
Dorothy drove me to Chartwell in time for luncheon.

'So nice of you to come and visit me in my exile,' was Winston's greeting.

'I should have been quite willing to go on giving orders as long as I had breath, but I have handled so many of these situations that I do not grudge to another his chance.'

He lit his cigar.

'I am in good spirits. Once my mind was made up I had a feeling of relief. I don't care a damn now. I have never found time to do the things I wanted to do. Now I shall have to look for things to fill my time.

'I've got my book. The first volume will come out in the autumn. After that I shall lay an egg a year for three years.'

'Is there much to be done on them?' I asked.

'No,' he replied, 'they could appear tomorrow. They need only a little polishing. I am not satisfied with the Tudors.'

He told me that the four volumes of his *History of the English-speaking Peoples* had been written in a year and a quarter just before the war.

'I worked at them every night till two in the morning, though at the time I was fighting for rearmament. Of course I had a team to help, but I wrote every word myself.'

'What will you do when you've done the polishing?'

'Ah, then,' he smiled broadly, 'I shall be ready to stage a come-back.'

When we were seated at the luncheon table Winston raised his glass. 'I give you the toast of Lord Horder,'[1] and he grinned mischievously. 'What is the betting on the election?' he asked gaily. 'I shall come back for it.'

Winston complained that his sense of taste was not what it had been. 'I expect, Charles, just as one's sight deteriorates, so the taste nerves are blunted by age. I think if I went now I should get to sleep; it does me so much good.' He gave me the first chapter of his *History* to read while he rested. It begins in the year 55 BC.

Winston has received an avalanche of letters on his retirement, and Miss Sturdee has come back to lend a hand. She said to me: 'He comes into the office and asks if anything has happened, just as he used to do. You know that for years he has been inundated with "paper" and with official business. And then, all at once, as if a tap has been turned off, it has ceased. All the bustle and stir have gone out of his life. Yesterday Sir Norman Brook sent him a message by a despatch rider. Sir Winston was delighted. Not with the message, but with the messenger. It was an echo from the past.'

Someone asked Winston if he had seen a film *Carmen Jones*, in which the chief character was a Negress. Winston replied that he didn't like 'blackamoors', and had walked out early in the proceedings. He asked, a little irrelevantly, what happened when blacks got measles. Could the rash be spotted? When he was told that there was a very high mortality among Negroes from measles he growled: 'Well, there are plenty left. They've a high rate of production,' and he grinned good-humouredly.

April 10, 1955

'I could have stalled them off in the House and stayed for another year,' he said half to himself. 'But it would have served no purpose.'

Then, turning to me, he said:

---

[1] There is an annual election for the office of President of the Royal College of Physicians. For nine years Lord Moran was re-elected President; on each occasion Lord Horder was the runner-up. Lord Moran retired in 1950. Sir Winston was under the impression that he was still President.

'You've had nothing to do with my going; it was an act of free will. I think Anthony is already feeling the strain.

'I know you think that I shall not thrive in retirement. You have had that feeling all along. I had it myself. But I am not so sure now that we were right. I have my book. Besides, I have other plans. You know this strike is causing great damage to the country and great inconvenience to millions of people. The State cannot stand by and allow this sort of thing. It is wrong that an insignificant number of people – only seven hundred men are involved – should be able to hold the community to ransom. I have been thinking of a Bill which would apply to a number of scheduled trades, where a small minority can injure the public in this way. Each man in these industries would have to sign a certificate when he began his trade undertaking to give three months' notice. In return he would receive every year five pounds from the employer and five pounds from the State, so that at the end of five years he would have fifty pounds in Savings Certificates.

'Meanwhile, before I go to Sicily I am going to read the history of the island. Clemmie says it's very interesting. Aristophanes – in a translation – is not at all dry reading; quite amusing in fact.'

London, April 27, 1955
Two hours after he had arrived at the airport from Sicily Winston telephoned:

'I'm fine, but I'd like to see you. No, it will do in the morning.'

Coming out of the lift on the seventh floor of the Hyde Park Hotel, I was directed to 708, a good room, looking down over a wide stretch of the Park in its spring dress, where I found Winston doing nothing. I stopped by the door to look at two of his pictures propped against the wall.

'I didn't find it easy to paint that cave,' he remarked. 'It isn't good, but it has depth. The other I did from the hotel garden; there is no sunlight in it, but we had no sun while we were there. Of course, I could put it in. I was delighted to find that I still got pleasure in painting. I wanted to do it.'

He gazed at his picture for some time.

'I painted with great vigour,' he repeated. 'What mattered was that I found I could concentrate for three hours – I got interested in it, and was always late for luncheon. I played a lot of cards with Jock.'

Not much, I gathered, had been done on the book.

He struck me as pale, and perhaps a little subdued.

'I have been going through considerable psychological changes,' he said. 'I have had to let things drop from my mind. I have had to shed responsibility and become a spectator. Unless there was a crisis I could not now get back to the point where I was before I resigned. I could have gone on till October if they had said, "For God's sake, don't go." But it would have done harm to trade to have an election hanging over the country. Besides, I have no desire now for anything that means effort. I have had my life – a very full life.' He grinned. 'I have got to kill time till time kills me. When, Charles, you wouldn't tell me, I asked my solicitor what my expectation of life was, and he told me four and a half years. Of course, I know I may die at any moment, but I don't care. I'm prepared for an emergency.'

His plans, he said, depended on the result of the election:

'I think we may win. If we do, but the majority is only five, I may have to attend the House; if it's forty I need not go.'

I asked him how long he would be in England.

'Until June 13 at any rate,' he answered. The Queen had commanded him to be present at the Garter ceremony at Windsor. He went on:

'I had a lovely letter from her, eight pages in her own writing. It took me a whole morning to reply. Besides, I have some horses running at Ascot and I have to see to some domestic things. My secretariat has broken up.'

I talked about the chances of a railway strike. He grinned:

'I have a car. That is the measure of my detachment from things.'

CHAPTER THIRTY-FOUR

The End of Make-believe

May 12, 1955

Today, without any warning, Winston threw in his part. He could no more pretend to himself that it was all for the best when he resigned. The brave attempt at make-believe has been scrapped. He looked up as I entered the room.

'Since I retired and relaxed I have noticed a decline in my interest in things – oh, in everything. I hate London. I don't want to see people. They don't interest me. I am bored with politics. This election prevents me getting down to my book.'

In matters which did not affect him personally he had never taken much interest. Have things now gone a stage further? This had been his answer:

'I shall die quickly when I retire. There would no longer be any purpose in living.'

Since his resignation he has not once telephoned to me about his health, and when I do call on him he is quite different. He does not say to me any more: 'I want to be at my best on Tuesday in the House.' I do not find him keyed up for some exacting test – what he called a hurdle. There are no tests now, and in any case, in his own words, what does it matter to anybody whether he is or is not at his best?

May 19, 1955

'I shall be glad when this election is over,' Winston said this morning.

'You find it tiring?' I ventured.

'No,' Winston grumbled, 'boring. I am out of it all. It means nothing to me. I am only doing my duty.'

I tried to say that after the election, when he could get down to his book, things would be better. He hardly seemed to be listening.

'No, I'm finished. I'm only waiting.'

To turn his thoughts I told him of an article about the Presidential election in America. There seems to be no market in an election there for close reasoning; all they appear to want are vague generalities and a comfortable personality like Ike.

Winston commented drily: 'It is as well to build up a personality on a solid structure of sound argument. In America,' he went on, 'when they elect a President they want more than a skilful politician. They are seeking a personality: something that will make the President a good substitute for a monarch. Adlai Stevenson will have to build himself up gradually if he is to do any good.'

Only once did I get a glimpse of the old pugnacity when he handed me a crumpled morning paper. 'Read that.'

'Don't be draft, Sir Winston' was the leader heading. It was all about a little bickering between Attlee and Winston. When that was done with, the writer, gaining momentum, said: 'Dear old Sir Winston in fact had a rather bad day.' And in support of this printed this specimen of 'the gloriously vituperative things' that Sir Winston had thrown at the Tories in the good old days when he was helping Lloyd George to float his famous Budget. 'A party of great vested interests banded together in a formidable confederation, a party of the rich against the poor.'

The little flutter of wind died away, and in the flat calm it seemed as if he had never been interested in politics.

May 31, 1955

A slight relapse. One Forbes had written a 'poisonous article', in the course of which he said that Anthony had increased his majority while Winston's had fallen.

'It is not true,' said Winston vigorously, 'it is quite untrue.'

I asked him why he did not lie down, he seemed so somnolent.

'Ah,' he said, 'I like lying in bed, but I must not become bedridden. I feel very stupid,' he muttered, giving a succession of noisy yawns.

'I'm not always like this. This morning I did three hours on the book. Oh, it was simple, just rearrangement, and picking out an unnecessary passage here and there. It's thinking and composing I find difficult.'

Ringing for a secretary, he said he would like to see a list of his horses. For a long time he stood looking over the Weald, his eye feasting on the different shades of green in the evening light. At last he turned to me and said: 'I bought Chartwell for that view.'

June 2, 1955

Winston telephoned in the morning that he would like to see me; he was not very happy about things. Christopher also telephoned that he was troubled about the old man. Winston had dined with them at the farm. He was in great form, but after dinner he said he felt light-headed as if he had drunk too much. 'Of course he hadn't,' Christopher added, 'we only had a bottle of champagne between the four of us.'

'Ah, Charles, I am glad to see you,' Winston began. He said his head had felt queer when they were at dinner. However, when he woke in the night the light-headedness had gone, but in the morning his right hand was clumsy. I asked him what he had noticed.

'It is no longer trustworthy. When I think about it, it is all right. Look,' and he held out his cup without a tremor. 'But in ill-considered acts it is bad. Twice I have knocked over my cup and upset the coffee.'

He demonstrated what he could do yesterday with his hand.

'I can't do now what I did then – nothing like it.' He reached for his pen and wrote his name several times. He held the paper out to me. While I was still examining the writing he took it away from me, and was on the point of destroying the sheet of paper, when I suggested that it would be a good thing to keep it, to compare with his writing in a few days' time. Thereupon, folding the paper up and putting it in an envelope, he sealed it and scribbled 'W.S.C.' on the front.

'My writing is not good. I know that something has happened.'

As he was speaking, his cigar slipped from his mouth; he caught it so that it lay flat against his cheek.

'I don't mind a bit,' Winston continued, 'I'm not despondent. Yesterday when I lunched with Max I kept dropping my cigar and Max kept picking it up.'

When Winston tried to touch my finger with his right hand he made a circle round it, though he had a good strong grip, and when he attempted to walk I was afraid that he might fall, his right leg shot out unsteadily in the air, as if he was goose-stepping.

'Have I had another go?' he demanded.

I told him that there was a spasm of an artery.

'You mean in my head?'

It soon became plain that Clemmie and Christopher wanted me to accompany him to Chartwell and to stay the night there. Anthony, he told me in the car, had sent him a very nice letter of four sheets. He rambled on. I had to lean towards him to catch his words. Three times he popped off to sleep. At Chartwell he rejected angrily all attempts to help him up the steps. He made his way to the office in a succession of darts, bumping against the wall, first to the right and then to the left, so that it seemed he must fall. In the office he flopped into a chair.

'Anything come in?' he demanded.

June 3, 1955

When I went to his room this morning the notice on his door 'Don't disturb' had not been taken down; half an hour later he was still sleeping. I began to feel uneasy and listened outside his door, but I could not hear his breathing. I kept wondering whether this business had spread in the night. Should I find his leg and arm para-lysed? However, when he woke he said he felt different.

'You mean better?'

'Yes,' he responded cheerfully.

He fiddled clumsily for his pen on the table by his bed, and began writing his name. Nine times he wrote with great care and deliber-ation 'Winston Churchill'. Opposite the fourth of these signatures he scribbled 'No noticeable improvement' and at the bottom of the sheet of paper '20% down'. Just then Kirkwood appeared with his breakfast. I was poring over his signature when he said:

'This is the thing to look at, what I'm doing now.'

He was holding out his cup at arm's length.

'Pretty good, Charles.'

When he had put down the cup his attention wandered, and his right arm made a sudden purposeless and uncontrolled movement, upsetting the cup, so that his fingers ended in the coffee. Looking up, as if he wanted to say, 'There, you see, that's what I do,' he gave his dripping fingers a rueful look.

'How they hate us,' he said sadly, handing me the *Daily Worker*.

June 4, 1955

'I think I am definitely better,' Winston began.

He had put his cup on the left of the breakfast tray so that he could use both hands when he lifted it to his mouth.

'Give me a bit of paper, Charles. I feel I shall write better.'

Once again he wrote out his name; four times he repeated it. Below the signatures he wrote 'I'm a very good autographer. I've had a lot of practice with other people. It's not as difficult as it seems.'

He held the paper away from him.

'Yes, the first signature is almost normal. I am better, definitely better.'

Tonight I tried, without any success, to persuade Winston that a film tires him. He insisted that he must see a thriller, *Les Diables*. He said he enjoyed a film and he was sure it did him no harm. Half an hour afterwards Christopher knocked at my door.

'Winston,' he said, 'came out of the film because his heart was pounding, and he did not feel up to much. He has gone to his room.'

There I found him stretched on his bed. He held out his wrist.

'Take my pulse, it must be 120. I don't think you'll find it too good.'

He was right. It was rapid and irregular.

'It's the first time the story of a film has upset me like this,' he continued. 'It was very exciting.'

I told him his pulse would soon settle down, and pulled up a chair by his bed. He got out of his clothes gingerly, sparing himself.

'I'm glad you're here.'

After a little, he asked me what book I had in my hand.

'Ruskin,' I answered, '*Praeterita*.'

'Ah, he writes beautifully, lovely language. Don't go, Charles.'

There was a long silence.

'Go on reading Ruskin. Don't go away.'

He addressed Kirkwood. 'Would you like to go down and see the end of the film?'

Kirkwood thanked him and vanished. When he came back he was closely questioned about what had happened to the various characters. Winston held out his wrist.

'Take it again. I think it's quieter now.'

June 5, 1955

'When I woke this morning,' said Winston, 'I felt master. I was on top. I was in good health again. I haven't yet made up my mind about my appointments for the next month.'

He is trying to persuade himself that the stroke which clamped down on his effort to make the best of things has made no difference. But he is not so well as he was, he cannot control his feelings as he did, and I am fearful of the days that lie ahead.

June 6, 1955

It does not seem a long time since Winston did all the talking at every meal; now he sits all huddled up in silence; he can no longer hear what is being said, he is outside the round of conversation and not part of it, though at times, it is true, when there is a burst of laughter, someone will explain to him what it is all about.

He said he would like to give me one of his pictures. I was to choose three, so that there might be an alternative if my choice fell on a picture from which he could not bear to part. I had admired a painting of a lake with trees which faced me during luncheon.

'You must have that,' he said.

When I left him his eyes filled with tears.

'I am touched by your kindness and devotion.'

With that he turned away, murmuring: 'I don't think I shall be able to do very much in the future. It is wonderful that you have kept me going for so long.'

CHAPTER THIRTY-FIVE

Mournful Gestures

June 8, 1955

Found Winston in his bath in his most unreasonable mood.

'This tickle,' he grunted, 'is quite intolerable. It kept me awake. Yes, a bloody night. The skin man has given me fourteen ointments or lotions in turn without any theory behind any of them. Just doling out some potion or unguent to keep me quiet. It's a disgrace to the medical faculty.'

As the tenure of office of Winston's adviser seemed to be threatened, I had to explain to Winston that his skin had grown old with the rest of his tissues, and that none of us could put back the clock. He gave an impatient snort. He was not convinced. I explained to him that if he were willing to cut down the number of hot baths it might help the irritation of his skin very considerably. This he regarded as an outrageous suggestion.

He was due at St James's Palace at noon for a rehearsal of the Garter ceremony, but he was in no mood to hurry.

'I shall take my seat in the House this afternoon.'

Christopher said he would get an ovation. Winston rapped back irritably:

'I don't care a damn about that. I don't need their applause. What are those blue marks?' he asked, pointing to some bruises on his arm. 'Do you mean to tell me that all my veins are going to burst?

'I think Anthony will have to give way to the strikers. The T.U.C. have passed the buck. I don't see why the Government shouldn't negotiate before the strike ends. It would not be right to allow pique, pride or procedure to hold up negotiations. There would be no sympathy with the Prime Minister if further injuries are inflicted on the public merely on account of pique. Certainly if there is a general strike it would be ridiculous for Anthony to prance about in his Garter robes.'

June 9, 1955

When I came into his room today he said at once: 'Have you seen the *Manchester Guardian*? Attlee was very kind to me when I took my seat in the House.' It appears that when a Member caught sight of Winston advancing up the floor – he was not very steady on his feet – he cried in his excitement, 'Churchill.' At that, before anyone could check it there was an unashamed clapping of hands in the public gallery, while all the Members crowding the benches waved their order papers, cheering madly. Where would he take his seat? It could only be in the seat below the gangway alongside the Treasury Bench. It was from this seat that he had warned the nation of its danger in the years before the war. Members must have wondered what was passing through his head at that moment – the rush of memories.

When they thought of him their feelings welled over into little signals of affection. Mr Shinwell gaily beckoned him to come over to the Labour benches. And then, when no Member dared trust himself to speak, Mr Attlee rose from his seat and, quickly crossing the floor, took Winston by the arm, pushing him forward in front of him towards the table. Sir Winston must take the oath before him; while the whole House, seeing what was being done, rose to applaud.

Herbert Morrison, who was following Attlee, touched Winston affectionately on the back, and Winston, turning round, grasped Morrison's hand and shook it warmly. Then he signed the roll of members, writing his name for the thirteenth time in the roll of the Parliaments of Great Britain, very carefully, very deliberately – no doubt he had in mind what had happened at Chartwell.

Chartwell, June 17, 1955
'The Guildhall people[1] want me to make a world pronouncement on Tuesday. It's not the time for a world pronouncement. Anyway, I'm not fit for anything. I shall speak for ten minutes.'

When Winston had said this he looked gloomily across the Weald:

'And I shall worry all day over that ten minutes' speech. I'm interested in my book, that's all I care for now. I'm tremendously interested in it. If I die tomorrow the business arrangements would not be altered. It's all written. But I'd like to make it as good as I can; just taking out something here, and perhaps adding a sentence there.'

His accountant came through the garden gate.

'Ah,' said Winston, 'I shall not be very long with Lord Moran. Perhaps you would return. My finances are intricate, though not unfavourable. I have to keep moving about, when I'd like to stay here for a month. You cannot realize how much I hate doing anything.'

I tried to reassure him about Tuesday. 'We'll get you through Guildhall without any trouble.'

'Are you sure?' he said, looking at me like a child.

June 21, 1955
Yesterday Winston appeared to be finished. He became impatient, demanding how long this must go on, and then, a moment after, it was plain that he was frightened about himself. He seemed to have given up the struggle since his stroke. Low-spirited and querulous, we could not interest him in anything. Today he is not so sure that he wants to die. The City's warm patriotism, that is as Victorian as his own frock-coat, is the medicine he needs. All the same, I was glad that this was his last public appearance. If he got through this with credit he would at any rate have avoided a breakdown in public. It was in that mood that I waited in Guildhall. But immediately I caught sight of him walking slowly but steadily up to the dais I knew it was all right.

[1] Churchill's statue in Guildhall was to be unveiled on June 21, 1955.

No one, I thought, would notice anything wrong with his gait. It is a good weather-vane. When he walks all right his mental processes are more or less normal. I sat back with a great feeling of relief.

Standing there on the dais beside his statue, he might have been the 'Spy' cartoon of Winston, or for that matter of his father, Lord Randolph. His white hands laid out above his groin, fingers spread wide apart, thumbs uplifted, they seemed to be caressing the nap of his black frock-coat.

He did not say very much of serious import. He did not believe that humanity was going to destroy itself, though a period of relaxation of tension might well be all that was now within our grasp.

After dinner I called at Hyde Park Gate. I found him playing bezique with Clemmie, tired but happy.

'This afternoon at Guildhall,' he said, 'restored my confidence. It was a formidable ordeal. Did you like my speech? It would be easy,' he continued, 'on such an occasion to say foolish, conceited things. I carefully avoided that.'

No one is more adroit at disarming criticism of that sort by a discreet levity. He told me how agreeable to him was the prospect of his statue, resting beneath those of Gog and Magog, between Nelson and Wellington, with Pitt and Chatham. He liked it as much as he had disliked Graham Sutherland's portrait.

Then, with a toss of his head, he said:

'All is vanity. Many have done more than I have, but no one has been so kindly treated. I do not deserve it.'

I advised him to go early to bed, but he explained that he had slept for more than an hour after his return from Guildhall. Sleep did him almost as much good as a 'minor'. He thought there was something, after all, in resurrection.

'Why, if I slept for a million years I should wake up full of meat.'

June 22, 1955
Winston said cheerfully,

'I know now I can do this sort of thing. I believe Sir Russell would give me a good report.'

Guildhall has done a good job of work; he will not give in without a fight. I clutched at the opening to consolidate the gain and brought Brain to Hyde Park Gate before he changed his mind.

Without any preliminaries Winston began his story:

'Three weeks ago to the day I bumped up against the wall. I thought I was drunk, but in the morning my writing was bad. I put my signatures in an envelope, but I have left it at Chartwell.'

He reached for his pen and wrote his name several times. This he handed to Brain.

'That is like my normal writing, whereas that morning my hand lingered so that I upset things – I cannot sprinkle sugar as well even now. I wondered if it would get worse as in 1953, when I did things the day after my stroke, and I was not paralysed until the following day. But this time the other channels opened up.' He grinned. 'I'm getting rather good at that. And Charles watched me like a cat, night and day, for five days. I can walk all right if I set my mind to it.'

He flung off the bed-clothes and stalked across the room. Then he stood and lifted first one leg and then the other.

'I'm still not very steady.'

Brain made a careful examination, and then sat back in his chair and said nothing. 'Charles is right,' he said at last. 'It was spasm, and now the artery has opened up again. I see no reason why you should not in a short time be as good as before.'

'You mean before I resigned?' Winston asked incredulously. 'Of course,' he went on, 'putting down responsibility is a very relaxing affair. My whole psychological position had to be changed. After my return from Sicily I had to begin my election address. The quality of thought, such as it is, was not diminished, but I had become very slow. I got it out all right in the end, but I dislike original composition. I am not ambitious any more. I only want not to make an ass of myself. I began my Guildhall address on Monday. I did 300 words in the car coming up from Chartwell, and another 300 between 10 o'clock and midnight. In the morning I finished it off only just in time. My bad time is from noon until half-past four. I am embarrassed by the midday blur.'

He complained of his memory, particularly for names. He looked at the glass of whisky by his bed.

'I keep it by me all day. Oh, it is only weak, and I only sip it. It is more a companion than a stimulant.'

Russell listened attentively to Winston's story, but offered no comment. Winston waited impatiently for suggestions, but they did not come. He had told Brain the whole story that he might get his help. He wanted to be told that his mind was not giving way. He wanted to do something. 'No,' Brain said shortly, 'there is nothing I can add to the treatment.'

Brain is an honest man, he has no patter. He told me, when I saw him to the door, that he noticed Winston a good deal changed. But of course he had not seen him for a year. There was really nothing to be said. He did not try to say comforting things. He would be more popular with Winston if he did.

July 10, 1955

Norman Brook is staying with us at Marshalls. He has an honest mind, and is on the whole more approachable than Bridges; it is easy to understand how the whole Cabinet trust him and rely on his judgement. He is very fair to Anthony. People talk of Anthony's impatience and his moments of petulance and irritability, but generally these soon vanish, the cloud is gone and the sun is shining again. Norman thinks, looking back, that he was very patient. Winston tried him pretty hard. For a long time he would make no plan of any kind about his resignation; then when at last he did talk about it, he still refused to name any date. I got the impression that Winston did not contribute much in his last six months in office. He wasn't really up to his job. In the end he made no effort to master anything.

'What brought things to a head?' I asked.

'The Party,' Brook answered, 'had wanted for some time to go to the country. The real reason why they wanted an election was that the economic situation was as good as it was likely to be. In the autumn it might not be so good. Incidentally, the fact that they came back with a good majority proved they were right. And then when everything was fixed up Ike announced, out of the blue, that he would like to come over. His idea was that there should be a great celebration of the tenth anniversary of VE day, which he would use to bring the French up to the scratch; he thought they could be persuaded, in these surroundings, to ratify the Paris agreement. This plan did not appeal to me,' Brook went on, 'because it could not be very attractive to the Germans. Besides, nothing could have been less opportune for the Government. Winston had agreed at last to name a date in April when he would resign. Now he was sorely tempted by the prospect of a Conference with Ike to hang on. Anthony's patience at last gave way.

' "But," he said mildly. "I thought we had an understanding." '

' "I cannot discuss this," Winston said in truculent tones. "It is not a matter for the Cabinet to decide."

'I suppose it wasn't,' Brook conceded. 'However, this time the Party knew all about the date, and Anthony could not have given way even if he had wanted to. So Ike was told privately that the Conservative Party had a General Election in view. Then when all this was settled, Anthony decided to take a chance and go to the country directly he took over from Winston.'

Brook was certain this was not just a trick to get Winston out; the Party believed it was the right moment to go to the country. They were sick of delays, they refused to put it off any longer. He thought for a time and then said:

'You know, if Anthony had not been ill when the P.M. had his stroke in 1953, Rab and Salisbury might have acted very differently. You see, the Party had accepted Anthony as Winston's heir; he was ill, so there was nothing for it but to carry on with Winston, however incapacitated he might be.'

Brook, too, marvelled at the strength of Winston's personality. He had begun the practice of sending a minute to a Cabinet Minister, writing across the top of the paper. It was a good plan, but no one had done it before him. When Attlee succeeded he imitated Winston's practice almost automatically. I told Brook of a conversation with

Shuckburgh[1] when he was staying at Marshalls. We were talking of who would ultimately come out on top in the Tory Party, Anthony, Rab or Harold Macmillan. To my surprise, Shuckburgh, who had been Anthony's secretary said; 'If toughness is the decisive factor, it will be Anthony.' When I pressed him for his reasons, he went on:

'Of course Anthony always gave way to Winston. We were often furious with him at the F.O. He would return and say Winston had been very nice to him and they had agreed. But this was because he cannot bear scenes or any sort of unpleasantness. However, when his mind is made up on a policy, no one sticks to it with the same tenacity as Anthony.'

Brook thought well of Shuckburgh, and said he was intelligent, exceptionally tough and thoughtful.

The conversation kept returning to Winston. I had said that Arthur Bryant was editing Alanbrooke's[2] diaries, and that I feared he might be critical of Winston as a strategist. Neither Alanbrooke nor Marshall, I said, took the old man seriously in the field of strategy. Brook thought from what Billy Collins[3] had told him that the diaries would not be published for a long time, anyway in their complete form. Then he rallied to Winston's side:

'The P.M. prevented any quarrelling between the three Services and co-ordinated their work. Winston's courage in 1940 will, I am sure, survive any criticism of his conduct of the war. He had two valuable qualities: he never frittered away his time attending social functions, public dinners and the like (he must have gone to only a fraction of those Attlee attended), and he was ruthless during the war in selecting the two or three subjects which he decided to master.' Brook smiled. 'After the war he was even more determined to cut down what he had to do, until in the end he made no effort to master anything.'

---

[1] Sir Evelyn Shuckburgh, Principal Private Secretary to Secretary of State for Foreign Affairs, 1951–4.

[2] General Sir Alan Brooke, wartime C.I.G.S., had become Viscount Alanbrooke.

[3] William Collins, publisher.

I told Brook that Winston had said during the war: 'Portal has everything,' and I asked him why Portal had fallen in his sight. A flicker of a smile crossed Brook's face:

'Winston invited Portal to call on him; he wanted him to take on the Ministry of Defence. Portal arrived and told him he had influenza. Winston was frightened he would get it. Portal obstinately refused to accept office. When Winston realized he had run the risk of picking up Portal's microbes for nothing he was very angry. From that day the P.M. seemed to write him off.'

I tried without success to get out of Brook his explanation of the way Winston would write off a man for good simply because he had refused a job. I quoted Trenchard: 'Portal was as good a pilot as he was a staff officer, a very rare combination.' Brook agreed: 'Yes, he is a remarkable figure; he goes through life like a lone wolf.'

One day last year Lord Wavell's son, who had been given a year's leave to put his father's paper in order, said to me: 'Why did Mr Churchill dislike my father?' I was about to put the question to Brook when N— joined us and answered my questions. It seems that after the first bitterness there had been a reconciliation, so that Winston said he was not sure that he had been quite fair to Wavell in his book. At this point the official history of the war came out. Wavell was praised, he was a very fine general, and there was a broad hint that Winston had failed to discern his merits. Then Winston seemed to revert to his original verdict. 'If only,' I put in, 'Wavell had possessed something of Ismay's gift for putting himself across.'

When David Maxwell-Fyfe replaced Lord Simonds as Lord Chancellor Winston asked me what I thought of the change; he appeared uncertain how it would be taken. Winston himself, on another occasion, remarked that he liked David, but that he was a poor politician and had given him the wrong advice on Crichel Down, and on television.

Brook, who had been silent, joined in: 'David was very conscientious. What I like about him is that if you have a problem he will at once offer to help and take any amount of trouble to find a solution. He has good judgement, and when his report is ready every aspect is considered. Nothing is left out. It is pretty dull stuff, but when David has done the Cabinet doesn't want to discuss it any further, but is ready to pass on to the next item on the agenda.'

July 12, 1955
'I feel I'm breaking up quickly. I have divested myself of everything. I only want to help. I have no desire to be a rival to anyone or to be a counter-attraction. Lots of people want to see me, but I am not fit to see them.' He brooded. 'Of course if the Party had come on bended knees and said I must help them and asked me to stay I could have done it. I think I should have been up to it. I slept from midnight to nine this morning. A lovely sleep. I did not get out of bed till one-fifteen and when I had been up less than two hours I went back to bed and slept for an hour and a half. Some day soon the sleep will go on for ever. I spend most of the twenty-four hours recumbent.'

He dragged himself wearily out of bed, and sitting in front of the looking-glass, sprinkled some lotion on his scalp before he took up his brushes. 'It makes me look a little more alive,' he said. Winston rose and went to the bathroom.

Montague Browne: 'I got hold of Walter Raleigh's *Life* and his last letter to his wife. I gave them to Winston to read. He wept. "James I was a bloody man," he said angrily. And Winston didn't like Henry VIII either. He hated his cruelty to his wives; Anne Boleyn, in particular, had put up a good show.'

Moran: 'Winston doesn't read much. I don't suppose he read the book I gave him.'

Montague Browne: 'You mean *Melbourne*? You're quite wrong. He came into the office the other day muttering:

' "Intelligent, yes. Good looking, yes. Well-meaning, yes. But not the stuff of which Prime Ministers are made."

'I said: "But would Rab have been any better?"

'Winston looked blankly at me. "I was thinking of Melbourne." '

July 20, 1955
This morning Winston began:

'I had an interesting dream. I was talking to Edward Grey, forty years ago. It was a long conversation. But I never can remember my dreams. They are very precise, even about detail, but they vanish.'

The budgerigar alighted on Winston's hand, and he held it to his lips. He went on:

'I can't pick up the points in conversation now. Yesterday when I went to Kempton I talked to no one but Christopher and my trainer. I avoided other people. I'm empty-headed, woolly. It's a ghastly condition. I have been making innumerable corrections in three volumes of the book. It's very confusing keeping the different periods apart. I must not do too much of it,' he said wearily, and then with a burst of impatience, 'I can only die.'

I wonder how long he can go on in this twilight state.

July 29, 1955
Called at Chartwell on my way to Marshalls. Winston had lunched with Anthony at No. 10. Anthony, he said, was 'very sensible about things'. He was not particularly optimistic, but said the Russians had been 'simple, friendly and natural'. Winston took a long time to finish a sentence and more than once I could not follow what he was trying to say.

'I' . . . (pause) . . . 'I think' . . . (pause) . . . 'that I have' . . . (long pause) . . . 'lost my memory. I'm no good . . . very stupid.'

'You mean on waking up?'

'No . . . it's more than that . . . I don't talk . . . I've . . . nothing to say . . . Anthony must have noticed . . . it. I don't care . . . I am conscious I . . . am much worse. I don't think I could make a speech now. It's extraordinary I'm not any good for anything.'

All this he mumbled as if he were speaking of someone else and was not really interested. Some of the pauses were so long that it seemed he was beginning a new sentence.

'Clemmie has made up her mind to go to Switzerland.'

'Where?'

It was some time before he answered.

'I don't remember the place, though I . . . know it quite well. Did you like the chapters I gave you?'

For a moment there was a flicker of animation. It passed. I looked at his vacant face; the skin was still smooth and pink, like a baby's skin after a bath. There is none of time's etching round the eyes. Nor could I detect a white hair, but in his mind he has rather gone to pieces.

August 7, 1955

Christopher says it is not necessary to warn Clemmie that Winston is not so well. She knows the position. She had thought of scratching her month in Switzerland, but decided that she must get better so that she might be ready on her return to look after him. She hoped nothing would happen while she was away. I mentioned that Winston had said he wanted sometimes to tell me what was in his mind.

'I can tell you what that is,' Christopher said grimly, 'he thinks he is dying.'

August 9, 1955

Deakin[1] told me that Winston had an illusion about the book. 'He has an idea that it should be his main interest now, but he hasn't any longer the energy to handle great masses of material. He can't enter into the rhythm of the book.' I said Winston realized that original composition, as he called it, is now beyond his reach, but he felt that he could grapple with the necessary corrections to the text. I asked Deakin about them. He said sadly that they were frankly not of much value. Deakin had not seen Winston for some months; in the past he had come only when invited. Now it is different.

We found Winston in poor heart. Proofs were scattered about the bed. Deakin said to Winston: 'How many millions of words have

[1] F. W. D. Deakin, historian, Warden of St Anthony's College, Oxford, who helped with Winston's books.

been dictated in this room?' That took him back before the war, and he seemed happier and talked a little about his other books.

When we were alone Winston made no attempt to talk. I asked him at last how he was.

'I suffer,' he replied slowly, 'from these pauses. It . . . is the state . . . of my mind . . . that troubles me.'

He turned abruptly.

'Am I going off my head?'

August 10, 1955

Lunched with Harold Macmillan. 'Of course Winston is older,' he said, 'but when I took the conversation back to Lloyd George his memory was surprisingly good.' Macmillan asked me how long he would go on like this. I replied that was guesswork.

August 14, 1955

I got nothing out of Winston during my visit. He did not speak unless I asked a question, and then only to mumble 'yes' or 'no', like a man talking in his sleep. I asked him if he had had any visitors. He said, 'Yes.' I asked him if Pug Ismay had been in form. He said, 'Yes,' without looking at me.

I learnt that Lady Violet Bonham Carter was staying in the house. I found her on the lawn. 'I saw Winston last at Clemmie's birthday party,' she said. 'I don't count the time you took me to his room for a few minutes. We had a very vigorous argument then. I am shocked by the deterioration in him since then. I made a point of talking about the past: I went back to the Leicester by-election which he fought as a Liberal.' Violet poked her nose in my face: 'You know Winston left the Liberal Party at that time because he did not agree with my father's action in putting Labour into power. My father thought that if Liberals and Conservatives combined to keep Labour out of office it would embitter Labour. It was, Lord Moran, a turning-point in Winston's career. But all he said was, "I can't remember . . . I can't remember these things as you do." '

CHAPTER THIRTY-SIX

When Life Was Over

November 18, 1955

This morning, as I entered his room, Winston looked up glumly.

'I have to speak tonight, and I don't know what to say. I am quite impotent. I hope I get through all right. I shall only speak for five minutes.'

He was expecting Christopher, who is going to help him with the speech; meanwhile he kept looking at the small clock by his bedside. He was not interested in my ministrations, he was entirely taken up with what he was going to say. Every word is written down; all Winston has to do is to read it out. Yet he is (to quote his secretary) 'in a panic lest things go wrong'. What is at the bottom of his nagging apprehension? Sir John Simon once said to me: 'When I get up in the Law Courts I don't turn a hair. But I never rise to address the House of Commons without feeling that it is a mill-stream running away from me.' His confidence in the Courts came from long experience; he knew that what he said would be accepted. Whereas in the House he rightly felt no such certainty. Is this the explanation of Winston's lack of assurance at the end of his life? Have even the war years, when he had the House in his pocket, failed to pluck from his mind the bitter memory of his time in the wilderness?

Henry Fairlie has an article on Winston in this week's *Spectator*. He wants him to get up in the House of Commons in the course of the debate on Geneva and make another Fulton speech that would change the mind of the nation. I thought it might give a fillip to Winston's morale. He read the page slowly and then put it down without a word. He knew it was not true. He would make no more speeches that mattered. If he had to get on his legs all he could now hope for was that he would not make a fool of himself.

Chartwell, November 21, 1955

Winston had asked me to call at Chartwell on my way to London. He was reading a section of the book, now in page form. 'I have 25,000 words to write and then it is done. It might take a year, there is no hurry.' He smiled. 'No, there is a hurry. Only my book,' he went on, 'commands my ability and my interest. All the rest is drudgery.'

Without a flicker of a smile he added:

'I find the fifteenth century more interesting than the twentieth. It has more reality.'

December 28, 1955

Winston looked very glum when I appeared today.

'I'm waiting about for death,' he said sombrely.

There was a long pause while he stared in front of him.

'But it won't come.'

When Winston's mind is not taken up with the imminence of death it is brooding on the safety of the Realm.

Winston's distaste for what is left to him of life makes him yearn for release; he wants to die, but he is fearful that he may leave the country without either the will or the means to defend herself.

I congratulated him on Christopher's appointment as Under-Secretary for Air.

'Yes, it will be very interesting at this time. England may be indefensible. But I think we may be able to make other countries indefensible. The Government has lost ground in the last six months. I'm glad the Chancellor of the Exchequer has gone. You see me at my best. I'm stupider . . . I . . . well, let me see . . .'

January 2, 1956

There was not a vestige of a smile when Winston looked up as I came into his room.

'I woke at four o'clock this morning with a pain in my throat, here,' and he put my hand on his neck. 'It lasted an hour, and I coughed a great deal. I wished you'd been here. I have had it before. It's been going on for some time. Is it cancer?' he demanded abruptly.

Before I had time to answer he muttered:

'I don't care if it is.'

January 3, 1956

I took C. P. Wilson to look at Winston's throat. He had just arrived from Chartwell and was sitting in a chair as if he felt a great distaste for the world.

'I feel pretty bloody,' he grunted, 'I'm getting older.'

Wilson said nothing.

'I'm getting older,' he said again.

Wilson thought that the cutting off of all his activities must be a great deprivation.

'Yes,' Winston muttered, 'a lot dropped away with that.'

When Wilson had examined his throat he said:

'It is nothing serious. That is definite. There is nothing organically wrong.'

'I wasn't alarmed at all,' Winston said. But he became all at once almost cheerful. He got up and crossed the room, briskly for him. Turning to Wilson, he said with a little smile:

'Well, anyway, what's the remedy for the pain and what is causing it?'

Wilson thought that it was rheumatic. Winston seemed pleased with the diagnosis; he said he thought it was that, and that Wilson had shown discernment in divining the nature of the pain.

January 12, 1956

I asked Winston about the pain in his throat and told him that Wilson was sure it was nothing serious. He stopped me.

'I don't trouble whether it is serious, but I do if it is not serious.' He really means this. He no longer finds any fun in life.

February 13, 1956

I asked Winston if he had been better in France than he was at Chartwell. He hesitated for a long time and then mumbled: 'I don't know.'

I asked him about his painting. He showed me a copy of a painting by Cézanne that he had taken from a book. It represented a brick-red château half-hidden by dark-green foliage. I asked him why he had chosen this particular picture to copy.

'I liked it,' he answered, 'because of the contrast between the red and the green.'

I told him that the Press was saying that the coming Budget was Harold Macmillan's opportunity to make a bid for the succession to the leadership of the Party.

'If he can find a way out,' Winston said, half to himself. 'There mightn't be a way out. He would have to take very unpleasant measures to make anything of the situation.'

Winston would go to the House on Thursday to vote on hanging.

'I'm a hanger,' he went on. 'It is one of the forms of death of which I have no horror. I never thought about breaking my neck out hunting.'

I marvelled at the number of books in his library that I had not read. Most of them were embellished with Lord Randolph's book-plate. 'You inherited them all? This, for example,' I said, picking out Froude's *History of England* in twelve volumes.

'I bought it,' Winston answered. 'I have read every word of it.'

February 18, 1956

I was creeping up the stairs to Winston's bedroom, having experienced of late some discomfort under my breastbone on taking stairs in my stride, when his door opened and he appeared, leaning back on Kirkwood, who was supporting him under both armpits, like an artist's dummy, while he pushed him into the passage. Winston gave me a blank, unsmiling, rather stupid look. When Kirkwood had taken him to Clemmie's room he returned explaining that Sir Winston has only just woken up. 'I had to rouse him, as he is going to see her ladyship off.'

When Winston came back into his own room he was walking very badly.

'I shall improve when I am properly awake. People must regard me as very frail. I lurch about. I don't think I shall live very long.'

When I expostulated he asked me like a child:

'Do you think I may get any better?'

He was full of the hanging debate, and even when Kirkwood had brought his breakfast he kept picking up a newspaper and reading the headlines: 'Hanging to Go'; 'By 31st. No more Hanging'; 'Wild cheers as M.P.s decide.'

'That's the *Mirror*,' he said grimly. 'It will do harm,' he muttered. 'The Tory Party will be furious, and it will be very unpopular in the country. There will be a murder, and then people will be shocked.'

I drew my chair nearer to the bed. I could not follow his speech.

What troubled Winston was the 'unmasculinity of the island'.

'It was mad of the Tories to bring in commercial television. It is no wonder the country is going soft. My interest in politics has come back,' Winston said, as he fiddled with the papers.

I thought that the atmosphere of the House had stirred the past. I said so.

'No,' he said half to himself, 'it's the loss of masculinity, of virility, that is troubling me. I would like to speak about it in the House, to warn the country. I think I could speak clearly enough if I made the effort.'

As he said this he took great care to make every syllable clear and distinct. He shook his head sadly.

'There is no longer the necessary clarity of thought.'

CHAPTER THIRTY-SEVEN

Germany Honours Sir Winston

April 22, 1956

Winston was sitting at a card table in his room, waiting patiently for Anthony Montague Browne. The bezique cards and markers were ready. He looked up and I could tell that he was glad to see me. He is in the mood to be pleased with the small change of political life.

Winston: 'The dinner [at No. 10] was a good show, because I was made the central figure. I sat next to Khrushchev. The Russians were delighted to see me. Anthony told them I won the war.'

At that moment Montague Browne came into the room and in his quick way picked up the thread of the conversation.

Browne: 'Could you tell which of the two, Bulganin or Khrushchev, was Number One?'

Winston: 'I've no doubt whatever; it was Khrushchev.'

Moran: 'Do you think he is a major figure, another Stalin?'

Winston: 'No, only a minor. But I am sure Bulganin and Khrushchev are in the main honest. They gave me a feeling of confidence. I am sure it is not all humbug. Their visit means something.'

Browne: 'You don't think it was a mistake?'

Winston: 'No, it will do good. At least it ought to.'

Browne: 'What are they up to?'

Winston: 'Russia is developing and getting richer. They may want to take part in the affairs of the Western nations. They may want us to help them to be better friends with the Americans. But

I should not be in favour of Bulganin and Khrushchev going to the States. The Americans aren't sure of themselves as we are. They might have difficulty after a visit in turning sour again with Russia.'

The Cabinet, I hear, is more critical. Winston has a busy week before him. 'I like something to do. But not too much. Often I do nothing.'

Dorothy had been talking to the policeman while we were in the house. He said there were four of them in the house guard; they did an eight-hour shift. They were told that Chartwell must be guarded night and day; they must keep awake, even when Sir Winston was away in London, on account of the number of secret documents in the house.

May 3, 1956

Winston is full of his visit to Germany. That he, the chief architect of Germany's downfall, should be their guest excites him, but he is bothered by his speech for Aachen.

'The Foreign Office brief was drivel, rubbish; what any Minister would spout. I have to say something, but it isn't easy. You see, Charles, it is an important speech. Awful,' he grunted. 'Charlemagne worked for the unity of Europe, and that is the purpose of this award. The Nazis set out to rule the world, and something went wrong.'

'They are not all dead,' I interposed. 'You will find some of them in your travels.'

'Oh,' he rejoined lightly, 'I'm a hero in Germany. It's very curious.'

I asked him if he had read the *Manchester Guardian*.[1] The editor of the weekly *Deutsche Zukunft*, a member of the Free Democratic Party, had devoted a whole page to Winston's alleged mistakes; extracts from this filled nearly a column on the centre page of the *Guardian* under two headings: 'The Misdeeds of Sir Winston; A German Attack'. The author of the article affirmed: 'Churchill did not wage war against Hitler out of any idealistic belief in freedom, but in order to maintain the balance of power. . . . Few politicians of recent years

[1] May 3, 1956, p. 7.

have made so many monumental mistakes as the 81-year-old British statesman.' He had done far more, it went on, to split Europe than to unite it. He had signed the Morgenthau Plan, which planned the systematic destruction of German industry, he had introduced illegal partisan warfare into territories occupied by the German Wehrmacht. Finally, he was responsible for the systematic bombing of undefended German cities. In his 'blind hatred' of Germany he had 'gambled away the British Empire and driven out the devil, Hitler, with the aid of Beelzebub, Stalin'. The Bonn correspondent of the *Guardian* introduced this tirade with the dry comment that it 'does not suggest that the award [of the Charlemagne Prize] has the general approval of the German people'.

Winston these days is not accustomed to minority reports; he read it through in silence, nursing his forehead in his left hand. When he had done he said: 'I shall have a great reception.' He had interrupted his breakfast to read the column in the *Guardian*, now he munched toast in silence. He cannot hide his feelings, and I saw he was disconcerted. As I was leaving his room he looked up: 'Is there a Leader on this?' and with that he pushed away his breakfast and picked up the *Guardian*.

May 6, 1956

It was about three o'clock in the afternoon when I arrived at Chartwell. Winston was sitting on the lawn doing nothing. It still seems strange to find him idling away the hours, not reading or dictating or even playing cards. I asked him about his speech for Aachen.

'It worried me,' he replied, 'but it's finished.'

He called to the policeman standing on the terrace.

'Officer, ask the young lady to bring me my speech.'

When it came he handed it to me.

'How does it read?'

I read it again before answering. I had not expected that he would take the line he did. It appeared to be a plea that the new Russia should be invited to join N.A.T.O. Winston has never shifted his position: German re-unification will only come when Russia realizes that the forces of the West have become so strong that she must accept the inevitable. Winston brushed aside my doubts, scoffing at the idea that Germany would ever take sides with Russia. 'I don't want,' he said, 'to put Germany against Russia or Russia against Germany. I want to be friends with both.'

May 14, 1956

I was all agog this morning to find out if Winston's visit to Germany had gone off without mishap. I went to the office on my arrival at Chartwell. Miss Maturin, who had gone with him, said she thought there had been no mishap.

'The large crowds in the streets were silent – a few cheered – rather as Londoners received Bulganin and Khrushchev. At the Town Hall a hostile demonstration had been planned, but it rained heavily, and the only people who turned out were friendly. In the Hall itself Sir Winston spoke in English, and they did not really understand what he said, but they seemed to like his looks and were quite warm in their feelings. The papers, when they appeared, were more critical. I think they misunderstood what he said. They thought he wanted to invite Russia to join N.A.T.O., whereas what he really said was that if there had been a real change of heart and B. and K. were sincere, then he did not see why Russia should not work with the West for a united Europe. He knows you're here,' she added, so I went to his room.

Winston himself had no doubts whatever.

'The Germans were very friendly, very friendly indeed,' he repeated. 'The first night was not a success. I did not get to sleep till three. The clothes were tucked in at the bottom of the bed, which was very hard. And the sheets were coarse, and the blankets heavy. But I woke at eight and I did not feel tired. I was surprised at my own strength. I spoke without notes, except for one speech. I found things to say. I don't know what I shall do now. I felt there that I could do things.'

He knew that Christopher and I had been anxious about the visit, and he felt very pleased with himself. It had stirred up the old longing to play a part again. Had he been too impatient? Had he retired prematurely?

'What would you like to do?' I asked.

His animation vanished. His face lost its life. He came to earth with a bump.

'There is nothing to do except to die,' he answered in a low voice.

CHAPTER THIRTY-EIGHT

The Flesh Was Weak

Chartwell, June 19, 1956

Winston is in a contrite mood this morning. He confessed, a little sheepishly, that he had walked in the procession to St George's Chapel for the Garter Ceremony.

Moran: 'You must have been nearly all in at the end of your walk, with all those stairs and your heavy robes.'

Winston grunted: 'I had to sit down during the Service. Even when they sang "God Save the Queen" I did not stand up. My legs felt wobbly. It wasn't the length of the walk that tired me, but the way they tottered along and dawdled. I'm very much of a cripple. All I can do is a little turn round Chartwell. I used to visit the cowhouse. Now I have had to give that part up. You know, Charles, I'm not particularly interested in things.'

Moran: 'You mean in the House of Commons?'

Winston: 'No. In anything. In living. I find life pretty dull.'

Moran: 'The American reviews of the book are very friendly.'

Winston: 'Yes, pages of unending flattery. I'm busy now doing Queen Victoria.'

Moran: 'Isn't that easier than, say, Richard III? You already know so much about it.'

Winston (*musing*): 'No, that's what makes it difficult. I know too much.'

Moran: 'Are you coming right up to the present?'

Winston: 'No, no. I stop in Victoria's reign. I could not write about the woe and ruin of the terrible twentieth century.' (*Sadly*) 'We answered all the tests. But it was useless.'

Marshalls, June 24, 1956

Norman Brook is staying here again. I am not surprised that successive Prime Ministers feed out of his hand. His judgement is hardly ever at fault. He was interesting on the defeatism after Dunkirk.

Moran: 'But, Norman, I don't remember people being jumpy. Extraordinarily phlegmatic they seemed to me.'

Brook: 'I agree about the public, but there were a lot of jitters among those at the top. Brooke was imperturbable, but his Staff weren't.' (He mentioned other soldiers and Cabinet Ministers.) 'If it had not been for Winston anything might have happened. He steadied the ship.'

Moran: 'Did he contribute a great deal to the actual conduct of the war?'

Brook: 'Winston had an extraordinary capacity for seizing on things that mattered, concentrating on them and mastering them. Of course, he liked to pretend that he was looking after everything. It wasn't true. All the same, no one knew when this searchlight, sweeping round, would settle on them, so everyone worked like blazes.'

Moran: 'I sometimes wonder if Winston's habit of doing the job of all his Ministers made them feel less responsible.'

Brook: 'There might be something in that, but he animated us all.'

Moran: 'Yes, Portal made that point when Alanbrooke affirmed that in strategy Winston had contributed nothing at all.'

Brook: 'And I give Winston full marks for his long struggle to postpone the invasion of France until the American infantry was seasoned. His stubborn resistance, when the Americans wanted to get at the Germans, was quite wonderful.'

Moran: 'Winston didn't discover the Russian menace till 1944.'

Brook: 'He may have been late in tumbling to the danger, but he was, after all, the first to notice it. Anyway, far sooner than the

Americans, who were badly taken in by Stalin. Look at the Iron Curtain telegram.'

Moran: 'It fascinated Monty.'

Brook: 'Winston was very cross when he discovered the boundaries of the agreed zones, and found we had already crossed our limit and had to go back. But though he tries to get away from it, he must have agreed to the zones.'

Moran: 'How do you account for that?'

Brook: 'I wonder if Winston had ever bothered to study them, or for that matter whether he had even read them. You remember, Charles, if anyone talked to him about things after the war he would say impatiently, "Cannot you see I have as much on my hands as I can deal with? Pray do not bother me with these things." '

Moran: 'What about the debit side?'

Brook did not answer my question.

'Winston has no knowledge of men,' I persisted.

Brook: 'How could he have? He disliked meeting strangers. He wasn't interested in people. When they came to see him he did not listen to them. He did all the talking. How could he find out about them?'

Moran: 'Maynard Keynes affirmed that Winston lacked instinctive judgement.'

Brook: 'If he had been like ordinary people it might have diminished his power. If he had been a sound judge of human nature it might well have interfered with his supreme virtues. As it was he was entirely self-centred, listening to nobody's views, so that in 1940 he just went straight ahead.'

Moran: 'I remember when Winston was in the doldrums after the incident of the telegram to Monty, Viscount Waverley said: "After all if he'd been cautious and had taken no risks he would have been of less use to us." '

Brook (*knocking out his pipe as he smiled affectionately*): 'Winston never talks like other people. Once in Cabinet I handed him a report. He weighed the documents in his hand before he said: "This Treasury paper, by its very length, defends itself against the risk of being read." At most Cabinets he coined at least one remarkable phrase.'

Moran: 'For instance?'

Brook (*grinning*): ' "I'd rather be right than consistent." "During a long life I have had to eat my own words many times, and I have found it a very nourishing diet." '

When Norman had dug a dandelion out of the lawn with his knife he looked up:

'And yet Winston knows nothing of self-criticism.'

Moran: 'I have always been defeated when I tried to put a case to him.'

Brook: 'It was almost impossible to change his mind once it was made up. The only chance was to go to him with the news, and put your view before he had made up his mind.'

Moran: 'Nothing happened unless I had the sense to put things on paper.'

Brook: 'Yes. That meant he did not have to make up his mind forthwith. He had time to think it over.'

July 21, 1956
The political world is full of Eden's moods at No. 10; all this is known to Winston, and he is anxious about the future. He sees that things cannot go on like this for long. At the back of his mind, as I keep finding out, is the disconcerting fact that he put Anthony where he is.

August 1, 1956
Winston is very angry about Nasser's seizure of the Suez Canal.[1]

Moran: 'Nasser is not the kind of man to keep his job for long?'

Winston: 'Whoever he is he's finished after this. We can't have that malicious swine sitting across our communications.' (He said this with something of his old vehemence.) 'I saw Anthony on

[1] On July 26, in retaliation for the withdrawal of American and British funds for the building of the Aswan Dam.

Monday. I know what they are going to say. Anthony asked me to treat it as a matter of confidence.'

Moran: 'What will the Americans do?'

Winston snapped: 'We don't need the Americans for this.'

Moran: 'Will you speak in the House?'

Winston: 'I might. I shall dictate something and see how it goes.'

Moran: 'Was your lunch with the King of Denmark at the Pool of London amusing?'

Winston (*grunting*): 'No. It was a damned bore.'

When he noticed I had picked up a book he went on:

'I am working at the part after the American Civil War. I read four or five books on it before I dictated anything.'

September 16, 1956

Found Winston playing bezique with Clemmie, a happy picture. They insisted on stopping the game, and Clemmie went off to bring Dorothy in to tea.

Winston: 'I don't like the way things are going. After the first debate in the House I came away encouraged, even elated. When there was danger to the country the Opposition seemed behind the Government, and Gaitskell[1] showed himself capable of playing an Englishman's part. But the second debate undid all the good; in fact, it did a good deal of harm. Gaitskell went back on things – the feeling in his party was too strong for him. I want our people to take up a strong point on the Canal with a few troops and to say to Nasser: "We'll get out when you are sensible about the Canal."'

He was silent for a time. Then he said sadly: 'I am afraid we are going downhill.' The fallen state of Britain troubles him more than his own parlous condition.

Winston insisted that I must take *The Wonderful Visit* to read on my way to Spain; Clemmie rose and went over to the bookshelf, where Wells's books were. Winston directed operations from his

[1] Hugh Gaitskell, Leader of the Labour Party.

chair. I began looking through the edition. On the flyleaf of *First and Last Things* Wells had written:

Reform Club,
Pall Mall, S.W.

My dear Churchill,

Here in a sort of intellectual hari-kari is my inmost self. I place it at your feet.

Very sincerely Yours
H. G. Wells

Clemmie invoked my aid to get Winston to persevere with a hearing aid. She got up and, speaking into his ear, said playfully; 'It's just a question of taking a little trouble, my dear. Quite stupid people learn to use it after a short time.' His eye twinkled as he put his hand affectionately on hers. He is flying to France tomorrow.

Government House, Isle of Man, October 20, 1956
The Governor called me: 'France wants you on the telephone.' When I could not hear what Winston said, he called Dr Roberts to speak to me. Roberts was guarded on the telephone, but I gathered Winston had some kind of black-out this morning. No, he did not think it was necessary for me to see him. He was already much better. All day I have had a feeling of disquiet. When Winston telephoned, did he want to see me?

October 26, 1956
I hear from France that Winston has had an attack of cerebral spasm. During the attack he lost the use of his right leg, right arm, left side of face and Broca's area. It appears that he fell down and lost consciousness for about twenty minutes.

Chartwell, November 4, 1956
Winston was still breakfasting when I entered his room, though it was after ten o'clock. He began a sentence and then lost the thread, looking at me as though he wanted help to finish what he was saying.

'I find it difficult to write letters,' Winston complained. 'I mean to compose them. I find it difficult to do anything.'

I noticed that he was drowsy and apathetic. He gazed at me blankly, so that I was not sure whether he had heard what I had said, but when I told him that it looked as if Dulles had cancer he woke up. 'What makes you say that?' he demanded.

He pushed away the bed-rest as if it was almost too much effort. He had hardly touched his breakfast and held out his wrist. 'What is it? You haven't counted it,' he said reproachfully. Winston spoke to Wright, who let down the wooden shelf by his bed and put the birdcage within his reach. Leaning over, Winston opened the cage and the budgerigar flew out, and fluttered twice across the room, finally perching on his head. Winston put up his hand and the bird perched on it, whereupon he drew his hand towards his lips murmuring, 'Darling.'

I telephoned to the farm that I should like to see Christopher about Winston. I found him in the hall.

He greeted me cheerfully, but soon disappeared, leaving me to Mary. As a Junior Minister he is absorbed in his job.

'I know there is nothing to be done,' Mary began. She had noticed a marked deterioration in her father when he came back from France. 'Of course, you cannot be certain what he takes in. When Anthony tells Papa something he follows it all right, but it goes in at one ear and out at the other. He doesn't attempt to work out its implications. It is just an isolated fact that has little connection with the past and none at all with the future. What I find rather sad, Charles, is that he doesn't seem interested in anything any longer. He doesn't want to do things. Mama didn't want him to make the speech at the unveiling of the Smuts Memorial, but she was sure he would not listen to her. "Are you very set, Winston," she began gently, "on this speech?" He told her, "No, I don't think I can do it." When he had sent off the telegram he seemed so relieved. He was really looking for a way out. Papa tries to get out of speeches now. It is all so different,' she added sadly. 'Of course, he varies a good deal. Last night, though we all bellowed, it seemed as if he heard nothing. And then – not very often now – he will perk up and for a short time take an interest in the conversation.'

November 11, 1956

When we were alone Winston held out his wrist.

'Seventy-eight? That is too fast, but it will soon come down. Let us go to my room,' he said, rising with difficulty from his chair. 'Take my pulse now, Charles. It may have fallen. Seventy-two? Why, that is normal. I'm worried,' he went on, 'about what I said to my servant the other day. I talked gibberish, as I did in France.'

I assured him that his pulse was quite good.

'Any time the bloody thing may stop,' he retorted. 'I'm not afraid to die.'

There was a long pause and then he added in a more subdued tone:

'At least I don't think I am.'

I told him that I would call in the morning.

'Do,' he said, 'I'd like that. I want you, Charles, to keep a watch on things.'

'I have a feeling of timidity about myself,' Winston confided to Brendan yesterday. Old age, by blanching the seat of reason, may cut off the fear of death even in a once imaginative mind, or it may, on the other hand, undermine fortitude, softening the will.

That Winston should own to a feeling of timidity is a measure of his decay. The mournful gestures that I have recorded were the consequence of his stroke on June 2. His plan for making the best of things then was laid in ruins. A second stroke on October 20 put an end to his project for helping the country in the Suez crisis. Each stroke seems part of a plot to destroy his reason and his will to act, leaving him more and more a physical wreck.

As I was leaving the room I picked up a book from his table.

'It's a good book,' Winston said, 'it describes very well a phase of the war. It's the diary of a woman who went to France in a destroyer, I think she went five or six times, coming back with perhaps two or three airmen whom she had helped to escape. Then the Germans noticed that she looked right before crossing the street and spotted that she was an Englishwoman. That is as far as I have read, where the page is turned down.'

Winston had read 129 pages since yesterday.

November 22, 1956
Winston's face was quite expressionless when I entered his room this morning. I took his temperature and pulse, and listened to his chest before he spoke. He told me without any bluster that he was going to dine at the Other Club. He said this with an air of great finality, and I knew that there was nothing to be gained by an argument. Clemmie repeated hotly that if he went, everyone in the constituency would know that his 'cold' was just an excuse for cutting their function last night. If Winston heard, he took no notice. After all, he had a huge majority; besides, he would never take part in another election. One thing might weigh with him. If I could get it into his head that if he took harm there was a real risk of pneumonia, I am pretty sure he would stay at home. In spite of his bravado he does not want to die.

As I rose to leave I said that if he decided to go to the club I would like him to take his temperature in the morning so that we might catch any trouble early. He glared at me. I knew my shaft had gone home. He will not go to the Other Club.

Clemmie must find me a doubtful ally. Winston is selfish, of course, he can't help it, he is just made that way, and she is trying to protect his name in the constituency. But I cannot bring myself to be hard with him now. It's little enough we can give him. Once he had plenty of enemies. Now he has none. Everyone is very kind to him, for he matters no longer. No one asks him what he thinks of a crisis. How long must he go on like this, of no use to anyone? Why should we baulk him of any fun that is left in life? Why did I intervene? Why shouldn't he go to his club? After all, he is eighty-two, and he can't expect to live for ever.

November 26, 1956

Moran: 'What made Anthony leave the country?'[1]

Winston: 'I am shocked by what he did, and I'm an Anthony man.'

Winston said this as if it had hurt him, adding in a low tone: 'I should not have done half the work he has been doing. I'd have got others to do it. He let them wake him up at all hours of the night to listen to news from New York – our night is their day.'

Moran: 'Will Anthony be able to take over when he returns from Jamaica?'

Winston (*hesitating*): 'I am very doubtful. I'd like to see Harold Macmillan Prime Minister, but they may ask Lord Salisbury. I cannot understand why our troops were halted. To go so far and not go on was madness.'

Moran: 'A lot of people are wishing you had been in charge.'

Winston (*shaking his head*): 'I am not the man I was. I could not be Prime Minister now. The aftermath of Suez might be serious. There may be unemployment.'

Moran: 'It is a rotten business from beginning to end.'

Winston nodded assent. 'But I'm not worrying about it.'

Is that true I wonder? Does Winston feel he is responsible for Anthony? The Prof. told me that when he was in the Cabinet he was so worried by Anthony's weakness that he spoke to Winston about it. 'I've gone too far in building him up,' Winston answered, 'to go back on it now.'

January 12, 1957

Winston was delighted when the Queen summoned him to the palace to advise about the new Prime Minister.[2] Christopher asked

---

[1] On October 31, 1956, British and French troops went into action against Egypt, in order to police the Suez Canal zone. The United Nations General Assembly voted overwhelmingly against this action, and Eden was forced to order a cease fire on November 6. Eden was visibly a tired man, and on November 19 he was persuaded by his medical advisers to take a rest, and flew to Jamaica on November 23.

[2] Sir Anthony Eden resigned as Prime Minister on January 9, 1957.

him if he had remembered his top hat. 'Oh, yes,' Winston replied, 'but it's getting very shabby; as there may be more than one of these consultations in the future I must get a new one.'

January 14, 1957
Winston had gone to bed when I arrived at Hyde Park Gate about half-past three. 'Macmillan has kept Selwyn Lloyd,'[1] I said.

Winston (*rather aggressively*): 'Did you expect that he would drop him? Lloyd stands for the position of the nation in this dispute. We haven't gone back on that. I am shocked by what Anthony did.'

He has said this to me on three separate occasions. I asked him if he had read the memoir by Sir Timothy Eden, Anthony's brother, about their father, Sir William Eden. Winston shook his head. It makes sad reading, I told him. Sir William's uncontrolled rages terrified his children, who were always on tenterhooks, fearing that they might say something that would start an explosion. A barking dog might give rise to a terrible tornado of oaths, screams and gesticulations. Sir William was a gifted egoist without any control, so that at any time there might be a terrible scene of rage and tears. Anthony did not inherit his father's instability, but it must have been a handicap to be brought up in such an atmosphere.

Winston: 'Will Anthony live long?'

Moran: 'Well, his nerves won't kill him, and if his belly was really troubling him I don't believe that his doctors would have let him go off to New Zealand.'

Winston: 'Do you think I shall be all right for a month? I may have another stroke.'

[1] Selwyn Lloyd, Secretary of State for Foreign Affairs, 1955–60.

CHAPTER THIRTY-NINE

Defacing the Legend

April 10, 1957

Anthony Montague Browne telephoned this morning:

'Lady Churchill and I are rather worried about Winston, he is so quiet and uncommunicative. We wonder if anything has happened. Could you suggest calling?' I went immediately to Hyde Park Gate.

'Anthony isn't really worried,' Clemmie began. 'It was me. I wonder whether Winston is brooding over the Alanbrooke *Diaries*?[1] You see, this book has upset him more than he will admit. He asked me a few days ago if I had seen that thing in the *Daily Mail* about the *Diaries*. And yesterday it was the *Evening Standard*.'

She went on:

'You know Winston has become a legend. I wonder why? I think that the speeches in 1940 had a lot to do with it. When Winston enters a theatre everyone rises. The other day when our car drove up to Hyde Park Gate there was an angry man in the road quarrelling with a woman. I feared there was going to be a scene. But when he saw Winston in the car, a different look came over his face. "It's the Guvnor," he said. "Are you very well, sir?" You know, my dear Charles, I am not really angry with Alanbrooke. We must get

---

[1] Viscount Alanbrooke, *The Turn of the Tide* (Collins, 1957). Alanbrooke was highly critical of Winston's war strategy.

used to criticism of Winston. I realize the poor darling cannot be a demi-god for ever.'

Clemmie smiled:

'You know as well as I do, he has some faults. The common people love him for these faults – his cigars, his extravagance. He loves Chartwell passionately. He wants the people of Westerham to like him, he has a feeling he is rather aloof. That's why he won't have the gates closed; the police have very strict orders. When he sees a crowd at the gate he will go nearer and wave to them. Sometimes he takes them in and shows them his fish. I asked him: "Are you happy?" He replied: "Yes, as happy as I can be." '

She seemed to forget about me, looking out of the window. After a time she turned round.

'Do you suppose, Charles, Winston is thinking about death?'

I asked her what had put that into her head.

'Oh,' she murmured, as if her thoughts were elsewhere, 'he suddenly said to me that he would like to go to a theatre. I was very much surprised, as you see the poor darling cannot hear what is being said on the stage. But he persisted. He was sure he would be able to follow the play.'

'It was on his mind that this might be his last theatre?'

She nodded.

April 16, 1957

Lunched with Jock Colville at his club. I suppose nobody really understands Winston, but Jock comes as near to it as anyone. Certainly if I were at a loss to fathom why Winston did a certain thing I should go to Jock. He loves the old man, and is very sad because 'his mind seems to be wearing out before his body.' Jock went on:

'He can still deal with business. He wants to die. How long do you think he can go on like this?'

I asked Jock which of Winston's gifts had been of most value to the country in the war. He said at once:

'Winston's capacity for picking out essential things and concentrating on them.'

It came into my mind that Norman Brook singled out the same quality.

'What next?'

Jock needs a good deal of jogging to make him communicative. He pondered, but nothing happened. At last he added:

'I think his great moral courage. If something went wrong he would patiently start again at the beginning. And his vivid imagination. It was always coming to his help in the war. His magnanimity of course, and his power of inspiring everyone he met.'

Jock grinned and went on ruefully:

'He always got his way. He could persuade anybody to do anything. When he asked me to be his secretary for the second time I was determined to refuse. I knew exactly how the interview would go, and I had thought out what I should say at each turn. I would have my excuses ready. But ten minutes later I came out of the room his secretary.'

'I see all that. But, Jock, you must admit that Winston's judgement was often wrong.'

Jock was not going to admit anything of the kind.

'More than once during the war Winston would come to the right decision when everyone else was on the other side.'

'Give me an example.'

'Oh,' said Jock, 'sending the Armoured Division to Egypt in 1940 when it was obvious to us all that we needed it at home in case of invasion. And his refusal to allow any more pilots and aircraft to fight in the Battle of France; everyone wanted to send them to France. But if Winston had given way we should have lost the Battle of Britain.'

I stuck to my guns.

'Take his judgement of men. Do you really think Winston knew that Anthony Eden wasn't made of Prime Minister stuff?'

Jock took me up at once.

'One day, it would be just after Winston resigned, I went with him to his bedroom. He sat on the bed shaking his head. "I wonder," he said. And stopped short. "You wonder what?" "I wonder if he can do it. Courage," he muttered. "Anthony has courage. He would charge a square, but would he charge at the right time and in the right place?"'

Jock gave me an expansive smile.

'Yes. Suez was the answer.'

We talked of nothing but Winston. With criticism of him in full spate, I find it reassuring to listen to Jock. As I rose to go I mentioned the Alanbrooke *Diaries.* Jock had crossed in the *Queen Mary* with Sir William Dickson.[1] He was very upset by the book.

June 6, 1957

William Haley, the Editor of *The Times*, has read more widely than anyone I know. I thought it would be fun to give him a book that he had not read. Dining with him tonight, I took with me *Impressions*, by Pierre Loti, with an introduction by Henry James. I picked it up in a bookshop in Alexandria before the First War, and found that Haley had not read it. John Reith was there, the old Covenanter decked out in a crimson smoking jacket. He came across to me after dinner and without any preliminaries began:

'I intensely dislike your man, more than I have ever disliked anyone.'

Moran: 'You find Winston wanting in consideration?'

Reith: 'No. You cannot expect consideration from a Prime Minister in war. But Winston prints in his war book innumerable directives and never once lets us see a single answer. Why, he vituperated me for not doing something, though I had been trying to get the Government to do this very thing for months. And even when I wrote to him and explained this, the same directive appeared unaltered in the next edition.'

Reith spoke without anger or vehemence, as if he were puzzled. Haley came up and, catching the drift of our talk, said that he had been reading Halifax's book,[2] and that what had struck him was the

---

[1] Sir William Dickson, Marshal of the Royal Air Force, Chairman of the Chiefs of Staff Committee, 1956–9.
[2] *Fulness of Days* (Collins, 1957).

author's dislike of Winston. All through the book he is trying to put him in the dock if he can. Up till now, Winston has had things all his own way. Apart from debates in the House, hardly a breath of criticism has reached him since the war. The Alanbrooke *Diaries* seem to have loosened men's tongues. I wish they had held their peace until Winston had left us.

Marshalls, June 23, 1957

Oliver Franks is with us for Glyndebourne, and since none of his opinions is borrowed from other people, I have been seeking enlightenment on some things that have puzzled me. Did he, for example, find difficulty in reconciling the legend of Winston Churchill with some of his faults?

Franks: 'Winston has, of course, many excellencies and many deficiencies. And if you are going to measure him with that foot-rule, I should be as baffled as you are. But surely it is the size of the man and the way history met him, giving him an opportunity which multiplied his size, that sweeps away, for me at any rate, all difficulties of that kind. Luck you may call it. But even greater men need luck. Calvin had it; Luther too.'

Moran: 'What do you mean by size?'

Franks (*musing*): 'Well, that is difficult. Winston embodied the soul of the nation. He succeeded in being the nation, for that is what he was. In the simplified conditions of war he could be that, whereas in the more complex days of peace he never was, never could be, that. Asquith, on the other hand, as war minister, was only the chairman of a committee trying to make wise decisions.'

Moran: 'Joan of Arc, I suppose, played that role, and Chatham perhaps.'

Franks: 'Yes. And Elizabeth to be sure, at the time of the Spanish crisis and the speech at Tilbury. Winston became a prophet. We can't explain him, any more than we can understand Isaiah or Elijah. I remember early in the war attending a meeting on the roof of the Ministry of Supply when Winston addressed us. I came away more happy about things. He dispelled our misgivings and set at rest our fears; he spoke of his aim and of his purpose, so that we knew that somehow it would be achieved. He gave us faith. There was in him a demonic element, as in Calvin and Luther. He was a spiritual force.'

Moran: 'It is twelve years since the end of the war. Why hasn't the legend been defaced?'

Franks: 'Nothing but a colossal blunder could have undone the work of those five years.' (*Smiling*) 'Something like an attempt to reconquer India.'

Moran: 'You thought Suez was a blunder?'

Franks: 'Oh, yes. The consequences will be felt for many years. It is as if we had lost a major battle – without casualties. We were disembowelled.'

Moran: 'What consequences have you in mind?'

Franks: 'Well. It is possible that America may meet Russia in conference without us being at the table. After the war we acted as a Great Power, though we had not the resources. A kind of confidence trick. It came off as long as the decisions we made were acceptable to the other Powers. The trouble with these island empires has always been the same: they had too few men. America and Russia can afford a holocaust, we cannot.'

Franks spoke of the importance to a politician of another life beside politics, something he can fall back on. If things go wrong in the House, Harold Macmillan, for instance, can go back to his publishing; that makes him independent.

Moran: 'Are you gloomy about the future?'

Franks: 'I think the period 1945 to 1975 may be like 1815 to 1845. We have a good many old men at the top living in the past. Macmillan tells how he was in Darlington in 1931 at the time of mass unemployment, and he was horrified by what he saw. There is a Labour leader, too, who says bitter things to the T.U.C. because for ten years his father was out of employment, and tramped up and down the Great North Road, looking for a job. They think more about this than of the last war. Nothing much will happen until a new generation takes over; we need younger men who are not obsessed with the past, men who are thinking over where they want to go.'

Winston's measurements will not, I believe, shrink with time. Oliver Franks had given the reason why. When he had gone I went to see Winston at Chartwell, full of 'the size of the man'. He was in bed, alone in the great house, reading *The Duke's Children*.

'Back to Trollope?' I asked.

'I don't know,' he mumbled, 'why you say, "Back to Trollope." I have never read him before.'

I asked if he found Trollope interesting, and he answered:

'It passes away the day.'

CHAPTER FORTY

Brendan's Verdict

February 19, 1958

Last night Dr Roberts telephoned from France: Sir Winston was feverish and coughing. This morning I flew to Nice, and when I examined Winston's chest found that he had bronchopneumonia.

The day before his illness began, Winston had lunched with Onassis on his yacht. About three o'clock Winston expressed a wish to go to the Rooms at Monte Carlo to have a little gamble. Reves suggested that they might play chemin-de-fer on the yacht instead. They played for high stakes and drank more alcohol than usual. Winston got very excited. As the afternoon wore on it was noticed that he was very white and tired. About seven o'clock Reves ventured to remind him that they had been invited for lunch. Was it not time to go home? Winston grumbled that Reves was breaking up the party. When they got home, Winston seemed 'all in'.

February 20, 1958

Looking into Winston's room about noon, I found him shivering violently, his teeth chattering. A rigor on the third day meant that the infection was spreading. I decided to change the antibiotic and get a blood count. The arrival of a French bacteriologist this afternoon led to a sharp protest:

Winston: 'Are you going to hurt me? Oh, no, I don't want that. It will hurt.'

Moran: 'It's over now.'

Winston: 'You said it wouldn't hurt. It hurt like hell.'

The Frenchman had gone about his job in silence.

Winston: 'Why doesn't he speak to me? You have told me nothing. I don't like it.'

The Frenchman smiled and held out his hand to take his leave. Winston took it grumpily without looking at him.

February 21, 1958

Winston demands to see the bulletins. 'I would be more candid and less revealing,' he complained. To Anthony Montague Browne he was more explicit. 'If I didn't push them along, nothing at all would happen.' He wants to stir up his doctors because he is bent on returning to England in time for the Other Club on Thursday.

February 22, 1958

I am not really anxious about Winston, but at 83 it is all guesswork. Perhaps if he felt ill he would be more amenable. This morning he announced that he intended to go downstairs to luncheon, although he has not yet been out of bed. Dr Roberts, in order to dissuade him, said something about his heart.

Winston (*raising his voice*): 'It has been a comfort to me that my heart is sound and that I shall not lurch into the next world without warning. And now you talk about my heart as if it were diseased.'

Winston seemed upset. After we left the room it appears that he let himself go. 'It's bloody rot about my heart,' he said. 'I know a great deal. I'm not dependent on my doctors. I know what I can do.'

March 7, 1958

Since the meeting of the Other Club has been postponed the tension has fallen. Winston feels that his troubles are at an end, and I am flying back to England this afternoon. He plans to go home for a week, partly because he is getting bored – there is nobody exciting out here – and partly because he wants to go to the Other Club. After breakfast he got going about Suez.

'I made a great mistake giving in to them when we left the Canal. I feel responsible. All the Cabinet were for withdrawing. They persuaded me that we must get out of Suez. But if I had been in better health, if I had been stronger, we might have stayed on the Canal and all this would not have happened.'

As I was leaving the room I picked up a Bible. 'Do you read it?' I asked him. He did not answer for some time. Then he said: 'Yes, I read it; but only out of curiosity.'

March 24, 1958

Staying with the Freybergs in the Norman Tower at Windsor, I had to take my telephone calls from France in the prison room. Montague Browne rang up yesterday saying that Dr Roberts wanted to speak to me. Since my return to England Sir Winston, he said, had had two bouts of fever. I said I thought I ought to see him. At this Dr Roberts went off to bring Clemmie to the telephone, and I was left reading the names of Cromwell's prisoners which they, while waiting to be taken to the Tower to be beheaded, had carved in the stone wall above the place where the receiver now hangs. When I had spoken to Clemmie I arranged to fly to Nice this morning.

Winston hardly looked at me as I entered his room. He said not a word. I took no notice of this wintry reception and began questioning him. He admitted grudgingly that he had been very worried on Saturday, and had wanted to see me; but now it was too late, his illness was all over. It had been noticed that Winston was yellow, but this was thought to be due to the antibiotic I had prescribed. In fact, he is suffering from obstructive jaundice, caused either by a stone or by an infection of the bile passages. I shall be glad when we get him back to England.

London, April 10, 1958

I have seen Winston twice since his return from France exactly a week ago, and on each occasion he poked fun at me as a prophet. I had urged him to get back to England in case he was stricken by a third attack of jaundice. 'Pray, at what moment may I expect this mysterious malady to appear?' He said this with an assumption of gravity, and I am bound to admit that he has not seemed so alert and free from symptoms for a long time. But when I went to his room this morning he looked glumly at me. He had a pain over his lower ribs on the right side. 'Yes,' he muttered, 'it might be the same pain that I had in France.' The car was coming for him at ten o'clock. An important gallop had been arranged for one of his horses, and he was very anxious not to miss this trial. I told him the wind was bitter, and that judging by the course of events in his first two attacks I thought he might well be running a temperature by tea-time. I said this not as if I were opposed to his going, but just to bring before him a few relevant facts. Then I left him. About five o'clock Wright telephoned that Sir Winston's temperature was 100. He had stayed in bed all day.

April 11, 1958
This morning Winston did not seem to take in what I said, and he has been feverish all day.

April 12, 1958
Shepherd telephoned before breakfast: Sir Winston was jaundiced, and his pulse had gone up from 64 to 110. I asked Dr Hunt[1] to see him with me, and took my kit prepared to stay at Chartwell. As I pulled aside the curtain that separates his room from the study, Wright and Shepherd were removing the bed-clothes to get him into his vest and bed-coat. Winston sleeps naked, and I noticed that his chest and belly were bright yellow. Wright said Sir Winston had been talking rubbish; he was sure he was wandering. When I sounded him his heart was fibrillating. It looks as if we may be in for trouble.

Dined alone with Clemmie. She did not appear depressed and talked without a break. Rufus, who was stretched on the mat, began dreaming in his sleep.

'You see, Charles, Rufus has been a great failure. When Winston's dog was run over, Walter Graebner, you know who

---

[1] D. T. C. Hunt, senior physician, St Mary's Hospital.

I mean, scoured the country for a poodle in the championship class. That is how he came to us. He is very highly strung. Do you know what chorea is? He had that, and the poor dog is never happy. Winston ought not to keep a dog. He hasn't the time. He will say "good morning" to Rufus, and when Rose brings his dinner, Winston will give it to him. But nothing more. You must love and give up time to a dog and try to make him happy. Now Christopher is a dog man; he understands them, and they love him.'

Rufus began whining, and Clemmie rose from the table to wake him. She went on:

'Do you know Lord Crookshank? When Winston became Prime Minister for the second time I discovered that he was a Chamberlain man, and that he gave parties for Tories who had been admirers of Mr Chamberlain. I thought I would try and see if I could not make him more friendly to Winston. But when I found he hated him I gave it up. I asked Winston whether he liked Crookshank. "Why do you ask, my dear? Oh, I don't mind him." You know, Charles, Winston never tries to placate men who are against him. Of course, the Tories never really liked Winston. It was Labour that made him Prime Minister in 1940.'

I was anxious about Winston and found it difficult to keep my mind on the conversation. When Clemmie left the table I crept into Winston's room in case he was asleep. He has held his own all day, and is perhaps a little more alert tonight.

April 13, 1958
Wright came to me about noon because Sir Winston was jibbing at the treatment. 'He refuses to take the glucose. He says, sir, that it is all damn nonsense, and he hasn't drunk anything but a cup of coffee since dinner-time yesterday evening.'

When I saw Winston he burst out irritably, 'I've got my temperature down below normal. What more do you want?' 'You are still yellow,' I persisted. 'Let me see. Wright,' he shouted, 'bring me a mirror!' He gazed at himself for some time. He is still a little muddled, but there is a noticeable all-round improvement since yesterday. Only the jaundice persists.

Chartwell, April 16, 1958

'I have still got the pain. It's no better.' It was with these words that Winston greeted me this morning, and I am pretty sure that there must be a small stone holding up the bile. Anyway, at his age no one is keen on surgery. Besides, he is not so yellow, and is following the Budget debate as if it really interested him. Speaking of Heathcoat-Amory[1] he said: 'He always sat opposite me in Cabinet when I was Prime Minister and he impressed me. I spoke to Harold about him. Fortunately his ideas about Amory were the same as mine.'

Winston came down to dinner for the first time since his illness. Clemmie was dipping happily into the *Oxford Book of Verse*. She pushed her plate forward to make room for it. I recalled to Winston how after his stroke in 1953 he had recited the first fifty lines of 'King Robert of Sicily' with only two mistakes. He tried to repeat the feat, but only succeeded in recalling a line or two. 'My memory,' he said sadly, 'is much worse; in the last nine months it seems to have deteriorated.' I took the book from Clemmie and turned to Arthur Hugh Clough. Winston's eyes lit up. 'Give it to me.' He looked up and began declaiming, but after a few words he was stumped and had to look at the book. His voice grew stronger. He used to gabble poetry; now he spoke it with fervour:

> *For while the tired waves, vainly breaking,*
> *Seem here no painful inch to gain,*
> *Far back, through creaks and inlets making,*
> *Comes silent, flooding, in, the main.*
>
> *And not by eastern windows only,*
> *When daylight comes, comes in the light;*
> *In front, the sun climbs slow, how slowly!*
> *But westward, look, the land is bright!*[2]

[1] Derick Heathcoat-Amory, Chancellor of the Exchequer, 1958–60.
[2] From A. H. Clough's 'Say not the Struggle Naught Availeth'.

When Winston came to the last line he sat up, making a vague gesture as if he were directing our eyes to the light, as he had done, long ago, in the war. And then he slumped back, the effort had been too much for his tired mind.

After a time he rose from his chair, slowly and not without difficulty, and asked me to go with him to the study. There he flopped into a chair and sat looking into the great log fire. A warm soft glow from the red curtains fell on the shelves of books. I asked him about the dark painting that hung above the mantelpiece. 'It's Blenheim Palace.' 'And the flag hanging from that beam?' Winston's face brightened. 'That was the first Union Jack to be taken ashore in the invasion of Italy.' It is his room, and he has it to himself, except when he plays bezique. At other times he reads by the fire, often for hours at a time. Tonight Clough's words have stirred up the past. He did not want to talk; we sat for a long time in silence.

April 17, 1958
Yesterday I found Winston halfway through the second of six volumes of a first edition of *Tom Jones*, bearing the date 1749; it might have been a wedding present, Winston thought. 'I think I have got his measure,' he said, putting down the book. His interest was plainly flagging, and he was looking for another book. But today he seems to have changed his mind. I suspect he wants to know what happened to Tom Jones.

Jock arrived to dinner. He came to my room to get the hang of things before he saw Winston. Jock is full of the Churchill College which is to be built at Cambridge. Its purpose is to make known to industry what is being done by those engaged in fundamental research in science. It will do this by training a new race of technologists in the college, cheek by jowl, as it were, with the Cavendish Laboratory. I wonder if the idea came from Winston. If it did, it is a fine curtain to a life that owes little to the scientific habit of mind; a final gesture on his part to the English people. The summons to do their best in this struggle for survival is perhaps less urgent than in 1940, but once more only Winston's voice can reach the people.

Jock gave me the papers to read. An appeal is to be made next month for three and a half million pounds, and Winston will open the fund with a gift of twenty-five thousand pounds. Jock wants Winston to give a luncheon to the trustees, and asked me whether he would be able to do this.

Winston greeted Jock affectionately. I know no one who understands with such intuitive sympathy this baffling creature, who is so unlike anyone else in everything he says and does. Before Jock went to bed he came to my room. Winston had confided to him that he did not want to live. We agreed that he seemed to get little out of life. I told Jock that I often feared I was boring Winston. Jock grinned.

'When he gets very bored with me I have a special technique. I say to him: "Don't you think Napoleon was the Hitler of the nineteenth century?" Then he wakes up with a start. "How dare you say such a thing?" Winston exclaims, and it is some time before he relapses into a state of apathy. As a matter of fact, Charles, Winston hasn't got much kick out of life since he resigned in 1955.'

I lay awake puzzling why Winston finds Jock so congenial a companion. Some of his secretaries have been equally quick at detecting Winston's moods and tempers; they knew his little frailties in the manner that Max Beaverbrook can put a finger on a weak spot. In their case it was perhaps a kind of safety-first device to avert the wrath of their alarming master. They seemed to know instinctively when it was not a favourable moment to bring up some question for the Chief's decision. They knew, too, what the P.M. would do and what he would not do, and they could advise the most promising line of approach, how in a word to get him to do things in minor matters. They were, I am sure, as disinterested as Jock in their devotion to Winston's service. Jock knew all this. He knew more because he loved the artist in Winston and was captivated by the way he handled words.

Of course, Jock has ability, too, though it is not of the most practical kind. He has an ear for words when they are well handled and won a prize for Latin verse at Harrow. I have said that his ability is not of the kind to pay dividends in the market-place, but if he had to go into the City you may be sure that he would think and act there like one of those directors of the Bank of England, John Revelstoke, for instance, who appear to be set up as a cautionary tale to all money-making men. I do not mean that Jock is wanting in ambition, nor for that matter would I call him unworldly. Jock was not born with an intuitive knowledge of human nature. I sometimes think I detect in him a certain lack of sympathy with more erring mortals, an impatient repugnance towards standards that are not quite impeccable, a quiet intolerance, a cold aloofness. Of course it would not be fair to expect Winston's secretary to be an Elizabeth Fry, with her warm heart and deep compassion for all shades of malefactors.

When war came, and Jock was one of the P.M.'s secretaries, important as this work was, it would have violated the code that had come down to him if he had left the fighting to others. In spite of defective eyesight, he became a pilot, and cheerfully paid the penalty in some mishaps in landing.

I wonder what effect, if any, Winston's secretaries have had on him. The manner in which anything is presented to Winston before he has made up his mind – that is the crucial point – and the time chosen to bring it forward surely plays a part in shaping things. It would be easy, I think, to underrate the part they have played in the shaping of events.

April 27, 1958
Some time later, Anthony Montague Browne came into the office with rather an important air. There was something, he said cheerfully, that he thought I ought to know. 'I suppose it sounds macabre, but the Prime Minister is concerned about what they ought to do when Sir Winston dies, and I shall have to ask him what his wishes are in the matter.'

It all began with the Queen. When word came to her that Sir Winston was ill in France, it entered her head that he was very old and very frail and might die. The Queen felt it would be the wish of her people that there should be a lying-in-state in Westminster Hall. I first heard of this when Norman Brook telephoned. His practical mind came straight to the point. 'How is Winston, because the Prime Minister is fussing about plans for his funeral?'

The Queen had told her secretary, and the secretary told Sir Norman Brook, and Sir Norman Brook told the Prime Minister. And that was how I came to be summoned to Birch Grove for drinks. After Macmillan had greeted me, he put his arm through mine and marched me off to a sloping bank of daffodils. He lost no time in coming to the point: 'How do you think Winston is? I thought he was quite alert at the Other Club on Thursday; he talked a lot and seemed to hear pretty well, that is if no one else was talking at the same time. A good deal of Winston's deafness, of course, is just inattention. And then when I met him in the Lobby he seemed very frail. What is likely to happen? One doesn't like to talk about it, but I suppose we ought to do something. I wonder what he would like done? Wellington was buried in St Paul's. Yes, and Nelson too.' We had come to the end of the daffodils. 'Winston likes bands, I think.' And with this ambiguous remark, Macmillan hurried off to do his duty as host.

At Chartwell this morning Diana took me aside. 'What do you think of him?' Without waiting for an answer she gave me her view. 'He has aged a lot, and he is walking very badly. He went to sleep during luncheon.' There was a cold east wind, and I left Diana to get him indoors before he got harm. I followed him to the study, where with a long sigh he settled down to read *An Infamous Army*.[1] 'It is a good solid account of the three months in Brussels before Waterloo,' said Winston. Eileen Joyce, the Australian pianist, has taken Chartwell Farm where Mary used to live, and is dining with them tonight. I suggested they should ask her to play 'A Wandering Minstrel I', but they said: 'There's not a piano in the house.'

June 27, 1958
'You are very well, Winston.'

'I suppose I am. What the good of it is I don't know. I saw Brendan this morning.'

---

[1] Georgette Heyer, *An Infamous Army* (William Heinemann, 1953).

He stopped. I wanted to ask him about Brendan, but I feared it might upset him. Winston will not go near a hospital in the ordinary way, and poor Brendan is in a lamentable condition. We have been very apprehensive about this visit to the Westminster Hospital, and wanted it to be safely over. But Brendan so managed things that Winston did not appear distressed. It was in a steady voice that he began to tell me about it.

'Brendan was very animated. I was a quarter of an hour with him, and he talked all the time – good sense. He had a rubber tube hanging from his mouth. They feed him through it. Why do they do that, Charles?'

When I explained that his gullet was obstructed he said nothing. At last he looked up.

'The surgeons can do nothing for his kind of cancer?'

Brendan is a brave soul. The last time I saw him the hand of death was on him, but all he thought of now was to let Winston down gently. How many good deeds has this man done in the dark! For a long time he has been pressing me to write about Winston. When I did nothing he asked Moir, who is an authority on such matters, to advise me about the income-tax side of a book of this kind. He thought this might bring me to the starting-post. And all this kindness of heart in the last terrible stages of this illness. As I left I met Alan Hodge at the door. Winston had sent for him to write something about Brendan for his paper, the *Financial Times*.

July 3, 1958

I had tea with Halifax in the House of Lords. He thinks Winston's virtues were, in a sense, a handicap when we came to present our case in Washington in the war years. The Americans had never met anyone like him. He seemed to them a museum piece, a rare relic. When he told them that he had not become First Minister of the Crown in order to preside over the liquidation of the British Empire they felt that they were listening to a voice out of the eighteenth century. Later in the war, when Winston began to warn Roosevelt about Russia's designs, there still seemed to be an air of unreality about what he said, as if he was living in a remote past.

I asked Halifax point-blank: Had he seen any signs that Roosevelt was jealous of Winston as the acknowledged saviour of the free world?

He said at once: 'I'm sure he was jealous. Marshall told me that the President did not look forward to Winston's visits. He knew too much about military matters; besides he kept such shocking hours.

'No, I don't think of Franklin Roosevelt as a very great man,' Halifax added. 'He was, of course, a very adroit manipulator, without doubt a very astute politician. But what he did was to split the American people. I remember when I was in Washington a number of Republican Senators invited me to dine with them and to give them a short talk. "Before you speak, Mr Ambassador, I want you to know that everyone in this room regards Mr Roosevelt as a bigger dictator than Hitler or Mussolini. We believe he is taking this country to hell as quickly as he can." Even on the day of his death this bitterness welled up.'

Halifax is the only British Ambassador that Americans seem to remember; unusual men, like Roger Makins and Oliver Franks, are already half-forgotten. I cannot explain this, but I have a feeling that if I could it would tell me something about the American people. I am sure that we do not yet fully realize the influence of Halifax and Dill in America during the war. It is interesting that two men, who at the crisis of their lives were both found wanting, should later have exercised that influence on so great a scale.

July 24, 1958
A message from Brendan yesterday. He has left hospital and asked me to come to his flat at Grosvenor House. Though his nurse had warned me that I should find him a good deal changed, I was not prepared for his dreadful emaciation: the heavily built figure had become a white wraith. Even the mop of hair had gone. He walked to a chair without help, and began talking at once, as of old, while the nurse put a rug round his shoulders and another over his knees.

He wanted to tell me about his illness. He had been lunching with some people when he noticed that he could not swallow properly. There were investigations, and at the end Price-Thomas told him that it was too complicated for surgery. So he had the cobalt ray. They gave him too much radiation, he thought. At this point a fit of coughing stopped him. 'There is a fistula from my oesophagus into the lungs,' he explained when he had got his breath. 'That's why I get these damned spasms of coughing. I want you, Charles, to find out for me some statistics. Does this fistula ever close? And if so, in what percentage of cases? I am not prepared to live an invalid's life, fed through a tube. If that is the position, the doctors will have to help me out of the world.' It was an old story. His doctors had not told him everything; they held out hope, but he was beginning to have his doubts. Another spasm shook him; he must come to business:

'Now, Charles, I haven't brought you here to talk about my troubles. Let's get down to something more interesting. I want to talk to you about Winston. Where shall I begin?'

'You once told me that Winston was full of apprehension,' I said. 'What made you say that? The public would think it out of character.'

'But, Charles, you know Winston better than anyone. You must know all about his fears.'

I repeated the story that Winston had told me a long time ago, how when a small boy he had been frightened by other boys throwing cricket balls at him, and he had taken refuge behind a tree, and how afterwards he had brooded on this. It was to him a shameful memory, and he was determined that one day he, too, would be tough.

Brendan took up the story. 'I was riding once with Winston and we got talking about courage. Winston insisted that it was quite wrong to suppose that men were courageous by nature. They weren't. He had always been full of apprehension, and had had to school himself to face anything. The House of Commons in particular used to frighten him. Oh, for years, perhaps up to the war. Yet, Charles, look what happened during the Abdication debate in the House of Commons. The House began yelling at him, and from all parts of the Chamber there were loud cries: "Sit down! Get out!" I broke out into a cold sweat, but Winston stood there with folded arms, very pale, but quite resolute. He was not going to give in to bullies. I went with him to the smoke-room. Members pushed away from him. There was a pair of waiters, Wright and Collins, who seeing this, stopped serving other Members and went over to Winston to attend to him. Only Wedderburn – you know, Dundee – stood up for him. He came over and said to Winston: "That was the best speech you ever made in your life." I took Winston off to Lord North Street. He was miserable beyond belief; to be howled down in the House of Commons was a disgrace. But he kept saying to me he would never give in.

'There is in Winston,' Brendan went on, 'the old aristocratic contempt for consequences. Do you remember the Lord Alfred Douglas case? He was a pervert kind of fellow, and he made a series of extraordinary accusations against Winston. Winston was terribly upset, and at last he sued him. Each day he had to listen in Court to some dreadful statements. He knew, of course, the political and financial consequences if he lost the case, but he remained cool and calm, while the attacks of the defending counsel became more and more bitter, more and more insulting. I can see him now, standing in the witness-box, twisting his ring round his finger; his answers were devastating. When the jury found for Winston a very curious thing happened: Winston appeared very cast down; we found that he could not bear the thought of this poor devil being sent to prison.

'You know, Winston has been so successful in controlling his fears that most people think of him as reckless. But he has had to struggle with a fearful handicap. Have you read Rowse on the Later Churchills?[1] Oh, you ought to get it; it is very well written. He says that of the last seven Dukes of Marlborough five suffered from melancholia. You and I think of Winston as self-indulgent; he has never denied himself anything, but when a mere boy he deliber-

[1] A. L. Rowse, *The Later Churchills* (Macmillan, 1958).

ately set out to change his nature, to be tough and full of rude spirits.

'It has not been easy for him. You see, Charles, Winston has always been a "despairer". Orpen, who painted him after the Dardanelles, used to speak of the misery in his face. He called him the man of misery. Winston was so sure then that he would take no further part in public life. There seemed nothing left to live for. It made him very sad. Then in his years in the wilderness, before the Second War, he kept saying: "I'm finished." He said that about twice a day. He was quite certain that he would never get back to office, for everyone seemed to regard him as a wild man. And he missed the red boxes awfully. Winston has always been wretched unless he was occupied. You know what he has been like since he resigned? Why, he told me that he prays every day for death.

'This strain of melancholy, a Churchill inheritance, is balanced in Winston by the physical and mental robustness of the Jeromes. There was in his formidable grandfather a touch of the frontiersman. When he had angered the mob he promptly put a machinegun on the roof, which he himself could operate.'

I interrupted: 'Like the machine-gun which Winston put in the stern of the small boat which was to take him off the *Queen Mary* if she was torpedoed.'

'Exactly,' said Brendan. 'The healthy, bright red American blood cast out the Churchill melancholy. But not entirely. Winston has always been moody; he used to call his fits of depression the "Black Dog". At other times, as you know, he goes off into a kind of trance. I have seen him sit silent for several hours, and when he is like that only a few people can make him talk.'

'Who, for instance?'

'Oh, Mrs Edwin Montagu. She was a Stanley of Alderley. Venetia used to laugh at Winston, and take him by the scruff of the neck and tell him not to go on looking at his plate like a booby. And Mrs Dudley Ward. She would let Winston drink a glass or two of champagne and then get him going. You knew her, Charles? Oh, she was a brilliant talker.

'Winston knew that these attacks of depression might come on him without warning, and he avoided anyone or anything that might bring them on. That's why, as you say, he won't go near a hospital, and why he dislikes people of low vitality. After all, lots of people feel like Winston. Eustace Percy wrote of British politicians after the First World War: "Gusto indeed was what we lacked; the best of us were a low-spirited lot."[1] But he pointed out that the two great exceptions were F.E.[2] and Winston. Bonar-Law was a listless old cove. Only F.E. and Winston laughed aloud. Winston has always liked buoyant people around him. F.E. was his closest friend. Oh, from 1910 to 1927. You never saw them together? Well, you missed a good sight. They both had tearing spirits – that is, when Winston wasn't in the dumps – a kind of daring, a dislike of a drab existence, a tremendous zest in life. Clemmie disapproved of F.E. because she thought he led Winston into strange ways. There was no truth in this; Winston could control his drinking. When F.E. went, Max became the bogey-man. And F.E., of course, had an unattractive side; he used the giant strength of his mind to down people. Winston never did that. Indeed, he disliked personal attacks. Why, you know that if you want to remain friends with Winston you must keep a civil tongue in your head when you are talking of the Royal Family or of his father.' Brendan's words came faster. 'Lord Rosebery could make Winston talk at any time. But when he called Lord Randolph a "scug" he fell out of favour, and Winston published the life of his father[3] without Rosebery's preface.'

'I suppose, Brendan, that Winston has had many friendships?'

'Yes,' answered Brendan, 'but few deep ones. I do not mean that he is not affectionate; he would go to the stake for a friend. And I don't think he has ever lost one. You can generally tell what he finds attractive in his friends; a V.C. is in his good graces before he begins.'

---

[1] Eustace Percy, *Some Memories* (Eyre & Spottiswoode, 1958).
[2] F. E. Smith, 1st Earl Birkenhead.
[3] Winston S. Churchill, *Lord Randolph Churchill* (Macmillan, 1906).

'Don't you think, Brendan, that his liking for romance is just another means of switching off his sad thoughts?'

'I don't know about that,' answered Brendan. 'But he has always fallen for heroes. Winston, you know, is not a simple character.' A flicker of a smile came and went. 'If you are going to write about him, as of course you must, you won't learn much from his letters. No one, he says, but a fool writes letters for pleasure. Winston is very credulous, he has always been easily taken in. Clemmie often saved him from the charlatans he gathered round him. He is at the same time ingenuous and cunning.'

I asked Brendan what he meant by cunning.

'Oh, of course, in getting his own way. His tenacity was always remarkable. Violent, irrational, superstitious,' Brendan murmured. 'You don't think of Winston as cautious, but he can be very much on his guard.

'Well, Charles, we began with a small boy hiding behind a tree, and I want to tell you before we end about a sandy-haired boy, a kind of portent, prepared to contradict anyone, ready to challenge the world. I want to tell you this because to understand Winston you must go back to his childhood.'

Brendan thought his bluster as a young man was a form of shyness, and told me of an occasion when Winston was lunching with Linky and the Duke of Marlborough. Linky's erudition made him feel a schoolboy; he was so ashamed of his ignorance that he made up his mind that he would educate himself. So he read and read and read. 'You know who I mean by Linky?'

'Yes, Lord Hugh Cecil. He was Winston's best man; they seemed to drift apart; perhaps they were never really buddies.'

Brendan told me that he first met Winston when he was thirty-seven years of age. He was beginning to lose some of his hair, but he had a good figure and was bursting with energy.

The nurse came in. Had I stayed too long? When I put my hand on Brendan's shoulder the spine of his scapula felt like a razor's edge. I keep thinking of him; I cannot get him out of my head.

CHAPTER FORTY-ONE

The Dying Gladiator

April 13, 1959

When I called at Chartwell on my way to London I found Clemmie in the cottage, which was full of books; she explained that Winston had about ten thousand, and she was trying to reduce them by half. I sat for a time in the garden shelter with Winston. Presently he levered himself to his feet and walked towards the house. He appeared more cheerful than he has been of late, and was reluctant to go indoors.

Clemmie telephoned about eight o'clock:

'After you left, Winston went to bed. Later on he rang his bell, and when Shepherd answered it he noticed that Winston was not speaking properly. He came to me and said that he appeared confused. Winston wanted to stay the night at Chartwell, but I had to explain that there were no servants. We shall be at Hyde Park Gate by ten o'clock. Do you think you could call?'

When I asked Winston how he was I could not understand what he was trying to say to me. He knew what he wanted to say, but he could not say it. I gave him my pen and he wrote something very slowly and very carefully. I took the paper from him, but I could not read what he had written. I noticed that his little finger was white and cold. When I asked if it was painful he nodded. When I left him Clemmie took up the story:

'Winston is usually very silent in the car, but on the way to London he kept trying to say something. I was not sure whether he wanted to tell me things or whether he was experimenting to find out for himself what he could say and what he could not. When he failed to get the words he exclaimed: "Damnation! Is it a stroke, Charles?" '

I went back to his room and reassured him. He had been like this before, and it had all cleared up. I told him that in a day or two he will be all right. He said he was worried.

April 14, 1959

This morning it is impossible to detect that there is anything wrong with his speech. But Clemmie is distracted, and she has good reason for her cares. A few days ago I noticed that the pupils of his eyes did not react to light, and now there is this speech defect and the little finger; there seems no end to these wandering clots. I keep wondering what will happen next. But Winston has made up his mind to go to the Other Club on Thursday.

April 15, 1959

When Brain had examined Sir Winston he told him that a small artery had been blocked, cutting off the circulation to his speech centre for a time. But the circulation had been re-established. I had advised Russell to ask Winston if he had made any plans, and if he had, to urge him to cancel them. Winston said that he was speaking to his constituents:

'I cannot cancel it without giving a reason. I should have to tell them about this, and I could not then take part in the election. Macmillan has asked me to take some part. What does it matter if I do break down?' He broke out impatiently:

'I am quite content to die.'

Russell could think of nothing to say. He sat looking at Winston for quite a time. Then he half turned to me as if he would say: 'Cannot you do something to put an end to this visit?'

Clemmie awaited us in the library. 'Well,' she asked, 'what did he say? Did you persuade him not to speak on Monday?' Brain told her what had happened. There was a long pause. At last he said:

'Does Sir Winston worry?'

'No,' Clemmie answered. 'Winston isn't a worrier. But he is profoundly depressed. The days are very long and very dull. It was never like this in the past. He found a hundred things to do. He reads a lot, but he does not enjoy what he reads. He cannot paint now. He painted two pictures in five weeks at Marrakesh. He wants to stay in bed. Today an agreeable, amusing woman came to luncheon. Winston likes her, but at the last moment he decided to lunch in bed. He has given up America, thank God. But what about this speech? Cannot you do anything, Charles?'

June 8, 1959

The scene of *Der Rosenkavalier* at Glyndebourne last night, the pretty woman's farewell to all that made life to her worthwhile, has set me thinking. The audience was plainly moved by the pathos of her abdication, yet the same people remain cold and indifferent when someone who once was famous draws out his leave of the world, alone and half forgotten.

I must not become morbid about Winston, though he is never far from my mind. The people I meet at Chartwell ask about him, but do they, I wonder, try to get into his mind as he sits there in the great house, through the interminable days, often alone, waiting for the end? His job is done. Will posterity say that it was well done? I sometimes wish that he would not think so much about posterity, because it seems to bring one of his black moods.

When did he begin to be troubled about his place in history? I suppose that in the war his days were so taken up with the conduct of operations that there was no time left to live with his own mistakes.

It was, however, the loss of the election in the summer of 1945 that gave me my first clue to the gnawing discomfort in his mind. He was hurt by the size of the majority, he felt that the whole conduct of the war had been called in question. When he had partly recovered from the blow he resolved to prepare his defence and to put it on paper. He must have known that he had a tired mind, but he would not be turned from his purpose. In 1949 – it may have been about the turn of the year – when he was halfway through the third volume of *The Second World War* it became plain that he no longer had the energy of mind to do the job properly. I tried to argue with him. Surely he had done enough, had not the time come to take in sail? 'You do not understand,' he said sadly. He could not bring himself to talk of it. Nor was it necessary.

Yet only on one occasion, as far as I can remember, did he show me his scars. It was in the summer of 1953, after his stroke, when he thought he was dying and his head was confused. Even his speech was difficult to follow; he kept trying to say something and I was able at last to pick up what he wanted to say:

'I ought not . . . I must not . . . be held to account . . . for all . . . that has gone wrong.'

He still lives in the war. On Thursday I found him with a glum face, brooding over his bed-rest. I taxed him with giving way to the Churchill melancholia. 'Why,' he retorted, 'do I get stuck down in the past? Why do I keep going over and over those years when I know I cannot change anything? You, Charles, have spent your life puzzling how the mind works. You must know the answer.' He thinks I know more than I do. Indeed, much that he has told me has been no more than a cry for help. I rack my brains, wondering what I can do. That I am so useless to him torments me.

August 3, 1959
Lunched at Birch Grove.[1] Harold Macmillan said: 'I miss Brendan. Who will be Winston's Boswell? He should have a Boswell. He is very witty. I always hoped Brendan would be. He must have had a wonderful fund of stories about Winston. Now he's gone I can't think who could do it. We are all getting on, the people who know him, I mean.'

The Prime Minister's face twitched with mirth.

'You know Winston's remark when he heard of the illness of someone he particularly disliked: "Nothing trivial, I trust."'

[1] Mr Macmillan's home in Sussex.

The smile widened.

'And the quip about Attlee. It must have been in 1947 when Winston was making speeches in the House. You remember Winston was never quite in step with the rather revolutionary people elected in 1945. One day Attlee answered one of these speeches very neatly and sensibly. Winston got up at the end and went to his room. He was feeling depressed about things when Colonel R. came up to him.

'Colonel R.: "Don't you think Mr Attlee's manner in the House has enormously improved?"

'Winston: "Oom, oom, oom."

'Colonel R.: "But really, sir, I can't help feeling that he is greatly changed for the better."

'Winston: "Oom, oom, oom."

'Colonel R.: "I must say one can hardly credit that it is the same person speaking, he is so much improved."

'Winston: "Oom, oom. Have you ever read Maeterlinck?"

'Colonel R.: "No, sir."

'Winston: "Well. Go and read him. You will see that if any grub is fed on Royal Jelly it turns into a Queen Bee."'

Macmillan: 'Jelly is such a splendid word. And you know to this day, the Colonel doesn't know what Winston was talking about.'

Dorothy said she had received a very agreeable letter from Mrs Clifford. Had the Prime Minister read Clifford's book[1] *The Young Samuel Johnson*? The Cliffords had been touring the Hebrides in Johnson's footsteps. They found a gull's egg in almost the same place where Johnson had found his egg.

Macmillan: 'Boswell's *Tour of the Hebrides* is a wonderful travel book. The best, I think. I've been reading it again. I haven't time to read new books, but I like taking up a book I know well. I like reading lives of statesmen. Of course, we all read them when we were young and decided they gave a good picture of the man and his life. But it is quite different reading them when you know the

---

[1] J. L. Clifford, Professor of English Literature, Columbia University.

machine. I've just been reading Philip Magnus's *Gladstone*. I felt very envious. He was Prime Minister for – was it fourteen years? and in all that time he never spent less than five months of the year at Hawarden. After all, it was a long way off, much further than Birch Grove,' he added with a quizzical smile.

Dorothy asked the Prime Minister how he had kept his garden so green. Hers was brown and parched. When she wanted to cheer herself up she looked at Norman Brook's photograph of the water garden taken with the camera Khrushchev gave him.

Macmillan: 'What do you think of Norman? Do you think he looks better than he used to? I like to keep to office hours. I don't keep him up half the night. Norman has most wonderful judgement. He is always right. Pure inborn judgement, because, as I expect you know, he had no background.

'I think,' he went on, 'Eton is a wonderful school. I think you learn there to take knocks. You learn not to make a fuss if you are criticized unfairly. Everybody at school is criticized unfairly some time or other. You learn to take it as part of the day's work. You don't write home to your mother and complain. You know, Alan Lennox-Boyd couldn't have endured the last fortnight without that training.[1]

'I try to make the Cabinet laugh sometimes, to take things lightly. After all, it's no use working oneself into a state. One just does one's best, that's all one can do.'

He spoke of Winston's kindness. Winston kept him in cigars. The Prime Minister showed me one of the cigar boxes from Cuba which Winston had given him. He thought Winston had mellowed. Then he asked me abruptly how he was. The Prime Minister thought it was very unusual for a man to go on so long in Winston's state. Women did, of course. Lady Dorothy's mother did, her last two years had been rather sad – more dead than alive. He looked over the distant prospect. He could not understand why people went

[1] Secretary of State for the Colonies, 1954–9. Lennox-Boyd was fiercely attacked in 1959 over the Hola camp affair in Kenya, in which eleven Mau Mau prisoners died of violence. The issue caused widespread feeling in Britain, and a motion of censure was put down in the House of Commons in June.

abroad; England was so lovely. The country was very prosperous. People ought to be happy. He turned to Dorothy: 'Do you think they are happy?'

This was a Prime Minister interested in other people's lives and in their backgrounds. He liked young people round him, and his eye brightened as he spoke of his grandson, who had just gone to Eton.

'I asked him a very silly question: had he come across the Headmaster? As if a Lower Boy would.'

' "Well, Grandpapa, as a matter of fact I did run into him the other day. And I am bound to tell you, Grandpapa, he made a very poor impression on me." '

October 22, 1959
I had gone to my room in the Fernley Hotel, Bath, to unpack when there was a knock on the door. The porter wanted to know if I would take a telephone call from London.

'It is Anthony. Yes, Montague Browne. I am telephoning about Sir Winston. He isn't very well. We are at Hyde Park Gate. We were talking when he yawned twice. Then he went white, face and hands, and became unconscious. I was alarmed. I thought he was dying.'

'How long was it before he came round?'

'Oh, I suppose not more than a few minutes. When he did come round he seemed dazed. He said he felt very ill, as if he had been turned upside down. I don't know if I did right, but when I couldn't get you I telephoned to Sir Russell Brain, and he'll be here any minute. I will ring you again when Sir Russell has seen Sir Winston.'

I am in the middle of a tour of meetings about merit awards in the West Country, but I must see him tonight. It doesn't sound too good.

I found Clemmie with Winston in his bedroom. 'It's Charles, Winston,' said Clemmie. A flicker of recognition crossed his face. He said nothing, but I found that he could answer my questions. As Clemmie put it, he was 'very quiet and withdrawn'. 'Winston did not recognize Sir Russell.' There was a troubled look in Clemmie's eyes as she said this. He took no heed of us. He sat propped up in bed looking at his dinner on the bed-rest; he was not interested in food. He had a quiet pulse, his colour was good and he was falling asleep as we left him. I do not think anything will happen.

October 23, 1959

This morning when Russell and I saw Winston he seemed much as usual. He did not feel ill. Russell thought his attack was due to 'petit mal', a mild form of epilepsy, the 'falling sickness' from which both Caesar and Napoleon suffered. It was not uncommon as a sequel to a sluggish cerebral circulation. Even if there was a recurrence, the risk that he would die in one of these attacks was small, but Russell did not think that he would be alive in six months' time.

October 24, 1959

Found Winston playing bezique with Clemmie as if nothing had happened. 'He is much better,' she said, watching Winston as he collected the cards. I asked him if he could detect any difference between his condition before the attack and now. He hesitated.

'If there is any difference it is for the worse.'

'In what way?' I persisted.

'It's not really a headache, but . . .'

I helped him out. 'Muzziness?'

'Yes, muzziness. Shall I have another attack?'

I asked him how he was getting on with his book.

'There's not much in it,' he grunted.

'You don't think Tolstoy makes out his case about Napoleon?'

His face lost its vacant expression and lit up in amusement. 'Oh, I put him on one side in order to read the second volume of the bloody diaries. Tolstoy must wait until I see what Brooke has to say. I was told that the second volume was worse than the first, full of venom, but as far as I have read I don't find it so. I had forgotten, my dear, that I called you a bloody old man. I apologize to you,' he said gravely.

*

Clemmie is at pains to bring Winston's friends to see him. It appears that Rupert Gunnis's[1] visit was a great success. He took him an old picture postcard of a house party with the King of Portugal and Winston in it. Winston was thrilled, and talked about each member of the party in turn. This went on till half-past three. Clemmie pressed Rupert to come again, any time. 'What card will you play next visit?' I enquired. Rupert thought for a little: 'Marie Lloyd, I think.'

November 17, 1959

Clemmie telephoned.

'Is that you, Charles? I'm very worried about Winston. He had another of his attacks when he was lunching with Lord Beaverbrook. It seems that Bullock, his chauffeur – you know he is a very sensible fellow – noticed that when Winston got out of the car he lurched to the right; he would have fallen but for Bullock. I telephoned Max to ask how Winston had been during luncheon.'

'What did he say?'

'Terrible. Winston could not get the words he wanted. Apparently he realized this and kept very silent.'

When I saw him about an hour later he still had difficulty in finding his words. When I asked him how he felt he replied, 'Frightfully stupid,' but he demurred when I said that he would not be able to see Adenauer. I explained that he might use wrong words. It might be very noticeable. He turned to Montague Browne and told him not to scratch any of his appointments for the moment. 'Anyway,' I added, 'the dinner at No. 10 is out of the question.' When he looked very glum, I asked him if he would like to see Russell Brain. He did not answer.

When Russell came he sat by Winston's bedside, staring at him; for what seemed an interminable period he went on gazing very intently at Winston, but saying nothing. Winston did not look at Russell, he just sat with his eyes fixed on his bed-rest; then it seemed

---

[1] The date of Rupert Gunnis's visit has been torn off my diary.

that he could keep them open no longer and he dropped off to sleep, waking in a few minutes with an uncomprehending, vacant and rather startled look. Clemmie came in and said that he would miss Adenauer unless we sent him a message now. Brain looked round at me as if he wanted to say: 'What do we do now?' I got up and we trooped out.

'How do you find him?' Clemmie asked Russell, and without waiting for an answer continued: 'Winston was very disappointed. He wanted terribly to see Adenauer. You see, Sir Russell, there will not be many of these occasions in the future.'

Clemmie got nothing out of Brain, but to me he was more forthcoming. His view is frankly pessimistic. The right carotid artery had been blocked before, and it looked now as if the left was affected. He thought that one day Winston would be found in bed unable to speak. 'You mean he will have a stroke in the night?' Brain nodded.

November 18, 1959

Clemmie greeted me cheerfully this morning.

'You wouldn't know anything had happened; maybe he is a little subdued. Adenauer expressed a great desire to see Winston if it was at all possible before he left London, and it has been arranged that he will come to Hyde Park Gate this afternoon. Oh, he has promised not to stay long.'

'What happened?' I enquired later of Clemmie.

'Oh, Winston was thrilled with the interview. You see, Charles, I speak German, and I think that helped.'

'Did Winston get very tired?'

'No, not at all. The first quarter of an hour he was hesitant and his voice was not very strong, though his answers were all sensible. Then he blossomed. His voice got stronger, and he asked a lot of intelligent questions. They talked a lot about the Summit Conference. Adenauer does not trust Khrushchev. He wants to keep Russia out of everything. I think, Charles, it went off very well.'

It may have been an hour after this that I saw Winston.

'I saw . . . I saw . . . that man.'

'Adenauer, you mean?'

He nodded.

December 20, 1959

Norman Brook spent nearly two hours with Winston after lunch.
I wondered what he would make of Winston's waning faculties.
When he came out he said:

'Of course there were long pauses, and sometimes Winston began
a sentence and then could not remember what he meant to say.'

'But,' I said, 'what happened when you discussed serious problems?'

'We didn't. To my mind Winston hasn't been capable of discussing anything that matters for the last six months. I just started
a line, and if he didn't seem to connect I moved on to something
else. I didn't do much more than make agreeable noises. The
trouble, Charles, for all who love Winston, is that you feel you can't
do anything to help him.'

March 8, 1960

It had been planned that Winston should join the Onassis yacht at
Gibraltar, but when our plane made an emergency landing at
Madrid to refuel we learnt that the rough weather might make difficulties at Gibraltar. The pilot, however, was determined to deliver
Sir Winston to the Governor waiting on the airfield, and he made
two abortive attempts to land; in the second Dorothy was thrown
sideways, bumping her head against the window, and everything on
the tables was swept off with a clatter. Then the pilot decided to
make for Tangier. When, in the war, we came down through low
clouds before landing at Gibraltar, Winston became apprehensive,
muttering: 'I hope we shan't collide with the Rock.' Now the blanching of his brain has wiped out his fears. Though it appears that those
who were waiting on the tarmac were full of trepidation, he himself
did not even seem interested, only growling irritably: 'What are
they doing?'

The Nairns,[1] who had heard of our plight, met us at Tangier, and a little procession of cars carried off our party to their house on the outskirts of the town. The guests for a dinner party were already arriving, their spruce evening clothes made us feel battered and dishevelled, and, perhaps, a little in the way. T. S. Eliot, one of the guests, said it would make a wonderful scene for a play. I took him over to Winston, who gazed at him in an uncomprehending way; his name evidently meant nothing to him. Eliot drifted away, and Winston was left sitting apart, looking at the carpet, a little puzzled perhaps about what it all meant. He could not understand why they did not announce dinner. 'I am very hungry, Charles.' Raising his voice, he repeated this, so that I was afraid Mrs Nairn would hear. I tried to explain that dinner was waiting for us at the Rif Hotel. He seemed too tired to make a move; sunk in his chair, he took no notice of the guests who were sitting about. They had given up making conversation, though one of them said to me that they would talk about this for a long time. It was a very great occasion.

It was nearly ten o'clock when we reached the Rif Hotel. Winston at once summoned the head waiter and ordered consommé. It was a long time coming. He kept grumbling: 'What about my soup? I gave the order a long time ago.' His voice got louder: 'Oh, damn it, what are they doing about it?' However, when dinner came he gradually began to thaw. Looking out into the courtyard, he watched the gusts of wind blow up the awning so that he could see the fairy lamps swinging in the wind and catch their light reflected in pools of water left by the storm.

'Look, Charles, at the shape of that foliage. That tree is like an animal pawing the air. You see the one I mean? It has a yellow belly. And that one is just like a crouching cat.'

Winston went on to explain that he often sees the shape of animals when he looks at trees and shrubs. I told him it was very late and urged him to go to his bed. He had been travelling for more than twelve hours. 'Oh,' he retorted, 'that doesn't tire me, it's the

---

[1] The Consul-General and his wife.

walking.' It was after midnight when he pulled himself to his feet with some help and tottered to the door. As he left the people in the room got up and others, appearing from nowhere, gathered round the door. They began to sing 'For he's a jolly good fellow' with a fine and touching fervour. When Winston tumbled to what was going on he gave them the victory sign twice, and then lurched, very slowly, to the lift. He was still giving the V-sign when he disappeared from their sight.

Yacht Christina, *March 9, 1960*

When we were gathering in the saloon of the yacht for luncheon Ari Onassis addressed a question to Winston across the length of the table. Winston waited till he had located the direction of the sound, then he looked at Onassis with dull, expressionless eyes. 'I can't hear you,' he muttered, but he did not ask his host to repeat his remarks. He did not seem to want to talk. However, tonight Winston came to life; he appeared quite alert and ready to join in the fun.

Martinique, March 17, 1960

Waves from the choppy sea washing the deck drove us in for luncheon. After the ladies had left us Winston, Ari and I were left alone at the table.

Ari: 'Sir Winston, Sir Winston, I think the Prefet is a nice man. I liked the Prefet. I told him that Martinique ought not to depend on sugar. They must attract American capital. They must do something. When nature provides a perfect climate and enough food people sleep all day and do nothing. If the climate in the north of England had been less harsh and the soil more fertile people would not have gone to sea so much. Necessity plays a big part in what men do.'

Winston: 'You need not talk so loud, it must be a great effort. I can hear quite well.'

Ari (*lowering his voice*): 'I'm sorry, Sir Winston. If people have to work very hard for subsistence, if they have to rub their hands to keep warm, they have no time for leisure. They cannot attend to the arts. Things of the spirit, things of the soul are left out of their lives.

You told me, Sir Winston, your father died very young, if he had lived to your age you might not have had to struggle so hard. Your life would have been easier, and you might not have done what you did.'

Winston, who did not appear to be listening very attentively, broke in:

'No, we were very different people.'

Ari: 'Yes, of course, you were different, but you would not have been driven on by necessity. My mother died when I was six. If she had lived I might not have worked as hard as I have done.'

Winston: 'Would you like to play a little cards instead of talking philosophy?'

Ari: 'Not philosophy, but history.'

Winston: 'They are not very different. I like living on your ship.'

Ari: 'I wish you'd return on her. You would avoid the strain of flying.'

Winston: 'It is very kind of you to press your hospitality, but I feel I ought to return to London in time for my commitments. There is the Budget, and the ceremonies in connection with de Gaulle, and the Other Club dinner – a special, rather unique occasion. I want to keep alive links with the past. I do not feel I can brush aside anyhow my relations with people of high consequence, higgledy-piggledy. I do not want to do anything more; I have had enough of power, but I should not like to lose touch altogether with these occasions. I have reduced them to a minimum.'

Ari: 'You must decide, Sir Winston. You must do what you like.'

When they left the table Ari took the captain to Winston's cabin and made him sit on his bed while various speeds were tried – thirteen knots seemed to produce the least vibration.

A flying-fish landed on the deck when we were at dinner. Louis[1] brought it in, flapping its wings. 'Put it back quickly,' Winston broke in, 'or it will die.' Clemmie says that Winston is disappointed in Harold Macmillan. He thinks that Harold ought not to have gone

[1] Onassis's servant.

to Africa, encouraging the black men.[1] About midnight Ari made a move. Winston was not at all ready for sleep: 'Of course, if you want to leave me, pray do not let me detain you.'

November 12, 1960

Clemmie telephoned me about midnight:

'Is that you, Charles? Winston has had an accident.' They had been dining with the Salisburys, and Winston had come to her room to say goodnight. He had kissed her, when stepping back he lost his footing and fell backwards; his head struck the wall, and then he fell heavily to the ground.

'Can you come? How long will it take you?' When I got to the house Howells said that he found Sir Winston lying on the floor; he looked like marble; he had no pulse; he thought he was dead. With the help of the policeman on duty they carried him to his bed. He seemed to understand what I said and there were no signs of shock. I decided to stay with him for the night.

November 13, 1960

Winston complains of pain round the shoulder, the pain is worse when he moves. It looks as if he has injured his spine and I called Professor Seddon to see him. He decided to take him in an ambulance to Harley Street to have his spine X-rayed. There is a fracture of the fifth dorsal vertebra which appears crushed. But we could not get a good picture of the cervical vertebrae, because it hurt him so much to move. When a man is in his eighty-seventh year and fractures his spine anything may happen, but in the bulletin we were content to record that Sir Winston had fallen and had broken a small bone in his back. Seddon's sound judgement and good sense are a great comfort. I do like a man who knows his job.

[1] During his African tour (January–February, 1960) Macmillan made his 'Wind of Change' speech to the South African Parliament on February 3, in which he asserted the British Government's opposition to Apartheid.

November 17, 1960

In old age an accident of this kind often does more hurt to the mind than to the body. Winston is being very difficult, swearing at the nurses. Last night he shouted at Howells till at last the poor man's patience gave out and he answered back. This morning Winston told me that Howells was mad; he would have to leave. I asked Howells what Winston had said.

'Oh, he just shouted abuse at me. You see, sir, even when Sir Winston is well he never says anything to me, unless, of course, he has to ask for something.'

November 22, 1960

Winston cannot raise his left arm properly. I don't think that it is connected with his spinal injury. Probably his cerebral circulation is playing its old tricks. This morning he objected most vehemently when the nurse tried to move him, he was afraid of bringing on the pain.

December 4, 1960

A bad night. 'Very confused and aggressive,' nurse reports. Sometime after midnight Sir Winston lost his temper and picking up his urinal bashed it against the wall with such force that it made a hole in the wall.

December 5, 1960

Seddon is worried because he had noticed a slight angular deformity in the neck, and insists on a second X-ray examination. It was found that three of the vertebrae of the neck had become fused into a solid block of bone, the result no doubt of some accident years ago. Seddon tells me that without this protective block it is probable that one of the cervical vertebrae would have been fractured in his fall, and then we should have been in real trouble. Winston, as I have said before, seems to have nine lives.

December 19, 1960

A bad day. Winston knows what he wants to say but cannot say it; he cannot get the words he wants. To make matters worse, the

Prime Minister chose today to visit him. Later I asked him how he got on.

'Did you find talking any easier?'

'No', grunted Winston, 'I was dumb, I could not think of anything to say.'

I gather the meeting was rather a flop, and they are afraid that the Prime Minister will talk. Winston asked: 'How long have I to go on like this, waiting for death?'

*

It is eleven years since the summer of 1949 when Winston received a tap on the shoulder – a notice to quit. Moreover, in that space of time the circulation in his head had faltered many times; old age, always an affliction, had become to him a source of embarrassment – in his own words, a feeble substitute for life. My diary for those years, five of them during his retirement, is in part a sad record of the advancing signs of decay, a catalogue of lamentations over faculties that had gone.

I have explained in the preface why I thought it right to recount the stages of his decline as long as he possessed political power, and even afterwards when his advice was still sought. But there is no point in continuing the story beyond the time when it ceases to be of any historical significance. I have therefore ended it in 1960, five years before his death.

Epilogue

Winston's eightieth birthday had brought him the homage of the free world, but when at the end of November, in the year of 1964, he came to the great age of ninety, the long chronicle of boredom and despair was hardly broken by the celebrations, which were only a half-hearted affair. Those near to him made suitable noises, but they knew that it was all make-believe, and that he did not wish to live. Christmas brought excited grandchildren to see their grandfather before being despatched to the pantomime. They came to him in turn and kissed him, and it may be that he knew what it was all about.

A time was coming when it was noticed that he did not like to be left alone. One day, as I was taking my leave, he put his hand on mine mumbling, 'Don't be too long, my dear, before you come again.' In the great days when I could help him he had not said as much. I think he was a lonely man, as I suppose he had been always.

Early in January, 1965 there was a change. He still seemed to know me, but he was drowsy and confused. At half-past eleven in the morning of January 10, Howells telephoned to me. He did not think Sir Winston was so well. He could not rouse him. I found him propped up by pillows in his bed, his head bent forward, his hands laid out on the sheet, arranged for death. I lifted his left arm, and when I let it go it fell to the bed. I could not feel a pulse. His hands were cold and he was blue about the mouth. I thought it wise to warn the public in my bulletin that he had had another stroke and that his condition was critical.

But Winston had never taken orders from anyone. He had always been unpredictable; he was to be like that to the end. Day after day I was persuaded that he would be gone before the morning, but when the morning came he was still there. In bulletin after bulletin I felt I must prepare the public for his passing, until I was at a loss what to say.

From time to time the door of the bedroom was gently pushed open and one of the family would appear and stand by the bed and whisper: 'How long can it go on?' When I did not answer I was left alone in the room, listening to the sound of his breathing. Randolph came in. I got up, and as I closed the door I saw him lift his father's hand to his lips. Lady Churchill drifted through the rooms. There was no expression on her beautiful face; she seemed to be in a trance.

One night in the small hours I was summoned to his side. The nurse on duty thought that he was dying. But when I came to him there was no change. Meanwhile the world seemed to stand still, half-incredulous that this man whom they held in reverence for what he had done was about to be taken from them. The narrow street was blocked by reporters. They did not speak to one another; they appeared numbed by what was happening behind the great black door. As I came out, there was a shuffling of feet as they pushed forward to catch my words.

For fourteen days he was not seen to move. His strength left him slowly, as if he was loath to give up life. On the night of the twenty-fourth of January it appeared that a crisis was at hand. His breathing became shallow and laboured, and at eight o'clock in the morning it ceased. Mary, sitting by his side, looked up at me. I got up and bent over the bed, but he had gone.

He was taken at night to Westminster, to the Hall of William Rufus, and there for three days he lay in state, while the people gathered in crowds that stretched over Lambeth Bridge to the far side of the river, to do honour to the man they loved for his valour. On the fourth day he was borne on a gun-carriage to St Paul's. There followed a long line of men in arms, marching to sorrowful music. With all the panoply of Church and State, and in the presence of his Queen, he was carried to an appointed place hard by the tombs of Nelson and Wellington, under the great dome, while with solemn music and the beating of drums the nation saluted the man who had saved them and saved their honour.

The village stations on the way to Bladon were crowned with his countrymen, and at Bladon in a country churchyard, in the stillness of a winter evening, in the presence of his family and a few friends, Winston Churchill was committed to English earth, which in his finest hour he had held inviolate.

Lord Moran,
Taken from the original edition

APPENDIX

List of Hitherto Unpublished Material Included in this New Edition

1. *August 25, 1949*
New remarks by Lord Moran on Churchill's health, from Box 65 – PP/W/K.5/5/2.

2. *September 29, 1951*
New remarks by Lord Moran and Churchill on the appointment of the new Cabinet, especially the Minister of Health, from Box 65 – PP/W/K.5/5/2.

3. *December 30, 1951*
New remarks by Lord Moran on Pug Ismay, from Box 65 – PP/W/K.5/5/2.

4. *February 21, 1952*
New remarks by Lord Moran on the appointment of the Minister of Health from Box 60 – PP/CMW/K.4/3.

5. *February 22, 1952*
New remarks about Churchill's future in the Lords, the award of the Garter, and Churchill's relationship with the Queen (the Queen Mother), from Box 60 – PP/CMW/K.4/3.

6. *April 19, 1952*
New remarks by Lord Moran about the failure to appoint John Anderson, from Box 65 – PP/W/K.5/5/2.

7. *March 7, 1953*
New remark by Lord Moran about Churchill's loss of energy, from Box 65 – PP/W/K.5/5/3.

8. *June 9, 1953*

Speaker on Churchill's vanity identified as Christopher Soames, from Box 65 – PP/W/K.5/5/3.

9. *June 26, 1953*

New footnote, from Box 65 – PP/W/K.5/5/3.

10. *June 28, 1953*

New remarks by Lord Moran about the strain Clemmie, Churchill's wife, was under, from Box 65 – PP/W/K.5/5/3.

11. *July 12, 1953*

New remarks by Lord Moran on Churchill's health, from Box 65 – PP/W/K.5/5/3.

12. *August 5, 1953*

New remark criticizing choice of Randolph Churchill as biographer, from Box 65 – PP/W/K.5/5/3.

13. *August 12, 1953*

New comments on Churchill's health by Lord Moran and Sir Russell Brain, from Box 65 – PP/W/K.5/5/3.

14. *September 2, 1953*

Churchill identifies a critic as Sir Anthony Nutting, from Box 65 – PP/W/K.5/5/3.

15. *October 27, 1953*

New comments by Lord Moran, Christopher Soames and Jock on Churchill's possible retirement, from Box 65 – PP/W/K.5/5/4.

16. *December 2, 1953*

New remarks by Lord Moran about Anthony Eden, from Box 65 – PP/W/K.5/5/4.

17. *January 12, 1954*

New remark by Lord Moran about Churchill's plans for retirement, from Box 65 – PP/W/K.5/5/4.

18. *March 26, 1954*

New comment by Churchill on Frank Owen, from Box 66 – PP/CMW/K.5/5/5.

465 of Hitherto Unpublished Material

19. *March 31, 1954*

New entry on Winston's comments on hydrogen bomb, and
US/UK agreement, from Box 66 – PP/CMW/K.5/5/5.

20. *April 8, 1954*

New remarks by Christopher Soames on Churchill's health and
retirement, from Box 66 – PP/CMW/K.5/5/5.

21. *July 30, 1954*

New comment by Norman Brook on Anthony Eden, from Box 66
– PP/CMW/K.5/5/5.

22. *August 6, 1954*

New comment by Montague Browne on Anthony Eden, from
Box 66 – PP/CMW/K.5/5/5.

23. *September 14, 1954*

New entry: Montague Browne and Lord Moran's discussion of
Churchill's relationship with Eden, from Box 66 –
PP/CMW/K.5/5/6.

24. *October 5, 1954*

New entry: Montague Browne on Churchill and Anthony Eden,
from Box 66 – PP/CMW/K.5/5/6.

25. *January 9, 1955*

New remarks by Harold Macmillan on Anthony Eden, and by
Lord Moran on Harold Macmillan, from Box 66 –
PP/CMW/K.5/5/6.

26. *March 3, 1955*

New comments by Churchill on his health, from Box 66 –
PP/CMW/K.5/5/6.

27. *November 12, 1960*

New entry: Churchill has a fall, from Box 69 –
PP/CMW/K.5/6/5.

28. *November 13, 1960*

New entry: Lord Moran's comments on Churchill's injuries, from
Box 69 – PP/CMW/K.5/6/5.

29. *November 17, 1960*

New entry: Lord Moran's comments on Churchill's state of mind, from Box 69 – PP/CMW/K.5/6/5.

30. *November 22, 1960*

New entry: Lord Moran's comments on Churchill's health, from Box 69 – PP/CMW/K.5/6/5.

31. *December 4, 1960*

New entry: Lord Moran's comments on Churchill's state of mind, from Box 69 – PP/CMW/K.5/6/5.

32. *December 5, 1960*

New entry: Lord Moran's comments on Churchill's injuries, from Box 69 – PP/CMW/K.5/6/5.

33. *December 19, 1960*

New entry: Lord Moran's comments on Churchill's health and state of mind, from Box 69 – PP/CMW/K.5/6/5.

Index